WARFARE IN HISTORY
Deception in Medieval Warfare

WARFARE IN HISTORY
ISSN 1358-779X

Series editors

Matthew Bennett, Royal Military Academy, Sandhurst, UK
Anne Curry, University of Southampton, UK
Stephen Morillo, Wabash College, Crawfordsville, USA

This series aims to provide a wide-ranging and scholarly approach to military history, offering both individual studies of topics or wars and volumes giving a selection of contemporary and later accounts of particular battles; its scope ranges from the early medieval to the early modern period.

New proposals for the series are welcomed; they should be sent to the publisher at the address below.

Boydell and Brewer Limited, PO Box 9, Woodbridge, Suffolk ip12 3df

Previously published volumes in this series are listed at the back of this volume

Deception in Medieval Warfare

*Trickery and Cunning
in the Central Middle Ages*

James Titterton

THE BOYDELL PRESS

© James Titterton 2022

All rights reserved. Except as permitted under current legislation
no part of this work may be photocopied, stored in a retrieval system,
published, performed in public, adapted, broadcast,
transmitted, recorded or reproduced in any form or by any means,
without the prior permission of the copyright owner

The right of James Titterton to be identified as
the author of this work has been asserted in accordance with
sections 77 and 78 of the Copyright, Designs and Patents Act 1988

First published 2022
Paperback edition 2024
The Boydell Press, Woodbridge

ISBN 978-1-78327-678-3 (Hardback)
ISBN 978-1-83765-131-3 (Paperback)

The Boydell Press is an imprint of Boydell & Brewer Ltd
PO Box 9, Woodbridge, Suffolk IP12 3DF, UK
and of Boydell & Brewer Inc.
668 Mt Hope Avenue, Rochester, NY 14620-2731, USA
website: www.boydellandbrewer.com

A CIP catalogue record for this book is available from the
British Library

The publisher has no responsibility for the continued existence or accuracy of
URLs for external or third-party internet websites referred to in this book, and
does not guarantee that any content on such websites is, or will remain, accurate
or appropriate

This publication is printed on acid-free paper

For Ellie

Contents

List of Illustrations	viii
Acknowledgements	ix
List of Abbreviations	x
Notes on the Text	xv
Introduction: Low Cunning in the High Middle Ages	1
1 Trickery in Medieval Culture: Source and Problems	9
2 Military Intelligence: Misdirection, Misinformation and Espionage	27
3 The Element of Surprise: Ambushes and Night Raids	53
4 The Feigned Flight	72
5 Disguises	88
6 Bribes and Inducements	123
7 Oaths and Truces	134
8 The Language of Deception	151
9 The Morality of Deception	171
Conclusion	202
Appendix: Taxonomy of Deceptions in Medieval Chronicles c. 1000–1320	207
Bibliography	245
Index	265

Illustrations

Plate

Jim Shoenbill, "Trojan Horse", original version printed in *Private Eye*, issue no. 1535, 20 Nov. – 3 Dec. 2020, p. 38. Reproduced by kind permission of the artist.   xx

Maps

Great Britain and Ireland	xvi
France and the Low Countries	xvii
Southern Italy and Sicily	xviii
The Holy Land and Near East	xix

Acknowledgements

First and foremost, my thanks go to Alan V. Murray and Karen Watts, who were instrumental in the research that forms the basis of this volume. It would not exist without their encouragement, patience and insight.

Especial thanks go to Jonathan Jarrett, a constant source of support and advice about the strange world of academia.

My thanks to William Flynn and Matthew Strickland for their advice and encouraging me to publish my research.

Thank you to Caroline Palmer, Elizabeth McDonald and Anne Curry for your understanding as I tried to finish this project during a pandemic and for helping me to turn it into a 'real book'.

Many thanks go to the members of the University of Leeds Medieval Warfare Colloquium (a.k.a. Fight Club) – Natalie Anderson, Samuel Bradley, Jacob Deacon, Sophie Harwood, Joanna Phillips, Trevor Russell Smith, Iason Tzouriadis – for their insights and encouragement.

To Rachael Gillibrand and Rose Sawyer, for their friendship through good times and bad.

To all my friends and family, who have helped me in ways both large and small.

To my wife and best friend, Eleanor. 'Two are better than one, because they have a good reward for their toil. For if they fall, one will lift up the other; but woe to one who is alone and falls and does not have another to help' (Ecclesiastes 4. 9–10).

To Calcio and Nimueh, my hard-working editorial team.

And hello to Jason Isaacs.

Abbreviations

AA	Albert of Aachen, *Historia Ierosolimitana: History of the Journey to Jerusalem*, ed. and trans. Susan B. Edgington (Oxford, 2007)
AG	*Annals of Ghent*, trans. Hilda Johnstone (London, 1951)
AM	Amatus of Montecassino, *Ystoire de li Normant*, ed. Michèle Guéret-Laferté (Paris, 2011)
Amb	Ambroise, *The History of the Holy War: Ambroise's Estoire de la guerre sainte*, ed. Marianne Ailes and Malcolm Barber, trans. Marianne Ailes (2 vols, Boydell, 2003)
BB	Baldric of Bourgueil, *Historia Ierosolimitana*, ed. Steven Biddlecombe (Woodbridge, 2014)
BoS	Aelred of Rievaulx, 'Relatio de standardo', in Richard Howlett (ed.), *Chronicles of the Reigns of Stephen, Henry II and Richard I* RS, 82 (4 vols, London, 1884–9), vol. 3, pp. 181–201
Bruce	John Barbour, *The Bruce*, ed. and trans. A. A. M. Duncan (Edinburgh, 1997)
CCA	*La Chanson de la croisade albigeoise*, ed. and trans. Eugéne Martin-Chabot (3 vols, Paris, 1931–61)
CDH	Guy (bishop of Amiens), *Carmen de Hastingae proelio*, ed. and trans. Frank Barlow, 2nd edn (Oxford, 1999)
Clari	Robert de Clari, *La Conquête de Constantinople*, ed. Philippe Lauer (Paris, 1974)
CM	J. Stevenson (ed.), *Chronica de Mailros* (Edinburgh, 1835)
DEL	Charles Wendell David (ed. and trans.), *De Expugnatione Lyxbonensi* (New York, 2001)
Dermot	Denis J. Conlon (ed. and trans.), *Song of Dermot and Earl Richard Fitzgilbert* (Frankfurt, 1992)
DK	Gerald of Wales, 'Descriptio Kambriae', in *Opera*, ed. J. S. Brewer, RS, 21 (8 vols, London, 1861–91), vol. 6, pp. 155–227
Dudo	Dudo of St Quentin, *De moribus et actis primorum normanniae ducum*, ed. Jules Lair (Caen, 1865)
EH	Gerald of Wales, *Expugnatio Hibernica*, ed. and trans. A. B. Scott and F. X. Martin (Dublin, 1978)
FB	Falco of Benevento, 'Chronicle', in G. A. Loud (ed. and trans.), *Roger II and the Creation of the Kingdom*

of Sicily: Selected Sources (Manchester, 2012), pp. 130–249

FC Fulcher of Chartres, *Historia Hierosolymitana, 1095–1127*, ed. Heinrich Hagenmeyer (Heidelberg, 1913)

FH Henry Richards Luard (ed.), *Flores Historiarum*, RS, 95 (3 vols, London, 1890)

GB Galbert of Bruges, *De multro, traditione, et occisione gloriosi Karoli comitis Flandriarum*, ed. Jeff Rider (Turnhout, 1994)

GCA 'Gesta consulum Andegavorum et dominorum Ambaziensium', in Paul Marchegay and Andre Salmon (eds.), *Chroniques d'Anjou* (2 vols, Paris, 1856), vol. 1, pp. 1–226

GF Rosalind Hill (ed.), *Gesta Francorum et aliorum Hierosolimitanorum et aliorum Hierosolimitanorum* (London, 1962)

GG William of Poitiers, *Gesta Guillelmi*, ed. and trans. R. H. C. Davis and Marjorie Chibnall (Oxford, 1998)

GH 'Gesta Herwardi incliti exulis et militis', in Thomas Duffus Hardy and Charles Trice Martin (eds.), *Lestorie des engles solum la translacion Maistre Geffrei Gaimar* (2 vols, London, 1888), vol. 1, pp. 339–404

GM Geoffrey Malaterra, *De rebus gestis Rogerii Calabriae et Siciliae comitis et Roberti Guiscardi ducis fratris eius*, ed. Ernesto Pontieri (Bologna, 1927)

GN Guibert de Nogent, *Dei geta per Francos et cinq autre textes*, ed. R. B. C. Huygens (Turnhout, 1996)

GND Elisabeth M. C. van Houts (ed. and trans.), *The Gesta Normannorum of William of Jumièges, Orderic Vitalis, and Robert of Torigni* (2 vols, Oxford, 1992–5)

GPA William the Breton, 'Gesta Philippi Augusti', in François Delaborde (ed.), *Ouevres de Rigord et de Guillaume le Breton: Historiens de Philippe-Auguste* (2 vols, Paris, 1882), vol. 1, pp. 168–320

GRA William of Malmesbury, *Gesta regum Anglorum*, ed. and trans. R. A. B. Mynors, R. M. Thomson, and M. Winterbottom (2 vols, Oxford, 1998), vol. 1

GRH William Stubbs (ed.), *Gesta Regis Henrici Secundi Benedicit Abbatis*, RS 49 (2 vols, London, 1867)

GS Potter, K. R. (ed. and trans.), *Gesta Stephani*, rev. R. H. C. Davis, rev edn (Oxford, 1976)

GT Ralph of Caen, *Gesta Tancredi*, ed. Edoardo D'Angelo (Turnhout, 2011)

GV Geoffrey de Villehardouin, *La Conquête de Constantinople*, ed. and trans. Edmond Faral, 2nd edn (2 vols, Paris, 1961)

HA	Peter of les Vaux-de-Cernay, *Historia albigensis*, ed. Pascal Guébin and Ernest Lyon (2 vols, Paris, 1926–30)
HG	'Historia Gaufredi ducis Noramnnorum et comitis Andegavorum', in Paul Marchegay and Andre Salmon (eds.), *Chroniques d'Anjou* (2 vols, Paris, 1856), vol. 1, pp. 227–310
HH	Henry of Huntingdon, *Historia Anglorum*, ed. and trans. Diana Greenway (Oxford, 1996)
HN	William of Malmesbury, *Historia novella*, ed. Edmund King, trans. K. R. Potter (Oxford, 1998)
How	Chr Roger of Howden, *Chronica*, ed. William Stubbs, RS, 51 (4 vols, London, 1868–71)
HPA	Rigord, *Histoire de Philippe Auguste*, ed. and trans. Élisabeth Carpentier, Georges Pon, and Yves Chauvin (Paris, 2006)
HWM	*History of William Marshal*, ed. A. J. Holden, trans. S. Gregory (3 vols, London, 2002–6)
HT	Herman of Tournai, *Liber de restauratione monasterii S. Martini Tornacensis*, MGH, Scriptores 14 (Hanover, 1883), pp. 274–317
IK	Gerald of Wales, 'Itinerarium Kambriae', in Gerald of Wales, *Opera*, ed. J. S. Brewer, RS, 21 (8 vols, London, 1861–91), vol. 6, pp. 3–154
IP	'Itinerarium peregrinoum et gesta regis Ricardi', in William Stubbs (ed.), *Chronicles and Memorials of the Reign of Richard I*, RS, 38 (2 vols, London, 1864–5), vol. 1, pp. 3–450
JF	Jordan Fantosme, *Chronicle*, ed. and trans. R. C. Johnston (Oxford, 1981)
JH	John of Hexham, 'Historia', in Roger Twysden (ed.), *Historiae Anglicanae scriptores x* (London, 1652), pp. 257–84
JT	John of Tynemouth, 'Extracts from the *Historia aurea*', in V. H. Galbraith, 'Extracts from the *Historia aurea* and a French "Brut" (1317–47), *The English Historical Review* (1928), 203–17
JW	John of Worcester, *Chronicle*, ed. and trans. P. McGurk (3 vols, Oxford, 1998), vol. 3
LA	Lambert of Ardres, *Historia comitum Ghisensium*, MGH, Scriptores, 24 (Hanover, 1879), pp. 550–642
Lanercost	Joseph Stevenson (ed.), *Chronicon de Lanercost* (Edinburgh, 1839)
LE	Margaret Ruth Morgan (ed.), *La Continuation de Guillaume de Tyr, 1184–1197* (Paris, 1982)
MFW	William Stubbs (ed.), *Memoriale fratris Walteri de Coventria*, RS, 58 (2 vols, London, 1872–3)

MGH	*Monumenta Germaniae Historica*
MSB	E. de Certain (ed.), *Les Miracles de Saint Benoit* (Paris, 1858)
NT	Nicholas Trivet, *Annales sex regum Angliae, qui a comitibus Andegavensibus originem taxerunt*, ed. Thomas Hog (London, 1845)
OD	Odo of Deuil, *De profectione Ludovici VII in orientem*, ed. and trans. Virginia Gingerick Berry (New York, 1948)
OP	Oliver of Paderborn, 'Historia Damiatina', in H. Hoogeweg (ed.), *Die Schriften des Kölner Domscholasters, späteren Bischofs von Paderborn und Kardinal-Bischofs von S. Sabina, Oliverus* (Tübingen, 1894), pp. 159–282
OV	Orderic Vitalis, *Ecclesiastical History*, ed. and trans. Marjorie Chibnall (6 vols, Oxford, 1969–80)
PL	Peter of Langtoft, *Chronicle*, ed. Thomas Wright, RS, 47 (2 vols, London, 1866–8)
RA	Raymond of Aguilers, 'Historia Francorum qui ceperunt Iheruslaem', in *Recueil des historiens des croisades: Historiens occidentaux tome troisième* (Paris, 1866), pp. 231–310
RC	Ralph of Coggeshall, *Chronicon Anglicanum*, ed. Joseph Stevenson (London, 1875)
RD	Ralph of Diceto, *Historical Works*, ed. William Stubbs, RS, 68 (2 vols, London, 1876)
RdB	Wace, *Roman de Brut: A History of the British*, ed. and trans. Judith Weiss, rev edn (Exeter, 2002)
RG	Robert of Gloucester, *Metrical Chronicle*, ed. William Aldis Wright, RS, 86 (2 vols, London, 1887)
RH	Richard of Hexham, 'De gestis regis Stephani et de bello standardii', in Richard Howlett (ed.), *Chronicles of the Reigns of Stephen, Henry II and Richard I*, RS, 82 (4 vols, London, 1884–9), vol. 3, pp. 139–80
RM	Robert the Monk, 'Historia Iherosolimitana', in *Recueil des historiens des croisades: Historiens occidentaux tome troisième* (Paris, 1866), pp. 717–882
RdR	Wace, *Le Roman de Rou*, ed. A. J. Holden (3 vols, Paris, 1970–3)
RS	Rolls Series; *The Chronicles and Memorials of Great Britain and Ireland during the Middle Ages*
RT	Robert of Torigni, 'Chronicle', in Richard Howlett (ed.), *Chronicles of the Reigns of Stephen, Henry II and Richard I*, RS, 82 (4 vols, London, 1884–9), vol. 4

RW	Roger of Wendover, *Chronica*, ed. Henry O. Coxe (5 vols, London, 1841–4)
SSD	Suger of St Denis, *Vie de Louis VI le Gros*, ed. and trans. Henri Waquet, 2nd edn (Paris, 1964)
TG	Thomas Gray, *Scalacronica 1272–1363*, ed. and trans. Andy King (Woodbridge, 2005)
TH	'Topographia Hibernica', in *Opera*, ed. J. S. Brewer, RS, 21 (8 vols, London, 1861–91), vol. 5, pp. 3–206
TW	Thomas Wykes, 'Chronicon', in Henry Richards Luard (ed.), *Annales monastici*, RS, 36 (5 vols, London, 1864–9), vol. 4, pp. 6–354
VES	N. Denholm-Young and Wendy R. Childs (eds.), *Vita Edwardi secundi* (Oxford, 2005)
VSL	Joinville, *Vie de Saint Louis*, ed. and trans. Jacques Monfrin (Paris, 1995)
WA	William of Apulia, *La Geste de Robert Guiscard*, ed. and trans. Marguerite Mathieu (Palermo, 1961)
WC	Walter the Chancellor, *Bella antiochena*, ed. Heinrich Hagenmeyer (Innsbruck, 1896)
WG	Walter of Guisborough, *Chronicle*, ed. Harry Rothwell (London, 1957)
WN	William of Newburgh, *History of English Affairs*, ed. and trans. P. G. Walsh and M. J. Kennedy (2 vols, Warminster, 1988–2007)
WP	William of Puylaurens, *Chronique*, ed. and trans. Jean Duvernoy (Paris, 1976)
WR	William Rishanger, *Chronica et annales*, ed. Henry Thomas Riley, RS, 28 (London, 1865)
WT	William of Tyre, *Chronique*, ed. R. B. C. Huygens (Turnhout, 1986)

Notes on the Text

All the translations that follow are the author's unless otherwise stated. For the sake of clarity and readability, I have chosen to render the historical present, commonly used by Latin chroniclers for dramatic effect, as the past tense in English.

I have followed Dunbar's convention of leaving the Latin *castrum* untranslated when translating passages relating to southern Italy, as it may refer to either a free-standing castle or a fortified village. See Amatus of Montecassino, *History of the Normans*, trans. Prescott N. Dunbar (Woodbridge, 2004).

For Arabic and Turkish names, I have followed the Anglicisation used in *The Crusades: An Encyclopaedia*, ed. by Alan V. Murray (2 vols, Oxford, 2006).

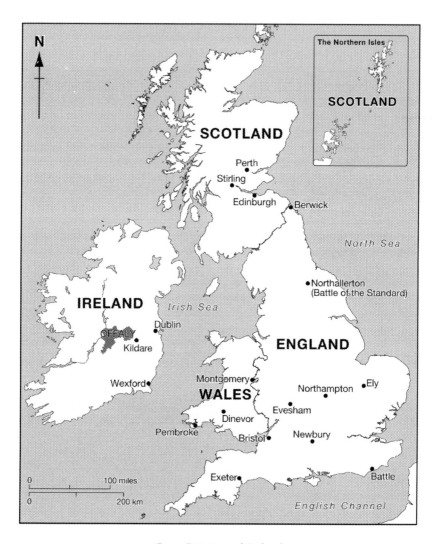

Great Britain and Ireland

France and the Low Countries

Southern Italy and Sicily

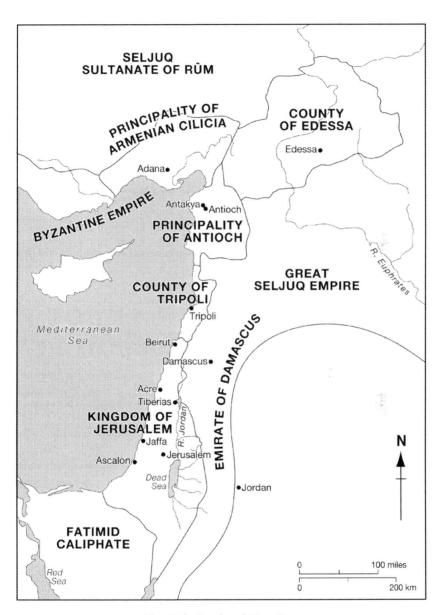

The Holy Land and Near East

Jim Shoenbill, "Trojan Horse", original version printed in *Private Eye*, issue no. 1535, 20 Nov. – 3 Dec. 2020, p. 38. Reproduced by kind permission of the artist.

Introduction

Low Cunning in the High Middle Ages

The daring commando raid behind enemy lines. The dummy pass that outwits the defender and enables the match-winning try. The superhero concealing their true identity behind a mask. Examples of admirable deception abound in our culture. Yet deceit and trickery are also the tools of the con-artist, the spin doctor and the terrorist. In April 2017, Afghanistan's Defence minister, Abdullah Habibi, and army chief of staff, Qadam Shad Shahim, both resigned after a Taliban force was able to enter an Afghan army base disguised as injured soldiers, wearing bandages and arm drips, resulting in the death or injury of up to 170 people.[1] Our attitudes to deception are profoundly ambiguous and contextual.

Medieval Europeans could be similarly ambiguous in their opinions on deception. Medieval literature is full of tricksters, both heroic and surprisingly amoral. Clerics, charged with guarding society's spiritual and moral health, diligently preserved exemplars of military deception inherited from the Classical world and recorded similar tales in their contemporary histories. And combatants, even chivalrous knights and nobles, appear to have been perfectly willing to use ambush, disguise and other forms of trickery to gain an advantage in battle.

The idea of a 'chivalrous trickster' may sound like a tautology to many modern readers. When we talk about 'chivalry', we associate it with honour, good manners and 'fair play' and assume that these values have some distant origin in medieval culture. This view is compounded by a simplistic depiction of medieval warfare in certain popular histories: 'Opposing armies generally continued to form up a thousand meters apart and basically to leap, grunt, and hack at each other […] campaigns were conceived of in terms of individual battles and victory was something to be exploited for plunder rather than pursuit'.[2] Specialist study over the past fifty years

---

[1] Sune Engel Rasmussen, 'Afghan defence officials quit over Taliban attack as Pentagon chief flies in', *The Guardian*, 24 Apr. 2017 <https://www.theguardian.com/world/2017/apr/24/afghan-defence-officials-resign-deadly-taliban-attack> [accessed 24 Oct. 2020].

[2] Christon I. Archer *et al.*, *World History of Warfare* (Lincoln, NE, 2002), pp. 143, 145.

has greatly advanced our understanding of medieval warfare beyond this crude stereotype. For the period 1050–1320, commonly referred to as the Central or High Middle Ages, the work of scholars such as John France, John Gillingham and J. F. Verbruggen has revealed a level of strategic and tactical complexity to medieval warfare that is greatly at odds with the image of primitive warriors charging headlong at one another.[3] Medieval armies engaged in elaborate conflicts of move and counter-move, preferring to attack their enemy's supply lines and strongholds rather than seek open battle. Similarly, we now possess a more nuanced understanding of the martial culture of the medieval West, what modern scholars call 'chivalry'. No longer dismissed as mere vanity, a glamour to hide the ugly reality of war, or a dogma that robbed fighting men of their reason, chivalry is appreciated as a complex socio-cultural phenomenon, one that both reflected the values of the medieval aristocracy and challenged them to reform their behaviour.[4]

One aspect of medieval warfare that has been under-represented in modern scholarship is that of military deception, or stratagem: deliberate attempts to deceive or mislead an enemy in order to gain a strategic or tactical advantage.[5] At best, it is acknowledged in passing, treated as an amusing curiosity. At worst, incidents are dismissed as pure fantasy and not worthy of the serious historian's attention. Marjorie Chibnall dismissed an account of how Ranulf of Chester captured Lincoln castle

---

[3] Medieval military history is a large and evolving field. The following represent good introductions for the general reader or student: John France, *Western Warfare in the Age of the Crusades 1000–1300* (London, 1999); John Gillingham, 'William the Bastard at War', in Christopher Harper-Bill, Christopher J. Holdsworth and Janet L. Nelson (eds.), *Studies in Medieval History Presented to R. Allen Brown* (Woodbridge, 1989), pp. 141–58; Helen Nicholson, *Medieval Warfare: Theory and Practice of War in Europe 300–1500* (Basingstoke, 2004); J. F. Verbruggen, *The Art of Warfare in Western Europe during the Middle Ages from the Eighth Century to 1340*, trans. Summer Willard and Sheila C. M. Southern, 2nd edn (Woodbridge, 1998). For readers interested in specific topics, the following bibliography is an ideal starting point, along with the 2003–6 update of the same: Kelly DeVries, *A Cumulative Bibliography of Medieval Military History and Technology* (Leiden, 2002).

[4] As with medieval military history, the history of chivalry is vast. Keen remains the touchstone but any of the following texts would be a good introduction to the field: Richard Barber, *The Knight and Chivalry*, rev edn (Woodbridge, 1995); Robert W. Jones and Peter Coss (eds.), *A Companion to Chivalry* (Woodbridge, 2019); Richard Kaeuper, *Medieval Chivalry* (Cambridge, 2016); Maurice Keen, *Chivalry* (New Haven, CT, 1984); Matthew Strickland, *War and Chivalry: The Conduct and Perception of War in England and Normandy, 1066–1217* (Cambridge, 1996).

[5] The strategic theorist Barton Whaley defined deception as any action '*intended* [sic] by its perpetrator to dupe or mislead a victim'. This excludes instances in which the victim merely misunderstands an enemy's intent and is surprised: the deception is intentional or is at least perceived to be so. Barton Whaley, *Stratagem: Deception and Surprise in War* (Norwood, MA, 2007), p. 47.

by trickery in 1141, recorded by the Norman chronicler Orderic Vitalis, as 'part of the fictional element that crept into history at every level, like the fables decorating the borders of the Bayeux Tapestry'.[6] Helen Nicholson was more equivocal about this kind of story: 'The similarity of these accounts indicates that either this was a standard tale to demonstrate the ingenuity of the young warrior-hero, or that this sort of trick was used rather frequently'.[7]

Only a handful of scholars have dedicated entire works to medieval military deception. Emily Albu analysed Norman and Byzantine historians' shared interest in stories of trickery and their mutual appreciation for cunning, with particular reference to Anna Komnene's story of how Bohemond escaped her father's patrols by faking his own death.[8] David Whetham's 2009 monograph is based on a detailed study of attitudes towards deception in later medieval theological and legal texts, primarily Honoré Bovet's treatise *L'Arbre des batailles* (1387). He concluded that these theorists viewed deception as licit because pitched battles between kings, the only licit form of warfare, were believed to be akin to judicial duels, in which God would award victory to the righteous, and such duels were to be fought by any means necessary.[9] At the time of writing, Yuval Noah Harari is the only scholar to have studied medieval accounts of military deception in detail. He used six case studies of stealthy expeditions, ranging from the capture of Antioch by the first crusaders in 1098 to the French officer Blaise de Monluc's raid on the Provençal town of Auriol in 1536. Harari calls these expeditions 'special operations', although (as he himself acknowledges) medieval armies possessed no equivalent to today's highly trained special forces.[10] These case studies brilliantly illustrate the daring and ingenuity that medieval combatants could employ to achieve their aims. The present volume can be read in conjunction with Harari, placing these remarkable incidents in their broader historical context.

In order to provide this context, it is necessary to identify the various kinds of deception that were employed in medieval warfare and to analyse what contemporaries thought about them. Specifically, was trickery seen as a licit or illicit way of waging war? Was deception honourable and

---

[6] Marjorie Chibnall, 'Orderic Vitalis on Castles', in C. Harper-Bill, C. J. Holdsworth, and J. L. Nelson (eds.), *Studies in Medieval History Presented to R. Allen Brown* (Woodbridge, 1989), pp. 43–56, at p. 55.
[7] Nicholson, *Medieval Warfare*, p. 130.
[8] Emily Albu, 'Bohemond and the Rooster: Byzantines, Normans, and the Artful Ruse', in Thalia Gouma-Peterson (ed.), *Anna Komnene and her Times* (London, 2000), pp. 157–68.
[9] David Whetham, *Just Wars and Moral Victories: Surprise, Deception and the Normative Framework of European War in the Later Middle Ages* (Leiden, 2009), p. 103.
[10] Yuval Noah Harari, *Special Operations in the Age of Chivalry, 1100–1550* (Woodbridge, 2007), pp. 34–7.

shameful? Were some forms of deception permissible and others not? To answer these questions, I will make a close textual analysis of the incidents of military deception reported in contemporary narrative histories. I have chosen to focus primarily on texts produced in the Francophone world during the central Middle Ages (c. 1000–1320), as this enables me to explore a theme within a single culture, that of England, France and the Low Countries. These regions were dominated by a powerful, landed aristocracy which shared a common religion, language and value system. In addition, by choosing this particular period, I am able to use sources for the various conflicts between this culture and the racially, culturally or religiously 'other', who did not always fight in the same manner or hold the same ethical values. This was an age of conquest and expansion, when Francophone armies fought and settled on the fringes of Europe: in Wales and Ireland in the British archipelago, in Sicily in the Mediterranean and in Syria and Palestine in the Near East. By studying what Francophone Europeans considered strange or abhorrent in the 'other', we can better understand their own self-image and cultural mores.[11]

The central Middle Ages also represents a relatively well-defined period in the history of European warfare. It is distinguished from preceding centuries by two key innovations. The first was the armoured horseman, whose combination of speed, training and heavy armour made him the core of every significant military force.[12] Foot soldiers, by contrast, were often relegated to an auxiliary role, as they lacked the necessary discipline to engage horsemen in the open (although they could be highly effective in defence).[13] The second factor that dominated warfare was the castle: stone or wooden fortifications, either built independently or as part of an urban settlement. Contemporary siege technology had difficulty breaching fortifications, meaning that forces had to commit many resources to either capture or contain enemy strongholds. Campaigns often centred around

---

[11] As the focus of this volume is Francophone Europe and its sources, sources produced by these other cultures will be consulted only for comparison with the narratives from the main corpus. A comparative study of Muslim and Latin Christian sources, for example, and their depiction of military deception in the Levant would be of immense value but it is beyond the scope of this present volume.

[12] France, *Western Warfare*, pp. 53–65; Nicholson, *Medieval Warfare*, pp. 53–7; Michael Prestwich, '*Miles in armis strenuus*: The Knight at War', *Transactions of the Royal Historical Society*, 6 (1995), 201–10; Verbruggen, *The Art of Warfare*, pp. 276–350.

[13] Matthew Bennett, 'The Myth of the Military Supremacy of Knightly Cavalry', in *Armies, Chivalry and Warfare in Medieval Britain: Proceedings of the 1995 Harlaxton Symposium*, ed. Matthew Strickland (Stamford, 1998), pp. 304–16; Stephen Morillo, 'The "Age of Cavalry" Revisited', in *The Circle of War in the Middle Ages: Essays on Medieval Military and Naval History*, ed. Donald J. Kagay and L. J. Andrew Villalon (Woodbridge, 1999), pp. 45–58.

the control of key strongholds.[14] Over the course of this period the European aristocracy and the horsemen who made up their retinues came to regard themselves as a distinct social group, the *militia* or 'knighthood' of Christendom. United by a common language, a common set of cultural values that we would call 'chivalrous' and a common Catholic Christian religion, they formed a reasonably homogenous group whose attitudes can be assessed through historical enquiry. Towards the end of this period and into the fourteenth century there were fundamental shifts in the practice of warfare in the medieval West: the 'feudal vassals' whom princes could call upon for a limited period of military service ceased to play a significant role in armies and waged soldiers became the basis for most forces. Furthermore, social and technological changes led to the emergence of foot soldiers as a potentially battle-winning force, demonstrated by the victories of infantry armies at Courtrai (1302), Bannockburn (1314) and Morgarten (1315).[15] While this was not the end of the armoured horseman's dominance, it marked a shift in the practice of warfare that sets the fourteenth century apart from those that preceded it.[16]

The evidence for this study will be drawn mainly from chronicles, contemporary narrative histories mainly written in Latin but with an increasing number of vernacular texts appearing in the thirteenth and fourteenth centuries. As will be discussed in Chapter 1, there are significant problems with using these texts for military history. The majority of chronicle authors were monks or clerics with little first-hand experience of war. Although they claimed to accurately record contemporary events, based on reliable testimony or personal experience, medieval standards and expectations of what constituted 'good' or 'truthful' history were very

---

[14] Charles L. H. Coulson, *Castles in Medieval Society: Fortresses in England, France, and Ireland in the Central Middle Ages* (Oxford, 2003); Kelly DeVries and Robert Douglas Smith, *Medieval Military Technology*, 2nd edn (Toronto, 2012), pp. 187–249; R. Rogers, *Latin Siege Warfare in the Twelfth Century* (Oxford, 1992).

[15] Rogers is the main proponent of this interpretation of the period. Clifford J. Rogers, 'The Military Revolutions of the Hundred Years' War', *Journal of Military History*, 57 (1993), 241–78; Clifford J. Rogers, 'Tactics and the Face of Battle', in *European Warfare, 1350–1750*, ed. Frank Tallett and D. J. B. Trim (Cambridge, 2010), pp. 203–35. DeVries provides an informative survey of infantry warfare at the turn of the 14th century. Kelly DeVries, *Infantry Warfare in the Early Fourteenth Century: Discipline, Tactics and Technology* (Woodbridge, 1996). Stone has provided valuable criticism of Rogers's thesis, shifting the argument away from technological explanations for the rise of 'infantry warfare' and identifying the more fundamental social and economic causes. John Stone, 'Technology, Society, and the Infantry Revolution of the Fourteenth Century', *Journal of Military History*, 68 (2004), 361–80.

[16] Similar periodisation is used in a number of notable survey texts such as Philippe Contamine, *War in the Middle Ages*, trans. Michael Jones (Oxford, 1984), pp. 208–37; Maurice Keen (ed.), *Medieval Warfare: A History* (Oxford, 1999); Verbruggen, *Art of Warfare*.

different from modern standards of objective reporting. Nevertheless, chronicles remain our best sources for the conduct of medieval warfare. Clerics preserved and copied Roman manuals on war but there is little evidence that these were used by medieval commanders or that they produced equivalent texts themselves.[17] Contemporary literary works, such as the Old French epics or Arthurian romances, written for and about the military aristocracy, can be fruitfully used as sources for the history of warfare but their highly stylised accounts of combat, focusing on heroic individuals, present their own problems of interpretation.[18] History and literature were more closely intertwined in medieval thought than they are today but, in order to compare like with like and maintain a clear focus on a single genre, this volume will focus primarily on those texts which contemporaries regarded as 'historical' records of contemporary events, with occasional reference to literary texts for illustration.

Furthermore, even if we doubt whether a chronicler's version of events, the narrative can still provide a valuable insight into the culture that produced it. Clerical authors were often aristocrats themselves and wrote for aristocratic patrons. What they chose to record, how they chose to portray certain events, what they chose to redact or leave out, tells us something about the author's views and those of his intended audience. This makes them excellent sources for learning about medieval *attitudes* towards deception in warfare, even when we may doubt whether a particular deception took place exactly as described.

As one of the goals of this volume is to demonstrate the ubiquity and diversity of the deceptions recorded in chronicles, it has been helpful to construct a taxonomy of trickery, which can be found in Appendix 1. The taxonomy contains over four hundred individual incidents of deception that I have identified in my corpus, which I have classified into ten categories based on their common features. As with any classification, there is a degree of artifice about this exercise: some incidents share features with multiple different categories. Most notably, the categories of 'ambushes' and 'feigned flight to lead an enemy into a pre-prepared ambush' have significant overlap but I felt it was necessary to distinguish the latter as a separate entity, characterised by the use of a decoy force to lure the victims into the ambush, which is not present in most descriptions of ambushes. In the main text, I analyse only a selection of representative incidents

---

[17] See Chapter 1 for a discussion of these texts and their influence on medieval chronicles.

[18] For examples of military history based on Old French literature, see Matthew Bennett, 'Wace and Warfare', in *Anglo-Norman Studies XI: Proceedings of the Battle Conference 1988*, ed. R. Allen Brown (Woodbridge, 1989), pp. 37–57; Catherine Hanley, *War and Combat 1150–1270: The Evidence from Old French Literature* (Cambridge, 2003).

from this wider body of material. The taxonomy has been included to demonstrate that the incidents discussed in this volume form part of a broader trend within chronicle writing. Whatever contemporaries may have thought about the rights and wrongs of deception in war, they clearly did not think it was uncommon.

The main text considers specific kinds of deceptions, how contemporaries used them and how they are presented in the chronicles. This involves a close analysis of the text: how the author presents a given incident of deception, how the ordering of events, the inclusion or exclusion of particular details, and the vocabulary used indicate what the author thought about the incident and what message they wanted to convey to their audience. The order of chapters has been chosen to reflect the order of Frontinus' *Strategemata* (see Chapter 1), which is divided into stratagems to be employed before battle, during battle and in siege warfare. Thus, Chapter 2 discusses forms of military deception that occur on the strategic level of war, such as feigned manoeuvres, and what we would today call 'information warfare'. This involves the dissemination of false information and the use of deception to gather accurate information by employing spies. Chapter 3 is the first to consider actual tactics, analysing accounts of surprise attacks in which one force attacked another unawares, either from ambush or under cover of darkness. Chapter 4 studies the feigned or false flight stratagem and the controversy surrounding its use at the Battle of Hastings (1066). Chapter 5 analyses various forms of disguise. While these are among the more fantastical stories of deception in the chronicles, they nevertheless provide valuable information about the link between appearance and social status in medieval society. This chapter also features a section on the development of battlefield heraldry and how it created new opportunities for combatants to disguise themselves by discarding or changing their coat of arms. Chapter 6 considers the role of bribery in siege warfare, in which an attacking force would offer some form of inducement to gain access to a stronghold. Also associated with siege warfare, Chapter 7 discusses the oath in medieval culture and the circumstances in which combatants swore false oaths or broke their word to an enemy in order to gain a tactical advantage. Finally, Chapters 8 and 9 move beyond analysis of specific ruses to focus on contemporary attitudes towards deception and the associated quality of cunning. Chapter 8 uses analysis of specific Latin terms to reveal how authors viewed trickery and how subtle variations in vocabulary reveal significant ambiguity in their attitudes. Chapter 9 looks at the (considerably rarer) explicit discussions of military deception and its morality in both canon law and chronicles, as well as how trickery was perceived in the culturally or religious 'other'. No one method can definitively capture 'the medieval attitude' towards military deception but, by presenting evidence in this impressionistic way, I hope to convey a sense of the broad trends in contemporary thought.

Many of the stories discussed below probably never happened or have been grossly exaggerated in the telling and re-telling. Nevertheless, they are entertaining stories and should be remembered for that reason alone. If subjected to careful analysis, they become something more: an insight into the grim business of medieval warfare and what people thought and felt about it. By throwing light on this neglected aspect of the history of war, I would like to stimulate conversations about the intersection of military, cultural and textual histories and encourage scholars to look again at the implausible, the absurd and the fanciful in their own sources.

1

Trickery in Medieval Culture: Sources and Problems

Before we can analyse how deception was used in medieval warfare, we must establish the cultural framework within which the combatants operated: the social values by which they and contemporaries judged their conduct. It is also necessary to understand how our sources were written, what the authors and their audience expected from a narrative history and particularly a history of war. As noted above, medieval chronicles are often far removed from our notions of impartial reporting. They are conscious literary constructions, drawing on over a thousand years of Classical and medieval writing. Each chronicle author had their own agenda and nuances that influenced how they depicted warfare.

Foxy Outlaws and Outlaw Foxes: Trickery in Medieval Literature

We begin by noting that one of the most enduring and recognisable images of the European Middle Ages is a trickster figure: Robin Hood, the greenwood outlaw who uses his cunning as often as his bow and arrow to resist the Sheriff of Nottingham.[1] Modern audiences are familiar with Errol Flynn leading his men into Nottingham Castle disguised as monks (1938, dir. Michael Curtiz and William Keighley) and Kevin Costner's band emerging from foxholes to ambush wagonloads of ill-gotten tax money (1991, dir. Kevin Reynolds).[2] This use of deception reflects the original fifteenth-century ballads. In *Robin Hood and the Potter*, after losing a fight with the

---

[1] Robin Hood studies is a vast field, but the following texts are good, general introductions to both the search for a 'historical' Robin and the literary tradition: David Crook, *Robin Hood: Legend and Reality* (Woodbridge, 2020); J. C. Holt, *Robin Hood*, rev edn (London, 2011); Maurice Keen, *The Outlaws of Medieval Legend*, rev edn (London, 1977); Stephen Knight, *Robin Hood: A Complete Study of the English Outlaw* (Oxford, 1994); Stephen Knight and Thomas Ohlgren (eds.), *Robin Hood and Other Outlaw Tales*, 2nd edn (Kalamazoo, MI, 2000).

[2] Even Ridley Scott's abysmal 2010 adaptation had a common-born Robin impersonating a nobleman, Sir Robert Loxley.

titular potter, Robin exchanges clothes with him and uses the disguise to work his way into the Sheriff's confidence.[3] Similarly, in *Robin Hood and Guy of Gisborne*, having killed Gisborne and mutilated his severed head, Robin dresses himself in Gisborne's clothes and passes his enemy's head off as his own in order to rescue Little John.[4]

Although these ballads were likely composed much later than the period studied in this volume, similar tales of forest-dwelling outlaws have survived from the central Middle Ages.[5] The infamous pirate Eustace Busquet (d. 1217) was portrayed as a cunning anti-hero in the thirteenth-century Old French poem *Li Romans de Witasse le moine*, fighting against the unjust count of Boulogne from his refuge in Hardelot Forest. He adopts many disguises, including a shepherd, a carpenter, a pastry cook, a prostitute and a potter.[6] The same motifs appear in the Anglo-Norman prose *Fouke fitz Waryn*, which combines a life of the historical Fulk fitz Waryn III (c. 1201–57) with both outlaw and romance tropes, including jousting, dragon-slaying and a love affair with a Muslim princess. Fulk, an Anglo-Norman lord of the Welsh marches, renounces his homage to King John and flees to the woods to live as an outlaw. He outwits and humiliates John's agents, disguised variously as a monk, a merchant and a charcoal burner. In one episode, he defeats a man sent to capture him and then passes off his would-be captor as himself by switching their coats of arms.[7] Tales of cunning outlaws who used guile and deceit to achieve their ends were clearly popular long before the Robin Hood tradition emerged.

Of particular interest for the present study is the twelfth-century *Gesta Herwardi*, a pseudo-historical life of Hereward (sometimes referred to as 'Hereward the Wake', after Charles Kingsley's 1866 novel of the same name), an English nobleman who led a brief campaign of resistance

---

[3] 'Robin Hood and the Potter', in Knight and Ohlgren (eds.), *Robin Hood and Other Outlaw Tales*, pp. 57–79.

[4] 'Robin Hood and Guy of Gisborne', in Knight and Ohlgren (eds.), *Robin Hood and Other Outlaw Tales*, pp. 169–83.

[5] The earliest surviving ballad, *Robin Hood and the Monk*, appears in Cambridge University manuscript Ff. 5. 48, dated c. 1450, while the first textual reference to Robin Hood appears in William Langland's Middle English poem *Piers Plowman* (c. 1377): 'But I kan rymes of Robyn hood and Randolf Erl of Chestre'. This suggests that tales of Robin Hood were already current in the later fourteenth century, originating earlier in that century or even the thirteenth century. Holt, *Robin Hood*, pp. 11–13; 'Robin Hood and the Monk', in Knight and Ohlgren (eds.), *Robin Hood and Other Outlaw Tales*, pp. 31–56, at pp. 31–4.

[6] Denis Joseph Conlon (ed.), *Li Romans di Witasse le moine* (Chapel Hill, NC, 1972). An annotated English translation can be found in Glyn S. Burgess, *Two Medieval Outlaws: Eustace the Monk and Fouke Fitz Waryn* (Cambridge, 1997), pp. 50–78.

[7] E. J. Hathaway, P. T. Ricketts, C. A. Robson, and A. D. Wilshere (eds.), *Fouke le fitz Waryn* (Oxford, 1975). An annotated English translation can be found in Burgess, *Two Medieval Outlaws*, pp. 134–83.

against the Normans from the Cambridgeshire Fens.[8] The author of the *Gesta*, a monk of Ely named Richard, claimed to have translated the text into Latin from an earlier account in Old English.[9] The author mixes the historical career of Hereward with elements of French romance, depicting him as a knight [*miles*] who fights in tournaments, rescues damsels and is dubbed, 'in the English manner', by the abbot of Peterborough.[10] Hugh M. Thomas has theorised that the author sought to elevate Hereward in the eyes of his (presumably Francophone) readers, perhaps in response to accusations that the English had been conquered in 1066 because they were weak or cowardly.[11] The *Gesta* is particularly significant for this volume because it was written in Latin, concerns an unambiguously heroic figure and contains numerous episodes in which the protagonist employs trickery against his enemies. Not only do Hereward and his men frequently ambush their enemies, Hereward feigns flight in battle, disguises himself a potter to infiltrate William the Conqueror's court, dresses as a fisherman to infiltrate a Norman camp at Cottenham and, on one occasion, instructs his men to put their horses' shoes on backwards to disguise their movements.[12] These stories may seem implausible, even fantastical, to us (and perhaps to their original audience too) but it is important to note that the author *chose* to include them. He clearly thought his readers would be interested in this kind of story and that they would not see trickery as incompatible with martial heroism.

If we look beyond historical and pseudo-historical accounts, we find numerous tricksters and deceivers in medieval literature. The anonymous black or red knight is a staple of medieval romance, while the enduring legend of Tristan and Isolde emphasises the elaborate deceptions the couple employ to keep their affair hidden from King Mark.[13] The most

---

[8] For a modern English translation, see Michael Swanton, 'The Deeds of Hereward', in Thomas H. Ohlgren (trans.), *Medieval Outlaws: Ten Tales in Modern English* (Stroud, 1998), pp. 12–60.
[9] 'Gesta Herwardi incliti exulis et militis', in Thomas Duffus Hardy and Charles Trice Martin (eds.), *Lestorie des Engles solum la translacion maistre Geffrei Gaimar* (2 vols, London, 1888), vol. I, pp. 339–404, at p. 339: 'videlicet primitiva insignia praeclarissimi exulis Herwardi, editum Anglico stilo a Lefrico Diacono, ejusdem ad Brun presbyterum'.
[10] 'Gesta Herwardi', p. 368.
[11] Hugh M. Thomas, 'The *Gesta Herwardi*, the English and their Conquerors', in Christopher Harper-Bill (ed.), *Anglo-Norman Studies* XXI: *Proceedings of the Battle Conference 1998* (Woodbridge, 1999), pp. 213–32.
[12] 'Gesta Herwardi', pp. 374, 384–9, 393. The trick with the horseshoes also appears in *Li Romans de Witasse* at lines 1494–515. and in *Fouke fitz Waryn* at folio 32, lines 4–10.
[13] For Tristan as trickster, see Merrit R. Blakeslee, 'Tristan the Trickster in the Old French Tristan Poems', *Cultura neolatina*, 44 (1984), 167–90; Nancy Freeman Regalado, 'Tristan and Renart: Two Tricksters', *L'Esprit créateur*, 16 (1976), 30–8.

famous trickster in medieval literature is undoubtedly Renart the Fox. First appearing in a supporting role in the twelfth-century Latin 'beast epic' *Ysengrimus*, Renart became the central character in a series of forty tales known as the *Roman de Renart*, compiled between 1170 and 1240.[14] The *Roman* was very popular; it was adapted into German as *Reinhart Fuchs* by Heinrich der Glîchesaere, into Flemish as *Van den Vos Reinaerde* and into Italian as *Rainardo e Lesengrino*.[15] Inhabiting a world of anthropomorphic animals, Renart is portrayed as a gleefully duplicitous anti-hero, unable to enter into any agreement without immediately seeking a way to break it to his advantage. Lacking the strength of his archfoe Isengrin the Wolf, he is forced to rely on ruses, dissimulation and lies to obtain food and avenge himself upon his enemies.[16] Roger Ballon argued that Renart embodies the Old French concept of *engin*, which may mean 'a trick, wile or dodge' but can also stand for 'an attitude of mind, a rule of conduct, and an approach to life […] all Renart's other characteristics are subordinated to his innate and unfailing trickery'.[17] It is a profoundly ambiguous term, as Robert W. Hanning has noted: it can refer to the marvellous creations of human ingenuity and wit, such as machines or beautiful buildings, but also to acts of manipulation and deceit.[18]

The *Roman* is a burlesque, a carnival-like upending of social norms: 'overturning all the positive values and aspirations of the day'.[19] Bawdy, vulgar and cheerfully amoral, the stories invite the reader to alternately laugh with Renart as he escapes the consequences of his crimes and to laugh at him when he himself duped, an example of the 'trickster tricked' motif found throughout world folklore.[20] Nobility and chivalric conventions are among the *Roman's* many targets, not least in Renart's encounter

---

[14] R. Anthony Lodge and Kenneth Varty (eds.), *The Earliest Branches of the Roman de Renart*, (Leuven, 2001), p. xiv.
[15] Kenneth Varty, *Reynard the Fox: A Study of the Fox in Medieval English Art* (Leicester, 1967), p. 23.
[16] An image of Renart wounding Isengrin in battle appears on the cover for this volume.
[17] Roger Ballon, 'Trickery as an Element of the Character of Renart', *Forum for Modern Language Studies*, 22 (1986), 34–52, at p. 34.
[18] Robert W. Hanning, *The Individual in Twelfth-Century Romance* (New Haven, CT, 1977), pp. 105–38.
[19] Lodge and Varty, *Earliest Branches*, p. xiii. For a specific example of how the *Roman* satirised the sacred symbols of the crusade, see Sarah Lambert, 'Translation, Citation, and Ridicule: Renart the Fox and Crusading in the Vernacular', in Sarah Lambert and Helen Nicholson (eds.), *Languages of Love and Hate: Conflict, Communication, and Identity in the Medieval Mediterranean* (Turnhout, 2012), pp. 65–86.
[20] Stith Thompson, *Motif-Index of Folk Literature: A Classification of Narrative Elements in Folktales, Ballads, Myths, Fables, Mediaeval Romances, Exempla, Fabliaux, Jest-Books and Local Legends*, rev edn (6 vols, Copenhagen, 1955), vol. 4, pp. 413–21.

with Tibert the Cat. Renart, having enlisted Tibert to fight with him against Isengrin, immediately breaks the rules of 'chivalrous companionship' by trying to push Tibert into a trap he has laid.[21] It is therefore surprising to find a positive reference to Renart in the famous knightly text, the *History of William Marshal*. In 1208, having regained the favour of King John of England, William Marshal, earl of Pembroke, was permitted to leave the royal court and visit his lands in Leinster, which were under attack from Meiler fitz Henry, the king's justiciar in Ireland. Landing at Glasscarrick in Wexford, he was met by his vassals but was disturbed to see that one of them, John of Earley, was wearing armour: 'The Marshal said to him: "How did this happen? Don't hide anything from me. Sir John, why are you wearing a habergeon? There's a peace now, is there not? Is this a joke?" "Sir, not everybody keeps it". He answered with subtlety, like Renart the fox'.[22]

We can be reasonably sure that this comparison was meant to be flattering. John of Earley, who joined the Marshal's household as a squire c. 1187, became one of his closest companions and was still alive at the time of the *History*'s composition. In his introduction to the text, David Crouch argued that it was 'likely to have been his recollections on which much of the key detail of the Irish exile and the [Marshal's] deathbed narrative depend'.[23] It is possible that Earley himself told the poet about this conversation or that his answer was remembered as a famous *bon mot* in the Marshal's household. Regardless, the poet would have been unlikely to compare the much-honoured (and still-living) Earley to Renart if this would have been taken as an insult. It is worth remembering that a knight could be admired for his fox-like *soutilz* as we go on to discuss their conduct in war in the following chapters.

Cunning was not just useful on the battlefield. In her study of the fourteenth-century MS Paris BnF fr. 19152, Tracy Adams has proposed that this anthology was compiled to teach readers the importance of 'cunning intelligence' in navigating the difficulties of life. The anthology contains around 88 works, including Marie de France's fables, texts with religious or courtly themes, and a variety of *fabliaux*, comical and bawdy tales. This amalgamation of different material disregards the critical distinction between the courtly and the non-courtly, allowing the emergence of 'a new type of character [...] from stories of all registers, one whose success

---

[21] Lodge and Varty, *Earliest Branches*, pp. xlvi–xlvii.
[22] HWM, lines 13953–60: 'Li Mareschal li dist: "Comment / Avient? nel me celez naient. /Sire Johan, par que raison / Avez vos vestu herbergon? / Dont n'est il pais? est ço dont gas?" / "Sire, tuit ne la tienent pas." / Il respondi comme soutilz: / Issi dist Reinart li gorpilz'.
[23] HWM, vol. 3, p. 32.

depends upon his or her cunning intelligence'.[24] The anthology opens with a series of framed tales, *Le Chastoiement que li pères ensaigne à son filz*, a vernacular adaptation of the twelfth-century *Disciplina clericalis* by Petrus Alfonsi.[25] In this text, a father teaches his son, through a series of illustrative tales, the two important qualities necessary to attain success in life: *sens et savoir*. This is not the amoral *enging* of Renart, however: the father's first admonition is that his son should fear God and not be a hypocrite:

> Sens et savoir, which at first seems to present two qualities, is rather cunning intelligence practiced within a framework of traditional Christian morality [...] The world is full of all varieties of false friends, cheating wives, and con artists. The wisdom to identify the cheats of the world is not sufficient: to be successful, one must employ trickery oneself. Still, one must fear God.[26]

The theme of cunning intelligence, tempered by Christian ethics, continues throughout the anthology, reframing the classic, hierarchical relationship between the sexes as portrayed in traditional courtly texts as 'exercises in calculated negotiation'. The prologue to the romantic *Lai de l'ombre*, which depicts the ploys of two lovers seeking to test one another's fidelity, derides the one who lacks the *sens* to distinguish between mere copulation and acts of mutual love. Adams proposes that this ideal of cunning intelligence would have been 'more appealing and useful than the "courtly" values of sincerity, prowess and passivity' to the French nobility, who had to navigate the shifting loyalties and duplicitous culture of the royal and princely courts.[27]

As we can see, there was a widespread interest in stories about cunning in medieval culture. Outlaw tales, beast epics, fables and romances all indicate that people took pleasure in hearing about clever tricks or a wily trickster being outwitted. This should be expected: such stories form a fundamental element of world folklore.[28] Yet they are not confined to tales of talking foxes or greenwood outlaws. The medieval chronicles record incidents of trickery in battle that appear to be pure folklore. Scholars have

---

[24] Tracy Adams, 'The Cunningly Intelligent Characters of BnF fr. 19152', *Modern Language Notes*, 120 (2005), 896–924, at p. 898.

[25] The *Disciplina* is itself an adaptation of the Arabic mirror for princes *Kalila wa Dimna*. Adams, 'Cunningly Intelligent', pp. 907–8.

[26] Adams, 'Cunningly Intelligent', p. 905.

[27] Adams, 'Cunningly Intelligent', pp. 923–4.

[28] Stith Thompson, in his index of motifs found in folk-literature, listed 2399 individual motifs under 'Deception'. Of particular relevance to this study are the twenty motifs listed under the subheading 'Military Strategy', including such common ruses as 'Disguise as merchant to enter an enemy castle', 'Capture of castle by feigning death' and 'Hero causes confusion in enemy camp in dead of night', all of which appear in the chronicles discussed below. Thompson, *Motif-Index of Folk Literature*, vol. 4, pp. 231–3, 495–7.

long struggled to rationalise the chroniclers' seeming acceptance of the supernatural and fantastical, which they recorded alongside what appear to be sober historical fact, but much less has been written about the merely implausible or the unlikely: the colourful stories, the 'old chestnuts' which raise a wry smile but merit little more than a passing reference. We must now turn to the chronicles: their purpose as a genre, their relationship to historical fact and how we are to interpret them as sources for the history of warfare.

Writing War in the Middle Ages: The Classical Legacy

Medieval chronicles were not solely a product of the Middle Ages. Medieval historians looked back to the great Roman authors, such as Livy, Virgil and Cicero, imitating their style and structure, often lifting whole phrases or quotations to give their work an air of classical authority. To understand how medieval authors wrote about a given subject, such as military deception, it is important to understand what their sources and models said about it.

When writing about warfare, medieval authors looked to Roman exemplars, primarily Publius Flavius Vegetius Renatus's *De re militari* (On Military Matters). By his own admission Vegetius, a fourth-century civil servant, never intended to write an 'art of war', or even an original military treatise, but merely to summarise the work of older authorities.[29] As a result, much of *De re militari*'s content was already antiquated by the fourth century.[30] It has been suggested that Vegetius compiled his text in response to the empire's humiliating defeat at Adrianople (378), advocating that the imperial army should be reformed to resemble the legions of the Roman Republic.[31] The sections on strategy and tactics consist largely of banal commonplaces: do not attack an enemy who outnumbers you; it is useful to surprise an enemy; soldiers who are properly led fight better than those who are not etc.[32] Despite its out-dated and generic content, *De re militari* continued to be copied and transmitted throughout the Middle Ages and beyond: what Sydney Anglo dubbed 'the triumph of

---

[29] Publius Flavius Vegetius Renatus, *Epitoma rei militaris*, ed. M. D. Reeve (Oxford, 2004), pp. 4–5.
[30] For example, Vegetius' use of *principes*, *hastate* and *triarii* to describe the battle-order of the ancient legion comes from the Republican armies of the third and second centuries BCE. Publius Flavius Vegetius Renatus, *Epitome of Military Science*, trans. N. P. Milner, 2nd edn (Liverpool, 1996), p. xvii.
[31] Vegetius, *Epitoma rei militaris*, p. ix.
[32] Nicholson, *Medieval Warfare*, p. 15.

mediocrity'.[33] 220 copies of the complete text survive, in addition to forty collections of select extracts, making it one of the most widely copied classical texts during the Middle Ages.[34] Christopher Allmand has argued that the generic nature of *De re militari*'s advice actually contributed to its enduring popularity, as its commonplaces could be applied to a variety of different circumstances. Vegetius' style, favouring the 'terse, easily remembered and recognisable statement', also helped. Finally, it was the only text of its kind to survive into the Middle Ages.[35]

Although it was widely copied, there is no firm evidence to indicate that *De re militari*'s advice was read and applied by medieval commanders. Bernard S. Bachrach has argued that *De re militari* was both read and followed in this period, using the example of Fulk Nerra, count of Anjou, but the most he can say is that there are 'fragments of circumstantial evidence' to suggest that Fulk may have read it, conceding that 'there is no direct evidence'.[36] Likewise, John Hosler, in his study of the military career of Henry II of England, is only able to offer 'circumstantial clues' that Henry may have read *De re militari*.[37] As noted, Vegetius' advice is little more than common sense, so it is very difficult to determine when a commander was following his advice.[38]

Far more important than any hypothetical impact it may have had on the conduct of war is *De rei militari*'s clear and demonstrable impact on medieval authors' thinking *about* warfare. During the eleventh and twelfth centuries, copies were preserved in the libraries of monastic houses, cathedral chapters and, later, universities, although it was never included in any formal curriculum.[39] As the only 'art of war' to survive from classical Rome, Vegetius was regarded as a major authority on the proper organisation and conduct of warfare. *De re militari*'s emphasis on the role of the emperor and the soldier's duty to protect the *res publica* was particularly attractive to political theorists who wished to advocate a more centralised form of government and a limit on private warfare.[40] *De re militari*

---

[33] Sydney Anglo, 'Vegetius's *De re militari*: The Triumph of Mediocrity', *Antiquaries Journal*, 82 (2002), 247–67.

[34] Christopher Allmand, 'Vegetius' *De re militari*: Military Theory in Medieval and Modern Conception', *History Compass*, 9 (2011), 397–409, at p. 398.

[35] Christopher Allmand, *The 'De re militari' of Vegetius: The Reception, Transmission and Legacy of a Roman Text in the Middle Ages* (Cambridge, 2011), pp. 252–3.

[36] Bernard S. Bachrach, 'The Practical Use of Vegetius' *De re militari* During the Early Middle Ages', *The Historian*, 47 (1985), 239–55, at pp. 249, 254–5.

[37] John D. Hosler, *Henry II: A Medieval Soldier at War, 1147–1189* (Leiden, 2007), pp. 126–7.

[38] Contamine, *War in the Middle Ages*, p. 211.

[39] Allmand, 'Military Theory', p. 400; Allmand, *'De re militari' of Vegetius*, pp. 63–7.

[40] Allmand, *'De re militari' of Vegetius*, pp. 83–147; John D. Hosler, *John of Salisbury: Military Authority of the Twelfth-Century Renaissance* (Leiden, 2013), pp. 5–7.

also influenced the depiction of battles in medieval chronicles. As will be discussed below, battle narratives were often composed according to set tropes: a competent or successful commander would behave in such a way, a foolish commander in another. Authors could use key phrases and ideas from *De re militari* to demonstrate both their own learning and the martial skill of their subjects.[41] Vegetius taught that a commander should behave cautiously and reasonably; therefore a classically educated chronicler would be inclined to portray a successful commander acting according to these precepts.[42]

It is therefore important to note that Vegetius encouraged his readers to employ deception. For example, in Book 3.6, entitled 'How an army should be carefully protected when moving near the enemy', he encourages commanders to scout carefully, induce traitors from the enemy force to reveal their plans and to lay ambushes to attack the enemy on the march.[43] Similarly, in Book 3.9 he writes: 'But if [the commander] sees that the enemy is stronger, he should avoid an open engagement; for those who are few in number and inferior in strength, carrying out sudden attacks and ambushes under good commanders, often obtain victory'.[44] This is not to say that medieval commanders learned about such tactics by reading *De re militari*, or that every incident of deception in the chronicles is a fictional construct inserted by classicising historians; it simply means that we should be aware that these ideas were in circulation among the literate members of medieval society, in a text that was regarded as authoritative on the art of war.

Even more popular than *De re militari* was the first-century text *Facta et dicta memorabilia* (Memorable Deeds and Sayings) by Valerius Maximus; more medieval manuscripts of this text survive than any other Latin prose text, except the Bible. It is a handbook of *exempla*, not military theory, drawn mainly from ancient history and philosophy, intended to instruct members of the Roman elite in the rhetorical art of declamation.[45]

---

[41] Richard Abels and Stephen Morillo, 'A Lying Legacy? A Preliminary Discussion of Images Antiquity and Altered Reality in Medieval Military History', *Journal of Medieval Military History*, 3 (2005), 1–13.

[42] Allmand, *'De re militari' of Vegetius*, pp. 257–8.

[43] Vegetius, *Epitoma rei militaris*, p. 79: 'Ut nostra commoditas est sapienter ista vitare, ita, si adversariorum imperitia vel dissimulatio occasionem nobis dederit, non oportet amitti, sed explorare sollicite, proditores ac transfugas invitare, ut quid hostis moliatur in praesenti vel in futurum possimus agnoscere, paratisque equitibus ac levi armatura ambulantes eosdem vel pabula victumque quaerentes inproviso terrore decipere'.

[44] Vegetius, *Epitoma rei militaris*, pp. 87–8: 'Si vero adversarium intellegit potiorem, certamen publicum vitet; nam pauciores numero et inferiores viribus superventus et insidias facientes sub bonis ducibus reportaverunt saepe victoriam'.

[45] W. Martin Bloomer, *Valerius Maximus and the Rhetoric of the New Nobility* (London, 1992), pp. 2–4.

Despite its shortcomings as both history and literature, it was enormously popular during the Middle Ages: 'hardly a monastery will have lacked a Valerius, judging by the regularity of his appearance in extant medieval library catalogues'.[46] Instances of medieval authors quoting and citing the *Facta* were 'legion' and include Fulbert of Chartres, John of Salisbury, Peter the Chanter, Peter of Blois, Saxo Grammaticus, Gerald of Wales and Petrarch.[47] Like *De re militari*, its popularity likely stemmed from a combination of its antiquity and the short, memorable phrases that could be quoted to illustrate a point and demonstrate an author's erudition.

It is notable that such a popular text contains two chapters dedicated to examples of cunning. The first, 7.3, entitled 'Vafra dicta aut facta' (Cunning Sayings and Deeds) is a mixture of legal and political *exempla*. The following chapter, however, is dedicated solely to military ruses: 'But there is an eminent piece of cunning, far removed from all censure. These works, because they cannot be suitably expressed in a Latin term, are called stratagems, in the Greek manner'.[48] Brief as it is, the chapter describes an impressive variety of tactics: seeding false information, feigning flight, concealing troops and sending false deserters into the enemy camp, armed with hidden swords.[49] Valerius offers no condemnation of these actions but actively celebrates them. Describing how the Roman general Livius Salinator concealed newly arrived reinforcements from his Carthaginian opponent Hasdrubal, he says: 'So that Punic cunning, notorious throughout the whole world, was duped by Roman prudence'.[50]

This brief summary of stratagems was incorporated into another Roman text, one which consisted of almost entirely of incidents of military deception: the *Strategemata* by Julius Frontinus. Composed between 84 and 88 CE, it is the only surviving Latin example from a wider genre of stratagem collections.[51] It was intended as a companion piece to the author's treatise on the art of war, which is now lost and does not appear to have

---

[46] C. J. Carter, 'Valerius Maximus', in T. A. Dorey (ed.), *Empire and Aftermath: Silver Latin II* (London, 1975), pp. 26–56, at p. 49.

[47] Dorothy Schullian, 'Valerius Maximus', in *Catalogus translationum et commentariorum: Mediaeval and Renaissance Latin Translations and Commentaries* (11 vols, Washington, D.C, 1960), vol. 5, 287–404, at pp. 290–5.

[48] Valerius Maximus, *Facta et dicta memorabilia*, ed. John Briscoe (Leipzig, 1998), p. 466: 'Illa uero pars calliditatis egregia et ab omni reprehensione procul remota, cuius opera, quia appellatione Latina uix apte exprimi possunt, Graeca pronuntiatione strategemata dicantur'.

[49] Valerius Maximus, *Facta et dicta*, pp. 466–73.

[50] Valerius Maximus, *Facta et dicta*, p. 470: 'ita illo toto terrarum orbe infamis Punica calliditas, Romana elusa prudentia'.

[51] Everett L. Wheeler, *Stratagem and the Vocabulary of Military Trickery* (Leiden, 1988), p. 1.

survived into the Middle Ages.[52] The existence of this lost work is attested by Aelian, a near contemporary, and Vegetius, as well as Frontinus himself:

> Although I alone among those who study the science of military matters undertook to teach it, and I seem to have achieved that goal, to the extent that my concern was satisfied, yet I still think I ought to arrange a work in which I gather the clever deeds of commanders, which were covered by the Greeks in a single term, stratagems, into convenient notes.[53]

These 'notes' are arranged into three books, with a fourth, emphasising the importance of discipline and good conduct, added by an unknown interpolator at a later date, although this interpolation was not always recognised as such by medieval readers.[54]

Each book is subdivided into types (literally, *species*) of stratagem. Each *species* is composed of examples of how past commanders overcame problems or gained an advantage over their enemies through trickery. For example, in Book Two, under the heading 'On Disturbing the Enemy's Line', Frontinus recounted how Fabius Rullus Maximus sent troops to seize a hill in the rear of a Samnite army.[55] Under the same heading we find a story from Livy in which Marcus Marcellus commanded his camp followers to join in a battle cry in order to make his army appear more numerous.[56] In total there are fifty different *species* listed in the *Strategemata*, ranging from stratagems for concealing one's plans from the enemy, to choosing an advantageous battlefield, to inducing treachery in a besieged garrison, to moving supplies into a stronghold.[57] Frontinus rarely passed judgement on the stories he included, recounting stories of lying, bribery, ambushes and spying without comment.

Although not as widely disseminated as *De re militari*, the *Strategamata* was in circulation during the Middle Ages. One third of the 120 known manuscripts are physically bound to *De re militari*, suggesting that contemporaries saw the two works as complementing one another.[58] It

---

[52] Charles E. Bennett, 'The Life and Works of Sextus Julius Frontinus', in Mary B. McElwain (ed.), *The Stratagems and the Aqueducts of Rome* (London, 1924), pp. xiii–xxvii, at p. xix.
[53] Sextus Julius Frontinus, *Strategemata*, ed. Robert I. Ireland (Leipzig, 1990), p. 1: 'Cum ad instruendam rei militaris scientiam unus ex numero studiosorum eius accesserim, eique destinato quantum cura nostra ualuit satisfecisse uisus sim, deberi adhuc institutae arbitror operae ut sollertia ducum facta, quae a Graecis una στρατηγημάτων appellatione conprehensa sunt, expeditis amplectar commentariis'.
[54] Bennett, 'Life and Works', pp. xix–xxvi.
[55] Frontinus, *Strategemata*, pp. 42–3: 'De acie hostium turbanda'.
[56] Frontinus, *Strategemata*, p. 44.
[57] Frontinus, *Strategemata*, pp. 2–3, 30, 70.
[58] Christopher Allmand, 'A Roman Text on War: The *Strategemata* of Frontinus in the Middle Ages', in Peter Coss and Christopher Tyerman (eds.), *Soldiers, Nobles and*

was popular for its classical pedigree, as well as being a source of moral exemplars for sermons, encouraging the virtues of courage and perseverance.[59] John of Salisbury incorporated maxims from the fourth book, emphasising the importance of military discipline, into his *Policraticus*.[60] In the later fourteenth century, Simon de Hesdin and Nicholas de Gonesse added forty-nine examples from the *Strategemata* to their French translation of the *Facta et dicta memorabilia*. This material was later incorporated into the works of the influential chivalric writers Christine de Pizan and Antoine de La Sale.[61]

As with Vegetius, acknowledging that Frontinus was known, read and copied during the Middle Ages does not mean that commanders looked to him for instruction or inspiration. Nor does it mean that every stratagem described in medieval narratives should be dismissed as an imitation, with no foundation in historical reality. We must be aware that such influences were present, without dismissing the possibility that medieval warriors and authors could arrive at these conclusions independently. Furthermore, we should be conscious that the most popular, authoritative texts in warfare did not condemn trickery but actively advocated the use of stratagems to achieve victory.

Writing War: The Problem with Chronicles

Trying to separate 'historical fact' from classical imitations or outright inventions when reading a medieval chronicle has become increasingly complex over the past fifty years, following the so-called 'linguistic turn'. Traditionally, medieval narratives were studied primarily as windows onto the past. It was the historian's role to peer through different windows, disregard the distortions and resolve the contradictions into something resembling what they believed to be historical reality. If one uses this approach, then the miraculous, the strange and the implausible must necessarily be dismissed as products of superstition or credulity; sifted out to reveal credible historical fact. Recent trends, however, have led scholars to analyse the textual nature of the histories themselves. Instead of ignoring the artificial and the fantastical, they should be viewed as integral to the text and the medieval historian's interpretation of the events they recorded. This

---

Gentlemen: Essays in Honour of Maurice Keen (Woodbridge, 2009), pp. 153–68, at pp. 155–6.
[59] Allmand, 'Frontinus', pp. 156, 161.
[60] Allmand, 'Frontinus', p. 162.
[61] Craig Taylor, *Chivalry and the Ideals of Knighthood in France during the Hundred Years War* (Cambridge, 2013), p. 251.

'turn' has important implications for the study of deception in medieval military narratives, as these incidents have often been dismissed as fantasies, unworthy of consideration in serious military history. I propose that these tales of trickery and guile (some of which may be wholly fictitious) are worthy of serious study and that recent scholarship on fictionality in medieval narratives can help us to appreciate the role they played in the writing of medieval chronicles.

Gabrielle M. Spiegel described the linguistic turn as: 'a growing awareness of the mediated nature of perception, cognition and imagination, all of which were increasingly construed to be mediated by linguistic structures cast into discourses of one sort or another'.[62] It was derived from the structuralist theory of linguistics, which posited that language is not a reflection of an objectively perceived reality but rather constitutes our perception of reality. By extension, historical texts do not tell us about the reality of the past, only the language which described it. It is possible to take these ideas to an extreme and argue that there is no real distinction between reality and imagination, fact or fiction, as all are simply different kinds of linguistic construction.[63] This is, of course, absurd.[64] These ideas do, however, remind us that all history is narrative; that it is impossible to say anything meaningful about the past without resorting to narrative. Monika Otter expressed it this way:

> Reality does not come in narrative form; it is an unlimited, unstructured field of data with multiple connections. History, however, must translate it into narrative, a more or less orderly sequence, one or just a few causal chains, a beginning, middle, and end. The process is marked, at the very least, by selectivity and by some form of "emplotment," [...] Thus, whether fictional or not, narrative consists, first of all, of a selection from a potentially endless number of entities and events.[65]

---

[62] Gabrielle M. Spiegel, 'Theory into Practice: Reading Medieval Chronicles', in Erik Kooper (ed.), *The Medieval Chronicle: Proceedings of the First International Conference of the Medieval Chronicle* (Amsterdam, 1999), pp. 1–12, at p. 5.

[63] For a summary of this complex debate, see Gabrielle M. Spiegel, 'History, Historicism, and the Social Logic of the Text in the Middle Ages', *Speculum*, 65 (1990), 59–86, at pp. 59–72; Spiegel, 'Theory into Practice', pp. 1–2.

[64] 'No one really believes we are sealed in a linguistic house of mirrors, even if we are. The black-hole epistemology can be ignored with the same little lurch of faith that takes us out of bed each morning rashly confident that the floor will be where we left it [...] everyone eventually resorts to some version of "we have to assume...," from which follow Other Minds, and External World, and soon after, Descriptive Language or something that passes for, and the whole show carries on as usual. Except that we feel more sophisticated doing it'. Nancy F. Partner, 'Making Up Lost Time: Writing on the Writing of History', *Speculum*, 61 (1986), 90–117, at pp. 95–6.

[65] Monika Otter, *Inventiones: Fiction and Referentiality in Twelfth-Century English Historical Writing* (Chapel Hill, NC, 1996), pp. 10–11.

Making sense of the 'unlimited, unstructured' data of lived experience through narrative is especially relevant to medieval accounts of combat. It has long been recognised that an individual participant in even a relatively small battle has only the vaguest sense of how the overall conflict is unfolding.[66] Even in a pre-gunpowder era, a combatant's field of vision was limited by the terrain, the men around him, and the enemies before him, even before we consider the effect of adrenaline, terror and the general chaos of hand-to-hand fighting. The only way to relate the experience to another, or to account for a defeat that had no obvious cause, would be through narrative. This may help to explain why battle accounts in chronicles are so frequently described using topoi or formulaic language; they were an effective way of translating the inherent confusion of battle into meaningful prose.

It is important to remember that history was regarded as a form of literature in the Middle Ages, rather than an analytical science. Isidore of Seville divided the field of grammar into poetry and prose, then further subdivided prose into *fabula*, 'the story of fictional happenings', and *historia*, 'the narration of things that have actually taken place'.[67] This is extremely broad and encompasses a variety of medieval genres that modern critics would ideally like to distinguish from 'real' histories: hagiography, epic, romance, genealogy and biography. That is a modern problem, however, not a medieval one. Genre boundaries were indistinct in the Middle Ages, allowing myth to pass for history and history to emulate myth.[68]

If history was literature, then it followed that good history should be well-written. Gervase of Canterbury (d. 1210), influenced perhaps by Cicero's *De Oratore*, distinguished between the true historian, who wrote elegantly, with 'rhetorical flourishes', and the mere annalist who recorded events in a 'direct and straightforward' manner.[69] Elaboration, expressing things in an impressive style, was more highly regarded than conciseness or adherence to strict plausibility.[70] This explains why, in contemporary chronicles, French-speaking Anglo-Norman commanders suddenly launch into flights of Ciceronian rhetoric when they give a pre-battle oration; that

---

[66] John Keegan, *The Face of Battle* (London, 1976), pp. 46–54.
[67] Nancy F. Partner, *Serious Entertainments: The Writing of History in Twelfth-Century England* (Chicago, 1977), p. 195.
[68] See Graeme Dunphy, 'Chronicles', in Albrecht Classen (ed.), *Handbook of Medieval Studies: Terms, Methods, Trends* (3 vols, Berlin, 2010), pp. 1714–21; Chris Given-Wilson, *Chronicles: The Writing of History in Medieval England* (London, 2004), p. ix; Justin Lake, 'Authorial Intention in Medieval Historiography', *History Compass*, 12 (2014), 344–60, at pp. 345–7; Monika Otter, 'Functions of Fiction in Historical Writing', in Nancy F. Partner (ed.), *Writing Medieval History* (London, 2005), pp. 109–30, at p. 111.
[69] Lake, 'Authorial Intention in Medieval Historiography', p. 345.
[70] Partner, *Serious Entertainments*, p. 206.

was what readers expected a general to do before a major battle. Moreover, it was what they did in all the great Roman histories.[71]

Connected to this trend is the didactic element in medieval historical writing. History was thought to be instructive: 'the "universal truths" to be deduced from any specific episode were just as important as the need to provide an incontestably factual account of that episode'.[72] This is especially relevant for descriptions of warfare. A battle was not simply an event, it was 'an exemplar, providing models to imitate or avoid, lessons to be contemplated'.[73] The authoritative texts taught that an army should be disciplined and cautiously but purposefully led, so this was how victorious armies were often depicted. Conversely, the defeated party was usually described as ill-disciplined and burdened with a divided leadership. A story about a commander who avoided an enemy ambush could illustrate the virtue of prudence (by no means a purely martial quality), while a force that gained an advantage through a well-planned ruse showed the importance of foresight. This is not to say that such incidents are necessarily fictitious, only that historians wrote with a didactic agenda in mind and chose to interpret the information they gathered in particular ways.

We must be careful not to overstate the case, however. As Robert M. Stein has noted, the very act of writing in Latin affected how authors described events: 'with Latinity inescapably comes a particular set of ways of rendering the social world, of framing experience and of asserting value'.[74] The vocabulary of battle narratives, the very language used to describe warfare, was the same as that of Vergil and Vegetius, of the Old Testament and the *Civil Wars*. Medieval clerics not only sought to emulate the great histories, they learned much of their Latin by reading them. An author may not even have been conscious of such a borrowing, especially if it came from a popular text; this was simply the most elegant phrase he knew to describe an army on the march, or an ambush, or any number of phenomena.[75]

---

[71] See John R. E. Bliese, 'The Courage of the Normans: A Comparative Study of Battle Rhetoric', *Nottingham Medieval Studies*, 35 (1991), 1–26; John R. E. Bliese, 'Rhetoric and Morale: A Study of Battle Orations from the Central Middle Ages', *Journal of Medieval History*, 15 (1989), 201–26; John R. E. Bliese, 'When Knightly Courage May Fail: Battle Orations in Medieval Europe', *Historian*, 53 (1991), 489–504; Ruth Morse, *Truth and Convention in the Middle Ages: Rhetoric, Representation, and Reality* (Cambridge, 1991), p. 119.
[72] Given-Wilson, *Chronicles*, p. 2.
[73] Given-Wilson, *Chronicles*, p. 3.
[74] Robert M. Stein, 'Literary Criticism and the Evidence for History', in Nancy F. Partner (ed.), *Writing Medieval History* (London, 2005), pp. 67–87, at p. 74.
[75] Morse, *Truth and Convention*, p. 108. For a related argument, based on a study of Biblical quotations in William of Tyre, see Alan V. Murray, 'Biblical Quotations and Formulaic Language in the Chronicle of William of Tyre', in Susan B. Edgington and

History was literature and, ideally, it was to be well-written, but it was a branch of literature that was expected to record real events. As already noted, Isidore of Seville distinguished *historia*, which was about true events, from mere *fabula*, which were manifestly untrue. Most medieval historians relied upon the testimony of others for information. This was especially true for military matters, as very few combatants composed histories in this period, with a handful of notable exceptions. We must therefore question the standards by which historians judged the information they received.

As Chris Given-Wilson has noted, there were three ways a historian could acquire his information: read it, hear it or witness it themselves.[76] When it came to written testimony, the medieval respect of *auctoritas* once again had a powerful influence. The textual nature of Christianity certainly played a part in this; medieval clerics were predisposed to believe in the possibility of the miraculous because it was attested in Scripture, even if they regularly expressed scepticism about contemporary reports that occurred outside their prescribed theological framework. The antiquity of a text and its resemblance to other, respected texts was often enough to render a text 'authoritative' to a medieval scholar.[77] A notable example of this was the enduring popularity of Geoffrey of Monmouth's *Historia regum Britanniae*, with its list of spurious kings including, of course, Arthur Pendragon. It is uncertain to what extent contemporaries believed it to be historical fact but, as Given-Wilson stressed: 'what is incontestable is that is continued to be cited, repeated and embellished *as if* it were historical fact'.[78] Its resemblance to other histories and the lack of a plausible alternative helped to secure Monmouth's place among the historians, rather than the fabulists.

If an author had not read about an event (unlikely for events contemporary with their lifetime), then they would have had to hear about it or witness it themselves.[79] Historians were often at pains to assure the readers of both their personal trustworthiness and that of their witnesses. Trustworthiness appears to have been measured according to vocation (with senior clergy as the most reliable), status (the nobility being implicitly more reliable that the common mob) and close relationship to the histo-

---

Helen Nicholson (eds.), *Deeds Done Beyond the Sea: Essays on William of Tyre, Cyprus and the Military Orders Presented to Peter Edbury* (Farnham, 2014), pp. 25–34.
[76] Given-Wilson, *Chronicles*, p. 6.
[77] Otter, 'Functions', pp. 109–10; Partner, *Serious Entertainments*, p. 190.
[78] Given-Wilson, *Chronicles*, p. 5.
[79] Simon John, 'Historical Truth and the Miraculous Past: The Use of Oral Evidence in Twelfth-Century Latin Historical Writing on the First Crusade', *English Historical Review*, 130 (2015), 263–301.

rian, who could vouch for their personal virtue and honesty.[80] This is not to say that medieval historians were entirely gullible or that they were unaware that false rumour could be mistakenly reported as solemn truth; their very insistence on the reliability of their sources demonstrates that. Historians employed the phrase 'it is said', or 'it is rumoured', to indicate information for which they lacked a reliable chain of testators perhaps because, as Ruth Morse argued, they were 'loathe to lose any remnant of evidence, loathe to relinquish a way of inserting non-authorized opinions which could be attributed to anonymous sources'.[81] Nevertheless, there remained a certain naivety to the medieval historical process: 'there was no systematic or thorough effort to find ways to detect mistaken or biased "moral truth". The concepts of "trustworthiness" and "accuracy" were not sufficiently distinguished, just as the difference between "possibility" and "probability" in the twelfth century was less marked that it is now'.[82]

How, then, is the historian to categorise accounts of military deception? If one does not automatically assume that all such incidents were transcribed from the historian's favourite chapter of Frontinus, then it is most likely that they heard about them from somebody else; potentially the last in a chain of witness stretching back to an eye witness or a participant. Carol Sweetenham's work on anecdotes in the chronicles of the First Crusade is particularly relevant here. These anecdotes started as soldiers' gossip, growing and changing in the telling, before moving, in Sweetenham's memorable phrase, 'from chatter to chapter'.[83] They were preserved in crusaders' letters, in monastic or family records or in personal reminiscences with friends and acquaintances, before finally being set down in the chronicles. These anecdotes helped the historian to emphasise themes already present in their text, such as the cruelty of the Turks or the holy character of the crusade. They also drew the listener imaginatively into the text, providing 'human interest and light relief'.[84]

There are several possible explanations for the presence of stories concerning elaborate stratagems in medieval military narratives: the classical and Biblical pedigree of such stories, their folkloric and narrative power, the dissemination and exaggeration of soldiers' gossip. Yet many of the stories are not inherently implausible. It is a plain fact of warfare

---

[80] Given-Wilson, *Chronicles*, pp. 7–8; John, 'Historical Truth and the Miraculous Past', p. 288; Partner, *Serious Entertainments*, p. 190.
[81] Morse, *Truth and Convention*, p. 95.
[82] Partner, *Serious Entertainments*, p. 191.
[83] Carol Sweetenham, 'What Really Happened to Eurvin de Créel's Donkey? Anecdotes in Sources for the First Crusade', in Marcus Bull and Damien Kempf (eds.), *Writing the Early Crusades: Text, Transmission and Memory* (Woodbridge, 2014), pp. 75–88, at p. 85.
[84] Sweetenham, 'What Really Happened to Eurvin de Créel's Donkey?', p. 82.

that combatants will seek any possible advantage over their enemy, often through deception. The history of later, better documented wars contain similar tales of cunning. Scholars should not discount medieval accounts of deceit on the battlefield, *prima facie*, any more than they should uncritically accept their every claim as literal truth. Each story must be judged according to its own merits and the merits of its author, with an awareness of the influence that other texts, folklore and an unreliable chain of witnesses may have had on its composition. Furthermore, even when one has good reason to question the historical reality of a particular incident, it can still be analysed as a narrative device. Stories of stratagems tell us not only what authors and their audience thought was plausible but what constituted admirable or shameful behaviour. Although they may appear peripheral to the main narrative, they provide modern scholars with information about both warfare and aristocratic culture in the central Middle Ages.

The following chapters are written with these principles in mind. When the author is demonstrably straying from the history recorded in other primary sources, it will be discussed, but for the most part the question of 'did this *really* happen?' will not be addressed. It is both unanswerable and, worse, uninteresting. The focus of this study is what the chroniclers and their intended audience thought was plausible, normative and honourable behaviour in war. We begin with one of the most contentious and morally suspect aspects of warfare: spies and spying.

2

Military Intelligence: Misdirection, Misinformation and Espionage

In the rapid strikes and strategic raiding that characterised medieval warfare, knowing the location and strength of the enemy forces was crucial. An ill-informed army risked blundering unexpectedly into the enemy or being taken by surprise. Basic reason would have told commanders this much, even without Vegetius's maxims to remind them: 'In war, the one who is more vigilant in the field, the one who works harder training soldiers, will be less subject to danger'.[1] Likewise, a commander who was able to conceal his movements and intentions was more likely to operate freely and to be able to surprise his enemy: 'No plans are better than those you carry out while the enemy is unaware of them'.[2] All of which was easier said than done, especially in an age before dedicated military colleges, precise maps or specialist intelligence services. Nevertheless, the very fact that medieval armies assembled and campaigned effectively indicates that they were capable of a certain level of intelligence gathering. Chronicles contain a number of hints about how this might have been achieved and more than a few stories about cunning spies.

Misdirection: Achieving the 'Mastery of Space and Time'[3]

Carl von Clausewtiz, Prussian general and seminal military theorist, defined military strategy as follows:

---

[1] Vegetius, *Epitoma rei militaris*, ed. M. D. Reeve (Oxford, 2004), p. 117: 'In bello qui plus in agrariis vigilaverit, plus in exercendo milite laboraverit, minus periculum sustinebit'.
[2] Vegetius, *Epitoma rei militaris*, p. 117: "Nulla consilia meliora sunt nisi illa quae ignoraverit adversarius antequam facias'.
[3] Philippe Contamine, *War in the Middle Ages*, trans. Michael Jones (Oxford, 1984), p. 219.

Strategy decides the time when, the place where, and the forces with which the engagement is to be fought, and through this threefold activity exerts considerable influence on its outcome. Once the tactical encounter has taken place and the result – be it victory or defeat – is assured, strategy will use it to serve the object of the war.[4]

This was also true for medieval warfare. Verbruggen has demonstrated that medieval campaigns were conducted according to sound strategic principles: the maintenance of collective morale, coordinating and concentrating one's forces, attempting to attack with superior numbers and the element of surprise and, when necessary, seeking a decisive engagement with the enemy force.[5] Surprise is particularly relevant for this study, as it usually necessary to deceive the person you wish to surprise: if somebody is aware of your intentions and actions, they cannot be surprised by what you do. A simple form of strategic deception is the feint or feigned manoeuvre, in which one party tricks the other into believing that they are going to take a certain course of action, such as attacking a particular stronghold, when in fact they are intending to do something else. A successful feigned manoeuvre can fulfil all of Clausewitz's criteria for military strategy, allowing the deceiver to decide where, when and with what forces an engagement is fought.

A clear medieval example can be found in the English chronicle, *Gesta Stephani*. In 1138, while campaigning against the rebel Robert of Bampton in Somerset, King Stephen of England took the castle at Harptree with a feigned manoeuvre. Stephen left Castle Cary and marched north, 'as though he were advancing with his army to besiege the people of Bristol', some fifteen miles north of Harptree.[6] The castle garrison sallied out to harass Stephen's army, only for Stephen to suddenly turn back and storm Harptree while it was poorly defended. This deception was not achieved with words but actions. By marching towards the key stronghold at Bristol, Stephen tricked the castle garrison into believing that it had been ignored in favour of a richer prize. They took the bait, seeing an opportunity to attack an unsuspecting enemy. Stephen was able to take advantage of their mistake by rapidly manoeuvring to attack in strength where his enemy was weakest.[7]

---

[4] Carl von Clausewitz, *On War*, trans. Michael Howard and Peter Paret (Princeton, NJ, 1976), p. 194.
[5] J. F. Verbruggen, *The Art of Warfare in Western Europe during the Middle Ages from the Eighth Century to 1340*, trans. Summer Willard and Shelia C. M. Southern, 2nd edn (Woodbridge, 1998) pp. 278–88.
[6] GS, p. 68: 'quasi cum exercitu Bristoenses obsessurus progrederetur'.
[7] A similar strategy was used during a Muslim invasion of the kingdom of Jerusalem in 1105. The invaders detached a small force to launch a diversionary attack on Ramla, hoping to the lure the Franks away from Jaffa, their true target: FC, p. 497; WT,

In 1138, David I of Scotland attempted to surprise the army assembled by Thurstan, archbishop of York, at Northallerton. Wishing to take advantage of the thick fog that had fallen on the morning of 22 August, David forbade his men to burn the villages which they passed, 'in their accustomed manner', in order to conceal their advance through the countryside and come upon the English army unawares.[8] Although the stratagem failed (the English army was warned of the Scottish advance by a squire) and the Scots were defeated by the fully prepared English army, it offers a rare indication of how medieval combatants may have concealed their movements. By minimising their interaction with the local population, whether hostile or friendly, they greatly lessened the chance of their position being betrayed to the enemy forces by spies, informants or refugees fleeing the devastation. The account of the events leading to the battle of Brémule (Normandy, 20 August 1119) by the contemporary chronicler Orderic Vitalis illustrates the value of such a stratagem: Henry I of England was able to locate Louis VI of France's army by the smoke rising from a barn that the French had burned near Noyon.[9]

The feigned advance has its obvious counterpart in the feigned withdrawal.[10] According to the thirteenth-century English chronicler Roger of Howden, Malcolm III of Scotland used a form of this manoeuvre during a raid into Teesdale and Cleveland in 1070. After some initial successes, Malcolm sent part of his army back north with the plunder but kept the rest with him in England. 'By this cunning act' (*hac scilicet calliditate*) he was able to pillage those locals who, thinking the Scots had left, came out of hiding and returned home with their possessions.[11] Roger chose to interpret this manoeuvre as a ruse, motivated by greed: Malcom wished to rob the English twice over. It is possible, however, that the detached force's

---

vol. 1, sp. 465. Philip II of France reportedly used a similar manoeuvre at Le Mans, Maine in 1189. He pretended that he was only stopping at Le Mans on his way to Tours but unexpectedly attacked Le Mans on the day that he intended to depart: HowChr, vol. 2, p. 107.

[8] JW, vol. 3, p. 252.

[9] OV, vol. 6, p. 236.

[10] This discussion will be confined to feigned withdrawals on the strategic level of warfare, namely bodies of troops moving over distance with minimal contact with the enemy. The use of tactical retreats in combat, such as the feigned flight, will be discussed in Chapter 4.

[11] HowChr, vol. 1, p. 121: 'Hac scilicet calliditate, ut cum totus hostis putaretur abiisse, miseros indigenas, qui sese suaque propter hostile metum latibulis, quibus poterant, tute conservaverant, secure in villas suas domosque regressos, ipse subito incursu improvisos praeoccuparet' (By this cunning act, since everybody thought that the enemies had gone away, the wretched natives who, for fear of the enemy had preserved whatever they could, themselves and their belongings, in hiding places, were returning safely to their homes and villages, the king could suddenly attack them while they were unprepared).

primary role was to guard the main army as it returned north, weighed down with the spoils. Whatever additional looting they carried out on the locals may have been coincidental but, to Howden, it was further evidence of the Scots' greed and cruelty.

A similar manoeuvre is described in the *History of William Marshal*. When talks between Philip II of France and Henry II of England broke down at Gisors on the Franco-Norman border in August 1188, Philip ordered that the elm tree under which the kings of France and dukes of Normandy had traditionally met for conferences be chopped down. This may have been a political gesture, symbolising the young Philip's intention to establish a new status-quo between France and Normandy, or simply a fit of pique provoked by Henry monopolising the tree's shade in the hot weather.[12] According to the *History*, William Marshal, at that time a member of Henry's household, advised him to disband his army: 'but in secret tell them to return to us without fail on a day set by you'.[13] Once reassembled, Marshal proposed, they could ravage Philip's undefended lands, declaring: 'Ours will be a finer and more successful exploit [than cutting down one tree]'.[14] Henry was delighted with the proposal, saying: 'Marshal, you are most courtly and you have advised me very well'.[15]

While the scene itself is probably a fiction, intended to emphasise Marshal's favoured position at the royal court at this time, it provides an insight into contemporary attitudes. Marshal is commended as *corteis* for his recommendation. He performs the role of the ideal courtier by offering his lord good advice.[16] He did not recommend Henry fight a pitched battle or challenge Philip to single combat but to employ a trick: to feign withdrawal then attack when Philip did not expect it. The consequence of this would be the devastation of the countryside, a 'much finer' deed than Philip's attack on a single tree. For the *History*'s audience, and presumably the Marshal's contemporaries, avoiding direct conflict with one's enemy through strategic manoeuvre was both an appropriate and admirable way to wage war.[17]

---

[12] For an analysis of contemporary interpretations of this gesture, see Lindsay Diggelmann, 'Hewing the Ancient Elm: Anger, Arboricide, and Medieval Kingship', *Journal of Medieval and Early Modern Studies*, 40 (2010), 249–72.

[13] HWM, lines 7787–90.

[14] HWM, line 7798.

[15] HWM, lines 7800–1: 'Marescahl, molt estes corteis / E molt m'avez conseillié bien'.

[16] Stewart Gregory translates this use of *corteis* as 'an excellent man'. This is certainly the sense in which it is used but I have chosen to translate it literally because it makes it clear that the Marshal is being praised specifically for acting as a courtier, giving wise counsel.

[17] The anonymous poet depicts Richard I of England using a similar manoeuvre to attack the French stronghold at Milly in May 1197. HWM, line 11111. According to two regional chroniclers, Bursuq of Hamadām employed this stratagem in 1115 to trick

Misinformation: Putting Up a Brave Front

Pretending to attack or withdraw could be accomplished quite simply: sometimes it was sufficient to simply march in the right direction. Medieval chronicles report other, much more elaborate, methods of spreading misinformation among one's enemies, by pretending to have more men or more supplies than was the case.

This kind of ruse has classical antecedents. Frontinus dedicated a whole chapter of the *Strategemata* to them: 'How we can make it seem that the thing we are lacking is abundant'.[18] The first ruse in Frontinus's list, one of the most famous in Roman history, occurred during the Gauls' siege of the Capitol Hill in Rome in 390 BCE:

> Then, a truce having been made with the Romans, with the permission of the commanders, parleys were held in which the Gauls repeatedly taunted them on account of their hunger, calling upon them to surrender out of necessity. It is said that, in order to disabuse them of this notion, bread was thrown into the enemy outposts from many places on the Capitol.[19]

Ovid referred to this incident in his *Fasti* as an explanation for the presence of an altar to Jupiter the Baker (*Pistor Iovis*) on the Capitol.[20] It is also one of the handful of ruses to appear in the work of Valerius Maximus.[21]

The twelfth-century author Gerald of Wales reported a very similar story in his *Itinerarium Kambriae*. As part of his description of Pembroke, Gerald recalls that, in 1096, his paternal grandfather, Gerald of Windsor, defended Pembroke Castle against the men of south Wales on behalf of his lord, Arnulf of Montgomery. In order to conceal how little food they had left, and pretending that they were confident of relief at any moment, 'he had four hog's carcasses, which had survived up until that time, cut into pieces and thrown from the ramparts to the enemies'.[22] Although

---

Baldwin I of Jerusalem into believing that he had withdrawn from the principality of Antioch, allowing him to raid the land unimpeded: WC, pp. 93–4; WT, vol. 1, p. 503.

[18] Sextus Julius Frontinus, *Strategemata*, ed. Robert I. Ireland (Leipzig, 1990), p. 86: 'Quemadmodum efficiatur, ut abundare videantur, quae deerunt'.

[19] Titus Livy, *Ab urbe condita: Tomus* I, *libri* I–v, ed. Robert Maxwell Ogilvie (Oxford, 1974), p. 381: 'Indutiae deinde cum Romanis factae et conloquia permissu imperatorum habita; in quibus cum identidem Galli famem obicerent eaque necessitate ad deditionem uocarent, dicitur auertendae eius opinionis causa multis locis panis de Capitolio iactatus esse in hostium stationes'.

[20] Publius Ovid Naso, *Fastorum libri sex*, ed. E. H. Alton, D. E. W. Wormell and E. Courtney (Leipzig, 1978), p. 149.

[21] Valerius Maximus, *Facta et dicta memorabilia*, ed. John Briscoe (Leipzig, 1998), p. 469.

[22] IK, pp. 89–90: 'quatuor qui adhuc supererant bacones a propugnaculis frustatim ad hostes projici fecit'.

bacon is substituted for bread, the parallels with the Roman story are clear: the starving defenders pretend that they are so well-supplied that they can afford to throw food away. Gerald credits his grandfather with adding even more elaborate layers to this trick, sending false letters into the Welsh camp that stated the garrison had enough food to last four months.[23] As Gerald is our only source for this siege, we cannot corroborate the details. Whether these ruses were employed exactly as Gerald claims, the stories having been passed down to him as family legend, or whether he fabricated the incident to give his family history classical resonance, the resemblance to the defence of the Capitol enhanced Gerald's portrayal of his ancestors and, by extension, the Anglo-Norman conquest of southern Wales.

Shortage of food was not the only deficiency that a medieval army might wish to conceal. In January 1148, towards the end of its gruelling march through Anatolia, Louis VII of France's crusading army was encamped before the town of Adalia (mod. Antalya, Turkey). The Turks, believing that the French had no horses left, planned an assault on their camp. Learning of their plan:

> [Louis] hid with him the wealthy men who still had their chargers, although they were starving, and the Templars. When [the Turks] approached, [Louis], appearing unexpectedly, killing some, compelled them to return across the river without using a bridge and to believe thereafter that the army had many very fine horses.[24]

An incident during the crusader siege of Acre (August 1189 – July 1191) further emphasises the importance of making a conspicuous display of strength in order to discourage one's enemies. The French poet Ambroise records that, early in 1190, three 'Turkish' ships were wrecked attempting to bring supplies to the garrison which was under siege by the crusaders. Many of the crew drowned but the cargo was saved, reviving the garrison's spirits and encouraging them to attack the crusaders.[25] The Latin chronicle knows as the *Itinerarium Peregrinorum*, which made extensive use of Ambroise's account, added the following details: 'Then the besieged dissolved into immoderate joy, as if their prayers had been answered. With cymbals and flutes and high-pitched, wailing voices they testified that they were not confounded. This din was made as a sign, lest it be supposed

---

[23] IK, p. 90.
[24] OD, p. 134: 'Quod notum factum est regi et contra illos abscondit secum viros ditiores qui dextrarios suos, quamvis famelicos, adhuc servaverant et fratres Templi. Venientibusque apparens subito coegit eos occidendo sine ponte fluvium retransire et credere deinceps in exercitu equos optimos abundare'.
[25] Amb, lines 3433–56.

that they had sustained a loss'.[26] This was no ruse, as the garrison really had been resupplied, but it demonstrates that maintaining the appearance of strength could be a conscious element of medieval strategy, particularly during a long, psychologically wearying siege such as Acre. A parallel can be drawn with the troops holding Nottingham Castle on behalf of John Lackland in 1194. They initially refused to surrender to Richard I of England because they believed that he was still in prison abroad and that the trumpet calls that announced the king's presence had been arranged by the 'leaders of the army in order to deceive them'.[27] They were quickly disabused of this notion and surrendered four days later, but it is noteworthy that they reportedly considered this to be a plausible trick.

Misinformation: Rumours and Lies

All of the above incidents relied upon the enemy deducing certain information from the deceivers' actions. We will now consider a more direct method: actively supplying false information to the enemy. We are not always able to determine exactly how such information was transmitted. Combatants relied on an informal network of contacts for intelligence gathering, questioning travellers, local peasants and deserters from the enemy (see p. 42). In such an environment, it would have been relatively easy to deliberately plant false information among the gossip and rumours that flowed in and out of an army or garrison. For example, the chronicler Raymond of Aguilers reported that the crusade leader Raymond of Saint-Gilles retreated from the siege of Arqah in May 1099 because of false rumours, spread by the garrison, that the 'pope of the Turks' (*papa Turcorum*, presumably a reference to the caliph, al-Mustazhir) was approaching with a vast army. Raymond does not elaborate on how this information was received, saying only 'it was reported to us' (*nuntiatum est nobis*) and that, afterwards 'it was discovered to have been false; and that the Saracens had arranged it in order that, having frightened us away, they might enjoy a little respite from the siege'.[28]

Cultivating a double agent within the enemy force was an effective way of spreading false information. For example, in 1106 Baldwin I of Jerusalem assembled an army to defend Tiberias from an attack by Tughtagin, ruler

---

[26] IP, p. 86: 'Unde obsessi nimia dissoluti laetitia tanquam voto eorum fuerit satisfactum, cum cymbalis et tibiis ululantes vocibus altisonis testati sunt se perplexos non esse. Fit igitur plausus ad indicium, ne putentur sustinere dispendium'.
[27] HowChr, vol. 3, p. 238: 'sed sperabant totum hoc factum fuisse a principibus exercitus ad illudendum eis'.
[28] RA, pp. 277–8: 'Interim inventum est falsum; et quod Sarraceni illud composuerant, ut, nobis taliter deterritis, aliquantulum respirare possent obsessi'.

of Damascus. One night, five Turks came to Baldwin's camp: 'they were sent as envoys of the rest, speaking about various things and urging [him] to make peace'.[29] Baldwin entertained them and sent them away with many gifts. The envoys returned to their commander and reported that the Christian army was seven times greater than it actually was. Believing their report, Tughtagin withdrew without giving battle.[30]

We must be cautious when discussing such incidents, however. Not all incidents are as clear cut as Baldwin's bribery. We are often reliant on a chronicler's interpretation of events and motivations. What a hostile author interpreted as a malicious attempt to spread false intelligence may have been no more than an honest mistake. Take the German chronicler Albert of Aachen's account of the siege of the Syrian coastal town Jabala by the forces of the First Crusade in March 1099. Albert, consistently hostile in his depiction of Raymond of Saint-Gilles, says that the reports of a large army approaching Raymond at Arqah were nothing more than lies concocted to draw the rest of the crusaders away from Jabala, sixty miles to the north.[31] Albert goes further, claiming that the citizens of Jabala bribed Raymond to do this.[32] A similar incident is reported by Orderic Vitalis during a conflict in 1118 between the Norman magnate Richer of Laigle and Henry I of England over the inheritance of certain lands in Sussex. William Tancarville, chamberlain of Normandy and England, deliberately passed a false report to Henry that the forces of William Clito, the disenfranchised son of his brother Robert Curthose, had fortified the monastery of Holy Trinity near Rouen, in order to make Henry abandon the siege of Richer's castle at Laigle.[33]

In times of rebellion, when loyalties could shift back and forth, it could be difficult to distinguish good intelligence from bad. In 1079, during a rebellion in southern Italy against the Norman ruler Robert Guiscard, the Apulian town of Giovinazzo, which had remained loyal to Guiscard, was saved thanks to the timely use of false information. William fitz Ivo, the governor of Bitonto, six miles south of Giovinazzo, sent a messenger to Amicus II, count of Molfetta, who was besieging the town. The messenger gave Amicus 'false reports' (*ficti rumores*) that Guiscard's son, Roger Borsa, was approaching with a large army.[34] Amicus,

---

[29] AA, p. 742: 'qui legati ceterorum de diuersis negociis et pace componenda plurimum loquentes et agentes'.
[30] AA, p. 742.
[31] For Albert's hostility towards Raymond of Saint-Gilles, see AA, p. xxxii.
[32] AA, pp. 379–81. See also WT, vol. 1, p. 322.
[33] Orderic does not suggest a motivation for Tancarville's actions. OV, vol. 6, p. 199.
[34] For the case for translating *rumores* as 'reports' rather than 'rumours', see J. O. Prestwich, 'Military Intelligence under the Norman and Angevin Kings', in George

evidently thinking that William was his ally and that his information was reliable, broke camp and fled.[35]

A famous example of a combatant taking advantage of an uncertain political climate to employ false information occurred after the battle of Dorylaion (1 July 1097, near modern Eskişehir, Turkey). Qilij Arslān, the sultan of Rūm, fleeing through Phrygia ahead of the victorious crusaders, spread false information that enabled his forces to devastate the region. Here is the *Gesta Francorum*'s account of these events:

> Coming to every castle or city, lying and deceiving the inhabitants of those lands, [the Turks] said: 'We fell upon the Christians, and conquered them all' [...] Not only that, they took the sons of the Christians with them and burned or destroyed everything that was convenient or useful, being greatly terrified and fleeing before our face. Therefore, we pursued them through a barren, arid and uninhabitable land, from which we barely escaped or passed through alive.[36]

This use of misinformation differs from others discussed above inasmuch as it was directed against the inhabitants of Phrygia rather than Qilij Arslān's enemies. Nevertheless, even if the method was unusual, this kind of 'scorched earth' tactic was in keeping with conventional medieval strategy.

Some forms of misinformation could be gruesome. In 1102, while besieging Jaffa, an Egyptian army cut the head and legs off an unfortunate crusader named Gerbod of Windeke, whom they had captured in battle near Ascalon. Dressing the remains in purple (a colour associated with royalty), they displayed them to the garrison, claiming that they belonged to Baldwin I of Jerusalem and that no aid was coming to relieve the city. This claim was believed by Arda, Baldwin's queen, and the rest of the garrison. It was only the arrival of the real Baldwin by sea, alive and well, that dissuaded them from surrendering.[37] A similar ruse was reportedly employed at the Battle of the Standard (1138), in a rare example of misinformation being employed to inspire one's own forces. According to

---

Garnett and John Hudson (eds), *Law and Government in Medieval England and Normandy: Essays in Honour of Sir James Holt* (Cambridge, 1994), pp. 1–30, at p. 11.

[35] WA, p. 194.

[36] GF, p. 23: 'At illi uenientes ad cuncta castra siue urbes, fingentes et deludentes habitatores terrarum illarum dicebant: "Nos deuicimus Christianos omnes, et superauimus illos, ita ut nullus eorum iam unquam audeat erigere se ante nos; tantum permittite nos intus intrare". Qui intrantes spoliabant ecclesias et domos et alia omnia, et ducebant equos secum et asinos et mulos, aurum et argentum et ea quae reperire poterant. Adhuc quoque filios Chrisitanorum secum tollebant, et ardebant ac devastabant omnia conuenientia siue utilia, fugientes et pauentes ualde ante faciem nostram. Nos itaque persequebamur eos per deserta et inaquosam et inhabitabilem terram, ex qua uix uiui euasimus uel exiuimus'. See also BB, pp. 34–5; GN, p. 69; OV, vol. 5, p. 65; RM, pp. 114–15.

[37] AA, p. 645.

Aelred of Rievaulx, when Henry, son of David I of Scotland, led a charge through the English line and began to attack the English baggage train, the 'unarmed commoners, terrified, began to run away'. The situation was saved by a 'deception' (*figmentum*) improvised by a 'certain prudent man'. Holding up the severed head of a man he had killed, he shouted that King David was dead. The commoners, 'having been recalled, charged violently into their opponents in [their] usual manner'.[38]

The opposite form of this stratagem, pretending somebody was alive when they were in fact dead, also appears in a handful of chronicles. Sadly, the story of El Cid's corpse leading his army to victory over the Moors while propped up on his horse, as memorably portrayed by Charlton Heston (1961, dir. Anthony Mann), is a much later addition to his myth, apparently invented by the monks of the Castilian monastery San Pedro de Cardeña in order to foster a hero cult around the Cid's tomb.[39] The closest comparable tale in a contemporary chronicle is Albert of Aachen's bizarre account of the death of Baldwin I of Jerusalem while on campaign in Egypt in 1118. According to Albert, Baldwin was very concerned that his body should be returned to Jerusalem for burial and gave detailed instructions to his cook that his body should be disembowelled and salted for the return journey. This was carried out according to his wishes, then:

> [The corpse] was sewn up in a hide and wrapped in a carpet, placed on a horse and firmly bound, so that none of the gentiles would be able to learn by craft that he had died and so, brimming full of confidence, might be inspired to attack the bereaved army with boldness.[40]

Quite how a dead body wrapped in a carpet was intended to fool the Egyptians is unclear. Albert does note that the army returned to Jerusalem by 'trackless and deserted places', so clearly it was not intended to withstand close scrutiny. Perhaps it was simply enough that there was a figure riding in the king's place with the army, giving the illusion that all was well. Fulcher of Chartres, another chronicler of the early history of the kingdom of Jerusalem and Baldwin I's chaplain, does not mention these elaborate preparations, saying only that the king's intestines were preserved

---

[38] BoS, pp. 196–7: 'Hujus igitur admirabili impetu plebs inermis perterrita labebantur. Sed prudentis cujusdam viri figmento, qui, caput unius occisi in altum erigens, regem clamabat occisum, revocati, vehementius solito irruunt in obstantes'.

[39] P. E. Russell, 'San Pedro de Cardeña and the Heroic History of the Cid', *Medium Aevum*, 27 (1958), 57–79.

[40] The term 'gentiles', originally a Biblical word for non-Israelites, was adopted by Christian authors (who regarded the Christian Church as the 'new Israel') as a general term for non-Christians. See p. 196. AA, p. 869: 'corio consutum ac tapetibus inuolutum, equis impositum ac firmiter alligatum est, ita ut nulla gentilium astucia percipere posset eum obisse, et sic in audaciam persequendi exercitum desolatum undique ebullientes animarentur'.

in salt and placed in a coffin.[41] Fulcher did not accompany Baldwin on this campaign, however, so it is possible that Albert of Aachen had access to another, perhaps oral, source for this tale.

The twelfth-century Flemish chronicler, Herman of Tournai, provides a more plausible anecdote of a combatant concealing a death in order to gain a strategic advantage. According to Herman, when William Clito was fatally wounded before the castle of Aalst he was keen 'to bring the horsemen back safely' from the fighting in front of the castle, so secretly he sent word to his ally, Godfrey, duke of Louvain, who was also at the siege.[42]

> The duke, realising that fortune had turned against them, cunningly called Thierry out through messengers and, pretending that he wanted to make peace between him and William, safely led the army away and only told Thierry that William was dead when he was far away.[43]

Galbert of Bruges, another Flemish chronicler and Herman's contemporary, records broadly the same story, describing how William's household knights concealed that their master had taken a mortal wound: 'all that day, concealing his death from their enemies, without lamentation and wailing voices, they supressed their cries of pain'.[44] Godfrey negotiates a safe withdrawal from the siege, then reveals to Thierry that William has already died. These stories indicate how important personal leadership could be in these (relatively) small medieval armies. It is also noteworthy that in both this incident, and Albert's description of Baldwin I's death, that the bereaved are concealing their leader's death from the *enemy*, not their own troops. The goal is not to preserve morale in their own army but to conceal weakness from their enemies by pretending that all was well.

The same motive is explicitly ascribed to two separate ruses recorded in William of Tyre's chronicle of the kingdom of Jerusalem. The first is

---

[41] FC, p. 612: 'Cumque ad usque villam, quae dicitur Laris, pervenissent, infirmitate ingruente et illum penitus consummante, defungitur. Et locatis eius intestinis et sallitis atque in loculo conditis, Hierosolymam properaverunt' (And when they arrived at the town called 'Arish, the king, afflicted by illness and performing penance, died. Putting his intestines in a coffin together with salt, they hurried to Jerusalem).

[42] Herman of Tournai, *Liber de restauratione monasterii S. Martini Tornacensis*, MGH, Scriptores, 14 (Hanover, 1879), pp. 274–317, at p. 289: 'ut caute exinde equitatum reducere studeat'.

[43] Herman of Tournai, *Liber de restauratione*, p. 289: 'Dux sentiens adversa fortunam, callide per internuntios Teodericum evocat, simulansque se pacem inter ipsum et Guilelmum velle componere, caute exercitum eduxit, et cum iam procul esset Teoderico, mortuum esse Guilelmum, mandavit'.

[44] GB, p. 165: 'Quem milites sui collegerunt utpote dominum suum miserando occasu morientem, ac per totum illum diem mortem celando inimicis, sine planctu et ejulatu voces et clamores dolorum compresserant, tanto acriori mentis angustiati confusione'.

attributed to Baldwin III of Jerusalem, following a disastrous campaign against the Syrian town of Bosra in 1147. In order to disguise their losses from the Turks, the Frankish troops were ordered to 'put the bodies of the dead onto the camels and other animals which had been assigned to carry the baggage [...] likewise they ordered the injured and wounded to be sat upon mules, lest it be thought that all our other men were either dead or injured'. The wounded were ordered to ride with drawn swords, to give the appearance (*species*) of strength.[45] It is not clear whether the wounded were being mounted in order to prevent them straggling behind the rest of the army or if they were supposed to make the Franks' cavalry look more numerous. The trick of mounting non-combatants to mimic the appearance of cavalry occurs in both Roman and medieval sources (see Chapter 5), so William may be making a classical allusion. He attributed a very similar ruse to Saladin's army during a foray into the kingdom of Jerusalem in 1182. After an inconclusive battle near the village of Taibe, William reports that the Franks could not estimate how many Muslims had died:

> for, in order to hide their plight from our men, they carried back with them those killed in the front line and the next night secretly buried them in their camp, lest their death, being made known, should make our men more confident.[46]

William does not pass judgement on this incident, reporting it with neither praise nor condemnation. He is, of course, more laudatory about Baldwin III, declaring that the Turks marvelled to see that not a single Frank appeared to have been killed, either by their arrows or the heat, but it is still noteworthy that he attributed the same basic deception to both a Christian and Muslim commander.[47]

Misinformation could be employed in a variety of ways. It could be used to make a force seem stronger than it truly was, to trick the enemy into retreating or even to inspire one's own forces. All of which raises the question of espionage: how did armies and their commanders acquire reliable information about their enemies?

---

[45] WT, p. 730: 'Erat autem nostris indictum publice ut defunctorum corpora camelis et aliis animalibus ad sarcinas deputatis imponerent, ne nostrorum considerata strage redderentur fortiores inimici, debiles quoque et saucios iumentis imponi mandatur, ne omnino nostrorum aliquis aut mortuus aut debilis crederetur. His etiam datum erat in mandatis, ut gladios educentes saltem speciem validorum exprimerent'.

[46] WT, p. 1032: 'De numero tamen interemptorum hostium nichil certum colligere potuimus, nam, ut suorum casum nostris occultarent, eos qui in acie ceciderant secum deportabant, quos sequenti nocte in castris occulte sepelierunt, ne eorum manifestatus interitus nostros redderet securiores'.

[47] See Chapter 9 for a discussion of Christian chroniclers' attitudes towards Muslims' use of military deception.

Espionage: Spies and Spying

Studying espionage in the Middle Ages is difficult, not least because Latin does not possess a simple cognate for the modern term 'spy', meaning a person who gathers information secretly. Chroniclers frequently refer to *exploratores* being sent out to gather intelligence. Lewis and Short define *explorator* as 'a searcher out, examiner, explorer; a prying person, a spy'. In a military context, however, it can also mean 'scout'.[48] The Old French *espie*, from which we derive the English 'spy', can also designate either a scout or a spy.[49] This makes it difficult to determine exactly what is being described in a given instance. Take the following incident from the Book of Joshua, which would have been familiar to medieval clerics:

> And so Joshua, son of Nun, secretly sent two men, *exploratores*, from Shittim and said to them: 'Go and view the land and city of Jericho'. Going ahead, they entered the house of a woman, a prostitute named Rahab, and they rested there. And this was reported to the king of Jericho: 'See! Men from the sons of Israel entered here by night in order to reconnoitre the land'. And the king of Jericho sent to Rahab, saying: 'Bring out the men who came to you and entered your house. For they are *exploratores* and they came to view the whole land'.[50]

How should we translate *exploratores* here? These men were sent out in a military capacity, to reconnoitre the land ahead of the Israelites' attack on Jericho, so they could be called 'scouts'. Yet they were sent 'secretly' (*abscondito*) and concealed themselves within the city at Rahab's house, which seems more characteristic of a spy. The same ambiguity is present in medieval chronicles. The function of an *explorator* was to gather information but their precise methods are often left unclear. This makes the modern distinction between scout and spy unhelpful. For a medieval author, the two roles were not easily separated. *Explorator* described an individual's role, not their methods.

Little scholarship has been produced concerning espionage in the central Middle Ages. Until recently, J. O. Prestwich's essay on the intelligence

---

[48] Charlton T. Lewis and Charles Short, *A Latin Dictionary* (Oxford, 1879), p. 696.
[49] William Rothwell and others (eds), 'espie', *Anglo-Norman Dictionary: Online Edition* (London, 1977–92), <http://www.anglo-norman.net/D/espie[1]> [accessed 8 Nov 2017]. See also 'spy, n.', *OED Online*, <www.oed.com/view/Entry/188063> [accessed 15 November 2017].
[50] Joshua 2.1–3: 'misit ergo Iosue filius Nun de Setthim duos viros exploratores abscondito et dixit eis ite et considerate terram urbemque Hiericho qui pergentes ingressi sunt domum mulieris meretricis nomine Raab et quieverunt apud eam nuntiatumque est regi Hiericho et dictum ecce viri ingressi sunt huc per noctem de filiis Israhel ut explorarent terram misitque rex Hiericho ad Raab dicens educ viros qui venerunt ad te et ingressi sunt domum tuam exploratores quippe sunt et omnem terram considerare venerunt'.

networks of the Anglo-Norman kings was the only major publication on the subject. Lacking explicit evidence for eleventh-century intelligence gathering, Prestwich argued from inference. For example, William I was forewarned about the Godwinsons' rebellion at Exeter in 1068 and the Danish invasion of northern England in 1075. The chroniclers do not tell us how this intelligence was gathered but the fact that William anticipated and swiftly countered these threats demonstrates that he had access to reliable information from both England and the Continent.[51]

Susan Edgington has gone further and argued that Bohemond of Antioch 'made systematic use of professional interpreters/scouts/spies' on the First Crusade.[52] Edgington cites references to *cursores* (lit. runners, messengers) in the chronicle the *Gesta Francorum*, generally accepted as having been written by a member of Bohemond's army, as evidence that he employed specialist scouts: 'When we had begun to approach the Iron Bridge, our *cursores*, who were always accustomed to go ahead of us, discovered that innumerable Turks had gathered against us, hurrying to give aid to Antioch'.[53] Fulcher of Chartres, another chronicler of this crusade, refers to crusader *speculatores* (scouts). By contrast, the *Gesta* describes the Syrian and Armenian Christians who mingled with the crusaders before Antioch (see p. 43) as *ingeniose inuestigabant* ('cleverly investigating') the camp on behalf of the Turkish garrison, while Albert of Aachen calls them *delatores* (informers). 'The vocabulary of intelligence-gathering is significant', says Edgington: '"our" side has "scouts" or "runners", while the enemy has "spies"'.[54] This is not a fair comparison, however. The crusader *cursores* and *speculatores* appear in a purely military context, performing reconnaissance for the army. Edgington herself notes that the Turks are depicted deploying *praecursores* (lit. an advanced guard) for the same purpose.[55] The Antiochene Christians are a different case: they were non-combatants who came to the crusaders in bad faith, pretending to be in distress but intending to inform the Turks of the crusaders' plans, hence their condemnation by the chroniclers.

Although she refers to Bohemond using 'professionals', Edgington does not define what constituted 'professionalism' in this instance, saying

---

[51] Prestwich, 'Military Intelligence', pp. 4–9.
[52] Susan B. Edgington, 'Espionage and Military Intelligence during the First Crusade, 1095–99', in Simon John and Nicholas Morton (eds), *Crusading and Warfare in the Middle Ages: Realities and Representations. Essays in Honour of John France* (Farnham, 2014), pp. 75–86, at p. 79.
[53] GF, p. 28: 'Cum coepissemus appropinquare ad Pontem Farreum, cursores nostri, qui semper solebant nos precedere, inuenerunt Turcos innumerabiles congregatos obuiam eis, qui dare adiutorium Antiochiae festinabant'.
[54] Edgington, 'Espionage and Military Intelligence', p. 77.
[55] Edgington, 'Espionage and Military Intelligence', p. 77.

only: 'It is very probable that Bohemond had recruited Greek and Arabic speakers in southern Italy who had been selected and trained for their role as scouts and interpreters'.[56] It is almost certain that Bohemond's army, raised in the polyglot lands of Sicily and southern Italy, included people who spoke Greek and Arabic. This would explain why it was Bohemond, of all the leading crusaders, who established a relationship with the Greek-speaking Pirrus at Antioch but this is not the same thing as possessing 'trained [...] scouts and interpreters'. Edgington draws a contrast between Bohemond, who supposedly employed these specialists, and the other leading crusaders, who had to rely on ordinary troops to gather intelligence. She cites Raymond of Saint-Gilles's use of knights to reconnoitre Antioch in 1098 but the chronicle text suggests that, far from being an aberration, this was a prestigious task, performed by picked men:

> Therefore, taking counsel with his men, he chose those whom he would send ahead to carefully investigate and otherwise carefully reconnoitre. The viscount of Castillon, William of Montpellier, Peter Roasa and Peter Raymond, men of comital rank, not ignorant of military discipline, were appointed to this task together with many knights.[57]

It is not impossible that Bohemond's *cursores* were trained specialists: it is notable that references to scouting and spying disappear from the *Gesta*'s narrative once Bohemond breaks with the other crusaders.[58] However, we lack the evidence to state conclusively that such training was provided. *Explorator* may refer to a specialist in espionage but it is just as likely to be a functional designation: individuals assigned to 'explore' for the army at a given time.

As Yuval Noah Harari has observed, this lack of a dedicated intelligence 'branch', combined with the relatively small, geographically concentrated nature of medieval armies, meant that it was difficult to prevent information from circulating among the troops.[59] Incidents such as the crusaders' negotiations with the Portuguese at the siege of Lisbon in 1148 or the army's influence over Richard I of England's decision to march on Jerusalem in 1192 demonstrate how soldiers could use this 'operational knowledge' to further their own goals, sometimes in opposition to their

---

[56] Edgington, 'Espionage and Military Intelligence', p. 78.

[57] BB, p. 37: 'Igitur cum suis consiliatus, elegit quos praemitteret, qui rem diligenter inuestigarent et cetera curiosi explorarent. Ad hoc directi sunt consulares uiri, discipline militaris non ignari, uicecomes de Castellone, Willelmus de Monte Pislerio, Petrus de Roasa, Petrus Raimundi, cum militibus multis'.

[58] Edgington, 'Military Intelligence', p. 79.

[59] Yuval Noah Harari, 'Knowledge, Power and the Medieval Soldier', in Iris Shagrir, Ronnie Ellenblum, and Jonathan Riley-Smith (eds), *'In laudem Hierosolymitani': Studies in Crusades and Medieval Culture in Honour of Benjamin Z. Kedar* (Aldershot, 2007), pp. 345–56, at pp. 349–50.

commander's plans.[60] Furthermore, as has already been observed, this lack of effective secrecy meant that enemies could easily plant false information among the rumours and gossip that flowed in and out of a medieval army.

Espionage in the later Middle Ages has received more scholarly attention, in part due to the greater survival of written reports and records of payment.[61] Even here, however, it can be difficult to identify the spies themselves. By their very nature, their role was a secret one, often cloaked in euphemism: 'If a *nuntius*, a *vespilio*, a *coureur*, or a *chevaucheur* may have been a spy, an *espie* or an *explorator* was almost certainly one'.[62] John Alban and Christopher Allmand have established that, in the fourteenth century, the role of messenger or ambassador frequently overlapped with that of a spy. As individuals who had been granted safe passage through enemy territory, they were ideally placed to gather intelligence while ostensibly fulfilling another, legitimate function.[63] Bastian Walter described how the towns of Switzerland and the Upper Rhine used merchants to gather intelligence during their wars against Burgundy (1468–77): they were often multi-lingual, travelled widely and had connections across Europe.[64] It is likely that commanders of earlier centuries made use of similar, well-placed sources to gather information.

In view of the above, I have chosen to translate *explorator* and *espie* as 'scout' and confine my analysis to incidents in which chroniclers explicitly describe deception being used to gather intelligence. Such incidents are relatively rare, as should be expected: if done correctly, espionage should be entirely undetected. Chroniclers frequently employed generic phrases such as 'we learned' or 'it was reported' without identifying how or where the information was gathered. Much of it was probably acquired on an ad hoc basis by interrogating travellers, local peasants or enemy deserters, but the chronicles occasionally describe ploys to gather intelligence covertly.

Some of these tales reveal an alarmingly lax attitude towards camp security, leading the reader to marvel that commanders managed to conceal anything from their enemies. The opening passage of the *History of William Marshal* contains a series of vivid anecdotes about the Marshal's childhood. In 1152, King Stephen of England laid siege to John Marshal's

---

[60] Harari, 'Knowledge', pp. 351–4.
[61] See Bastian Walter, 'Urban Espionage and Counterespionage during the Burgundian Wars (1468–1477)', *Journal of Medieval Military History*, 9 (2011), 132–45, at p. 138.
[62] J. R. Alban and Christopher Allmand, 'Spies and Spying in the Fourteenth Century', in Christopher Allmand (ed.), *War, Literature, and Politics in the Late Middle Ages* (Liverpool, 1976), pp. 73–101, at p. 74.
[63] Alban and Allmand, 'Spies', pp. 75–9; see also James P. Ward, 'Security and Insecurity, Spies and Informers in Holland during the Guelders War (1506–1515)', *Journal of Medieval Military History*, 10 (2012), 173–96, at pp. 188–9.
[64] Walter, 'Urban Espionage', p. 135.

castle at Newbury in Berkshire. During the siege, John's infant son, the titular William, was sent into the king's camp as a hostage. One day, while playing with Stephen in his tent, William spotted a young man passing by outside and innocently exclaimed: 'Welcome, Wilikin, my friend. Tell me who sent you here! How is my lady mother? How are my sisters and my brothers?'[65] The unfortunate Wilikin, whom the poet tells us was 'a valet of his mother's chamber' and had been sent into the camp to check on William, promptly fled.[66] This anecdote may have been recorded solely for its comedic value but it may also have been intended to contrast the child-Marshal's innocence with the ruthless and cynical behaviour of the adults who controlled his fate. Upon hearing that Stephen was threatening to hang the boy if John did not surrender, the elder Marshal famously said that 'the child did not concern him, for he still had the anvils and hammers from which he could forge better ones'.[67] The presence of a spy in the siege camp is passed over in the narrative as an unremarkable detail. It is the child's unwitting betrayal that is notable, not Wilikin's presence, which suggests that it was quite conventional to send spies out in this way. If an individual could pass in and out of a besieged stronghold undetected, probably after dark or through a postern gate, it indicates that medieval armies did not, or could not, cut off a stronghold entirely from the outside world but had to be content with stopping large numbers of troops or supplies.

Infiltrating an enemy force of the same race and who spoke the same language would be relatively simple, as in the above example where an English army besieged an English garrison. It would have been more difficult when a force and its enemy looked different or spoke different languages. This may be one reason why so many references to secret intelligence gathering are found in crusade narratives. Operating in unfamiliar terrain, surrounded by a potentially hostile population, it is only natural that the crusaders regarded the locals with suspicion. The chroniclers of the First Crusade are universally hostile towards the Syrian and Armenian Christians who came into the crusader camp during the siege of Antioch (October 1097 – June 1098). Baldric of Bourgueil's description is typical:

> There were many Armenians and Syrians in the city. They were Christians but many were beholden to the Turks. Pretending to flee, they came boldly into the camp, begging and asking for public alms. They habitually

---

[65] HWM, lines 631–4: 'Bien vingiez, Wilikin amis, / Dies kui vos a ça tramis. / Que fait or ma dame ma mere? / Que funt mes sorors e mi frerer?'.

[66] HWM, lines 623–4: 'Un vailleit qu'il ben conoisseit, / De la chambre sa mere esteit'.

[67] HWM, lines 513–16: 'Mais il dist ke ne li chaleit / De l'enfant, quer encore aveit / Les enclumes e les marteals / Dunt forgereit de plus beals'.

returned to their family homes because their wives were in the city; and these ill-natured *exploratores* were faithfully telling the Turks whatever they were hearing in the camps.[68]

As noted above, we should be cautious about taking the chroniclers' accusations at face value. The Antiochenes probably did not endear themselves to the crusaders, short-supplied as they were, by begging from them. If they were in fact going between the city and the camp (another example of how porous a medieval siege could be), then it would be reasonable to suspect that they were passing information to the garrison. The Muslim chronicler Ibn al-Athīr suggests that the Antiochenes were distrusted as much by the Turks as the crusaders. He writes that Yāghī Siyān, the ruler of Antioch, ordered all the Christians to go out and help 'dig the moat', but then refused to open the gates to them when they had finished. He kept their wives and families within, ostensibly for protection but more likely as hostages.[69]

Walter the Chancellor records another episode of Turkish espionage, from the campaign that terminated at the Battle of the Field of Blood (1119). The Turkish commander Īlghāzī located Roger of Antioch's force in the Ruz Valley in late June 1119 by sending out scouts 'in the guise of birdsellers'. Thomas Asbridge and Susan Edgington, in their commentary on this chronicle, note that 'Walter does not comment upon this seemingly unusual choice of disguise. This might suggest that the Latins were used to purchasing supplies from the local Muslim population'.[70] This illustrates how difficult it was to keep a medieval army camp secure. Ordinary camp followers (leaving aside potential enemies disguised as pedlars) who passed in and out of an army as a matter of course, could be compelled or bribed into passing on information.

The crusaders were just as capable of using local informants. The *Itinerarium Peregrinorum* records that Richard I of England employed three scouts to locate caravans travelling from Egypt into Palestine in June 1192. The chronicle refers to one as 'Bernard, the king's *explorator*'. They were 'natives of that region, dressed in Saracen clothes [and] nobody spoke

---

[68] BB, p. 39: 'Erant autem in ciuitate Armenii multi et Suriani, ipsi equidem Christiani, sed Turcis multum obnoxii. Ipsi fugam simulantes audacter exibant in castra, mendicantes et stipem publicam postulantes. Hi, quoniam eorum mulieres erant intra ciuitatem, ad familiares redibant lares; et exploratores maligni quecumque in castris audiebant Turcis fideliter insinuabant'. See also AA, p. 220; GF, p. 29; OV, vol. 5, p. 71; RM, p. 121; WT, pp. 221–3.
[69] *The Chronicle of Ibn al-Athīr for the Crusading Period from al-Kāmil fi'l-ta'rīkh: Part 1. The Years 491–541/1097–1146, the Coming of the Franks and the Muslim Response*, trans. D. S. Richards (Aldershot, 2006), p. 14.
[70] WC, p. 115.

the Saracen language better'.⁷¹ Ambroise says that Bernard was 'a man born in Syria' (*Uns hom qui iert nez de Sulie*) but his Western name, combined with the chronicler's statement that they went into Egypt in Muslim clothes (suggesting that this was unusual), indicates that all three were Franks.⁷² Greek, Syrian and Armenian polyglots had been employed by the crusaders as interpreters and envoys since the First Crusade. By the Third Crusade, after a century of close contact and acclimatisation, some of the nobility of the kingdom of Jerusalem had become fluent in Arabic: Reynald de Sidon acted as an intermediary with Saladin for both Guy of Lusignan and Richard I of England. This was a specialist skill, however, and would have been highly valued by the newly arrived crusaders from Western Europe.⁷³ The fact that the three *exploratores* were paid a hundred silver marks each demonstrates just how highly Richard valued their service.⁷⁴ The *Itinerarium*'s description highlights how important language, appearance and local knowledge were for effective intelligence gathering.⁷⁵

The narrative continues with Richard leading his army from Bayt Nuba to 'Galatia' (Qaratiya, approximately 15 miles east of Gaza).⁷⁶ An *explorator* (presumably not one of the three mentioned above) informed him that a caravan was passing near Tell-Khuwailifa. Richard, however, was sceptical 'since that *explorator* was a native of that country', so he sent 'a Bedouin and two very prudent native Turcopoles [...] he made them swathe themselves up like Bedouins, so that they would look like Saracens'.⁷⁷ It is notable that Richard did not trust the scout because he was a native, whereas the three men sent into Egypt were both trusted and richly rewarded. This may have been because the latter were Franks or because they had proven themselves reliable. This appears to have been the case with the two Turcopoles sent out to confirm the caravan sighting. We are told that the Bedouin warned them not to speak when they encountered

---

⁷¹ IP, p. 384: 'cum alliis duobus, qui illius terrae fuerunt omnes indigenae, cum vestibus Saracenicis, qui de partibus Babyloniae venerunt, qui revera a Saracenorum in nullo discrepabant habitu'.

⁷² Amb, line 10242.

⁷³ K. A. Tuley, 'A Century of Communication and Acclimatization: Interpreters and Intermediaries in the Kingdom of Jerusalem', in Albrecht Classen (ed.), *East Meets West in the Middle Ages and Early Modern Times: Transcultural Experiences in the Premodern World* (Berlin, 2013), pp. 311–40.

⁷⁴ IP, p. 384: 'ecce Bernardus explorator regis, cum aliis duobus, qui illius terrae fuerunt omnes indigenae, cum vestibus Saracenicis [...] Nemo ipsis efficacius Saracenico loquebatur idiomate; horum trium quilibet, hujus gratia ministerii, prius acceperat a rege Ricardo centum marcas argenti'.

⁷⁵ Another *explorator regis*, named Jumas, is recorded by Ralph of Coggeshall. He acted as a lookout near Richard's camp at Bayt Nūbā in June 1192. RC, p. 39.

⁷⁶ Amb, vol. 2, p. 167 n. 649.

⁷⁷ IP, p. 339.

a Saracen patrol, as this would give them away, so they were obviously not selected for their ability to blend in. It is more likely that these were trusted men, sent along to protect the Bedouin or to make sure he did not defect to the enemy.

Although their activities are often hidden from us by euphemistic language or their own successes, we can learn something about military espionage from the chronicle sources. Commanders certainly valued individuals who could provide reliable intelligence. There is little to suggest that these individuals received special training for this role or that it was a recognised military 'role', but acting as an *explorator* nevertheless required certain qualities: discretion, loyalty, knowledge of the local area and, most importantly, the ability to speak the language. In local conflicts in Western Europe, it would have been easy to find individuals who possessed the latter skills. On crusade, or any conflict between markedly different forces on unfamiliar ground, they were much harder to acquire. This would explain the imbalance in the source evidence. In the West, such individuals were practically invisible in reality and the written record. In the Holy Land, they were noteworthy exceptions among an otherwise hostile population.

The Role of Clerics in Military Espionage

When it came to gathering intelligence, contemporary sources indicate that priests, monks and other clergy could make very effective agents. While the contemporary model of a society divided into those who pray, those who fight and those who work would appear to separate clerics from the world of warfare, recent scholarship has shown that the two intersected in a variety of ways.

Daniel Gerrard has described the fighting clergy as 'a defining paradox of the culture of the medieval church'.[78] It may seem strange to read about ministers of the Prince of Peace leading armies, or even hacking away in the thick of battle, but there are numerous accounts of medieval clerics taking to the field in defiance of Church strictures. Since the earliest days of Christianity, clerics have been prohibited from fighting: at the Council of Nicaea (325 CE), it was decreed that those who returned to the military life after renouncing it for a religious vocation must perform thirteen years of penance.[79] The collections of church canons assembled in the eleventh century by Burchard of Worms and Ivo of Chartres also forbade clerics from carrying arms. Gratian, in Causa 23 of his *Decretum*, stated

---

[78] Daniel M. G. Gerrard, *The Church at War: The Military Activities of Bishops, Abbots and Other Clergy in England, c. 900–1200* (London, 2017), p. 2.
[79] Craig M. Nakashian, *Warrior Churchmen of Medieval England, 1000–1250: Theory and Reality* (Woodbridge, 2016), p. 31.

that the clergy should not bear arms, nor should any offerings be made for clerics killed in battle.[80] It is important to recognise, however, that 'canon law was promulgated by segments within the "church" as a whole, and did not represent a unified and contested "voice of the church"'.[81] The historical record testifies that members of the higher clergy, who were often sons of the warrior aristocracy, felt able to ignore these prohibitions and take up arms when they felt it necessary. Odo, bishop of Bayeux (d. 1097), commanded armies in Normandy prior to the conquest of England, participated in the Battle of Hastings and held Dover for William I of England during the rebellion of 1067.[82] During the conflict between Robert Guiscard and Gisolf II of Salerno, Alfanus I, archbishop of the city (c. 1020–85), established four new bishoprics in the south of the principality that commanded approaches to the city, with the intention of blocking any attack by Guiscard while also increasing his own local power-base.[83] Hugh of Noyers (1183–1206), bishop of Auxerre in Burgundy, was praised by his biographer, Eustache of Auxerre, for his use of military force to stamp out dissent and heresy in his diocese.[84] Clerics might be criticised for adopting the trappings and lifestyle of secular lords but they could also be praised for defending the Church and its people in times of crisis.[85]

Even when they were not actively engaged in combat, clerics played an important role in war by interceding with God on behalf of the combatants through prayers and litanies. David Bachrach has examined the spiritual dimension of medieval warfare and the role played by clerics. Although he is often too ready to take chronicle accounts at face value, ignoring the religious and cultural pressure to depict victorious armies as overtly pious, Bachrach's study does indicate that medieval battles were frequently preceded or accompanied by religious rituals. Prayers of invocation might be made for protection and assistance, Mass celebrated, and sacred relics or banners displayed to assure the combatants of God's favour.[86] One of the most famous and ostentatious displays of this kind took place at the Battle of the Standard (1138), in which the clergy accompanying the English army carried banners and relics from local churches. The titular

---

[80] Nakashian, *Warrior Churchmen*, pp. 87–93.

[81] Gerrard, *Church at War*, p. 8; Nakashian, *Warrior Churchmen*, p. 88.

[82] Gerrard, *Church at War*, pp. 35–40; Nakashian, *Warrior Churchmen*, pp. 129–35.

[83] Valerie Ramseyer, 'Pastoral Care as Military Action: The Ecclesiology of Archbishop Alfanus I of Salerno (1058–1085)', in John S. Ott and Anna Trumbore Jones (eds), *The Bishop Reformed: Studies in Episcopal Power and Culture in the Central Middle Ages* (Aldershot, 2007), pp. 189–208, at pp. 201–5.

[84] Constance Brittain Bouchard, *Spirituality and Administration: The Role of the Bishop in Twelfth-Century Auxerre* (Cambridge, MA, 1979), pp. 99–120.

[85] Nakashian, *Warrior Churchmen*, pp. 22–3.

[86] David S. Bachrach, *Religion and the Conduct of War, c. 300–1215* (Woodbridge, 2003), pp. 78–95.

Standard, the rallying point for the English army, was a ship's mast erected on a cart, with the Host and other religious relics hanging from it.[87] There are also accounts of clerics hearing confessions from the combatants before battle, although this would have been very time-consuming for the whole army and was probably reserved for those wealthy enough to employ their own chaplain.[88] There are even reports of clerics continuing to invoke divine aid during combat. William the Breton, chaplain to Philip II of France, claims that he and another priest stood behind the king chanting psalms throughout the battle of Bouvines (27 July 1214).[89] All of the above suggests that clerics were not an anomaly on the medieval battlefield. Even when they were not physically engaged in combat, they performed an important spiritual and pastoral role to support those who were.

These pastoral duties may explain an unusual detail in the *Gesta Stephani*'s account of the siege of Exeter Castle in 1136. Reporting a stratagem used by Alred, son of Judhael, to enter the castle through the king's siege line (see Chapter 5), the chronicler describes how Alred informed the garrison of his arrival: 'Then, when a messenger had been sent into the castle, since captives and *religiosi* often went in and out for good reasons, he made his arrival known to Baldwin's knights'.[90] K. R. Potter translated *religiosi* as 'priests' but this appears to be an error. Later in the *Gesta*, the chronicler describes the Empress Matilda constructing a castle at Cirencester near 'the holy church of the *religiosi*'.[91] Cirencester Abbey, founded in 1117, was a house of Augustinian canons, which indicates that the author understood the word *religiosus* to mean a member of a religious order, such as a monk or canon, not a priest.[92]

The *Gesta* does not explicitly say that it was a *religiosus* who carried the message; it could have been one of the captives or somebody disguised as a *religiosus*. Yet it is significant that these clerics were permitted to enter and leave the castle. An exchange of prisoners during a siege is not particularly remarkable: they may have been captured in a skirmish, then ransomed, or the garrison may simply have been unwilling to use their precious supplies to feed prisoners (they were eventually starved into surrendering). So why were the *religiosi* permitted to go back and forth? They may have been

---

[87] Bachrach, *Religion and the Conduct of War*, pp. 154–5.
[88] Bachrach, *Religion and the Conduct of War*, pp. 95–8.
[89] It is not recorded whether Philip found this inspiring or simply distracting. Bachrach, *Religion and the Conduct of War*, p. 186.
[90] GS, p. 37: 'Deinde legato intra castellum misso (captivi siquidem et religiosi de causis introeundi vices frequentabant) Balduini milites de adventu suo certificauit'.
[91] GS, p. 189: 'tertium penes civitatem Cirencestriae, juxta piam religiosorum ecclessiam, tanquam alterum Dagon juxta Arcam Domini'. Author's translation.
[92] K. J. Beecham, *The History Cirencester and the Roman City Corinium* (Dursley, 1887), p. 53.

acting as messengers because they were perceived as trustworthy 'neutral parties' who could mediate between the two forces. Another possibility is that these *religiosi* were also priests and were admitted into the castle to provide pastoral care for the garrison: hearing confessions, saying Mass and burying the dead. This is speculation but their presence at the siege and their ability to move between the belligerent parties indicates that clerics were seen as impartial. Their vocation placed them beyond partisan politics.

If other sources are to be believed, this perceived neutrality was sometimes exploited for distinctly partisan ends. The Italian chronicler Amatus of Montecassino records that Robert Guiscard, Norman duke of Apulia, used a certain 'Peter the Deacon' to gather information on the city of Palermo in 1068. Hearing that Robert was making peace with the other towns and cities of Sicily, and fearing that he would be left isolated, the emir of Palermo sent gifts to Robert in the hope of currying favour. In response, Robert devised 'a great piece of cunning' (*une grant soutillesce*): he sent Peter to Palermo as a messenger to thank the emir for his gifts. Peter 'who understood [the Saracen language] and spoke like the Saracens' was instructed only to listen and observe what he saw in the city, presumably so that the citizens would speak candidly around him, thinking that they would not be understood.[93] Peter reported 'that the city was desolate and that [the people] of the city were like a body without a soul': an easy target for the next Norman conquest.[94] Graham Loud speculates that this Peter 'was probably a Greek Christian', one of many bilingual inhabitants of eleventh-century Sicily, although not one for whom Arabic was his first language, else the deception would not have worked.[95] This is an example of a spy employing a twofold cover: his holy vocation as a cleric and his diplomatic role as Guiscard's messenger. Of the two, the latter is probably the most significant here, as a Muslim ruler was unlikely to hold a cleric in the same esteem as a Christian would, but it is nevertheless notable that Guiscard chose a cleric for this covert task rather than a warrior or other secular person.

Another possible reason why certain clerics were so useful for gathering or disseminating intelligence was their connection to specific locations. While merchants and ambassadors were useful because they travelled widely, priests and monks were attached to a single place through their parish or monastery. They had intimate knowledge of the local geography and were likely to be familiar with the local news. In short, they were

---

[93] AM, p. 404: 'liquel entendoit et parloit molt bien coment li sarrazin'.

[94] AM, p. 404: 'Et Pierre fait assavoir a lo duc coment la cité est asoutillié, et ceuz de la cité sont comme lo cors san l'arme'.

[95] Amatus of Montecassino, *History of the Normans*, trans. Prescott N. Dunbar (Woodbridge, 2004), p. 142 n. 38.

ideal informants for a medieval army, especially one operating in unfamiliar territory. Conversely, as indicated in several chronicles, local clerics were well placed to spread misinformation to credulous enemies. Gerald of Wales records a humorous anecdote about how a deacon from Cantref Mawr, named Guaidan, duped a certain Breton knight. In 1163, Henry II of England was planning to assault Rhys ap Gruffydd, king of Deheubarth, at his castle at Dinevor (in mod. Carmarthenshire). The king instructed Guaidan to show an unnamed knight of 'Armorican Brittany' (*de Armorica Britannia*) the quickest and easiest way to the castle, presumably because of his local knowledge. Gerald describes what happened next:

> But the priest, having been ordered to show the better and easier road to the castle, instead deliberately led him through difficult and inaccessible approaches. And wherever they crossed through grassy defiles, the priest ate the grass while the knight stared in astonishment; stating that the inhabitants and native peoples, when starvation threatened, were accustomed to subsist on and enjoy grass and roots. So, when the knight returned to the king, he related everything which seemed worth telling or hearing; the land was certainly uninhabitable, the land was impassable and inaccessible, there were no people except those like beasts and it was necessary to adopt the habits of beasts to live there.[96]

Gerald's attitude towards the Welsh and their alleged propensity for deceit is complex and will be discussed in detail in Chapter 9. In this instance, at least, it would appear that Gerald is on the side of the Welsh, with Henry and his credulous vassal acting as the butt of Guaidan's joke. Henry, Gerald tells us, believing Dinevor to be inaccessible and the local area inhospitable, called off the assault and instead made peace with Rhys through an exchange of oaths and hostages.

As with all stories of deception, we must be conscious of authorial prejudice. Roger of Wendover, an English Benedictine, recorded a story of clerical deceit that cast the Welsh Cistercians in a dubious light. In July 1231 Llewelyn ap Iorwerth, king of Gwynedd, pillaged the Welsh marches, burning Montgomery, Radnor, Hay and Brecon in an act of vengeance against Hubert de Burgh, regent of England.[97] According to Roger, Llewelyn employed a local monk to lure the garrison of Montgomery Castle into

---

[96] IK, pp. 81–2: 'Presbyter autem, monitus ut per viam meliorem ad castrum et faciliorem militi praeberet iter, per magis difficiles et inaccessibiles aditus ipsum ex industria circumduxit. Et ubicunque per saltus herbosos transsitum faciebant, cum intuentium admiratione presbyter herbam pascebatur; asserens accolas et indigenas herbis et radicibus, ingruente inedia, vivere et vesci solere. Ad regem itaque milite reverso, cunctisque relatis quae vel digna relatu viderat vel audierat; terram scilicet inhabitabilem, terram inviam et inaccessibiliem, nullique genti nisi bestiali et bestiarum more viventi victui necessariam'.

[97] Frederick C. Suppe, *Military Institutions on the Welsh Marches: Shropshire, AD 1066–1300* (Woodbridge, 1994), p. 21.

an ambush, who told the garrison that Llewelyn was close at hand and that they could easily ride across the nearby meadow to attack him. In reality, the meadow was a bog and the garrison became stranded: 'Then the Welsh, seeing the submersion of their enemies, turned back to attack them with their lances and cruelly killed the knights and horses who were wallowing in the mire'.[98] It is difficult to believe that the garrison would have been so ignorant about the nearby terrain. The castle had been built in 1223 by Hubert de Burgh, who expended considerable effort to strengthen the garrison, including transferring all castle-guard service from nearby Shrawardine Castle to Montgomery.[99] Roger himself seems to have had reservations about the story's veracity, prefixing it with the chroniclers' ubiquitous phrase, *'ut dicitur'* ('it is said'), used to indicate information that they did not consider wholly reliable.[100] Nevertheless, he did not pass over an opportunity to disparage the Welsh or report the punishment inflicted on Cumhyre Abbey by Henry III.[101] Even if the incident is of dubious historicity, the garrison's use of a local cleric to gather information (and the subsequent opportunity to spread misinformation) corroborates stories from other chronicles. It was a plausible course of action for an army campaigning in unfamiliar terrain.

A full study of this topic, and the general role of clerics within medieval warfare as non-combatants, is necessary. Scholars have studied churchmen as fighters or victims but there is more to be said about their role as auxiliary figures: care-givers, pastors and informants. The handful of incidents presented above suggest that clerics, like women, were frequently non-combatant participants in war whose roles are obscured, often invisible, in the historical record. Their sacred vocation set them apart, allowing them to cross battle lines in ways that secular individuals could not. Their unique status in the society of Western Europe provided cover to clerics who chose to act as spies or *agents provocateurs* in secular conflicts.

Conclusion

Some of the incidents described above are difficult to credit, either because of implausible details or their resemblance to archetypical stories. Even if one disregards the less plausible tales, however, the chronicle sources testify

---

[98] RW, vol. 4, pp. 222–3: 'Tunc Wallenses, hostium submersionem cognoscentes, reversi sunt cum impetu super eos, et cum lanceis suis milites et equos in coeno volutantes crudeliter peremerunt'.
[99] Suppe, *Military Institutions on the Welsh Marches*, p. 137.
[100] Ruth Morse, *Truth and Convention in the Middle Ages: Rhetoric, Representation and Reality* (Cambridge, 1991), p. 95.
[101] RW, vol. 4, p. 223.

to the importance of military intelligence in medieval warfare. Commanders sought reliable information about their enemy and the local environment and were willing to pay significant sums to acquire it. Conversely, they attempted to prevent their opponents from gathering accurate intelligence about them. This appears to have been difficult, as medieval armies could be very lax in their security arrangements. Whether carried by pedlars, spies or just simple gossip, information flowed in and out of the medieval army camp, as well as between the tent of the commander and the common soldier. This made it very easy to deliberately spread misinformation. Sometimes there was little discernible difference, to either the commander or the chronicler, between a deliberate ruse and an honest mistake. The fact that so many of these incidents were recorded, even the more outlandish varieties, indicates just how confusing and difficult waging war in the Middle Ages could be.

3

The Element of Surprise: Ambushes and Night Raids

Surprise can grant a decisive advantage in battle. Barton Whaley calculated, based on a study of incidents across sixteen wars between 1914 and 1968, that 'while the usual non-surprise operations produce casualty ratios of about 1-to-1, those with surprise yield ratios of 5-to-1. That is, surprise may be rather reliably depended upon to quintuple the enemy's casualty rates, *relative to one's own* [sic]'.[1] We lack the data to make a comparable analysis of medieval warfare but Whaley's conclusions demonstrate the impact that a properly conducted surprise attack can have on its victims. It may challenge modern notions of fair and honourable fighting but the evidence presented below indicates that medieval combatants regularly sought to launch precisely these kinds of devastating attacks on their enemies and took precautions to avoid being surprised themselves.

Ambushes: Setting, Executing and Avoiding

Ambushes were ubiquitous in medieval warfare: they account for nearly a third of the incidents in the taxonomy presented in the Appendix. They were simple to arrange: all that was required was a suitable hiding place and sufficient patience to wait for the enemy to appear. If executed correctly, they could confer an overwhelming tactical advantage. The English 'ambush' comes from the Old French *embusche*, which is derived from the Latin *inboscāre*, a compound of *in* and *boscus*, 'woodland'.[2] Therefore, a literal definition of an ambush would be 'people concealed in woodland' to attack an enemy by surprise. Dense woodland can provide cover for a large number of people and was very common in the predominantly rural environment of medieval Europe, which is probably why it became

---

[1] Barton Whaley, *Stratagem: Deception and Surprise in War* (Norwood, MA, 2008), p. 130.
[2] 'ambush, v.', *OED Online*, < http://www.oed.com/view/Entry/6260> [accessed 7 March 2018].

synonymous with surprise attacks.[3] For the purpose of this discussion, I have defined an ambush as any incident in which troops were concealed (in woodland or elsewhere) in order to take their enemy by surprise.

While such incidents are relatively easy to identify in Old French narratives, Latin terminology presents some difficulties. *Insidia*, which can be translated as 'ambush' or 'ambush party', can also be used in a figurative sense for any sort of 'artifice, crafty device, plot [or] snare'.[4] For example, in Genesis 42, when Joseph accuses his brothers of having entered Egypt as spies, they protest: 'We are peaceable men and we mean no *insidiae*'.[5] Similarly, Augustine used *insidia* to stand for all the varieties of stratagem (which he contrasted with '*aperta pugna*' (open battle)) in his discussion of right conduct in warfare.[6] The ambiguity surrounding the possible meaning of *insidia* is also present in the medieval chronicles. For example, consider the *Gesta Stephani*'s description of Miles of Gloucester's actions following his defection from King Stephen's cause to the Empress Matilda in 1138:

> Now he abducted innumerable animals from the furthest limits of England, now he harassed with fire and sword those around him who were loyal and whom he knew had done homage to the king: here he wove *insidiae* for the king and his adherents, there he mostly cruelly devastated their lands and possessions until they became a desert.[7]

It is likely that Miles laid ambushes for Stephen's supporters at some point during this conflict, but the chronicler does not appear to be describing specific tactics here. This is a summation of Miles's behaviour, intended to emphasise his utter hostility towards Stephen's supporters. Furthermore, the use of the verb *texere* (to weave) suggests that this is a metaphor, depicting Miles as a hunter laying snares for his innocent prey. In view of this ambiguity, I have confined analysis in this chapter to incidents in which combatants are explicitly depicted intentionally concealing themselves in some manner, waiting for the enemy to approach and then attacking them unawares.

The chronicles give little indication that ambushes required specialist training or that they were performed exclusively by specialist troops. Depending on the situation, ambush parties could be mounted or on foot,

---

[3] Malcolm Barber, *The Two Cities: Medieval Europe, 1050–1320* (London, 1992), pp. 11–23.
[4] Charlton T. Lewis and Charles Short, *A Latin Dictionary* (Oxford, 1879), p. 964.
[5] Genesis 42. 31: 'cui respondimus pacifici sumus nec ullas molimur insidias'.
[6] See Chapter 9 for a detailed discussion of this passage. Augustine, *Quaestionum in Heptateuchum libri* vii, ed. Joseph Zycha (Vienna, 1895), pp. 428–9.
[7] GS, p. 90. 'Et nunc quidem de remotissimis Angliae finibus innumerabilis multitudinis animalia abducere, nunc quos circa se fide, et hominio regi allectos praenoverat, igne, et gladio validissime vexare; illic juges regi, suisque confraganeis insidias texere, istic eorundem terras, et possessiones usque ad solitudinem crudelissime nudare'.

but the chroniclers rarely describe how they were organised. Raymond of Aguilers's description of an ambush carried out by Raymond of Saint-Gilles in 1099, against Turks harassing the army of the First Crusade on the road to Damascus, implies a mounted ambush party:

> But when the Turks had passed by the ambush party, our knights, together with the count, coming out of their hiding places, assaulted, confounded and dismayed the enemy divisions; they killed them and led away their best horses to the army with great rejoicing.[8]

The description of the ambush party as *milites*, rather than foot soldiers or archers, combined with the description of them leading away the enemy's best horses (which would have been difficult on foot), suggests a mounted ambuscade.

The accounts of Henry II of England's relief of Rouen in August 1174 contain a rare description of specialist troops being employed to lay an ambush. Rouen had been under siege from the north bank of the Seine by the combined forces of Louis VII of France, Philip I of Flanders and Henry's eldest son, the Young King, since 22 July. Henry II, with characteristic rapidity, arrived on the south bank on 11 August. English chronicler William of Newburgh described his next move as follows:

> But in the night he secretly sent out a troop of Welshmen which he had brought from England, in order that, hidden in the shadows of the woods (for this race of men is agile and has experience of the woods), they might watch all the necessities that were being brought to the army. When the time was right, rushing out from the woods, they attacked a convoy.[9]

These Welsh troops were able to ambush the French supplies and effectively starve Louis into breaking the siege. Roger of Howden, who served for a time in Henry's household, calls these troops Henry's 'Welshmen' (*Walenses sui*) and describes the enemy reaction as follows: 'they were so terrified by this report that nobody thought of anything except flight'.[10] Robert of Torigni's account of the siege differs slightly, calling them 'Welsh marchers' (*marchisi Walenses*), suggesting that they may have been Cambro-Normans rather than native Welshmen.[11] The terror that they

---

[8] RA, p. 273: 'Sed quum jam praeterissent insidias, egressi milites nostri de occultis cum comite agmina hostium invadunt, conturbant et confundunt; atque ipsos interficiunt, et equos eorum optimos cum grandi exsultatione ad exercitum deduxerunt'.

[9] WN, vol. 2, p. 153: 'Porro ipse Walensium turmam ex Anglia accitam per noctem latenter emisit ut siluarum opacitate tecti (nam hoc genus hominum agile et siluarum gnarum est) locis opportunis obseruarent qua tanto exercitui necessaria conuehebantur. Hi nimirum captato tempore siluis erumpentes commeatum inuaserunt'.

[10] GRH, pp. 74–5: 'Quod cum nunciatum esset regi Franciae et exercitui ejus, tali rumore perterriti, jam nihil nisi de fuga cogitabant'.

[11] RT, p. 265.

reportedly inspired would seem to indicate native Welsh, however: a force that appeared suddenly out of the trees, shouting in an alien language, dressed in an unfamiliar way, could have had a profound psychological impact on the French and Flemings. Regardless, the sources identify these Welshmen as specialists, used to fighting in woodland, and employed by Henry for this purpose.[12]

As has been established, the very word 'ambush' derives from woodland. Not only could forests conceal large numbers of troops, the enemy were restricted to travelling along specific roads, which made them easy to locate. The crusader-chronicler Robert de Clari provides a description of such an ambush in his account of the Fourth Crusade. In the winter of 1203, while the crusaders were besieging Constantinople, Henry of Flanders led a raid on the nearby city of Philia. As he was returning, his force was ambushed by Greeks loyal to the Byzantine emperor, Alexios V. Robert's account conveys something of the panic and the vicious close-quarter fighting involved:

> When they saw the Greeks, they were very much afraid and many began to call upon the Lord God and Our Lady and they were so dismayed that they did not know what to do. Then they said to one another: '*Par foi*! If we flee, we are all dead: better to die defending ourselves than fleeing' [...] When the French saw that the Greeks were attacking them from all sides, they dropped their lances to the ground, drew the knives and *misericordes* which they had, and fought very fiercely to defend themselves and they killed many.[13]

The fact that the crusaders chose to use their knives and daggers suggests they were attacked in a tightly enclosed area, where they could not effectively use lances or even swords. In these circumstances, it would have been very difficult to form up for a cavalry charge: another advantage of conducting an ambush in woodland.

---

[12] This corroborates Gerald of Wales's description of the difference between warfare on the Continent and warfare in Wales, to which the armoured knight was quite unsuited. See Chapter 9 for a detailed discussion.

[13] I have chosen not to translate the exclamation 'Par foi' because a modern English rendering would be unnecessarily stilted. Clari, p. 66: 'Quant il les virrent, si eurent molt grant peur, et molt commenchierent a reclamer Damedieu et Nostre Dame, et furent si esmari qu'il ne se seurent conseiller, et tant qu'il disent entr'aus: "Par foi! se nous fuions, nous sommes tout mort; miex nous vient morir en desdendant que en fuiant" [...] Quant li Franchois virent que li Grieu leur couroient si sus de toutes pars, si laissierent les lanches caïr jus, si traient coustiaus et misericordes qu'il avoient, si s'acueillent a desfendre molt vigeureusement, si en ochient mout'. The misericorde was a short knife or dagger which was used to kill an enemy who refused to surrender or ask for mercy, hence its name. It was clearly a weapon of last resort. Victor Gay, *Glossaire archéologique du Moyen Âge et de la Renaissance*, ed. Henri Stein (2 vols, Paris, 1928), vol. 2, pp. 133–4.

Woodland was not essential for laying an ambush, of course. Any difficult terrain that allowed combatants to conceal themselves could serve. According to the English chronicler John of Hexham, in February 1138 David I of Scotland used a marsh near the town of Roxburgh to shelter his army in order to attack Stephen of England:

> But King David, composing himself and gathering his men inside a certain little marsh which was not far off and utterly inaccessible on all sides, save along a narrow path, ordered the citizens of Roxburgh to receive the king of England into their town generously if he arrived [...] But these *insidiae* were made known to King Stephen who, being angry and preparing to return, compelled Eustace [fitz John] to place the fortress of Bamburgh into his hands and swiftly returned to England.[14]

The *Gesta Herewardi* depicts both Normans and English laying ambushes in the Cambridgeshire Fens. In one incident, the earl of Warenne, learning that Hereward was travelling to the island of Ely, 'prepared many ambushes upon his road in secret hiding places in the marsh surrounding the island, and carefully set a watch around the waters near the land'.[15]

Passes through steep hills or mountains were also good locations to lay ambushes. As in a forest, the narrow pathways restricted the enemy's movements and made it easy to judge where the enemy force would have to pass. According to *The Song of Dermot and Earl Richard fitz Gilbert*, an Old French poem celebrating Richard Strongbow's conquests in Ireland, Strongbow was ambushed in 1172 while returning to his base in Kildare from a raid into Offaly, possibly through the Slieve Bloom mountains: 'Straightaway, at the end of the pass, he rushed upon them from all sides; O'Dempsey [king of Uí Failghe] and the Irish of Offaly rushed upon them; everybody from that region attacked the rear guard'.[16] The rearguard would have been particularly vulnerable in these situations, as the

---

[14] Eustace fitz John (d. 1157), a powerful magnate in Yorkshire and Northumberland and favourite of Henry I of England, would switch allegiances after this incident, handing over his castle at Malton to the Scots at Easter and fighting for David at the Battle of the Standard. JH, p. 260: 'Rex vero David colligens se & suos haud procul intra quandam paludem minutam valde et prorsus inaccessibilem circumquaque, nisi per angustias cujusdam semitae, praecepit civibus de Rochasburch magnanimiter excipere regem Angliae intra urbem si adveniret [...] Notae autem factae sunt insidiae regi Stephane, qui parans reditum iratus coegit Eustachium reconsignare in manu sua munitionem de Bahanburch et in Angliam festinus regressus est'.

[15] 'Gesta Herwardi incliti exulis et militis', in Thomas Duffus Hardy and Charles Trice Martin (eds.), *Lestorie des engles solum la translacion Maistre Geffrei Gaimar* (2 vols, London, 1888), vol. 1, pp. 339–404 (at p. 374): 'Quod audiens comes de Warenne, cujus fratrem jamdudum ipse Herewardus occiderat, in occursum ejus multas insidias per occultas latebras juxta paludem insulae exterius praeparavit, et circa aquas prope terram custodiam posuit caute'.

[16] Dermot, lines 2801–6: 'Tut dreit al issir del pas / lur currut sure tost vias / sur

narrow terrain made it difficult for the rest of the army to turn around and help. The *Itinerarium Peregrinorum* describes how Frederick, duke of Swabia, was wounded when the rearguard of the German contingent of the Third Crusade was caught in a similar ambush laid by Turkish forces among 'steef cliffs and rough ascents up narrow paths' near Iconium in Phrygia on 3 May 1190. Learning that his father, the Emperor Frederick Barbarossa, was under attack in the rearguard, the duke led a rescue party back up the pass: 'their horses were forced to gallop where they could hardly even walk'. The emperor was saved but the duke lost his front teeth when he was struck in his face by a stone.[17] This passage conveys the chaos and fear experienced by a force caught in an ambush, as well as the difficulties that horsemen faced when manoeuvring in a confined space. The duke's decision to turn back and help the rearguard was considered particularly heroic. The *Itinerarium* records that his wounds became a badge of honour: 'whenever he parts his lips his empty mouth bears witness to the glory of his victory'.[18]

Ambushes were not confined to warfare in the countryside. Fortifications and settlements also provided locations where troops might be concealed. French royal chronicler Suger of Saint-Denis describes how Louis VI of France was ambushed while attempting to storm the defensive works of the rebel castle at Toury in 1112:

> Meanwhile, Ralph of Beaugency, a man of great shrewdness and activity, fearing what had happened earlier, concealed an unknown army in part of the castle, hidden by the height of a certain church and the shadowiness of the nearby houses. When he saw the fugitives pass through the gate, the army having been brought to halt by the weariness of the king's knights, he attacked them very violently.[19]

---

lur currut O'Dymmesy / E les Yrreis de Offaili; / L'arere garde unt asailiz / Les tuz de cel païs'.

[17] IP, pp. 50–1: 'Erat locus quem rupes arduae, conscensus asperi, semitae strictiores, difficilem ad permeandum reddebant, qua cum prior pars agminis, filio imperatoris ductante, transisset, in postremam subito Turci undique ex indisdiis irruunt [...] Equi, qua ire non poterant, coguntur ad cursum. Denique dum huc illuc patrem quaerens, patrem vociferans, anxius et incautus discurrit, ictu saxi eliditur galea, excutiuntur dentes'. This incident is also recorded in the contemporary German chronicle, the *Historia de Expeditione Friderici Imperatoris*. See G. A. Loud (trans.), *The Crusade of Frederick Barbarossa: The History of the Expedition of the Emperor Frederick and Related Texts* (Farnham, 2010), p 102.

[18] IP, p. 51: 'nam quoties labra secedunt, victoriae gloriam os nudum testatur'.

[19] SSD, pp. 158–60: 'Interea Radulfus Baugentiacensis, vir magne sagacitatis et strenuitatis, idipsum quod contigit prius formidans, exercitum celaverat in parte castri, altitudine cujusdam ecclesie et opacitate vicinarum domorum incognitum. Qui, cum fugitivos suos jam per portam exire videret, pausatum exercitum lassatis regiis militibus apponit, gravissime impetit'.

Suger is at pains to excuse Louis's defeat, although it is important to note that at no point does he describe Ralph's tactics as dishonourable or illegitimate. Indeed, he criticises the knights (although not Louis directly) for fighting in a disadvantageous position: 'Too late they realised how much wisdom surpasses courage, since, if they had been awaiting them in order in the field, they would have subjugated them all to their will'.[20]

As mentioned above, it was important to be able to determine exactly where the enemy would be at a given time in order to ambush them. This was made easier if the enemy was short of supplies and had limited opportunities to replenish them. Several of the accounts of the crusaders' siege of Jerusalem in 1099 refer to the Muslims blocking or fouling local water sources and laying ambushes around others.[21] Amatus of Montecassino recounts a particularly cruel variant of this stratagem employed by the Norman force that besieged Palermo, Sicily in 1071. The inhabitants were starving and many were sick:

> And the malicious Normans made small loaves of bread and left them at the foot of the Saracens' walls: and twenty or thirty Saracens ran out to take the bread. And on the second day, they placed loaves of bread further from their ground; and the Saracens ran out to take the bread, and the Normans lay in wait for them, and more came out. On the third day, they placed loaves even further away, and when the Saracens all came out to get the bread, the Normans captured them all and kept them as slaves or sold them in distant lands.[22]

Ambush parties possessed a great tactical and psychological advantage. They were able to attack at a time and place of their choosing and with the element of surprise on their side. Several accounts suggest that ambush parties would try to make a loud noise as they attacked, by shouting or blowing horns, presumably to further confuse the enemy and increase the psychological impact of their assault. For example, in the Old French history of Britain, the *Roman de Brut*, a British ambush led by Cador, earl of Cornwall, is described as follows: 'The Saxons never heard a word, nor a cry, nor any sound until Cador shouted his battle-cry, attacking without hesitation. He killed more than half of them'.[23] In April 1128, the Flemish

---

[20] SSD, p. 160: 'quantum sapientia prestet audacie, licet sero, animadvertentes, cum, si eos ordinati in campo expectarent, voluntati sue eos omnino subjugarent'.

[21] AA, p. 410; BB, p. 105–6; GF, p. 89; GN, p. 128; OV, vol. 5, p. 163.

[22] AM, p. 429: 'Et li maliciouz Normant faisoient poiz de lo pain et lo lessoient a pié de li sarrazin: et corroient a.xx. et.xxx. pour prendre lo pain. Er lo secont jor, metoient un poi li pain plus loing de la terre; et cil corroient a prendre lo pain, et se asseguroient, et plus en venoient. Lo tiers jor, lo mistrent un poi plus loing, et quant vindrent li paien tuit defore, furent tuti pris et gardez pour serf, ou estoient vendut en longes part'.

[23] RdB, lines 9085–9: 'Unches li Saisne mot n'en sorent / Ne cri, ne noise oï n'en orent / Dessi que Cador s'escria, / Ke de ferir ne se targa. / Plus en ocist de la meitied'.

baron Lambert of Aardenburg laid siege to the castle at Oostburg in defiance of his nominal lord, Thierry of Alsace. Galbert of Bruges, a contemporary Flemish chronicler, describes how a relief force from Aardenburg (whose citizens were, somewhat confusingly, enemies of Lambert) terrified the besiegers into retreating:

> Those who had leapt forth, disturbing the air with clamour and infinite battle-cries, immediately rendered the besiegers so astonished that they began to flee and, throwing away their shields and arms, they tucked their clothes into their belts to run in flight.[24]

Roger of Wendover describes Richard, earl of Cornwall, employing similar tactics when ambushing a French force in the woods near Rieux in Gascony in 1225: 'and when they were passing the ambush party in the direction of the siege, earl Richard and his followers rushed on them with the noise of trumpets and brandishing spears'.[25]

There was another, uniquely medieval, factor that made ambushes so effective, which can be demonstrated by analysing an incident from the *History of William Marshal*. The poem describes how the Marshal's uncle Patrick, earl of Salisbury, was killed in an ambush in Poitou in 1168.[26] Patrick had been ordered to escort Eleanor of Aquitaine through the region, where the Lusignan family had risen in rebellion against Henry II of England. The poet describes the circumstances of his death:

> He did not want to flee either up or down the road; he called resolutely for his horse, but it was still a long way away, nor could he have it in his great need, for he did not have time to be armed. Unarmed, upon his palfrey, he rushed to attack them in a great rage, and his horse came there. His companions did not follow him, for they were intent on arming themselves. This story is very painful to tell: when he wanted to mount his horse, before he was properly seated in the saddle, a traitor, an assassin, struck him from behind with a lance, piercing him through the body, in such a way that he was slain on the spot, which was a great misfortune to all his men.[27]

---

[24] GB, p. 153: 'Statimque strepitum et clamores infinitos in aera moventes illi qui prosilierant, perterritos et prorsus attonitos reddiderunt obsidionem facientes in tantum ut fugam inirent et, clipeis et armis abjectis, ad cursitandum in fuga sese succingerent'.

[25] RW, p. 285: 'qui dum locum insidiarum versus obsidionem pertransissent, comes Richardus et socii ejus cum strepitu buccinarum et vibramine hastarum irruerunt in ipsos'.

[26] This much, at least, is corroborated by other sources such as RT, p. 236; HowChr, vol. I, p. 273.

[27] HWM, lines 1635–52: 'N'en vot fuïr n'amont n'aval; / Forment demanda son chival, / Mais uncor li esteit trop loing, / Nel pout aveir a grant bosoign / N'il ne pout a tens estre armé. / Sor son palefrei desarmé / Par grant ire lor corut sore, / E sis chivals vint en illore. / Si compaingnon pas nel sivirent, / Quer a els armer atendirent. / Ci a trop fot conte a conter: / Quant e son cheval volt monter, / Anceis qu'es archuns

Patrick was killed while trying to change horses in the midst of the fighting. When he realised that he was under attack he called for his horse, *son chival*. This does not mean that he was on foot at the time, however, as the poet says he attacked the Poitevins '*sor son palefrei*' (upon his palfrey), indicating that the horse he called for was a warhorse or destrier. A palfrey, an expensive horse trained to provide a smooth and comfortable ride, was evidently considered an unsuitable mount for combat, except in an emergency.[28] It is noteworthy that the poet did not feel it necessary to specify the type of horse Patrick called for: both he and his audience knew what he would have needed in that situation.

The second noteworthy detail is that Patrick is described as 'unarmed' (*desarmé*). Yet this cannot mean 'without a weapon', as he is depicted fighting, so it must mean 'not wearing armour'. This agrees with lines 1643–4: 'His companions did not follow him, for they were intent on arming themselves'. It would have only taken a moment to grab a lance or a sword but putting on a hauberk and other pieces of equipment would have been time-consuming and required the men to dismount.[29] Later in the *History*, Geoffrey Plantagenet, the future duke of Brittany, is said to have been able to perform the remarkable trick of putting on his hauberk while in the saddle.[30] When asked why he did this, he explained: 'the man who is armed in a time of need such as this, but his horse is far away, is more quickly taken and held if the enemy sees him, and they do him more harm and hurt than if he had been upon his horse'.[31]

Patrick of Salisbury is not censured by the poet for travelling without his armour, which suggests that this was considered normal behaviour. Other sources indicate that medieval combatants did not wear their armour unless they expected to fight imminently.[32] See, for example, the description of Charlemagne's behaviour the morning after the battle of

---

fust asis, / Uns traïtres, un hanseïs / Le feri d'un glaive desriere / Parmi le cors, en tel manere / Que tantost murir l'en estut, / Dunz a toz les suens mesestut'.

[28] R. H. C. Davis, *The Medieval Warhorse: Origin, Development and Redevelopment* (London, 1989), p. 67; Cynthia Jenéy, 'Horses and Equitation', in Albrecht Classen (ed.), *Handbook of Medieval Culture: Fundamental Aspects and Conditions of the European Middle Ages* (2 vols, Berlin, 2015), vol. 1, pp. 674–96 (here p. 682).

[29] The hauberk was made all in one piece, so the wearer was usually required to bend double or find assistance to put it on: Kelly DeVries and Robert Douglas Smith, *Medieval Military Technology*, 2nd edn (Toronto, 2012), p. 64.

[30] HWM, lines 2164–70.

[31] HWM, lines 2177–82: 'Qui est armez en tel bosoing, / Se son chival li est trop loing / E si enemi li sorvenent, / Plus tost le prenent e retienent / E li funt plus ennui e mal / Que s'il esteit en son chival'.

[32] See Roger of Howden's account of the death of Geoffrey, count of Vendôme, in 1189, when he was caught *inermus* in an ambush by the viscount of Mont Double: HowChr, vol. 2, p. 108.

Roncevaux in the *Chanson de Roland*: 'The king ungirded himself, and he removed his arms, and the rest of the army disarmed themselves too. Then they mounted, to ride hard upon those long ways and those great roads'.[33] Even though the men had slept in their armour because they expected to be attacked, they removed it when they had to ride a long way. It was unusual to wear armour on the march. Consider Fulcher of Chartres's description of Baldwin II of Jerusalem's army as it advanced against Damascus in 1126:

> But when the guides had begun to make their way along the path for travellers, also with blaring trumpets, they carefully joined the road which they knew would be more practicable for them. And when they had gone deeper into the enemy land, it was wiser that they endeavoured to advance with banners raised and protected themselves with their arms lest they be thrown into confusion by an unforeseen danger.[34]

Fulcher appears to be stressing how well-prepared the Christians were, prefiguring their eventual victory over the Damascene Turks. Advancing with banners raised was a generally recognised sign that an army was on a war-footing and seeking battle. Likewise, they took precautions against a sudden ambush by equipping themselves with their *arma*. As discussed in the introduction, chronicles often had a didactic purpose. Fulcher may have intended this as a lesson to his readers about prudence and the importance of thorough preparation, both in war and general life.

Ambushes were particularly effective in the Middle Ages because they allowed the attackers to catch defenders *unprepared* i.e. without their specialist equipment. An unarmoured man on a palfrey was a much easier target than the same man, fully armoured and mounted on a warhorse. Travelling without armour might seem reckless but it was so heavy and uncomfortable that contemporaries must have felt it was worth the risk when they were not expecting combat imminently. Furthermore, there was the need to keep the warhorses fresh and not tire them out through extended usage. If their scouts and informers could keep the knights well-informed, they would have sufficient time to equip themselves before combat, hence the attraction of catching an enemy unawares.

Several of the ambushes described above were directed against the rear of an enemy force, perhaps because it was easier to approach unseen.

---

[33] Gerald J. Brault (ed.), *The Song of Roland: An Analytical Edition* (2 vols, University Park, PA, 1978), lines 2849–52: 'Lis reis descent, si ad rendut ses armes, / Si se desarment par tute l'ost li altre. / Puis sunt muntet, par grant vertut chevalchent / Cez veiez lunges e cez chemins mult larges'.

[34] FC, p. 787: 'Cum autem praeduces viatoribus tramitem insinuare coepissent, cornibus item una personantibus, viam, quam sibi utiliorem noverunt, accurate carpserunt. Et cum terram hostilem profundius introissent, levatis signis incedere sapientius sategerunt et armis suis se munierunt, ne inopinato periculo perturbarentur'.

The ubiquity of ambushes, particularly when campaigning in enemy territory, made the rear of a medieval army a dangerous place and consequently appears to have been a station of special honour, reserved for the bravest or most reliable troops. The *Itinerarium Peregrinorum* tells us that Frederick Barbarossa took command of the rearmost division of his army on the march to Iconium in 1190, leaving the vanguard to Frederick of Swabia and placing the baggage and pack animals in the middle.[35] In the passage from the *Song of Dermot* discussed above, we are told that Strongbow entrusted the rearguard to his constable, Robert de Quency.[36] Robert was one of the earl's most trusted followers, the standard bearer for the whole force: 'In short, Robert de Quency was killed that day, he who bore the banner and the pennon of the region of Leinster, to whom the earl had given the constableship as a hereditary possession'.[37] Describing Simon de Montfort's retreat from the siege of Toulouse in 1217, the anonymous continuator of the *Chanson de la croisade albigoise* says that he retreated 'in close array, and formed the rearguard out of those with the best horses'.[38] In his account of the battle of Mansurah (8 February 1250), crusader-chronicler Jean de Joinville reports that, towards the end of the battle, Walter de Châtillon (nephew of Hugh, count of Saint-Pol) actually requested that Louis IX give him command of the rearguard.[39] He must have done well, as he also commanded the rearguard on the crusaders' retreat to Damietta in April of the same year.[40]

In summary, ambushes appear to have been a significant feature of medieval warfare. They were employed by every kind of force, in every region and terrain type. As well as conveying significant tactical and psychological advantage to the ambush party, the contemporary practice of travelling without armour made ambushes particularly effective. Contemporaries were aware of this and regarded it as an honour to command the rear division of an army on the march, where one was most likely to be ambushed.

---

[35] IP, p. 49: 'At ne molem tantam confusi ordinis turbaret seditio, in artem trinam, totus secessit exercitus; prima duci Suaviae, postrema imperatori, media summariis, et sarcinarum custodiae deputata'.

[36] Dermot, lines 2797–800: 'Li quens esteit al frunt devant / Od mil vassals combatant; / Le conestable esteit destrefs / En l'arere garde remés'.

[37] Dermot, lines 2807–12: 'Le jor enfin esteit occis / De Quenci Robert li [gen]tis / Que t[i]nt l'enseigne e le penum / De Leynestere la regiun, / A qui li quens aveit doné / La conestablerie en herité'. Author's translation.

[38] CCA, vol. 3, p. 46: 'E lo coms s'en repaira, streitament esarratz, / E fetz la reire garde dels ben encavalgatz'.

[39] VSL, p. 120: 'Sire, mon seigneur de Chasteillon vous prie que vous li donnez l'ariere garde". Et le roy si fist moult volentiers, et puis si se mist au chemin'.

[40] VSL, p. 152: 'Il me dit que il avoit lessié la seue bataille et c'estoit mis entre li et mon seigneur Geffroy de Sargines, et en la bataille mon seigneur Gautier de Chasteillon, qui fesoit l'ariere garde'.

Night Attacks and Dawn Raids

A sleeping enemy was even more vulnerable than one on the road. Although not mentioned as frequently as ambushes, attacks launched on an unsuspecting enemy by night or at the break of dawn also appear regularly in the chronicle narratives. This does not appear to have been regarded as dishonourable. Indeed, the Book of Judges provided a model upon which descriptions of such stratagems could be based. Having selected a force of 300 from among 32,000 Israelites, the judge Gideon leads a night attack on the camp of the Midianites at Moreh, blowing trumpets and waving torches. The Midianites, thinking that they are under attack by a very large force, panic and fall to fighting one another, making them easy prey for the Israelites.[41]

Dudo of St. Quentin, author of the semi-legendary *De moribus et actis primorum Normanniae ducum*, appears to have been influenced by the story of Gideon when describing a night attack allegedly carried out by the Normans' ancestors in 911. The 'Danes' were trapped on a mountain near Lèves, Chartres, by a much larger force of Franks and Burgundians, led by Ebalus, count of Poitou. An anonymous Frisian warrior in Danish service suggested how they might escape:

> Silently, in the dead of night, some of us should secretly go down from the mountain top and sound trumpet calls around the outside of the [enemy] tents. For they, having heard the noise of the trumpets, thinking Rollo, our duke, has arrived, will flee, being frightened, senseless and panic struck, scattered hither and thither.[42]

The parallels are not exact: the Danes had no torches and their primary aim was to escape, not kill their enemies. Nevertheless, the reference to sounding trumpets in the dark to spread panic in an enemy encampment suggests that Dudo may be have been influenced, perhaps unconsciously, by the Biblical narrative.

Just as Dudo did not think it was shameful to depict the Normans' ancestors engaging in a night attack, Henry of Huntingdon used a similar incident to demonstrate the great valour of the English in his *Historia Anglorum*. In 1019, King Cnut of England led a combined force of Englishmen and Danes to Denmark to fight against the Wends, a Slavic people on the southern shore of the Baltic. Without Cnut's knowledge, the English contingent attacked the Wends the night before they

---

[41] Judges 7. 16–20.

[42] Dudo, pp. 164–5: 'Intempestae noctis silentio, quidam nostrorum de cacumine montis clam descendant, et forinsecus circa tentoria buccina clangant. Illi namque, audito clangore tubarum, autumantes adesse Rollonem, nostrum ducem, formidolosi stupidque atque pavidi, fugitabunt, huc illucque divisi'.

expected to give battle. When Cnut awoke, he 'found only blood, corpses and spoils in the enemy camp. Because of this, he henceforth esteemed the English as highly as the Danes'.[43] Henry, writing over a century later, is the only source for this incident. The Anglo-Saxon Chronicle confirms that Cnut was in Denmark in 1019 but does not mention an expedition against the Wends. The *Life of King Edward* records that Earl Godwin earned praise for his conduct on an expedition to Denmark in 1025, suggesting Henry may have conflated the two campaigns.[44] Regardless, it is significant that Henry chose to depict a night attack as the means by which the English won Cnut's respect, rather than a stereotyped pitched battle. Cnut is shown valuing the English for their foresight and cunning as much as for their physical courage.

Roger of Wendover reports an unusual case of a commander demurring from joining in a night attack. On 11 November 1233, Richard Marshal and his Welsh allies learned that Henry III of England was encamped with his army before the castle at Grosmont (near Abergavenny, Monmouthshire) and arranged to attack them by night. Wendover, who was a great partisan of Richard and consistently depicted him as the wronged party in his quarrel with the king, made it clear that Richard did not take part in the night attack himself and that the Welsh showed great restraint: 'the victors did not want to injure or capture any of them; only two knights out of all the king's army were killed'.[45] Roger's claim that Richard was not present, and therefore not guilty of treason, may be spurious but the stated rationale clearly had nothing to do with the tactics employed: Richard was a loyal subject who refused to attack the king in person, by day or night.

As mentioned above, making a loud noise could greatly increase the psychological impact of a surprise attack. This was particularly true for night attacks, when a small force could easily be mistaken for a large one. Orderic Vitalis reports that one Arnold of Échauffour, who spent three years ravaging the Lieuvin region of Normandy after William the Conqueror confiscated his lands in 1061, seized the castle at Échauffour with a force of only four knights:

> One night he came to Échauffour with four knights; and, secretly entering the castle with his men, he rushed forth with a great yell. When the duke's

---

[43] HH, p. 365: 'Rex uero summo mane cum Anglos fugisse uel ad hostes perfide transisse putaret, acies ordinatas in hostem dirigens, non inuenit in castris nisi sanguinem, et cadauera, et predam. Quamobrem summo honore deinceps Anglos habuit, nec minori quam Dacos'.
[44] HH, p. 364 n. 77; M. K. Lawson, *Cnut: England's Viking King, 1016–35*, 2nd edn (Stroud, 2011), pp. 88–90.
[45] RW, p. 60: 'nec ex eis quenquam laedere vel captum abducere voluerunt victores illi, praeter duos milites, qui ex omnibus interfecti fuerunt'.

sixty knights heard this, they thought there was a great army with Arnold and, terrified, they fled, abandoning the castle which they should have been guarding.[46]

Orderic also records that Raymond of Poitiers, prince of Antioch, carried out a night attack in which loud noises were used to spook the defenders. In 1137 the Byzantine emperor John II Komnenos laid siege to Antioch in retaliation for Antiocheone attacks on Byzantine possessions in Cilicia.[47] Raymond, who had been leading an army south to fight alongside Fulk of Jerusalem, turned back but, fearing that he would not be able to break though the emperor's lines to reach the city, took counsel with his men. One of them, a man of 'noble spirit' (*magnanimus*), proposed Raymond 'go silently among the imperial squadrons all the way to the tent of Augustus himself and enter the Ionian legions. Then cry out with frightful voices close to the emperor's ears and boldly declare your presence'.[48] Everybody agreed to the plan and the Latins infiltrated the Byzantine army. Their battle cry was so terrifying that the Greeks fled and did not stop running for three miles. It is a colourful story that reflects Orderic's pronounced anti-Greek prejudice but it is probably a fiction. William of Tyre, who was much better placed to gather reliable information about the campaign, simply says that Raymond entered the city by a gate near the citadel.[49] Nevertheless, the presence of this story in Orderic's chronicle gives us an insight into Anglo-Norman attitudes towards warfare. Attacking the Greeks by night was not considered shameful but the product of a *magnanimus* spirit. Raymond and his men are portrayed as brave and hardy, despite their 'sneaky' tactics, in contrast to the feeble and easily startled Greeks.

Fortifications were particularly vulnerable to night attacks, as there was less chance of the attacking force being spotted by sentries. Galbert of Bruges's chronicle provides a very detailed account of a dawn raid carried out by the men of Bruges on the comital castle (which had been occupied by the Erembald clan and their followers) on 19 March 1127. The Erembalds had left the outer defences undefended, preferring to shelter

---

[46] OV, vol. 2, p. 92: 'Quadam nocte cum quatuor militibus Excalfoium uenit; et in castrum cum suis clam ingressus in magnam uociferationem prorupit. Quam ut lx milites ducis audierunt; magnum cum Ernaldo exercitum adesse putauerunt, territique castrum quod custodire debebant relinquentes aufugerunt'.

[47] Andrew D. Buck, *The Principality of Antioch and its Frontiers in the Twelfth Century* (Woodbridge, 2017), pp. 27–31, 192–9.

[48] OV, vol. 6, p. 504: 'arma uestra uiriliter sumite, et armati tanquam de turmis imperialibus usque ad ipsius augusti tentorium silenter ite, et Ionias legiones penetrate. Tunc prope imperatoris aures terribiliter exclamate, et qui sitis audacter demonstrate'.

[49] WT, p. 670.

indoors due to the 'harsh cold and winds'.[50] The citizens scaled the wall with 'slender ladders and lattices', then set about securing the courtyard:

> they gathered themselves together in great divisions without a sound or a cry and, having prepared themselves to fight, immediately ordered that the lesser among them should go to the larger gates to remove from the door the earth and stones which had been piled up and to make an entrance for all those who were still outside, who were unaware that this had been done.[51]

This suggests a significant level of tactical co-ordination among the attackers, particularly the division of labour once they had occupied the courtyard. It is not clear what Galbert meant by 'the lesser' (*minores*) citizens, who were sent to clear the gates. These may have been men of lesser social status, and consequently poorly equipped, leaving the wealthier and more heavily armed citizens to do the actual fighting, or they may have been younger and less experienced.

It is notable that this attack was undertaken independently, without the knowledge of the rest of the army. Galbert is at pains to ascribe this successful attack to the citizens of Bruges alone, implicitly contrasting it with the failed assault launched by the 'foreigners from Ghent' the day before. At this time the besieging army included several forces from beyond Bruges, including a contingent from Ghent (traditional enemies of Bruges) and the army of Louis VI of France. There was frequent contact between the garrison and the besiegers, and several of the leading conspirators had secretly bought safe passage out of the castle.[52] There was so much mistrust among the besiegers, and a very real possibility that the plan might be betrayed to the garrison, that the citizens of Bruges felt it necessary to carry out the dawn attack alone and in secret.[53]

---

[50] GB, p. 90: 'namque ea securitate vigiles murorum praeconato die introierant in domum comitis ad ignem tepefacere se propter asperitatem frigoris et ventorum, in vacuum relicta curte castri'.

[51] GB, p. 90: 'cives nostri in meridionali parte, qua sanctorum reliquiae elatae fuerant, intro conscenderunt per subtiles scalas et latrices quas solus homo ferret. Intus quippe sine sonitu et clamore sese collegerunt in magnas acies et praemunitas ad pugnandum, statimque ordinabant minores inter se ituros ad portas majores ut terrae et simul lapidum congeriem sustollerent a portis et introitum facerent extra consistentibus universis, qui hoc factum adhuc ignorabant'.

[52] GB, pp. 69–73.

[53] For a detailed study of the 1127 siege, see Steven Isaac, 'Galbert of Bruges and the Urban Experience of Siege', in Jeff Rider and Alan V. Murray (eds), *Galbert of Bruges and the Historiography of Medieval Flanders* (Washington, DC, 2009), pp. 89–106; Marvin's study provides a thorough narrative of the siege but his argument that knights were nearly useless in siege warfare is spurious: Laurence W. Marvin, '"…Men famous in combat and battle…": Common Soldiers and the Siege of Bruges, 1127', *Journal of Medieval History*, 24 (1998), 243–58.

Galbert describes the surprise among the besiegers when they heard that their allies were inside and had forced a side gate: 'Our burghers immediately opened it with swords and axes, and then, having raised a great cry and noise of arms inside, threw the army around the castle into a tumult and confusion'.[54]

Night-time provided cover for more than just attacking one's enemies. Moving and erecting war machines or other equipment took a long time and left the crew vulnerable to attack. Moving it by night, although not without its risks, was safer and could potentially surprise the enemy. A number of chronicles of the First Crusade mention the Byzantine forces transporting boats across land by night to Nicaea in June 1097. The combined forces of the crusaders and Byzantines were besieging the city but could not cut off the garrison's supply route across the nearby lake, so an appeal was sent to Alexios Komnenos for boats to form a blockade. Boats were dragged across land then launched onto the lake under cover of darkness. The sudden appearance of a fleet on the lake thoroughly demoralised the garrison and the city surrendered shortly thereafter.[55]

During the crusaders' siege of Jerusalem in 1099, the force under the command of Godfrey of Bouillon encamped on the west side of the city and began to construct a mobile siege tower. The garrison, observing this, responded by strengthening their defences on that side of the city. On the night of 9 July, the crusaders disassembled the tower and relocated it to a comparatively undefended stretch of wall on the eastern side of the city. Although it took three more days to prepare the ground for an assault, the garrison was unable to sufficiently strengthen this section of wall to repel the attack when it finally came on 13 July.[56]

The late twelfth-century Flemish chronicler Lambert of Ardres describes another remarkable feat of night-time logistics: the transportation and construction of an entire castle. Lambert claims this took place c. 1137, during a conflict over the succession to the county of Guînes. The old count, Manasses, had died without a direct male heir. Henry of Bourbourg fought against the count's nephew, Arnold of Ghent, on behalf of Albert the Boar, husband of the late count's granddaughter. Although driven from the town of Audruiq, Henry still held Bourbourg, some seven miles to the north-east, and devised a plan to threaten Arnold at Audruiq. Conveniently for Henry, there was a large mound known as Amaurival, the remnants of an old siege castle, outside the town:

---

[54] GB, p. 90: 'Quam statim ipso accessu gladiis et securibus nostri burgenses aperuerant, et tunc concitato clamore et strepitu armorum intrinsecus in tumultum et concursum conturbaverunt exercitum in circuitu castri'.
[55] AA, p. 117; GF, p. 16; BB, p. 27; GN, pp. 151–2; WT, p. 160.
[56] AA, p. 414; GF, p. 90; RA, p. 298; GT, p. 101.

So, Henry, castellan of Bourbourg, sent surveyors and carpenters to Amaurival, or rather to the mound, to inspect the position with geometric instruments and, since Arnold and the people of Guines were unaware [of his plan], secretly build a tower and warlike defences and other engines near Bourbourg.[57]

These fortifications were then moved to Amaurival and silently erected by night. The psychological impact of a fully constructed castle appearing overnight before Audruiq must have been immense. This was clearly a wooden castle, similar to the 'flat pack' kind that William the Conqueror brought with him to England in 1066. It was a sturdy structure, as the garrison repelled the first attempt to storm it, only retreating back to Bourbourg when the enemy numbers grew overwhelming. Afterwards, Arnold of Ghent made sure to level both the castle and the mound to prevent it being refortified.[58]

Like ambushes, night attacks could convey a great tactical advantage to the attackers, potentially allowing a small force to overcome a much larger enemy, but the risks were very great. In an age without electric lights or communications technology, simply manoeuvring in the dark could be hazardous. In 1067 Eustace I, count of Boulogne, landed at Dover by night to help the men of Kent capture the town. This was supposed to be a prelude to an uprising against the Norman invaders but it swiftly degenerated into a farce, with many of his men stampeding over the cliffs in the dark.[59]

Coordinating the actions of separate forces has always been a challenge for commanders. Attempting to do so at night, without long-distance communications, only compounded the problem, as illustrated by John of England's failed attempt to relieve Château-Gaillard in September 1203. The fullest description we possess was written by Philip II of France's chaplain, William the Breton, and, as such, is openly hostile towards John and his followers. Nevertheless, if one can look past the anti-Plantagenet rhetoric, it illustrates the great difficulty that medieval commanders faced when trying to coordinate separate attacks in the dark. Two forces were to attack the French at dawn simultaneously: one from the land and the other from a fleet of ships on the Seine. It is unclear whether the landward force was too hasty or the fleet was delayed, but the landward force attacked before the fleet appeared and was repulsed after a stubborn defence led

---

[57] LA, pp. 589–90: 'Misit ergo Henricus castellanus Broburgensis secreto geometricos et carpentarios ad Almari-vallum vel aggerem, ut locum cum geometricalibus particis ambirent et ad mensuram aggeris proportionaliter metirentur et pro quantitate loci, ignorantibus Arnoldo et Ghisnensibus, apud Broburgum turrim et bellica propugnacula aliaque machinamenta clanculo construerent'.

[58] LA, pp. 590–1.

[59] OV, vol. 2, pp. 204–6.

by William de Barres. With the landward force defeated, and the French awake and ready to defend themselves, the fleet was also driven back.[60] The relief effort had failed and, although the garrison continued to put up a remarkably determined defence, the castle fell in March 1204. It is surely no coincidence that the *History of William Marshal*, whose subject was one of the commanders of the landward force, does not mention this battle.

Combatants were, of course, fully aware of how vulnerable an encampment or stronghold was during the night and most took measures to avoid being surprised, such as posting sentries or erecting temporary fortifications to protect the camp. The fact that we have so many records of successful night attacks is remarkable. Good intelligence could completely nullify the attackers' advantage. Roger of Howden reported that, at the siege of Acre, the Christians were regularly informed about the garrison's plans through letters written in Latin, Greek and Hebrew by an anonymous citizen. In the last days of the siege, on 5 July 1191, Saladin attempted to create a diversion that would allow his garrison to escape the siege but the Christians, 'were prepared through the message of the aforesaid man of God who was in the city'.[61]

When a commander had reliable intelligence that the enemy was at hand and was intending to attack, one solution was simply to keep the army in readiness all through the night. Several of the accounts of the Hastings campaign report that William the Conqueror did this upon learning that Harold Godwinson was planning to attack him by night: 'Meanwhile the king, seat and heir of deceit, active in the robber's art, ordered his divisions to arm under cover of night. He ordered this so that they would prevail if they attacked the duke's troops'.[62] This is a rare example of a text explicitly condemning a commander for attempting to carry out a night attack, describing it as a product of the 'robber's art'. It comes from the *Carmen de Hastingae proelio*, a Latin poem written by Guy, bishop of Amiens, shortly after the battle to both celebrate and vindicate William's conquest. It is a work of propaganda that denigrates Harold at every opportunity, portraying him as a wicked usurper. His attempt to attack the Normans unawares could be contrasted with William's decision to fight a pitched battle, trusting in God to vindicate his claim to the throne through trial by battle. Other chroniclers, writing with less partisan motivations, were usually more even-handed in their depiction of

---

[60] GPA, pp. 213–14.
[61] HowChr, vol. 3, p. 118: 'Sed reges inde praemuniti per mandatum praedicti viri Dei qui in civitate erat'.
[62] CDH, p. 18: 'Interea, sedes fuscate fraduis et heres / Nocte sub obscura, furis in arte vigens, / Rex acies armare jubet, ducis atque latenter / Mandat ut invadant agmina si valeant'. See also GND, vol. 2, p. 170; OV, vol. 2, p. 174.

such stratagems, accepting them as part of the reality of warfare or even celebrating them as demonstrations of skill and prudence.

In summary, despite the difficulties and risks of attempting to manoeuvre and fight in the dark, medieval combatants were willing to hazard an attack by night or at dawn. An enemy who was caught sleeping, or who panicked at the unexpected attack, was much more easily defeated than one who was fully prepared. Night was also a good time to move cumbersome machinery or equipment, and could surprise an enemy by suddenly appearing in an unexpected location. Conversely, the ability to resist a night attack appears to have depended on the intangible qualities of good morale and discipline. Any force that fell into confusion and panic in the dark was easily destroyed, whereas a force that maintained its composure and resisted the attack was much more likely to survive. Group discipline was also key to performing and responding to one of the most famous ruses employed in medieval warfare: the feigned flight.

4

The Feigned Flight

The feigned flight or retreat – pretending to run away in order to trick an enemy force into pursuing – was famously employed by the Normans at the Battle of Hastings (although this has been the subject of some debate, as outlined below). This makes Hastings a logical place to begin an analysis of this stratagem: whether such a manoeuvre was even possible, what may have happened during the battle and how it was portrayed by the various chroniclers. A wider reading of medieval narratives reveals that, far from being an isolated incident, the feigned flight was employed in a variety of conflicts and by a variety of forces.

The Battle of Hastings

Several scholars have claimed that the description of the Norman army feigning flight to draw the English off Senlac Hill on 14 October 1066 is a fiction, invented after the fact to cover up a very real and embarrassing retreat that almost cost the Normans the battle. The source of this theory appears to be Charles H. Lemmon, who argued that 'such a manoeuvre is contrary to the principle that troops once committed to the attack cannot be made to change their direction' and that it would be impossible to relay such an order to thousands of individuals, all fighting hand-to-hand. Furthermore, the feint would have been too obvious if the Norman army had fallen back at the same time, en masse.[1] This argument was taken up by John Beeler, who concluded that the story of a feigned flight at Hastings was nothing more than a 'legend', a historical 'hoax' perpetrated by the Norman chroniclers.[2] More recently, John Marshall Carter argued that there is limited evidence that the Normans were able to use this tactic

---

[1] Charles H. Lemmon, *The Field of Hastings*, 3rd edn (St. Leonards-on-Sea, 1964), pp. 47–8.
[2] John Beeler, *Warfare in England 1066–1189* (Ithaca, NY, 1966), p. 21.

and that the topography of the battlefield would have made it difficult for cavalry to perform such a manoeuvre.[3] Carter proposed that the story of the feigned flight was inserted into the Hastings narrative by the early chroniclers in imitation of Vegetius, in order to make the Normans appear more skilful.[4]

Bernard S. Bachrach provided a thorough criticism of this thesis, demonstrating that the feigned flight was employed by both the Huns and the Visigoths, many centuries prior to Hastings.[5] However, his own theories about the origin of the stratagem are equally dubious. Bachrach claimed that the Normans inherited the concept of a feigned flight from the Alans, a nomadic people who settled in Gaul under the Roman emperors and whose influence subsequently 'permeated the military tactics of western France'. Bachrach specifically highlighted the influence of the Alans, who settled in Armorica in the fifth century, stating that it was from them that the Normans, 'with their usual hospitality to effective military innovations learned the tactic'.[6] The basis for his extraordinary claim rests on a single sentence in the chronicle of Regino, abbot of Prüm (d. 915). Describing the arrival of the Magyars into Europe (a description which he adapted from that of the Scythians in the works of eighth-century chroniclers Justin and Paul the Deacon), Regino explicitly compared their military tactics to those used by the Bretons:

> For they do not know how to fight hand-to-hand in formation or when besieging cities. They fight by either running forwards on horses or turning back, indeed they often feign flight […] Their manner of fighting is more dangerous because it is unfamiliar to other peoples. There is only one difference between the Bretons' manner of battle and theirs, that one uses missiles, the others arrows.[7]

---

[3] John Marshall Carter, 'Une réévaluation des interprétations de la fuite simulée d'Hastings', *Annales de Normandie*, 45 (1995), 27–34, at pp. 31–3.
[4] Carter, 'Une réévaluation', p. 30.
[5] Bernard S. Bachrach, 'The Feigned Retreat at Hastings', *Mediaeval Studies*, 33 (1971), 344–7, at p. 346.
[6] Bachrach, 'Feigned Retreat', p. 347.
[7] Regino of Prüm, *Chronicon cum continuatione Treverensi*, ed. Friedrich Kurze, MGH, Scriptores rerum Germanicarum, 50 (Hannover, 1890), p. 183: 'Comminus enim in acie preliari aut obsessas expugnare urbes nesciunt. Pugnant aut procurrentibus equis aut terga dantibus, saepe etiam fugam simulant […] Quorum pugna, quo ceteris gentibus inusitata, eo et periculosior. Inter horum et Brittonum conflictum hoc unum interest, quod illi misilibus, isti sagittis utuntur'. For Regino's adaptation of earlier descriptions of the Scythians, see Simon MacLean, 'Introduction', in Simon MacLean (ed. and trans.), *History and Politics in Late Carolingian and Ottonian Europe: The Chronicle of Regino of Prüm and Adalbert of Magdeburg* (Manchester, 2009), pp. 1–60, at pp. 46–7.

From this slender evidence, Bachrach argues that there was direct continuity between the Alans, Bretons and the Normans.[8] While it is notable that a chronicler drew parallels between a Eurasian steppe people and the Bretons, this is not the stratagem that is described being used at Hastings. The Bretons are depicted employing hit-and-run tactics, throwing missiles at their enemies and refusing to engage in hand-to-hand combat, in a manner similar to the ancient Parthians or medieval Turks. Regino described exactly this kind of fighting in his account of a battle between Charles the Fat and the Bretons in 851: 'They assailed the densely packed Frankish formation in this way, and tormented all the men in the midst with their darts, now feigning flight they pierced their chests with darts just the same'.[9] The Norman stratagem at Hastings appears to have involved a number of charges to engage the English at close quarters, followed by a turn and a withdrawal to lure them into pursuing (see pp. 76–8). None of the chroniclers describe them throwing *missiles* or *spicula* from horseback. Bachrach fails to provide any further evidence that the Normans learned their horsemanship from the Bretons or that the Bretons had inherited their mode of fighting from the Alans. In fact, Bachrach's own work contradicts him on this point, as he had previously stated that the fifth-century Alans resembled the Roman cataphracts who 'fought as a mounted phalanx of heavy cavalry'.[10] This would be an example of *discontinuity*: between their settlement in Armorica in the fifth century and their wars with the Carolingians in the ninth, the Alano-Bretons modified their tactics to suit their circumstances.

The Normans did not need to learn or inherit the feigned flight from anybody else: it is a logical tactic to employ, especially for a force of skilled horsemen. As R. A. Brown has said, even if the Norman force did not feign flight en masse at Hastings, the individual units of knights, 'trained together over long, arduous years, and bound by the companionship of expertise, had ample discipline and the capacity not only to work and fight together but also to combine with other similar units'.[11] Nor was this

---

[8] Bachrach, 'Feigned Retreat', p. 347; see also Bernard S. Bachrach, 'The Alans in Gaul', *Traditio*, 23 (1967), 476–89, at pp. 488–9; Bernard S. Bachrach, 'The Origins of Armorican Chivalry', *Technology and Culture*, 10 (1969), 166–71, at p. 168.

[9] Regino of Prüm, *Chronicon*, p. 79: 'Brittones more solito huc illucque cum equis ad huiuscemodi conflictum exercitatis discursantes modo confertam Francorum aciem impetunt ac totis viribus in medio spicula torquent, nunc fugam simulantes insequentium nihilominus pectoribus spicula figunt'.

[10] Bachrach, 'Alans', p. 485.

[11] R. Allen Brown, 'The Battle of Hastings', in R. Allen Brown (ed.), *Anglo-Norman Studies III: Proceedings of the Battle Conference on Anglo-Norman Studies 1980* (Woodbridge, 1981), pp. 1–21, here p. 16; see also David Bates, *William the Conqueror* (New Haven, CT, 2016), p. 242; David R. Cook, 'The Norman Military Revolution in England', in R. Allen Brown (ed.), *Anglo-Norman Studies I: Proceedings of the Battle*

stratagem introduced to Europe in 'the mid-fifth century by the nomadic tribes of the Huns', as Georgios Theotokis has claimed.[12] This claim would have certainly surprised Frontinus who, in the first century, recorded that Romulus employed a feigned flight in the fifth century BCE:

> Romulus, when he had drawn near to Fidenae [a town five miles north of Rome], having stationed some of his troops in hiding, feigning flight, led the enemies, who were blindly pursuing him, to the place where his soldiers were lying hidden, who, rushing out and attacking from all sides, killed those who had incautiously pursued him.[13]

The stratagem is also depicted in the Bible. It was employed against the Benjamites by the other tribes of Israel in Judges 20 and against the citizens of Ai in Joshua 8:

> When the king of Ai saw this in the morning he hastened and came out with the city's whole army and, not knowing that Israelites were lying hidden in the rear, directed his formation against the desert. But Joshua and all Israel withdrew from there, feigning fear and fleeing along the road into the wilderness.[14]

The accounts of the Battle of Hastings form a useful case study in how different chroniclers could subtly alter the description of the same event to suit their narrative agenda. The two earliest descriptions of the battle refer to both a 'true' and a feigned flight by the Normans, although with significant differences. The *Carmen de Hastingae proelio* depicts the feigned retreat taking place first, as a deliberate stratagem to disrupt the English formation: 'Nor would they have been able to penetrate the dense forest of Englishmen if ingenuity had not bestowed strength to the men. The French, having been instructed in craft, skilful in waging war, feigned flight as if they had been defeated'.[15] According to the poet, the Normans

---

Conference on Anglo-Norman Studies 1978 (Woodbridge, 1979), pp. 94–102, at p. 99; Stephen Morillo, 'Hastings: An Unusual Battle', in Stephen Morillo (ed.), *The Battle of Hastings: Sources and Interpretations* (Woodbridge, 1996), pp. 219–28, at p. 225.

[12] Georgios Theotokis, *The Norman Campaigns in the Balkans 1081–1108* (Woodbridge, 2014), p. 159.

[13] Julius Frontinus, *Strategemata*, ed. Robert Ireland (Leipzig, 1990), p. 45: 'Romulus, per latebras copiarum parte disposita, cum ad Fidenas accessisset, simulata fuga temere hostes insecutos eo perduxit, ubi occultos milites habebat, qui undique adorti effusos et incautos ceciderunt'.

[14] Joshua 8. 14–15: 'Quod cum vidisset rex Hai, festinavit mane, et egressus est cum omni exercitu civitatis, direxitque aciem contra desertum, ignorans quod post tergum laterent insidiæ. Josue vero et omnis Israël cesserunt loco, simulantes metum, et fugientes per solitudinis viam'.

[15] CDH, p. 26: 'Nec penetrare valent spissum nemus Angligenarum / Ni tribuat vires viribus ingenium / Artibus instructi, Franci, bellari periti / Ac si deuicti fraude fugam simulant'.

subsequently panicked when a rumour circulated that Duke William had been killed. The feigned flight was in danger of becoming a true rout until William rode up, removed his helmet and rallied his troops. The *Carmen* depicts the final stages of the battle as an epic charge, led by William, that broke through the English lines and killed Harold.[16]

William of Poitiers, Duke William's chaplain, included a prose account of Hastings in his *Gesta Guillelmi* that depicts a different sequence of events. He placed the true flight before the feint. Furthermore, unlike the author of the *Carmen*, who emphasised the non-Norman contributions to Duke William's victory, William made it clear that it was not the Norman knights who fled, nor should the Normans be shamed for the blunder:

> See! The foot soldiers, and however many auxiliaries were in the left wing, together with the Breton horsemen, terrified by the fierceness [of the English], were driven back; they withdrew almost to the duke's division, if such a thing might be freely said of the invincible Norman nation. The majestic Roman army, containing the armies of kings, accustomed to conquering by land and sea, sometimes fled when their commander was known or believed to have been killed.[17]

The chronicler locates Duke William's heroic rallying of the troops here, saying that the left wing of the army turned and cut down the English who had pursued them off Senlac Hill. This was followed by a series of feigned flights, depicted as an adaptation to the tactical situation rather than a pre-conceived stratagem: 'The Normans, suddenly turning their horses around, slaughtered everybody they could cut off and encircle, sparing none. They used the same trick twice, attacking those who remained with greater enthusiasm'.[18]

Later accounts of the battle omit the true flight but retain the feint or series of feints. The anonymous *Chronicle of Battle Abbey*, composed sometime after 1135, is the most straightforward. There is no rout and the feigned flight is depicted as a deliberate stratagem: 'Finally, when the duke's army had feigned flight, the most active Eustace, count of Boulogne, since this skilful piece of craft had been secretly considered in advance, rushed

---

[16] CDH, pp. 28–32.

[17] GG, p. 128: 'Ecce igitur hac saeuitia perterriti auertuntur pedites pariter atque equites Britanni, et quotquot auxiliares erant in sinistro cornu; cedit fere cuncta ducis acies, quod cum pace dictum sit Normannorum inuictissimae nationis. Romanae maiestatis exercitus, copias regum continens, uincere solitus terra marique, fugit aliquando, cum ducem suum sciret aut crederet occisum'.

[18] GG, p. 132: 'Normanni repente regiratis equis interceptos et inclusos undique mactauerunt, nullum relinquentes. Bis eo dolo simili euentu usi, reliquos maiori cum alacritate aggressi sunt'. Orderic Vitalis's account of the battle, which is based on the *Gesta Guillelmi*, offers no significant variations in the depiction of the feigned flight: OV, vol. 2, p. 174.

upon the English from behind with a powerful hand while they were scattered in pursuing the Normans with great agility'.[19]

Henry of Huntingdon's description is more unusual. He appears to have conflated the feigned retreat and an incident that other chroniclers placed later in the day, when a group of Norman knights, pursuing the English as they fled, accidentally rode into a ditch and were crushed to death: 'Duke William instructed his men to feign flight: but while fleeing they came to a certain great pit that had been deceitfully concealed, whereby many of them, falling in, were crushed to death'. [20]

Wace's *Roman de Rou*, composed nearly a hundred years after the battle, is also noteworthy for its depiction of the feigned flight. Whereas other accounts suggest a series of short retreats followed by a turn, Wace depicts a gradual withdrawal, performed by the entire army: 'They did just as they had said, they attacked them while retreating, and made a great show of fear, and the English pursued them; the Normans fled little by little and the English followed after them'.[21] While this may not be an accurate representation of how the feigned retreat was performed at Hastings, it may nevertheless indicate how Wace's courtly audience expected such a manoeuvre would be performed.

Finally, William of Malmesbury presents the English at Hastings in a very sympathetic manner, whereas the Norman tactics are, at best, morally ambiguous. The English are depicted fighting bravely, if not very shrewdly:

> All the foot soldiers, armed with battle axes, made an impenetrable formation, linking a *testudo* of shields before them; which, having been accomplished, would have been their salvation that day if the Normans had not, in their usual manner, feigning flight, opened up their close-packed troops [...] So, having been surrounded through a ruse, they won a noble death in revenge for their country, nor did they neglect their revenge, but, having made a stand, they made many extraordinary mounds of casualties from among their attackers.[22]

---

[19] Eleanor Searle (ed. and trans.), *Chronicle of Battle Abbey* (Oxford, 1980), p. 38: 'tandem strenuissimus Bolonie [com]es Eustachius clam callida premeditata arte, fuga cum exercitu duce simulante, super Anglos sparsim agiliter insequentes cum manu ualida a tergo irruit, sicque et duce hostes ferociter inuadente, ipsis interclusis utrinque prosternuntur innumeri'.

[20] HH, pp. 392–4: 'Docuit igitur dux Willelmus genti sue fugam simulare: fugientes autem ad quandam foueam magnam dolose protectam deuenerunt. Vbi multus eorum numerus corruens, oppressus est'.

[21] RdR, lines 8189–94: 'Si com il l'orent dit si firent, / retraanment les assaillirent / e du fuïr grant semblant firent, / e li Engelis les parsuïrent; / poi e poi vont Normant fuiant / e li Engleis les vont sivant'.

[22] William is clearly describing a 'shieldwall' formation here but I have chosen to translate it literally in order to retain the classical resonance. William may have deliberately used Roman military terminology here to emphasise the English army's discipline and virtue. GRA, vol. 1, pp. 452–4: 'Pedites omnes cum bipennibus, conserta

This passage includes two noteworthy phrases. The Normans are described as feigning flight in *suo more*, which could mean 'in their usual manner' or 'according to their custom'. This may mean that William associated this specific stratagem with the Normans or that it was in keeping with their reputation as cunning and ruthless warriors to use stratagems to deceive their enemies. The second phrase is even more ambiguous: the English were surrounded due to *ingenium*. This has multiple possible meanings. It can mean a trick or clever scheme but it can also mean somebody or something's nature, their innate character, or the cunning that conceives of such a scheme.[23] So the above phrase can be interpreted as saying that the English were surrounded due to a trick (the ruse of a feigned flight) or due to the ingenious character of the Normans (who were accustomed to employing such ruses). The double-meaning of these two phrases contribute to William's portrayal of the English defeat as a tragedy: they fought bravely, winning a 'noble death', but were undone by a more cunning enemy.

Feigning Flight: Western Armies

Perhaps the most convincing argument against the feigned flight at Hastings being a fiction is the fact that Norman forces are depicted employing the same ruse at other times and in other places. For example, during Roger I of Sicily's raid against Messina in 1060: 'But the count, most astute and cunning in military matters, having been attacked, first pretended to be afraid. When he had led the citizens a long way from the city, he rushed fiercely upon them and put them to flight'.[24] Similarly, Bohemond of Taranto was depicted employing the feigned flight against the Turkish garrison at Baalbek, Syria, which harassed him as he travelled north from Jerusalem in 1111: 'when they had feigned flight for a short while, escaping through narrow passes in order to lead the Turks on, they deliberately withdrew, but soon, having turned around, they scattered their dispersed enemies as it pleased them'.[25] Gerald of Wales describes how, in 1169,

---

ante se scutorum testudine, impenetrabilem cuneum fatiunt; quod profecto illis ea die saluti fuisset, nisi Normanni simulata fuga more suo confertos manipulos laxassent [...] Ita ingenio circumuenti pulchram mortem pro patriae ultione meruere, nec tamen ultioni suae defuere, quin crebro consistentes de insequentibus insignes cladis aceruos facerent'.

[23] Charlton T. Lewis and Charles Short, *A Latin Dictionary* (Oxford, 1879), p. 950.

[24] GM, p. 30: 'Porro comes, ut semper astutissimus et militia callens, primo timore simulato, cum eos longius ab urbe seduxisset, impetu facto, acerrime super eos irruens, in fugam vertit'.

[25] GRA, vol. 1, 664: 'namque simulata paulisper fuga, ut ipsi de angustiis locorum

a Cambro-Norman force led by his uncle, Robert fitz Stephen, used a feigned flight to draw the men of Osraige out of the forests and marshes, where they were accustomed to fight, and into the open: 'Assured by their previous successes, they now pursued them all the way onto the plain. But Fitzstephen's horsemen turned back against them, and at once began assaulting them fiercely'.[26]

This tactic was not unique to the Normans, of course. Chroniclers depict other Western European forces employing feigned flight.[27] William of Malmesbury's description of the battle of Nar al-Kalb (24–26 October 1100) contains a vivid description of two forces, commanded by Baldwin I of Jerusalem and Duqāq, ruler of Damascus, attempting to employ the feigned flight as they fought on the narrow coastal road near Beirut:

> Then Duqāq sent some men ahead to provoke and entice the incautious to give battle, holding most of his men in advantageous positions. So, at first these men came forward in a great rush, then immediately withdrew, in order to draw our men into the narrow places. This sort of cunning did not deceive Baldwin; but, skilled in ancient military practice, he indicated to his men that they should feign flight, and also, to reinforce the suspicion of fear, he ordered them to pick up the burdens and baggage which they had just put down and to drive the pack animals on with goads and, in fact, to open up the ranks so that the enemies could attack them.[28]

This is an unusually detailed description of how an army might give the appearance of panicking: carrying their gear, driving the baggage animals ahead, and breaking formation. We can extrapolate from this to learn how a brave or resolute army was expected to behave: dropping their burdens in order to fight more effectively, sending the pack animals away and maintaining a close formation. Malmesbury's description of how Baldwin's army turned once it had reached an open plain corroborates this, as he emphasises how the troops were able to reform and attack in the correct

---

euadentes Turchos inducerent, consulto cessere, sed mox retro uersi dispersos hostes pro libito fudere'.

[26] EH, p. 36: 'Unde et solitis confisi successibus, ipsos etiam usque in ipsa campestria longe persequuntur. Stephandie vero equites in eosdem reversi, statim acriter irruentes'.

[27] For example, Llewellyn ap Iorwerth, who sent a Cistercian monk to misinform the garrison of Montgomery Castle in 1231, as discussed in Chapter 1, feigned flight to draw members of the garrison onto boggy ground where they sank and were easily killed: RW, vol. 4, pp. 11–12.

[28] GRA, vol. 1, p. 668: 'Tunc Ducah mittit aliquos qui prelia prima lacessant elitiantque incautos, retentans ampliores uires in locis oportunis. Itaque illi primo magno impetu uenire, mox subinde subterfugere, ut nostros in angustias deducerent. Non latuit Balduinum huiuscemodi calliditas; sed, antiquae militiae usu instructus, suis ut fugam simularent innuit, simul et, ut suspicionem metus urgeret, sarcinas et impedimenta quae iam deposuerant resumi et iumenta stimulis agitari, quin et ordines laxari ut hostes incurrerent edixit'.

manner: 'when it appeared that they had pretended to be afraid for long enough, their ranks having been reformed and the banners having been turned around, rushing forward, they now surrounded the enemies'.[29]

We must be cautious when using Malmesbury's account of this battle, however. Fulcher of Chartres, whose chronicle was Malmesbury's main source for events in Outremer, describes a very different sequence of events. After an initial clash with the Turks, and a sleepless night during which they were attacked from both land and sea, the Franks took the decision to make a fighting retreat back down the coast.[30] Fulcher attributes the army's subsequent decision to turn and charge when it had reached the plain to divine inspiration, with no mention of any feint or prearranged stratagem:

> But God, of great mercy and power, observing our humility on earth from heaven, and the affliction and the danger into which we had fallen for love and service of Him, moved by pity, which always comes to rescue His people, supplied such great boldness of prowess to our knights, that they should in no way desire to defend themselves, in order that, having suddenly turned back along the three-forked road, those who had been fleeing could put [the enemy] to flight.[31]

It is possible that Malmesbury had other sources of information about the battle and that Baldwin's flight was indeed a ruse but it is more likely that he chose to reinterpret a potentially embarrassing incident in a way that showed Baldwin in a better light. Even if this were so, it is still noteworthy that he chose to portray Baldwin as a skilful and cunning general, refusing to be drawn by the Turks' feint and tricking them in turn into pursuing him, when he could have simply rewritten the battle as an epic cavalry charge.

Lemmon may have been incorrect in asserting that it was impossible for a medieval force to realistically and effectively feign flight, but his suggestion that the incident at Hastings was invented because the chroniclers 'dared not record that the Norman cavalry ran away' does raise an important question: how can we be certain that a particular retreat was actually a feint?[32] It is plausible that combatants, recounting the events of a battle, may have claimed that their flight was intentional, part of a

---

[29] GRA, vol. 1, p. 668: 'Namque, ut uisum est satis metum finxisse, consertis ordinibus et conuersis signis inimicos iam iamque incursantes inclusere'.

[30] FC, pp. 359–62.

[31] FC, pp. 362–3: 'Sed magnae Deus clementiae atque potentiae prospiciens de caelo in terram humilitatem nostram atque angustiam necnon periculum, quod incideramus propter amorem eius atque seruitium, motus pietate, qua rite semper praesens suis subuenit, tantae probitatis audaciam militibus nostris praestitit, ut recursu repentino per uiam trifurcam fugarent eos fugientes, ut nunquam animum defendendi se haberent'.

[32] Lemmon, *Field of Hastings*, p. 48.

masterful strategy, rather than admit that they panicked and ran. There is also the possibility that a chronicler might have deliberately reinterpreted a shameful incident of this kind to fit their narrative agenda. Consider Galbert of Bruges's account of the battle of Akspoele (21 June 1128), fought between William Clito and Thierry of Alsace near Bruges. Galbert reports that, after the initial clash between William Clito and Daniel of Dendermonde, William's division fled:

> While both sides were labouring hard, one in fleeing, the other in pursuing, the second part of Count William's division, which was lying in ambush, rushed in front of Daniel and his men. And because they had been encouraged by fresh strength and unity of action, and trained for war, they opposed the pursuers with spears and swords without hesitation. Then Count William, swiftly returning from flight, recovered himself together with his men and, in a single charge, with a manly spirit and the strength of their bodies, pursued the cruel work of arms and the dispersal of his enemies.[33]

This was the decisive moment of the battle: Thierry's army broke and ran, leaving William in possession of the field. But how should we interpret William's flight? Galbert portrays it as a genuine retreat, which was only halted when the ambush party intercepted the pursuers. But it is possible that this was a stratagem: a feigned flight, designed to lure Thierry's vanguard into a pre-prepared ambush.[34] Thierry was, at that time, based in Galbert's home town of Bruges, so he would have been able to question members of the defeated army. They appear to have believed that the flight was genuine but that may just mean it was a very effective ruse. Galbert reports that other citizens of Bruges had their own interpretation of the battle:

> Again our foolish priests were saying that the consul Thierry and his men had been put to flight in the battle through the incantations of the presbyter from Aartrijke and the presbyter from Knesselare and the cleric from Odfried, even though God disposes and ordains all things.[35]

---

[33] GB, p. 160: 'Cumque utrimque laborarent, illi in fugiendo, illi in persequendo, secunda pars cuneorum Willelmi consulis, quae ad insidiandum latebat, prosiluit in adversas facies Danielis et suorum. Et quia recenti virtute et unanimi consensu exhortati fuerant et instructi ad bellum, in nullo hesitantes, hastis et gladiis persecutores illos interruperunt. Tunc comes Willelmus a fuga velociter resiliens, sese cum suis recepit, unoque cursu et animo virili, robore corporum suorum, crudelitati armorum, et dispersioni inimicorum insistebat'.

[34] J. F. Verbruggen, 'La Tactique militaire des armées de chevaliers', *Revue du Nord*, 29 (1947), 161–80.

[35] GB, p. 161: 'Iterum nostri sacerdotes idiotae dicebant presbyterum ex Artrica et presbyterum ex Cnislara et Odfridum clericum per incantationes fugasse in bello consulem Theodericum et suos, cum Deus omina disponat et ordinet'.

This is a salutary reminder for modern military historians. Although we look for mundane explanations for events, attributing victories to superior resources or strategies, medieval observers were just as likely to attribute the same events to supernatural forces. The priests of Bruges thought Thierry was defeated by magic, whereas Galbert thought it was the will of God. Neither ascribed it to William Clito's superior tactics. When studying medieval military narratives, we must appreciate that they are not written for us, for our culture or our conceptual framework, and resist trying to rationalise or simplify them to serve our particular interests.

Until now, this discussion has focused almost entirely on one form of the feigned flight, what might be called the 'Hastings variant', in which the retreating troops intended to lure their enemy away from their present location. Once they were on ground of their choosing, they could wheel round and attack their pursuers, who would have broken formation in their haste to take captives, making them vulnerable to a sudden charge. There was, however, another form of the feigned flight, in which the retreat was intended to lure the enemy into a prearranged ambush. The fleeing force, usually a smaller detachment of the main army, might still turn back and engage the pursuers but its primary role was to act as bait.[36] For example, William the Conqueror established a siege castle near Arques in 1052, which was held against him by his uncle, also called William. Henry I of France led an army to relieve Arques and encamped near Saint-Aubin:

> The duke's knights, learning of his arrival, sent out some of their number to see if they could perhaps draw off some men from the king's company, whom they, lying in wait, might capture while they were following them incautiously. When they had come there, drawing out no small part of the army, they fled in order to lead them into the ambushes.[37]

Geoffrey V, count of Anjou, is described employing similar tactics against the rebel garrison of Thouars (a strategically important town in southern Anjou) in 1129:

> The townspeople threatened them, the count's men falling back according to their purpose, and prolonged the feigned retreat past the location of the ambush. But those who maintained their hiding places, proceeding cautiously from the hiding places, pursued those who were pursuing their companions with reckless daring: but those who had made the feigned

---

[36] The taxonomy presented in the Appendix indicates that this latter kind of feigned flight was the more common of the two, with 22 examples of its use to 14 examples of the more famous Hastings variant.

[37] GND, vol. 2, p. 104: 'Cuius aduentum milites ducis comperientes de suis miserunt, si quos forte hostium a regio cetu abstraherent, quos illi in latibulis degentes incautos exciperent. Quo dum uenissent, non minimam exercitus partem inde protrahentes, in insidias induxere fugientes'. See also RdR, lines 3455–508.

retreat, seeing the others appear, turned their reins, with swords and lances drawn, vented their rage against those who were pursuing them.[38]

In this latter incident, Geoffrey's knights were aided by the defenders' overconfidence. They had been victorious in previous skirmishes and had put the count's men to flight, which made it easier to trick them into mistaking a feigned retreat for a real one.[39] A similar incident reportedly occurred in 1057 when Richard, the Norman count of Aversa, attempted to compel the Lombard prince, Guaimar IV of Salerno, to pay him tribute. Guaimar refused and the citizens of Salerno drove Richard away with arrows. The next day, Richard feigned flight in front of Guaimar to draw him into an ambush, which resulted in the citizens being killed or driven into the sea.[40]

According to Roger of Howden, overconfidence derived from a previous victory was crucial to the success of Robert de Breteuil, earl of Leicester, at Pacy-sur-Eure, Normandy in 1198. The castle had formerly belonged to Robert but he had been forced to surrender it to Philip II of France after he was captured at Gournay in 1194. Although he had been defeated by Philip's garrison the day before, Robert was able to lure it into an ambush in their next encounter by feigning flight: 'And when the knights of the castle, who the day before had put him to flight from the field, had seen him, they sallied out with fury and he fled before them until they fell into the ambushes, and eighteen knights and many commoners were captured from among them'.[41]

Far from being a 'hoax' perpetuated by William the Conqueror's propagandists, it is clear that the feigned flight was known and employed by the armies of Western Europe before and after 1066. The Normans and their descendants appear to have employed it frequently (accounting for 12 out of the 19 incidents of feigned flight by Western forces recorded in

---

[38] HG, pp. 262–4: 'Assuetis autem successibus insolentiores effecti, quadam die, spe abundantioris victoriae ducti, solito plures exierunt, sed praeter spem illud evenit. Comperto siquidem consulares eorum accessu, quingentos milites, in vicini nemoris umbrosa opacitate, in insidiis posuerunt, ipsi vero, tanquam contra eos congressuri, obviam processerunt. Instant oppidani, cedunt ex industria consulares, et ultra insidiarum loca fuga fallaci protrahunt. Illi vero qui latebras fovebant de latibulis suis caute progredientes, eos qui ausu temerario suos insequebantur insequuntur: illi autem qui simulatoriam fugam arripuerant sentientes suos adesse, vertunt habenas et ensibus strictis et lanceis in insecutores suos desaeviunt'.

[39] Stephen Morillo has discussed the importance of this aspect of medieval tactics in Stephen Morillo, 'Expecting Cowardice: Medieval Battle Tactics Reconsidered', *Journal of Medieval Military History*, 4 (2006), 65–73.

[40] AM, pp. 337–8.

[41] HowChr, vol. 4, p. 60: 'Cum autem milites castelli, qui pridie eum a camp fugaverant, vidissent illum, exierunt cum impetu, et ipse fugit ante illos, donec inciderunt in insidiantes, et capti sunt ex eis xviii. Milites et plebs multa'.

the Appendix) but it was not an exclusively Norman tactic. Nor is there any reason to suppose that other peoples learned it from the Normans, or that the Normans needed to learn it from this or that steppe tribe: it was a logical and achievable stratagem for any well-disciplined force of horsemen.

Feigned Flight: Near Eastern Armies

Having established that the feigned flight was known and used by Latin Christians, independent of any encounters with other military cultures, we now turn to the armies of the Near East. Turkish horsemen are also depicted employing feigned flight but with unique features that require separate analysis.

In the ninth century, the armies of the Islamic world came to be dominated by elite bands of Turkish horsemen from Central Asia. They were a nomadic people, famous for their endurance and skill as horse archers, who lived by plunder. In an effort to harness this potentially destabilising force, the caliphs encouraged the Turks to migrate to the fringes of the Islamic world, mainly Central Asia and Anatolia, to harass and displace the caliphate's external enemies. At the same time, Muslim rulers began to employ groups of Turkish soldier-slaves, either purchased in Central Asia or captured in battle, called *mamlūks*. These highly trained horse archers formed the core of most Islamic armies of the crusading period, supported by mercenaries, tribal forces and urban militia.[42] In battle, they did not fight in rigid formations but small groups that attacked the enemy continuously from all sides, dispersing when charged, before returning to the attack. The riders would charge towards their enemy, only to wheel away at the last moment and shoot as they retreated. The aim was to disrupt the enemy formation sufficiently to allow a final, decisive charge with sword and lance. These tactics disconcerted Latin Christians, who sought to maintain solid, close-order formation in battle.[43]

Chapter 9 will analyse how Latin sources discussed the morality of these tactics but for now it is sufficient to say that they were aware that the

---

[42] David Ayalon, 'From Ayyūbids to Mamlūks', *Revue des etudes islamiques*, 49 (1981), 43–57; Hamilton A. R. Gibb, 'The Armies of Saladin', in S. J. Shaw and W. R. Polk (eds), *Studies on the Civilization of Islam* (Boston, 1962), pp. 74–90; Hugh Kennedy, *The Armies of the Caliphs: Military and Society in the Early Islamic State* (London, 2001), p. 123.

[43] John France, *Western Warfare in the Age of the Crusades, 1000–1300* (London, 1999), pp. 212–13; John France, *Victory in the East: A Military History of the First Crusade* (Cambridge, 1994), pp. 147–9; Carole Hillenbrand, *The Crusades: Islamic Perspectives* (Edinburgh, 1999), pp. 439–44, 512–13; R. C. Smail, *Crusading Warfare, 1097–1193* (Cambridge, 1956), pp. 78–82.

crusaders had encountered a different mode of fighting, one that did not conform to their strategic or tactical mores. The *Itinerarium Peregrinorum* compares the Turkish horsemen to irritating flies:

> Indeed, the Turks were not burdened with armour, like our men, but, advancing lightly-armed, they often disturbed our men with many greater injuries [...] For it is the Turks' custom that, when they are fleeing and they see that those pursuing them have stopped, they themselves then stop fleeing, like a wearisome fly which will fly away when you drive it off but which returns when you stop, it will flee for as long you chase but is still there when you cease.[44]

These tactics (sometimes referred to as Scythian or Parthian tactics) involved a form of feigned flight but one that should be distinguished from the variants discussed above. The two former variants, intended to lure an enemy away from a strong position or into a pre-prepared ambush, were primarily and intentionally deceptive. They required the fleeing force to make a convincing show of fear in order to trick the pursuers into breaking formation and giving chase. They were effective because they played on conventional expectations of military behaviour in the Latin West. It was generally understood that, when a force stood facing another in close order with banners raised, it was prepared to give battle, which meant fighting at close quarters. A force that turned and moved away, refusing to fight at close quarters, was retreating and would not fight effectively if pursued. This was not the case for troops who employed Parthian tactics. The sudden turns, shooting and dispersing involved were not primarily intended to deceive but to protect the archers, who could not engage a heavily armed enemy at close quarters. This would not have been apparent to people used to fighting according to Western customs who, assuming that a force that was withdrawing in front of them was retreating, would have pursued, only to be surprised when it turned back and resumed the attack.

Latin Christians fighting in the East had to adapt to these unfamiliar tactics. John France has identified two principal changes in crusader warfare over the twelfth century in response to these tactics. First, the Latin states of Outremer began to recruit their own horse archers, known as turcopoles, made up a mixture of Turks, Syrian Christians and Franks.[45] They were never the primary arm of the Latin forces, however, and appear

---

[44] IP, p. 247: 'Turci denique non, ut nostri, armaturis sunt onerati, sed incedentes expeditiores nostros multo majori saepius perturbant gravamine [...] Turcorum etiam moris est, ut quando persenserint se fugantes a persequendo cessare, tunc et ipsi fugere cessabunt, more muscae fastidiosae, quam si abegeris avolabit, cum cessaveris redibit, quamdiu fugaveris fugiet, cum desieries praesto est'. See also Amb, lines 5629–66.

[45] Yitzak Harari, 'The Military Role of the Frankish Turcopoles', *Mediterranean Historical Review*, 12 (1997), 75–116.

to have operated as auxiliaries to the knights.[46] The other adaptation was the tactic of the mass charge. Rather than operating as smaller units that could be isolated and overwhelmed by the Turks, the entire Latin army would charge as one, breaking the enemy in a single, devastating attack. This required significant discipline among the Latin troops, especially the foot soldiers who had to protect the horsemen until the order was given to charge.[47]

Muslim forces did use the other variants of feigned flight, of course. After the armies of the First Crusade seized Antioch in June 1098, the Turkish commander Karbughā sent a force of horsemen to lure some of the Franks into an ambush: 'Thirty from among them, who seemed to have swift horses, occupied the land before the city in order to deliberately ride about, pretending to be ignorant and riding about incautiously'.[48] It is not clear what is meant here by acting 'incautiously'. It may mean they scattered in different directions, so that they would not be drawn up to fight should they be attacked. Whatever they did, it was clearly effective. One Roger de Barneville, who served under Robert Curthose, duke of Normandy, took the bait and sallied out with fifteen men to attack what he thought would be an easy target: 'He charged boldly with loose rein against the aforesaid enemies who were riding about, but they suddenly and fraudulently turned around in flight, continually fleeing for a long time until they reached their men's ambuscades'.[49] Roger and his men tried to retreat to the safety of Antioch but he was killed by an arrow and his body decapitated in sight of the city walls.[50]

An example of the Hastings variant of a feigned flight, which includes explicit description of Turkish horsemen pretending to be afraid, appears in Walter the Chancellor's account of the campaign that culminated in the Field of Blood in 1119. Roger of Antioch was encamped before Athrab when a detachment of Turks approached. The town garrison sallied out to give battle, in conjunction with men from Roger's army:

> the enemies held themselves as if faltering in spirit and as if afraid to fight, turning back with loud complaints, although they appeared to be supported by 60,000 knights or more, their reins tightened, their bows taken from

---

[46] John France, 'Crusading Warfare and its Adaptation to Eastern Conditions in the Twelfth Century', *Mediterranean Historical Review*, 15 (2000), 49–66, at pp. 58–9.

[47] France, 'Crusading Warfare and its Adaptation', pp. 60–1.

[48] WT, p. 308: 'Ex quibus triginta, qui equos videbantur habere velociores, usque ad urbem ceperunt discurrere, ex industria ignorantiam pretendentes et discurrentes incautius'.

[49] WT, p. 308: 'Qui dum laxis habenis in predictos excursores irrueret animosius, subito sed fraudulenter in fugam versi sunt, tam diu fugam continuantes, quousque ad suorum pervenerunt insidias'.

[50] See also AA, pp. 287–9.

where they were hanging and drawn from the arm to the breast, their shields taken from their shoulders to their arms. But these things had been deliberately hidden by deceit, in order that, by these signs, they could draw our men far out of the camp.[51]

The description of the Turks grumbling and complaining as they fled is another reminder of the importance of shouts and cries on the medieval battlefield: as means of identification (see Chapter 5), to raise morale, to increase the impact of a surprise attack and, as here, creating the illusion of discontent or fear.

Conclusion

The chronicles reveal several variations of feigned flight. Sometimes it was employed to disrupt the enemy formation and lure them away from their defensive positions. At others, it was to lure an enemy force into an ambush. The third variant, employed by the horse archers of the steppes and the Muslim Near East, was not intended to deceive as much as to keep them out of reach their enemies, although it might have been interpreted as such by those used to fighting hand-to-hand. We cannot always be certain that a particular incident of feigned flight was not a plain rout that was later recast as a cunning ruse but there is sufficient evidence to indicate that both Latin Christians and their enemies were capable of performing such manoeuvres and that they knew that their enemy might do the same.

---

[51] WC, p. 81: 'hostes, licet.lx. milibus militum uel ultra uallati uiderentur, retentis tamen habenis ac de parte pendula sumptis arcubus parmisque ab umeris ad brachia, a brachiis ad pectora reuocatis, quasi animo titubantes et quasi pungere [variant reading: *pugnare*] metuentes, terga uersi fremendo se habebant. Sed res erat tecta fraude ex industria, ut his indiciis remotius a castris nostros extrahere potuissent'.

5

Disguises

Disguises are a universal story-telling device, from superhero comic books to comic opera. They also have a long history in warfare, from camouflage pattern on modern uniforms to the inflatable 'dummy' vehicles deployed by Allied forces during the Second World War.[1] It is therefore unsurprising to find a variety of tales involving disguise in medieval chronicles. While the most of these disguises are visual (e.g. dressing up as somebody else), there is also an important verbal and performative element.

These incidents have been divided into categories according to their intended effect: to make a combatant appear to be some kind of non-combatant, to make a fighting force appear larger than it truly was and to make one combatant look like another, be that friend or foe. This will require a detailed discussion of how medieval combatants distinguished these categories in the first place and how they expected to recognise one another on the battlefield. Many of these disguises reveal important cultural assumptions about the visual markers that distinguished fighting men from other social groups in the central Middle Ages.

Escaping and Infiltrating Strongholds

One way of avoiding an enemy's attention was to look like someone (or something) harmless and beneath their notice. This left the deceiver free to escape from danger or to enter a stronghold or enemy camp unnoticed.

A disguise could be useful if one wished to escape from one's enemy after a major defeat. According to Robert the Monk, the Turkish governor of Antioch, Yāghī Siyān, fled the city in June 1098 'covered in cheap rags' (*vilibus pannis obsitus*) when he learned that the crusaders had seized the outer defences, probably attempting to pass himself off as a pauper or beggar. Unfortunately for him, he was recognised on the road by a band

---

[1] Charles Cruickshank, *Deception in World War II* (Oxford, 1981), pp. 194–9.

of Armenians, who killed him and presented his head to the crusaders.[2] While chivalric convention in the West offered a level of protection to a defeated nobleman, who could expect to be spared in return for a ransom, this was not guaranteed. Furthermore, ransoms could be cripplingly expensive, so it is no wonder that chroniclers occasionally reported that individuals evaded capture by adopting a disguise. The *Gesta Normannorum Ducum* records an elaborate disguise adopted by Hugh III, count of Maine, following his failed assault on the Norman castle at Tillières c. 1013, alongside Odo II of Chartres and Waleran I of Meulan:

> It is certain that Hugh, since the horse he had mounted had been killed, fleeing on foot, turned aside to a sheepfold, hiding the hauberk which he was wearing under a furrow of earth. Then, clothing himself in a shepherd's cloak, and, covered by these things, tirelessly carrying them from place to place, he encouraged the Normans to pursue all their enemies, who were close by, fleeing shamelessly. When they had withdrawn, led by a shepherd, taking a path through the wild forests, after three days he came at last to Le Mans, his feet and shins bleeding wretchedly from the thorn-bushes and briars.[3]

While the *Gesta Normannorum* does not explicitly comment on Hugh's adventure, Wace stated that this behaviour was shameful when he adapted the story for the *Roman du Rou*: 'When those who had been hunting him returned in that direction, in the evening, when it had grown dark, the count went forth on foot. Without shoes, disguised as a shepherd, he escaped dishonourably'.[4] A similar story can be found in Orderic Vitalis's *Historia*, concerning the Norman baron William Lovel, who had rebelled against Henry I of England in favour of William Clito. Lovel escaped after the battle of Bourgthéroulde (26 March 1124) to his stronghold at Ivry:

> But William Lovel, having been captured by a certain peasant, gave his arms to him as a ransom and, his hair having been cut in the manner of a squire by the peasant, taking a staff in his hand he fled to the Seine, and, disguised, he gave his boots to a boatman in place of a fare to cross the river,

---

[2] His pauper's disguise was clearly not very thorough, as the Armenians also gave the crusaders the belt he had been wearing, which was valued at sixty besants: RM, p. 806.

[3] GND, vol. 2, p. 24: 'Hugo nempe, equo cui insederat extincto, pede fugiens, ad caulas ouium diuertit, loricam quam indutus erat sub sulco tegens telluris. Dehinc clamide opilionis se amiciens, septaque gregum infatigabiliter humeris de loco ad locum ferens, Normannos ortabatur, ut quamtotius persequerentur hostes non longe ante illos turpiter abeuntes. Quibus recedentibus, preuio pastore siluarum lustra carpens, tandem post triduum Cinomannis uenit, uepribus et sentibus miserabiliter pedes ac tibias cruentatus'.

[4] RdR, lines 1675–80: 'Quant cil s'en furent repairie, / Ki cele part orent chacie, / Al seir, quant bien fu annuitie, / S'en est li quens ale a pie: / Nuz piez, a guise de pastur / S'en eschaps a deshonur'.

and he returned to his home with bare feet, rejoicing that, slipping away, he had escaped howsoever from the hand of his enemies.[5]

The reference to William's hair appears to be linked to the contemporary fashion for courtiers to wear their hair long, making long hair a sign of noble status.[6] As 'squire' (*armiger*) is more likely to refer to a low-born arms-bearer than a noble knight-in-training in the twelfth century, they would have been expected to wear their hair short.[7] It is not clear from the text if the peasant cut William's hair at his request (i.e. it was a deliberate part of his disguise) or whether it was forced upon him in order to humiliate him.[8] Shame is the overriding feature in both of these accounts: the deceiver removes his arms, dresses like someone of lower social status and reaches safety by walking barefoot. For a social group defined by its ability to fight on horseback, being forced to travel on foot in this way would have been particularly humiliating.

There are echoes of this idea in an episode from the *Gesta Tancredi*, in which the author explains how Tancred, alone among all the leaders of the First Crusade, avoided doing homage to Alexios Komnenos at Constantinople in April 1097:

> So, coming to Constantinople, he did not bow to the king like the others, nor did he send ahead trumpet calls or sound a trumpet: he crossed over in secret. For, when his knightly dress had been laid aside, he dressed himself as a foot soldier; since it was peasant garb, while it protected Tancred, it deceived Alexios.[9]

This scheme is not presented as humiliating or shameful but prudent: Tancred acted 'wisely' (*sapienter*). Nevertheless this ruse, like the two

---

[5] OV, vol. 6, p. 352: 'Guillelmus uero Lupellus a quodam rustico captus arma sua illi pro redemptione sui dedit, et ab eo tonsus instar armigeri manu palum gestans ad Sequanam confugit, et incognitus ad transitum fluminis pro naulo caligas suas nauclero impertiuit, nudisque pedibus proprios lares reuisit, gaudens quod de manu hostili utcumque prolapsus euaserit'.

[6] For an example, see Eadmer, *Historia in novorum in Anglia*, ed. Martin Rule (London, 1884), p. 214.

[7] Matthew Bennett, 'The Status of the Squire: The Northern Evidence', in Christopher Harper-Bill and Ruth Harvery (eds.), *The Ideals and Practices of Medieval Knighthood: Papers from the First and Second Strawberry Hill Conferences* (Woodbridge, 1986), pp. 1–11; for the significance of hair in Anglo-Norman aristocratic culture, see Pauline Stafford, 'The Meanings of Hair in the Anglo-Norman World: Masculinity, Reform, and National Identity', in Mathilde van Dijk and Renée Nip (eds.), *Saints, Scholars, and Politicians: Gender as a Tool in Medieval Studies* (Turnhout, 2005), pp. 153–72.

[8] The clause is passive, with no reference to William requesting or ordering the peasant to cut his hair.

[9] GT, p. 15: 'Constantinopolim igitur ueniens, non sicut ceteri declinat ad regem, non classica premittit, non tuba intonat: clam transit. Nam exuto milite, peditem induit; quatinus uestis rustica, dum Tancredum tegeret, Alexium falleret'.

described above, relied on the distinction between the usual appearance of a knight (*miles*) and that of a foot soldier (*pedes*) or peasant (*rusticus*). The use of *induere* in the main clause suggests that *miles* is referring to clothes here but the language indicates a fundamental connection between appearance and social status. By abandoning the distinctive clothes and equipment that marked him out as a *miles* and choosing to travel on foot, Tancred was abandoning an essential part of his identity.[10] What distinguished his disguise from that of Hugh of Maine or William Lovel was his motivation: Tancred adopted it to avoid the 'crafty devices' of Alexios (*Alexii tegnas*), whereas they adopted it out of fear.

Escaping in disguise often meant abandoning weapons and armour. Infiltrating a stronghold presented additional challenges: the deceiver had to appear harmless but still carry his arms as, once he was inside, he needed to be able to overpower the guards and seize the defences. The obvious solution was to choose a disguise that included a large cloak or similar enveloping garment. For example in 1263, during the Second Barons' War in England, Henry de Montfort allegedly gained access to Gloucester by sending two knights 'riding upon two woolpacks as if they were merchants [...] They were both covered with Welsh mantles'.[11] As soon as they were admitted, they threw off their mantles and revealed that they were armed and armoured. The porters immediately surrendered the keys and allowed the barons to take the town. When the royalists recaptured the town the following year, the unfortunate porters were hanged for their trouble.[12]

Louis VI of France took the town of Gasny in 1116 using a disguise, in a rare case of two independent, contemporary chroniclers reporting the same incident. Gasny controlled a strategically vital ford on the Epte, allowing the French to cross into Normandy. Louis's biographer Suger said that he sent a detachment ahead of his main army 'down the public road as if they were travellers, hauberks and swords hidden beneath their cloaks'.[13] When they revealed their true identity, the inhabitants assaulted them and Louis was forced to charge into the town with the rest of his

---

[10] This agrees with Kostick's conclusions on the meaning of *miles* and other related terms in the chronicles of the First Crusade: Conor Kostick, 'The Terms *milites, equites* and *equestres* in the Early Crusading Histories', *Nottingham Medieval Studies*, 50 (2006), 1–21.

[11] RG, lines 11,170–7: 'Sir Ion giffard come aday & sir Ion de balun þere / Ride vpe tueye wolpakces chapmen as hii were / To þe west ȝate ouer þe brugge & þe porters bede / To late in tueie wolmongers hor caffare in to lede / Biweued hii were boþe mid welsse mantles tueie. / Þo þe ȝates were vndo hii hupte adoun beye / Of hor hors & caste hor mantles awei anon / & þo stode hii Iarmed fram heued to þe ton'.

[12] RG, lines 11,294–7.

[13] SSD, p. 186: 'tanquam viatores, loricati sub cappis et gladiis cincti, publica via descendentes'.

force: 'he captured both the town hall and the fortified church with a tower without loss to his men'.[14] Orderic Vitalis, a Norman, recorded the same incident but with some significant variations:

> Also Louis deceitfully attacked the ford of Nicaise, which is commonly called Gasny, and entered it as if he were a monk, together with his household knights who had been dressed in black cloaks; and he built a castle there in the cell of the monks of St. Ouen and, in the house of the Lord, where solemn prayers should be offered to God, he disgracefully established a den of thieves.[15]

The basic story is the same: French troops enter and capture Gasny wearing cloaks, but Orderic's account explicitly portrays it as an immoral act. Not only does he use the adverbs 'deceitfully' (*fraudulenter*) and 'disgracefully' (*turpiter*), he includes blasphemous elements not present in Suger's version: instead of general 'travellers' (*viatores*), Louis and his men are explicitly dressed as monks (*monachi*).[16] Furthermore, whereas Suger implies that the monastery was already being employed as a fortress (*munita ecclesia*), Orderic states that it was Louis who turned this sacred space into a 'den of thieves', a reference to Christ's words during the Cleansing of the Temple: 'Was it not written: "Because this is my house, it will be called a house of prayer for all peoples"? But you made it a den of thieves'.[17] The truth of the matter is unclear. It would certainly have been surprising if the Norman dukes had not fortified Gasny against invasion. Orderic may have objected, not so much because Louis seized the monastery, but because he used it to raid into Norman lands, whereas formerly the 'thieves' garrisoning the town had been raiding in the opposite direction, into the Ile-de-France.[18]

---

[14] SSD, p. 186: 'tam ville atrium quam munitam turre ecclesiam non sine suorum damno occupat'.

[15] OV, vol. 6, p. 184: 'Porro Ludouicus uadum Nigasii quod Vani uulgo uocatur fraudulenter adiit, ac ueluti monachus cum sociis militibus qui nigris capis amicti erant ex insperato intrauit; ibique in cella monachorum sancti Audeoni castrum muniuit, et in domo Domini ubi solummodo preces offerri Deo debent speluncam latronum turpiter effecit'.

[16] It is possible that Suger used *viatores* to mean lay brothers, which would agree with Orderic's description of the French wearing monastic-style robes, but, as Suger does not use this word anywhere else in this chronicle, we lack a basis for comparison. I have therefore chosen to follow the more obvious interpretation of the word. For the alternate meaning of *viatores*, see Du Cange and others, *Glossarium mediae et infimae latinitatis*, ed. Leopold Favre (Niort, 1883–7) <http://ducange.enc.sorbonne.fr/VIATORES1> [accessed 3 May 2018].

[17] Mark 11. 17: 'Nonne scriptum est : Quia domus mea, domus orationis vocabitur omnibus gentibus ? vos autem fecistis eam speluncam latronum'. See also Matthew 21. 13 and Luke 19. 46.

[18] OV, vol. 6, p. 187.

While Orderic's account of this action was intended to be moralistic, Suger's account of another incident of infiltration by disguise was probably intended to be humorous. In 1109 Louis VI had laid siege to the castle at Ferté-Baudouin (mod. La Ferté-Alais) to rescue Odo, count of Corbeil, and Anselm of Garlande from Odo's brother, Hugh of Crécy. Hugh, finding himself outside the royal siege lines, attempted to pass through in disguise: 'He was troubled and distressed. He plotted how he might enter the castle, now on horseback, now on foot, adopting the likeness of a jester and a prostitute'.[19] Unsurprisingly, he failed and was pursued by Anselm's brother, William of Garlande. Hugh, however, escaped through a ruse worthy of Renart the Fox:

> Deceitfully pretending that he himself was William of Garlande, he cried out that Hugh was chasing him, William, and summoned the king's men to obstruct him as if he were an enemy. In this way and others, as much by a crafty tongue as by a bold heart, escaping through flight, one man made fools of many.[20]

While the elements of cross-dressing and slapstick comedy suggest that this tale is more salacious gossip than factual history, there is nevertheless a hint of admiration in Suger's description of Hugh's escape, the 'one who made fools of many': an example of admirable cunning, even in a rebel.

When Baldwin II of Jerusalem was captured by the Turkish ruler Balak, nephew of Īlghāzī, in April 1123 and imprisoned in his fortress at Kharput, north of the Euphrates, an extraordinary rescue mission was launched to save him.[21] Fulcher of Chartres reports that it was the prisoners themselves who arranged the mission, through the Armenians 'whom they consorted with':

> And when this had been confirmed, after many gifts and promises, with oaths of faith by both sides, about fifty of the wisest citizens were sent there from Edessa; and, when the opportunity arose, as if carrying and selling the poorest sort of goods all the way up to the gates of the inner castle, they let themselves in one by one.[22]

---

[19] SSD, p. 94: 'anxiatur, laborat, et quomodo castrum ingredi possit, modo eques, modo pedes, multiformi joculatoris et meretricis mentito simulachro, machinatur'.
[20] SSD, pp. 94–6: 'Nisi cum simulata fraude seipsum Garlandensem Guilelmum fallendo, Guilelmum autem Hugonem se sequentem conclamaret et ex parte regis ut eum tanquam hostem impedirent invitaret. His et aliis hujusmodi, tam lingue cautela quam animi strenuitate fuga lapsus, multos unus derisit'.
[21] For a comprehensive study of this operation and its context, see Yuval Noah Harari, *Special Operations in the Age of Chivalry 1100–1550* (Woodbridge, 2007), pp. 74–90.
[22] FC, pp. 678–9: 'Et cum post aliqua dona et promissa plurima hoc fidei nexu utrimque confirmatum esset, de Edessena urbe sagacissime L fere clientes illuc ob id missi sunt; et quasi pauperrimi merces ferentes atque vendentes usque ad portas interioris castri, occasione quadam nata, se paulatim intromiserunt'.

William of Tyre, doubtless reflecting the numerous tales that circulated about this adventure, describes two possible versions of the Armenians' plan:

> So they disguised themselves in monk's habits, carrying daggers beneath their loose clothing, directing their course to the aforesaid town as if they were conducting the business of monasteries, by word and gesture and facial expression they pretended that they had suffered violence and injury from somebody [...] Others say they entered the town as merchants, the bearers of cheap goods.[23]

The former version, in which the Armenians posed as supplicants seeking justice from Balak, is also found in Matthew of Edessa's chronicle.[24] Sadly for the Armenians, although they succeeded in penetrating Kharput and freeing the prisoners, no aid followed to bring them home. Balak laid siege to the fortress and, having recaptured it after a brief siege, executed the entire garrison, sparing only the king and two senior Frankish noblemen.[25]

The final variation of this disguise made the deceiver appear to be something entirely inhuman, such as an animal or inanimate object. Amatus of Montecassino reports that, in 1051, during a conflict between Guaimar IV of Salerno and one William Barbote, William's castle at Belvedre was destroyed after a peasant 'made a bundle of tree branches and placed himself inside, and shortly afterwards [the garrison] carried it in for firewood'. Once inside, the peasant set fire to the castle, forcing William to flee.[26] According to John Barbour, Robert Bruce's supporters took the peel (a fortification consisting of an embankment, ditch and palisade) at Linlithgow from the English in c. 1308 by hiding soldiers in a wagon. A local named William Bunnock hid eight men under the hay in his wagon, which he was accustomed to bring into the peel for safety. Once his wagon was in the gateway itself, he cut the traces on his oxen, preventing the garrison from shutting the gates in time, while Bruce's men rushed in and secured the defences.[27]

---

[23] WT, p. 568: 'Habitu ergo se simulant monachos, sicas sub laxis vestibus portantes, ad predictum tendunt opidum tanquam de negociis monasteriorum acturi aliquid, simulant verbo et gemitu et faciei modificatione se a quibusdam vim iniuriamque passos [...] alii dicunt eos quasi mercatores, vilium mercium portitores, opdium ingressos'.

[24] Ara Edmond Dostourian (trans.), *Armenia and the Crusades, Tenth to Twelfth Centuries: The Chronicle of Matthew of Edessa* (Lanham, MD, 1993), pp. 229–30.

[25] Harari, *Special Operations*, p. 86.

[26] AM, p. 303: 'Mes lo chastel, pour la hautesce de lo mont, non se pooit prendre, et o feu de un vilain fu ars. Et fu fait un fas de branchez d'arbre et et il se mist dedens, et poi a poi va portant la lainge; et lo lieu de lo castel garni, et o une pingnote qu'il portoit, lo feu arst tout lo chastel'.

[27] Bruce, Book 10, lines 187–252.

Ralph of Caen claimed that a similar trick was employed to capture the Cilician city of Adana. Having left the main crusading force on 14 September 1097, the Norman lord Tancred travelled to Adana where he was warmly welcomed by 'Ursinus', the city's Christian ruler. Tancred asked how Ursinus was able to maintain his rule there, as he was surrounded by the Turks. Ursinus responded with a detailed account of how he had recently liberated Adana from Turkish rule. The citizens of Adana, noticing that the hay carts they brought in from the fields were never inspected by the Turkish guards, conceived a plan to smuggle armed men into the city under the hay. Ursinus provided both the infiltrating force and a diversion, raiding in sight of the walls and then feigning flight to draw the garrison away. Once the infiltrators had seized the defences, Ursinus turned back and drove the Turks to the city gates, which were now shut against them, where they were all killed. According to Ralph, Tancred's only response to this tale was to exclaim: 'Thanks be to God!'[28]

Scholars have struggled to conclusively identify 'Ursinus'. F. C. R. Robinson, P. C. Hughes and Christopher MacEvitt all tentatively identify him with Oshin of Lampron, head of the noble Armenian family the Hethoumids. In 1072 Oshin was granted command of the Cilician fortress of Lampron by the Byzantine governor of Tarsus. Taking advantage of the disintegration of both Turkish and Byzantine power in the region, he may have sought to claim Ardana for himself in 1097.[29] While Ralph of Caen portrays 'Ursinus' as an eager ally of Tancred and the other Franks, Macevitt has interpreted his suggestion that Tancred attack the city of Mamistra as altogether more cynical. As a recent newcomer to the region himself, he was uncertain of his position and sought to play the crusaders off against one another and the Turks.[30]

How then should we interpret Ursinus's tale in the *Gesta*? It cannot be corroborated: no other crusading chronicle mentions it. Albert of Aachen does refer to Tancred's expedition to Ardana but his account is quite different: instead of Ursinus, he reports that the town had recently been captured by a Burgundian crusader named Welf, with whom Tancred later negotiated a trade deal.[31] Stephen Runciman attempted to square the two accounts by arguing that Oshin had captured only part of the city, while Welf held the citadel, but there is no contemporary evidence to support this.[32] The story of the troops hidden in the hay wagon is

---

[28] GT, pp. 39–41.
[29] Christopher MacEvitt, *The Crusades and the Christian World of the East: Rough Tolerance* (Philadelphia, 2008), pp. 55–7; F. C. R. Robinson and P. C. Hughes, 'Lampron: Castle of Armenian Cilicia', *Anatolian Studies*, 19 (1969), 183–207, at p. 184.
[30] MacEvitt, *Christian World*, p. 58.
[31] AA, pp. 153–55.
[32] Steven Runciman, *A History of the Crusades* (3 vols, Cambridge, 1951), vol. 1, p. 199.

probably a fiction, either repeated or invented wholesale by Ralph, but it is still significant that it was ascribed to the generally admirable figure of 'Ursinus' and that Tancred is depicted approving of the stratagem.[33]

Dead Bodies and Fake Corpses

Feigning death to enter or exit a stronghold, a variant of the 'category disguise', is simultaneously one of the least plausible tales of military deception in medieval history and one of the most widely circulated, being attributed to a variety of actors in a variety of sources. The first written account of the ruse appears in Dudo of St. Quentin's *Historia Normannorum*. Dudo's chronicle, commissioned by Richard I of Normandy c. 994–6, was composed to help legitimise the ducal dynasty as Christian lords, worthy to be counted among the princes of Western Europe. Rollo, the first duke, inspired by a divine vision, is depicted leading his people across the sea into a new land, where they are baptised into the Christian faith.[34] His foil in the narrative is Hasting, a violent and unrepentant pagan chieftain, who, although unrelated to Rollo by blood, serves as a symbolic ancestor to both the Norman dukes and their people: he is a representation of their dark past that was abandoned at the baptismal font.[35]

Hasting's chief outrage was the sack of the Italian city of Luni (which at the time he believed to be Rome). Realising that he could not take the city by force, Hasting 'invented a cunning stratagem of most abominable deceit'.[36] First, he sent word to the citizens that he was dying and wished to be baptised. The citizens believed him, agreed to a truce and permitted him to enter the city for baptism. Dudo makes much of this act of impiety: 'Meanwhile the bath is prepared by the bishop, which will be of no benefit to the faithless man [...] The faithless man enters the font, washing only his body. The wicked man receives baptism, to the ruin of his soul'.[37] Hasting then instructed his men to claim that he had

---

[33] Hanawalt has suggested that this may be because Tancred was reliant upon the local Armenians during these early campaigns and that he grew to 'genuinely' admire them: Emily A. Hanawalt, 'Norman Views of Eastern Christendom, from the First Crusade to the Principality of Antioch.', in Vladimir P. Goss (ed.), *The Meeting of Two Worlds: Cultural Exchange between East and West during the Period of the Crusades*, (Kalamazoo, MI, 1986), pp. 115–21, at p. 119.

[34] Dudo of St Quentin, *History of the Normans*, trans. Eric Christiansen (Woodbridge, 1998), p. xxiii; Benjamin Pohl, *Dudo of Saint-Quentin's Historia Normannorum: Tradition, Innovation and Memory* (York, 2015), p. 83.

[35] Pohl, *Dudo of Saint-Quentin's Historia*, pp. 135–6.

[36] Dudo, p. 133: 'dolosum reperit consilium nefandissimae fraudis'.

[37] Dudo, p. 133: 'Interim praeparatur ab episcopo balneum, perfido non profuturum

died in the night and that they wished to bring the 'corpse' into the city for a Christian burial. The citizens agreed and admitted the burial party, who had secreted weapons inside the funeral bier. Following the funeral Mass, once again conducted by the bishop: 'Hasting jumped off the bier, and drew his gleaming sword from its sheath. The cruel man attacked the prelate, who was holding a book in his hand'.[38] The city was pillaged and all the citizens either slaughtered or enslaved. When the raiders discovered that they were not actually in Rome but Luni, they burned the city and rampaged through the surrounding country in revenge.[39]

Hasting is the villain of Dudo's chronicle, the mirror image of the heroic Rollo, whose sincere baptism parallels the false one Hasting received to gain entry to Luni. As Benjamin Pohl has observed, Rollo's baptism cleanses him and the Norman people from the 'original sin' of Hasting.[40] This makes it all the more remarkable that the ruse of the fake corpse, the instrument of Hasting's greatest crime, was attributed to a variety of individuals over the twelfth and thirteenth centuries, usually in a laudatory context. Three separate chronicles claim Robert Guiscard employed it. Matthew Paris wrote that he used it to seize Monte Cassino:

> That mountain was impregnable, that is to say, accessible to only a few, unless the monks and the other inhabitants wished it; Robert Guiscard only captured the monks' *castellum* unexpectedly through a contrivance, by which he pretended to be dead and was carried inside on a bier.[41]

The *Gesta Tancredi* reports a conflict occurred following the sack of Jerusalem in 1099 between Tancred and Arnulf of Chocques, a cleric who had assumed the authority of the papal legate on the First Crusade. Arnulf lambasts Tancred for dividing the plunder from the Temple with his men, which ought to have gone to the Church:

[...] Intrat perfidus fontes, corpus tantum diluentes. Suscipit nefarius baptismum, ad animae suae interitum'.

[38] Dudo, p. 134: 'Alstignus feretro desiluit, ensemque fulgentem vagina deripuit. Invasit funestus praesulem, librum manu tenentem'.

[39] Dudo, p. 135.

[40] Pohl, *Dudo of Saint-Quentin's Historia*, p. 212. For further analysis of Hasting, see Pierre Bouet, 'Hasting, le Viking pervers selon Dudon de Saint-Quentin', *Annales de Normandie*, 62 (2012), 215–34; Frederick Amory, 'The Viking Hasting in Franco-Scandanavian Legend', in Margot H King and Wesley M. Stevens (eds.), *Saints, Scholars and Heroes: Studies in Medieval Culture in Honour of Charles W. Jones* (2 vols, Collegeville, MN, 1979), vol. 2, pp. 265–86.

[41] Matthew Paris, *Chronica majora*, ed. Henry Richards Luard, RS, 57 (7 vols, London, 1872–83), vol. 3, p. 538: 'Erat autem mons ille inexpugnabilis, immo inaccessibilis alicui, nisi ex voluntate monachorum et aliorum inhabitantium in eo; nisi tantummodo quod R[obertus] Guichard per excogitationem, qua se mortuum simulavit, in feretro in illum delatus, castra monachorum subito occupavit'.

But one ought to be kind to a Guiscard: for he followed in his forefathers' footsteps. Who, amidst embraces, amidst kisses, threw his own cousin tumbling from the walls? Guiscard, of course! Who was borne alive into Monte Cassino like one dead, living as if to be buried? Surely it was Guiscard! Who first poured hot water then cold upon his nephew, whom he had enticed into friendship? The same Guiscard! Yet he is said have been a founder of churches, not a destroyer: he did not despoil but furnished many.[42]

The context here, listing the 'fake corpse' ruse between two examples of familial treachery, is certainly negative. Tancred's response, however, indicates that this was not a universally held opinion:

You all heard him, there is no need for an external witness, with what persuasive force he savaged my ancestry: a man who has not seen any prince arise from his own lineage disparaged such a prince as Guiscard, second only to Alexander in boldness. The deeds of Guiscard are known throughout the world. It is impossible to disparage them, unless one always tried to paint white on black and black on white.[43]

The portrayal of Guiscard elsewhere in the *Gesta Tancredi* is more in keeping with Tancred's valourisation than Arnulf's criticism. Compare the opening section of the chronicle, which celebrates Tancred's relation to Guiscard through his mother: 'For who does not esteem the valour of Guiscard, before whose conquering banners, it is said, in one day the Greek and German emperors trembled?'[44]

The most detailed account of Guiscard's use of the 'fake corpse' trick is found in William of Apulia's laudatory *Gesta Roberti Wiscardi*. William does not name the town that Guiscard attacked, saying only that 'it was difficult for him to climb up to because there were many inhabitants, Greeks who lived there as well as monks, who would not permit strangers to enter'.[45] Unable to storm the town, Guiscard sent word that one of

---

[42] GT, pp. 112–13: 'At indulgendum est Wiscardidae: secutus est enim patrum suorum uestigia. Quis inter amplexus, inter oscula compatrem suum a menibus rota deiecit? Nempe Wiscardus! Quis uiuus pro mortuo, incolumis pro tumulando, in montem Cassinum perlatus est? Vtique Wiscardus! Quis nepotem suum, ad concordiam elicitum, prius calida mox gelida perfudit? Idem Wiscardus! Qui tamen fertur ecclesiarum fundator, non subuersor; nec denudasse, at multas ornasse'.

[43] GT, p. 114: 'Audistis ipsi, non est externo opus teste, qua ui persuadente genus meum corroserit: Wiscardo, secundae ab Alexandro audaciae, detraxit, tanto principi homo, de cuius sobole quispiam principem non uidit. Wiscardi acta nota sunt orbi, non est qui possit detrahere, nisi qui semper studuit candidum in nigra, nigrum in candida colorare'.

[44] GT, p. 6: 'Quis enim Wiscardi probitatem non probet, cuius signa sub uno, ut aiunt, die Grecus Alemannusque imperator tremuerunt uictricia?'

[45] WA, p. 150: 'sed eius / Difficilis conscensus erat, quia plurimus huius / Accola, grex habitans etiam monasticus illic, / Non alienigenam quemvis intrare sinebant'.

his men had died and he needed to bury him in the town's monastery. The monks agreed and the 'corpse' was prepared for burial. William adds the notable detail that he 'was placed upon a bier and a silk cloth spread over him, having been commanded to hide his face, as it is the Normans' custom to cover up corpses'.[46] The funeral procession entered the town but, in contrast to the story of Hasting, they never actually entered the monastery, only reaching the entrance (*limina*) before the deception was revealed and swords were drawn. Nor was there any great slaughter: '[the townsfolk] were all captured, and Robert established his first garrison in the *castrum*. The monastery was not destroyed, the Greek monks were not expelled from there'.[47] The essential story is the same but William has removed the sacrilegious and morally troubling elements from Dudo: the fake baptism, the slaughter of the clerics, the destruction of holy places. All that remains is an irreverent display of Guiscard's 'craft' (*arte*).

This ruse was also associated with other members of Guiscard's family. The twelfth-century German chronicler Otto of Freising attributed it to Roger II of Sicily, claiming that he employed it during the invasion of Corfu in 1147:

> Therefore, when certain men had been sent ahead, so it is said, who pretended to carry a corpse to be buried – for there is a community of clerics or monks in the citadel of the aforesaid fortress, in the Greek manner – they rushed into the fortress, occupied the citadel, and, when the Greeks had been ejected, they placed their own men there.[48]

Anna Komnene described Bohemond using a similar trick to escape from Antioch to Western Europe in September 1104. According to Anna, he spread the rumour that he had died. A special coffin was prepared, with hidden air holes, and the 'body' was carried onto a ship at Soudi. When the ship was out at sea, Bohemond would get out of the coffin and walk around but, when approaching the land, he would climb into the coffin with a dead cockerel 'in order that the corpse might appear to be in a state of rare putrefaction'.[49]

---

[46] WA, p. 150: 'Qui cum, quasi mortuus, esset / Impositus feretro, pannusque obducere cera / Illitus hunc facie iussus latitante fuisset, / Ut Normannorum velare cadavera mos est'. Reading *saeta* for *cera*.

[47] WA, p. 150: 'omnes capiuntur, et illic / Praesidium castri primum, Roberte, locasti. / Non monasterii tamen est eversio facta, / Non extirpatus grex est monasticus'.

[48] Otto von Freising and Rahewin, *Die Taten Friedrichs oder richtiger Cronica*, ed. Franz-Josef Schmale, trans. Adolf Schmidt (Darmstadt, 1965), p. 198: 'Igitur premissis quibusdam, ut dicitur, qui se quempiam mortuum humandi gratia deferre simularent – est enim in predicta arce castri, sicut Grecis mos est, congregatio clericorum seu monachorum – idem castrum irruunt, arcem occupant, Grecis eiectis presidiisque suis ibidem locatis'.

[49] Anna Komnene, *The Alexiad*, trans. E. R. A. Sewter (London, 1969), pp. 366–7.

There is a second, apparently independent tradition, that attributes the 'fake corpse' ruse to the Norwegian adventurer and monarch Haraldr Sigurðarson, also known as Harald Hardrada. Following the battle of Stiklarstaðir in 1030, Haraldr was exiled from Norway. In 1034 he entered the service of Michael IV the Paphlagonian, emperor of Byzantium, as a member of the elite Varangian Guard. Between 1038 and 1041, Haraldr fought under Georgios Maniakes in a campaign to reconquer Sicily for the empire.[50] It is in this context that the story of him employing the 'fake corpse' ruse appears in the *Morkinskinna*, the earliest surviving compendium of Norse kings' sagas, compiled c. 1220.[51] In this version of the tale, the plan is proposed by Haraldr to enter a city that the Byzantine army cannot storm. As in William of Apulia's account, the (empty) coffin never actually enters the monastery: it is dropped across the city gateway to wedge it open while the rest of the army rushes inside.[52]

As this compilation was written down long after their first composition, it is difficult to determine what its original sources were. Theodore M. Andersson and Kari Ellen Gade suggest that the descriptions of Haraldr's Byzantine service may have been based on oral testimony, as does Sigfus Blöndal, who described the spectacular adventures as 'much-expanded self-justifications, originally told by Haraldr [sic] and blown up by his flatterers'.[53] This fails to explain the similarities between the story in this saga and that of Hasting in Dudo's chronicle, which predated Haraldr's exile in Byzantium by some thirty years. While it is possible that both tales have their origins in a lost, oral motif from Scandinavian folklore or saga tradition, there is no textual evidence for this. The striking similarities between these two tales must lead one to prefer Dudo as the originator of the tale and the sagas as the imitator. It may have been transmitted orally, via Scandinavians in Byzantine service, from Normans in southern Italy, as Klaus Rossenbeck has suggested, or by Scandinavian scholars who travelled south and encountered the story in a Continental chronicle.[54] This would explain why the sagas depict a Muslim garrison permitting a Christian burial party to enter their city: it is a legacy from

---

[50] Sigfus Blöndal, *The Varangians of Byzantium: An Aspect of Byzantine Military History*, trans. Benedikt S. Benedikz (Cambridge, 1978), pp. 65–7.
[51] *Morkinskinna: The Earliest Icelandic Chronicle of the Norwegian Kings (1030–1157)*, ed. and trans. Theodore M. Andersson and Kari Ellen Gade (London, 2000), p. 1.
[52] *Morkinskinna*, pp. 141–3; this saga was also included by the Icelandic writer Sturlson (d. 1241) in his collection of kings' sagas, the *Heimskringla*: Snorri Sturlson, *Heimskringla: History of the Kings of Norway*, trans. Lee M. Hollander (Austin, TX, 1964), p. 585.
[53] *Morkinskinna*, p. 63; Blöndal, *Varangians of Byzantium*, p. 66.
[54] Klaus Rossenbeck, *Die Stellung Der Riddarassogur in Der Altnordischen Prosaliteratur: Eine Untersuchung an Hand Des Erzählstils* (Bamberg, 1970), pp. 78–9.

the original, Dudo's *Historia*, that becomes a nonsense when it became applied to Haraldr's historical campaign.

As stated at the beginning of this section, this is a highly implausible ruse. It is very unlikely that Guiscard, or any other commander, ever actually employed it. Yet its very survival, across multiple texts from different locations, tells us that it was a story that contemporaries enjoyed hearing. Stripped of the blasphemous elements that made the original so monstrous, it became an exemplar of cunning that could be comfortably ascribed to either a hero or a worthy foe.

Strength in Numbers: Looking More Numerous

The disguises analysed above were employed by, at most, a handful of individuals. The following section considers a form of disguise employed by entire armies: ruses to make a force appear more numerous than it truly was. Tales of these stratagems date back to the pre-Christian era. Frontinus records that in 109 BCE, during a battle with the Scordisci and Dacians of central Europe, the Roman general Minucius Rufus sent trumpeters into the hills to give the impression that reinforcements were approaching.[55] In 358 BCE the consul Gaius Sulpicius Peticus had mule drivers mount their animals to simulate a cavalry force in a battle against the Gauls.[56] The latter example, from Livy's *Ab urbe condita*, may have influenced Andrew of Fleury's *Miracula Sancti Benedicti*, a mid-eleventh-century chronicle of the region around Fleury Abbey in central France. According to Andrew, in 1038 Odo, count of Déols, refused to submit to the peace council convened by Aimon, archbishop of Bourges. Aimon assembled an army and confronted Odo's forces on the banks of the Cher. Andrew ascribes Odo's subsequent defeat to both divine intervention, in the form of a thunderbolt that fell in the midst of Odo's army, and the army's ingenuity:

> Furthermore, the people, seeing that they were fewer in number than their adversaries, who outnumbered the grains of sand in the sea, seized upon this strategy: that the foot soldiers, having climbed up onto whatever animals there were to hand, should mingle in the middle of the band of knights, to take the appearance of horsemen so that they might be thought to be such by the enemy knights.[57]

---

[55] Frontinus, *Strategemata*, ed. Robert Ireland (Leipzig, 1990), p. 43.
[56] Frontinus, *Strategemata*, p. 43.
[57] *Les Miracles de Saint Benoit*, ed. E. de Certain (Paris, 1858), pp. 196–7: 'Porro adversa partis populus multo se inferiorem prospiciens, cum illi numero maris superarent arenam, id consilii capiunt ut pedites, ascensis quibuscumque animalibus, mediis militum se miscerent cohortibus, ut tam ex figurata specie equitandi quoai ex

This story is another reminder of the importance of reading medieval military narratives in their full context, rather than selecting the 'plausible' details. Andrew of Fleury attributed Aimon's victory to both the miraculous thunderbolt and the ruse: both were evidence of the righteousness of the archbishop's cause and a demonstration of God's favour. His account probably tells us more about the political and religious significance of the Peace of God movement and the influence of Livy on medieval historians than about the realities of warfare.

One method of making a force appear larger that appears in multiple chronicles was the display of numerous banners. A banner (which should be distinguished from the smaller pennant or *gonfanon*) served as a rallying point and identification for a substantial group of combatants, such as the following of a great lord or members of an urban guild.[58] A force with many banners could be assumed to contain many people. Roger of Wendover reports that the commanders of the Anglo-French force besieging Lincoln on 20 May 1217, Thomas, count of Perche and the 'Marshal of France', made just this assumption when viewing the approaching royalist army.[59] Although their English allies reported that the royalists were few in number, the French were not convinced and insisted on counting them 'in the French fashion'. As each magnate flew two banners, one with the baggage, one with them in person, the French mistakenly believed that the royalist army was twice its actual size.[60] While this does not appear to have

---

oppositione armorum milites arbitrarentur ab illis. Nec mora, ad duo millia plebeiae multitudinis, ascensis asinis, medio equitum ordine partiuntur equestri'.

[58] See below for a discussion of the different methods by which combatants distinguished friend from foe in this period.

[59] Roger does not name the Marshal, presumably the same *mareschallus Franciae* who was listed among the French noblemen who escaped the ensuing battle: RW, vol. 2, p. 397. Identifying him is difficult. Henry Richards Luard, in his edition of Matthew Paris's *Chronica majora*, calls him Walter of Nismes but provides no supporting references: Paris, *Chronica Majora*, vol. 3, p. 20 n. 4. This would be Walter of Nismes the Younger, who fought at Bouvines and died while participating in the Fifth Crusade, but he does not appear to have been in England at this time: John W. Baldwin, *The Government of Philip Augustus: Foundations of French Royal Power in the Middle Ages* (Berkeley, CA, 1986), p. 108. The question is further complicated by the fact that, according to Baldwin, the title 'Marshal of France' was not yet a hereditary one in 1217: Baldwin, *Philip Augustus*, p. 113. A more plausible identification may be William of Beaumont, known as Rat's Foot, whom the *Histoire des ducs de Normandie* says accompanied Louis of France to England in 1216 and who 'was the marshal of many others': *Histoire des ducs de Normandie et des rois d'Angleterre*, ed. Francisque Michel (Paris, 1840), p. 161.

[60] RW, vol. 4, p. 56: 'Quibus comes Perticensis et Mareschallus respondentes dixerunt, "Vos aestimastis illos juxta scientiam vestram; et nos exibimus modo, ut aestimemus eos juxta consuetudinem Gallicanam". Exierunt ergo ut aestimarent exercitum regis venientem, sed in aestimatione decepti fuerunt; nam, cum primo vidissent a tergo exercitus bigas et sarcinas cum custodibus earum, qui cuneos jam ad bellum dispositos

been a deliberate stratagem by the royalists (Roger's intent was probably to highlight the arrogance of the French, who insisted on behaving in 'French fashion' rather than rely on English judgement) it illustrates the principle behind such ruses: raising many banners gave the impression that many men were at hand, which would intimidate the enemy and make them less inclined to stand and fight.

This appears to have been the intention behind the ruse employed by the 'yomen and swanys and pitaill [camp-followers]' who were left to guard the Scottish baggage train at Bannockburn (24 June 1314), as described by the poet John Barbour. Wishing to take part in the fighting, the guards raised sheets on poles 'in steid of baneris' and moved towards the battlefield in a body, shouting 'Sla! Sla! Apon thaim hastily!'. The English army, seeing them approach, thought that they were about to be attacked by 'sic a company [...] as that wes fechtand with thaim thar'. Barbour depicts this as the crucial point in the battle, causing the English morale to waver before a final charge (led by his hero, Robert Bruce, of course) broke them.[61]

The twelfth-century chronicler Ralph of Caen reports that this ruse was used by participants in the First Crusade at the siege of Antioch. As the Turkish ruler Karbughā's army approached to relieve the city in February 1098, the crusaders sent a force across the Iron Bridge to confront them, taking up position behind a small hill. The crusaders intimidated the Turks by 'affixing banners to their lances, one to each, as if there were as many divisions as there were banners'.[62] A similar incident, also from Outremer, was recorded by Guibert de Nogent. He reported that Baldwin I of Jerusalem exiled Gervais de Bazoches, lord of Tiberias, from the kingdom due to his 'insolence'.[63] Gervais departed Tiberias with only two knights, 'attended by many squires', when he was attacked by a large force of Muslims:

> Despairing of the number of his men, but constantly looking to God, cutting his shirt, which is called an 'under-tunic', he put it on a lance like a banner and ordered his men to do likewise. This being done, and having raised a battle-cry, they urged their horses on with their spurs, and

---

sequebantur, aestimaverunt unum esse per se exercitum, quia ibi multitudinem magnam cum vexillis micantibus inspexerunt; habuerunt enim singuli magnatum duo vexilla, unum, ut jam diximus, cum sarcinis a tergo remotius cuneos sequens, et aliud corpora singulorum praecedens, per quod cognoscerentur praelia conserentes; sicque comes Perticensis cum Mareschallo illusus ad socios remeavit incertus'.

[61] *Bruce*, Book 13, 225–309.

[62] GT, p. 55: 'Ipsum hoc simulantes, Christicolae hastas uexillis armant, singula singulis aptantes, quasi tot abderent agmina, quot proderent uexilla'.

[63] Guibert does not provide a date for this misadventure but, as Gervais was appointed to the lordship in 1106 and was executed in May 1108 after being captured by the Damascene Turks, we must assume it happened sometime between those two dates.

were carried into the enemies barring their way, who, being terrified by their unexpected daring, since they thought they were being followed by many cohorts, took flight and exposed themselves by withdrawing before those three.[64]

Gervais was victorious but, 'moved to repentance by God', he returned to Baldwin and threw himself on his mercy. While his stratagem appears to have been more makeshift than the one employed at Antioch, it was essentially the same plan, especially if one assumes that the *armigeri* were also equipped with fake banners. These two incidents underline the importance of performance in executing ruses, as previously discussed in relation to the feigned flight: it was not simply the display of the banners that deceived the enemy, it was the confidence with which the crusaders attacked that convinced the Muslims that they were facing a large and powerful force.

Banners were not the only means by which a small force could be made to seem large. On 16 February 1099, Raymond Pilet and Raymond, viscount of Turenne, detached themselves from the crusading army of Raymond of Saint-Gilles in order to attack the coastal city of Tortosa (mod. Tartūs, Syria). According to the *Gesta Francorum*, although they were unable to take it in the initial assault:

> when it was late in the day, they withdrew into a certain out-of-the-way spot, where they lodged; they made innumerable fires, as if the whole host was there. And the pagans, much frightened with dread, fled secretly in the night, and left the city full of all good things, which also has a most excellent port by the sea.[65]

Some of the descriptions of the battle of Ascalon (12 August 1099) suggest that the crusaders' army appeared much larger to the Egyptians because herds of animals had become intermingled with their formations. Fulcher of Chartres interpreted this as a miracle:

> See the aforesaid animals, on the right and left of the divisions, acting correctly, as if they had been commanded, advancing in step with them, although they are being driven by nobody: so that from a distance many

---

[64] GN, pp. 347–8: 'Qui suo diffidens numero, ad deum vero utcumque respectans, concisa camisia quam "subuculam" dicunt, hastae pro vexillo apposuit itidemque socios facere iussit. Fecerunt, et clamore sublato sonipedes calcaribus urgent obviosque feruntur in hostes, qui territi repentinis ausibus, dum estimant quod quasi previos sequerentur multae cohortes, fugam ineunt seque tribus illis cedendos exponunt'.

[65] GF, pp. 83–4: 'Sero autem iam facto, secesserunt in quemdam angulum, ibique hospitati sunt; feceruntque innumerabiles ignes, ita ut tota hostis esset ibi. Pagani uero timore perterriti nocte latenter fugerunt, et dimiserunt ciuitatem plenam omnibus bonis, quae etiam ualde optimum portum secus mare in se retinet'. See also RM, p. 854.

of the pagans, seeing them advancing with our men, reckoned that they were all an army of Franks.[66]

Albert of Aachen offered a more mundane interpretation, describing the animals as 'thunderstruck and amazed by the loud din'. Rather than acting as a separate division of the army, they became mixed up with the Franks: 'they advanced when they advanced, they stood when they stood, and by increasing the cloud of dust they struck fear in the Saracens'.[67] Both chroniclers are clear that the Egyptians were only deceived 'from a distance' (*a longe*) but the effect on their morale was believed to have been significant enough to be worthy of record.

Albert's reference to the great dust cloud raised by the herds at Ascalon is reminiscent of an incident recorded in Raymond of Aguilers's *Historia Francorum*. In June 1099, during the siege of Jerusalem, one Geldemar Carpinel was sent to collect supplies that had recently been landed at Jaffa. He was attacked near Ramla by a much larger force of Muslims and was on the verge of surrendering when a second force, commanded by Ramond Pilet, came to his rescue:

> But when our leaders, now greatly wearied from exhaustion rather than from fear, might have been willing to surrender, a cloud of dust being seen in the distance, the swift Raymond Pilet entered headlong into the fight, and so much dust was stirred up that the enemies believed a great many knights to be with him.[68]

It is noteworthy that all of these examples reportedly occurred on the First Crusade, the first major military encounter between Western Europeans and peoples of the Near East in the central Middle Ages. Some were caused by the geography: it is easier to raise a dust cloud during summer in Palestine than during winter in France. The ability to dupe enemies with false banners, however, may have been due to the Turks being unfamiliar with Western military custom. Westerners were unlikely to mistake a shirt tied to a lance for a banner (whatever John Barbour

---

[66] FC, pp. 313–14: 'videretis praedictam praedam tanquam monitu ducentium a dextra et laeva parte acierum gressum suum recte agere, licet a nemine minaretur: ita ut multi paganorum eam a longe cum militibus nostris euntem spectantes, totum aestimarent esse Francorum exercitum'.

[67] AA, p. 462: 'Vnde arrectis auribus stupefacti, et inmobiles diu persistentes tandem sociantur equitibus et peditibus, et sic armatis cuneis permixti, cum euntibus ibant, et cum stantibus stabant, ac nubem pulueris multiplicantes, Sarracenis rem ignorantibus sua multitudine copiosa a longe metum inferebant'. See also WT, pp. 435–6.

[68] RA, pp. 294–5: 'Sed dum nostri duces, jam magis fatigati ex lassitudine quam ex timore confecti, declinare vellent, cognito pulvere a longe Raimundus Pelet praeceps et festinus in pugnam intravit, atque tantum pulverem commovebat, ut crederent hostes cum eo plurimos esse milites'.

claimed) but, if this was the Turks' first encounter with a crusading force, they might have failed to make this distinction.

Marks of Distinction: Cries, Cognizances and Coats of Arms

If not trying to look like a non-combatant, or to make a few men look like many, disguises could also be used to make one combatant look like another. This begs the question of how medieval combatants were able to distinguish friend from foe in an age before standardised uniforms. This will, in turn, necessitate a discussion on heraldry, which first appeared in the twelfth century, and its practical function on the battlefield.

Some method of battlefield identification was clearly necessary, especially with the development of the great helm in the late twelfth century, which covered the wearer's entire head, rendering combatants practically anonymous. The problem of distinguishing one group of armoured men from another is aptly illustrated by an incident that occurred during King Stephen's siege of Baldwin de Redvers at Exeter in 1136. One of Baldwin's allies, Alred, son of Joel, arrived secretly at the siege with a band of knights, where they 'mingled with the king's knights under the appearance of aiding the king, for it was not possible, among so many wearing hauberks, to easily distinguish who was who'.[69] Sending messengers into the castle (as discussed in Chapter 2). Alred arranged for Baldwin's garrison to make a sally at a prearranged time. In the confusion, Alred's men were able to break away from the royal siege lines and enter the castle unhindered.[70]

A simple way of identifying oneself in battle was by shouting a distinctive word or phrase.[71] For example, Wace recorded the various battle-cries used by the commanders at Val-ès-Dunes (1047):

> As they spur their horses on, they shout out their particular war-cry: those from France shout '*Montjoie!*', it pleases them to hear that; William [the Conqueror] shouts: '*Deus aïe!*'; that's the war-cry of Normandy; Nigel [II, viscount of the Cotentin] cries: "*Saint Salveor*", that is the war-cry of his domain, and Ranulf [of Briquessart, viscount of the Bessin] shouts in a

---

[69] GS, pp. 37–9: 'Esoniamque cum fortissima militum manu frater illius latenter aduentans, inter regios milites (nec enim possible erat, inter tot loricatos, quis ille vel iste esset facile discernere), sub specie regem adjuuantium se commiscuit))'.

[70] If true, this incident would be another example of how lax security arrangements could be in a medieval army camp. One would have expected a newly arrived troop of knights to be at least questioned by somebody.

[71] Isabelle Guyot-Bachy, 'Cris et trompettes: Les Échos de la guerre chez les historiens et les chroniqueurs', in Didier Lett and Nicolas Offenstady (eds.), *Haro! Noël! Oyé! Pratiques du cri au Moyen Âge* (Paris, 2003), pp. 103–16, at pp. 109–13.

loud voice: '*Saint Saveir, sire Saint Saveir!*', and Haimo Longtooth [lord of Torigny] goes forward calling: '*Saint Amant, sire Saint Amant!*'[72]

It is noteworthy that the word translated above as 'battle cry' (*enseigne*) could also be used to mean a banner, standard or any sign or token, emphasising its purpose as a means of identification.[73] The French use of '*Montjoie*' can be traced back at least as far back as the Oxford *Chanson de Roland*: '[Oliver] does not want to forget Charles's war-cry, "*Munjoie!*" he cries, high and clear'.[74]

Unsurprisingly, some enterprising individuals adopted their enemy's war-cry in order to deceive them. Orderic Vitalis relates how in 1119 a certain Ascelin, son of Andrew, wishing to revenge himself upon Geoffrey, archbishop of Rouen, who had seized some of his land, approached Louis VI of France with a promise to betray the Norman town of Andely.[75] Ascelin was given a band of 'most valiant men' (*probissimos satellites*), whom he introduced into Andely, hiding them under some straw in his storehouse. The next day, as Louis's army approached the town gate:

> But those who had been lying under the straw suddenly rushed forth and, shouting the royal war-cry of the English together with the commoners, ran to the citadel; but, once they were inside, they changed to crying '*Meum gaudium!*', which is the French war-cry.[76]

Marjorie Chibnall is almost certainly correct to identify the phrase '*Meum gaudium*' as a translation of the vernacular '*Montjoie*', presumably mistaking *mont* for *mon*.[77] Note also the similarity between the Latin *signum* and the Old French *enseigne*: both can mean sign, banner or war-cry, depending

---

[72] RdR, vol. 3, lines 3877–950: 'si com poignent criant vont / itels enseignes com il ont. / Cil de France crient: "Montjoie" / ceo lor est bel que l'en les oie; / Guillame crie: "Deus aïe" / c'est l'enseigne de Normendie; / Neel crie "Saint Salveor!" / ceo est l'enseigne de s'enor, / e Ranof crie o grant poeir: "Saint Saveir, sire Saint Saveir" / e Ham as Denz vait reclamant: "Saint Amant, sire Saint Amant"'.

[73] 'enseigne', *Anglo-Norman Dictionary: Online Edition*, <http://www.anglo-norman.net/D/enseigne> [Accessed 07 Jun 2018].

[74] Gerald J. Brault (ed.), *The Song of Roland: An Analytical Edition* (2 vols, University Park, PA, 1978), lines 1973–4: '*L'enseigne Carle n'i volt mie ublier, / Munjoie escriet e haltement e cler*'. For a study of the use of '*Munjoie*' in the chanson, see Julian Harris, '*Munjoie* and *Reconuisance* in *Chanson de Roland*, *l. 3620*', *Romance Philology*, 10 (1956), 168–73.

[75] Andely, the future site of Château Gaillard, was a site of major strategic importance on the Franco-Norman frontier. The archbishops of Rouen had a fortified manor there: OV, vol. 6, p. 216 n. 2.

[76] OV, vol. 6, p. 217: '*Latitantes uero sub stramine subito proruperunt, et regale signum Anglorum cum plebe uociferantes ad munitionem cucurrerunt; sed ingressi "Meum gaudium" quod Francorum signum est uersa uice clamauerunt*'.

[77] OV, vol. 6, p. 217.

on the context.⁷⁸ Orderic's use of the phrase 'royal war-cry of the English', rather than 'the Normans', can be explained by the fact that the citadel of Andely was held at that time by Richard of Lincoln, an illegitimate son of Henry I of England, who was permitted to depart, together with his garrison, after the assault.⁷⁹

Peter of Les Vaux-de-Cernay, a chronicler and participant in the Albigensian Crusade, records that Peter-Roger, the lord of Cabaret, used a similar ruse in 1210 to escape from Simon de Monfort's men after a failed attempt to burn their siege engines in a night raid: 'likewise they might have captured the lord of Cabaret, Peter-Roger, two or three times, but he began to cry out with our men, "Montfort! Montfort!" out of fear, as if he were one of us'.⁸⁰ Peter reports a grim sequel to this incident that occurred after a crusader victory at Castelnaudary in 1211. The crusaders, upon capturing one of the fleeing enemy, forced them to kill one of the other fugitives to prove their identity, only to kill the captive regardless.⁸¹ This suggests that there was another way for the crusaders to identify their enemies, perhaps their appearance or the fact that the enemy spoke Occitan, unlike the crusaders, who mostly came from northern France. By contrast, it would have been much easier to pass men from the Ile-de-France for French-speaking Anglo-Normans, as Orderic claimed happened at Andely.

This form of disguise could work just as easily the other way, of course: shouting out false information to confuse or misdirect the enemy. As described above, Aelred of Rievaulx claimed that the English army was rallied at the Battle of the Standard when somebody held up a severed head, (falsely) shouting that the king of Scotland had been killed.⁸² A similar, if less gruesome, ruse reportedly saved Richard I of England from being captured in a skirmish outside Jaffa in September 1191. Richard and his men had gone out ahead of the main army and pursued a band of Turkish horsemen into an ambush. Richard was in danger of being captured when:

> one of the king's companions, named William of Préaux, cried out, shouting out in the Saracen language that he was the *melech*, that is 'king' in Latin, and the Turks, believing him, capturing that William, immediately led him away as a captive to their army.⁸³

---

[78] Charlton T. Lewis and Charles Short, *A Latin Dictionary* (Oxford, 1879), pp. 1697–8.
[79] OV, vol. 6, p. 217.
[80] HA, pp. 171–2: 'dominum etiam Cabareti, P. Rogerii, bis vel ter cepissent, sed ipse cum nostris cepit clamare "Mons Fortis, Mons Fortis" pre timore, ac si noster esset, sicque evadens et fugiens per montana, non nisi post duos dies rediit Cabaretum'.
[81] HA, pp. 270–1.
[82] See Chapter 2.
[83] IP, p. 287: 'Sed ecce, confuso certamine contendentibus, exclamavit unus sociorum

William's capture is also reported by Roger of Howden, although without any reference to a deception.[84] This act of self-sacrifice made an impression on the Muslim chroniclers too. Ibn al-Athīr describes how one of Richard's companions 'sacrificed himself' during the skirmish, allowing the king to escape, while Bahā al-Dīn says that the man was actually killed by a lance thrust intended for Richard.[85] Al-Ifahānī claims that Richard was fighting in disguise (*incognito*) and that the knight who saved him attracted the Turks' attention not with words but 'the beauty of his garments'.[86] The *Itinerarium*'s account is not implausible, however. William of Préaux, a Norman, was a member of Richard's household prior to the crusade but it is conceivable that he could have acquired a few words or phrases in Arabic during his three months in Outremer.[87] Richard was evidently grateful to

---

regis nomine Willelmus de Pratellis, idiomate Saracenio vociferans se esse Melech, quod Latine dicitur rex, quod Turci credentes confestim ipsum Willelmum comprehensum ad exercitum suum deduxerunt captivum'. See also Ambroise, lines 7083–175. *Mālik* is the Arabic for 'king'.

[84] HowChr, vol. 3, p. 133: 'Sed Willelmus de Pratellis, quidam familiaris suus, ibidem captus fuit, et Reginaldus socius ejus interfectus est, et unus destrariorum regis ibidem captus fuit, et ductor illius interfectus, et rex per vim evasit'.

[85] Ibn al-Athīr, *Chronicle for the Crusading Period from al-Kamil fi'l-ta'rikh*, trans. D. S. Richards (3 vols, Aldershot, 2006–8), vol. 2, p. 392; Bahā al-Dīn Ibn Shaddād, *The Rare and Excellent History of Saladin or al-Nawadir al-Sultaniyya wa'l-Mahasin al-Yusufiyya*, trans. D. S. Richards (Aldershot, 2002), pp. 181–2.

[86] 'Imād ad-Dīn al-Ifahānī, *Conquête de la Syrie et de la Palestine par Saladin (al-Fath al-qussî fi l-fath al-qudsî)*, trans. Henri Massé (Paris, 1972), p. 347: 'par la beauté de son vêtement, il attira l'attention de celui qui s'en prenait au roi, de sorte que cet homme ne s'occupa plus que de lui et le fit prisonnier'.

[87] William, son of Osbert, lord of Préaux, appears to have followed a parallel, if less exalted, career path to that of William Marshal. He actually appears in the *History of William Marshal*, together with four of his brothers, competing at a tournament at Lagny-sur-Marne (c. 1179) as part of the retinue of Henry the Young King. HWM, lines 4662–74. As mentioned above, he was a member of Richard I's household prior to the Third Crusade, witnessing royal charters at Geddington (Sept. 1189) and Canterbury (Dec. 1189) alongside another de Préaux brother, Roger, a royal steward: Lionel Landon, *The Itinerary of King Richard I* (London, 1935), pp. 17, 20. According to the Colbert-Fontainebleau version of *L'Estoire de Eracles*, William acted as Richard's envoy to Isaac Komnenos upon his arrival on Cyprus: *The Conquest of Jerusalem and the Third Crusade: Sources in Translation*, trans. Peter W. Edbury (Farnham, 1996), pp. 176–7. William remained in royal service under John, playing a key role in the defence of Normandy in 1204, where he remained following the French conquest. In October 1215 he relocated to England, where John courted his support during the First Barons' War with marriage to the heiress of Coleby and other land grants: S. D. Church, *The Household Knights of King John* (Cambridge, 1999), p. 27; S. D. Church, 'The Rewards of Royal Service in the Household of King John: A Dissenting Opinion', *English Historical Review*, 110 (1995), 277–302, at pp. 299–302.

him: Ambroise and the *Itinerarium* both record that he exchanged ten Turkish nobles for William's freedom.[88]

These verbal signs had several crucial drawbacks as a means of identification: they might not be heard, especially over the other sounds of battle, they did not protect against unforeseen attacks (you cannot warn a potential friend not to attack if you do not see them coming) and, as we have seen, they were easily imitated by the enemy. A clear visual signifier was obviously preferable, yet it is not always clear how medieval combatants used such visual tokens. Even with the development of heraldry in the late twelfth century, it is debatable what precise function it served on the battlefield.

The banner, or standard, was one means of visual identification on the battlefield, usually carried on behalf of a prince or great lord. It functioned as a symbol of the leader's presence: if the banner fell, it signified their death or retreat. It also served as a rallying point for their troops, to be followed and defended in the melee. As Robert W. Jones has argued, if such banners were to function as recognisable symbols, their designs would have had to remain consistent over a substantial length of time.[89] Like other means of identification, a banner could be employed as a disguise: we have already seen how raising additional banners could give the impression that more troops were present than there actually were. In December 1216, the royalist garrison of Berkhamsted Castle in Hertfordshire was besieged by baronial forces who had given their support to Louis the Lion, future king of France. During a sally, they captured the banner of one William de Mandeville. The same day, they attacked the besiegers' camp again, this time flying the captured banner.[90] The aim here does not appear to have been to pass for Mandeville himself (who was presumably still present at the siege) but simply to create confusion and disorder in the camp. A more explicit, and successful, attempt to pass for another force with captured banners reportedly occurred at the battle of Evesham (4 August 1265). According to the chronicler Walter of Guisborough, Edward, prince of Wales, approached the town from three sides, hoping to trap Simon de Montfort's force there, while flying the banners which he had captured from Montfort's son (also Simon) at Kenilworth the day before:

---

[88] IP, p. 440; Amb, lines 12257–70.
[89] Robert W. Jones, 'Identifying the Warrior on the Pre-Heraldic Battlefield', in C. P. Lewis (ed.), *Anglo-Norman Studies XXX: Proceedings of the Battle Conference 2007* (Woodbridge, 2008), pp. 154–67, at p. 158); Robert W. Jones, '"What banner thine?" The Banner as Symbol of Identification, Status and Authority on the Battlefield', *Haskins Society Journal*, 15 (2004), 101–9, at pp. 104–5.
[90] RW, vol. 4, p. 5.

And when the earl's scout, Nicholas, a barber who was an expert in the knowledge of arms, had seen the armed men coming from a distance, he said to the earl: 'See! Many armed men are coming from the north and, as can be recognised from a distance, they carry your banners'. And he said: 'It is my son; do not be afraid, but go and look around, lest perhaps we be caught, having been surrounded'.[91]

Nicholas climbed the bell tower of Evesham Abbey to look again. It was only then that he saw Edward and his allies flying their true banners, causing him to cry out to Montfort: 'We are all dead men!' (*Mortui sumus omnes*). We can assume that Edward raised his own banners once he felt sure that Montfort could no longer escape.

Another incident involving Simon de Montfort and banners occurred at the battle of Lewes (14 May 1264). It is an instructive example of how tales grow in the telling and the same incident could be interpreted in a variety of ways. Montfort had broken his leg in December 1263 and, although he fought on horseback at Lewes, he had been forced to travel long distances in a cart.[92] This cart, which was decorated with Montfort's banners, was left with the baggage during the fighting. When Prince Edward's division broke through the London militia, who were fighting for Montfort, they set about pillaging the baggage:

> And seeing a cart upon the plain, which had been made for earl Simon to ride, standing with the horses and without driver or guide for the road, they galloped up and tore it to pieces in a moment; and they also slew two burgesses [of London] with the sword, whom they found within it.[93]

The presence of the cart, and the death of the two burgesses, who had hidden themselves inside for safety, was subsequently interpreted by other chroniclers as some kind of stratagem. Thomas Wykes, a chronicler sympathetic to the royalist cause, described it this way:

> Therefore [the Londoners] abandoned the earl of Leicester's four-horse cart, to which he had dishonourably fixed his banner, if one may rightly say so, in order that it might be thought that he was lying quiet in there, as if he were powerless or sick. Certain citizens of London had been placed in there

---

[91] WG, p. 200: 'Cumque vidisset speculator comitis, Nicholaus scilicet barbitonsor eius qui homo expertus erat in cognicione armatorum, armatos sic a longe venientes dixit ad comitem: "Ecce veniunt armati multi a septentrione et, vt cognosci potest a longe, apparent vexilla tuorum". Et ille, "Filius meus est; ne timeas, sed vade et circumspice ne forte preocupemur circumuenti"'.

[92] For Montfort's breaking his leg, see 'Annales de Dunstaplia,' in Henry Richard Luard (ed.), *Annales monastici*, RS, 36 (5 vols, London, 1869), vol. 3, pp. 3–408, at p. 227.

[93] WG, p. 195: 'Et videntes sui in planicie currum, quem fieri fecerat comes Symon ad equitandum, stantem cum equis absque aurgia vel duce itineris, cucurrerunt et quasi in momento dilacerauerunt eum; duos etiam burgenses, quos inuenerunt in eo, gladio peremerunt'. See also FH, II, pp. 495–96.

[...] who, in order not to seem faithless to their lord king, had refused to put on their hauberks, in order that [Montfort] might abandon them to be victims of either the formidable or the faithless.[94]

The anonymous author of the *Chronicle of Melrose* also depicted this incident as a deliberate ruse but portrayed it as an admirable display of Montfort's cunning:

> So Simon ordered his banners, which are called penons, to be hung around the cart, so that the king and the army might be fooled into believing that Simon was in the cart, which Simon was not. However Simon was then hiding in a wooded spot, since it was surrounded on all sides by mountains and steep cliffs.[95]

In this account, the cart becomes a lure that draws the royalist army into a trap. The citizens are not killed but, by the time the royalists realised their mistake, the ambush has already been sprung.[96] The chronicler defends Montfort for using the burgesses in this way:

> So he carried them off justly. He did not, by means of the cart, betray those two native enemies who, out of madness, wished to prevent the city of London (which is greater than all the carts and towers of Christendom) from giving aid to the barons, since without the city's excellent and most powerful aid, they could not have expelled the foreigners on account of the king's power, which had beset them from all sides.[97]

As in other cases where chroniclers explicitly excuse the conduct of their subjects, it indicates that not all contemporaries approved of Montfort's actions.

During the crusader siege of Acre (1189–91), Saladin was able to send supplies and reinforcements to the garrison on ships, which he disguised

---

[94] TW, vol. 4, pp. 150–1: 'Relinquentes igitur quadrigam comitis Leycestriae, cui vexillum suum, si fas sit dicere, minus honeste infixerat, ut putaretur in eo quiescere tanquam impotens vel aegrotus, impositis in ea quibusdam civibus Londoniae viz. Augustino de Hadestok, Ricardo Pycard, Stephano de Chelmareford, qui ne viderentur infidi contra dominum regem loricas induere recusabant, ut eos tanquam formidolosos vel infidos exponeret ad victimam'.

[95] CM, p. 193: 'In giro ergo illius currus vexillula sua, que pensilia nominantur, Simon fecit appendi, ut per ea deluderetur rex et exercitus ejus dum putarent Simonem esse in curru, in quo non erat Simon. Erat autem Simon tunc delitescens in locis nemorosis, montibus et rupibus prearduis undique circumobsessis'.

[96] Compare William of Apulia and others removing the violent elements from the Dudo's story of the 'fake corpse' ruse in order to present their subject in a better light.

[97] CM, p. 195: 'Juste ergo tradidit, non prodidit pene duos contradictores indigenas per currum, qui civitatem omnibus Christianismi curribus et turribus meliorem, Londonicam loquor urbem, voluerunt alienando avertere a succursu baronum, cum sine tante civitatis eximio et permaximo auxilio, expulsionem alienorum nullatenus facere potuissent, propter potestatem regiam, que undique eos circumvallavit'.

in a variety of ingenious ways. According to Bahā al-Dīn: 'A number of Muslims boarded the buss in Beirut and dressed up as Franks, even shaving their beards. They also placed pigs on the deck, so that they could be seen from a distance, and flew crosses'.[98] This corresponds with the *Itinerarium Peregrinorum*'s claim that Muslim ships were able to intermingle with the crusaders' because they were 'furnished with both Christian language and Christian insignia'.[99] Roger of Howden reported that Richard I of England encountered a large Saracen ship off the coast of Cyprus in June 1191 'decorated with the banners of the king of France and his allies'.[100] Richard ordered the crew to join his fleet but they shot arrows at his messenger, leading to a brief sea battle in which the Muslim ship was sunk. This encounter is mentioned in other chronicles but none of them mention the Muslims flying French banners.[101] The *Itinerarium* directly contradicts Howden on this point, claiming that, when Richard came close enough to inspect the ship, he 'did not hear any French language, nor see any Christian sign or banner, that made him believe their answer [that it was a French ship]'.[102] Whether this particular ship was sailing under 'false colours' or not is unclear but the incident does illustrate the use of banners in the medieval West as markers of identity, as well as agreeing with Bahā al-Dīn's more general observation about Muslim ships 'flying crosses' to disguise themselves.

In land warfare, a banner could be used to locate a significant individual or to identify them and their followers from a distance. Combatants could also adopt signs and symbols to mark them out as individuals or members of a particular group. This practice was not exclusive to medieval Europe, of course, but the discussion is complicated by the appearance of heraldry in the late twelfth century. Simply put, heraldry refers to the use of unique devices, known as 'coats of arms', or simply 'arms', that individuals used to decorate their shields. What distinguishes 'true' heraldry from other forms of historical battlefield identification is an adherence to a system, the 'science' of blazon, governing the colours and symbols displayed on the shield, and the heritability of arms: the passing of the same coat of arms from one generation of a family to the next. In this sense, 'true'

---

[98] Baha al-Din, *History*, p. 124.

[99] IP, pp. 91–2: 'Interdum vero Gentilium classis nostrae furtim permixta procedit; et tam lingua quam insignibus Christicolarum mentita paratus, inopinos et subitos ad urbem cursus subducit'.

[100] HowChr, vol. 3, p. 112: 'Et crastino, scilicet feria sexta in hebdomada Pentecosten, cum ipse iter ageret versus Accon, vidit in mari ante se busciam quandam magnam, onustam viris bellicosis, et ornatam vexillis regis Franciae et sociorum suorum'.

[101] Baha al-Din, *History*, p. 151; Ibn al-Athir, *Chronicle*, p. 387; RC, p. 32; RD, pp. 93–4.

[102] IP, pp. 205–6: 'Quam cum responso reddito didicisset regis esse Franciae, rex in impetu ferventissimo eo versus appropians, nec Francorum idioma, vel aliquod signum vel vexillum attendit Christianorum, quod eorum responso faceret fidem'.

heraldry did not fully emerge until the mid-thirteenth century. Although many heraldic devices first appeared prior to 1200, Michel Pastoureau has deemed the period between 1000 and 1250 as an age of 'proto-heraldry'. It contained many of the features that would come to define 'true' heraldry but lacked certain crucial elements, particularly the transmission of coats of arms within families.[103]

Developments in military technology between 1000 and 1200 afforded combatants greater scope for martial display. The use of the couched lance, which was decorated with a small flag or pennant, the adoption of surcoats and caparisons, which covered both man and horse, and the disappearance of the shield boss all provided additional space for decoration.[104] Individual noblemen took to displaying distinctive devices on their shields, which were in turn carried by members of their household, the low-born knights, as a sign of loyalty but also to stake their claim to be considered part of the chivalric 'class'.[105] By the end of the thirteenth century, possession of a coat of arms became one of the defining characteristics of the medieval nobility.[106] Note that, from the very beginning of the period, heraldic devices and their informal antecedents were the preserve of the mounted elite. As we shall see below, the very act of bearing these symbols would have marked an individual as a member of the elite who was worth ransoming.

Heraldry is actually a pretty poor system of distinguishing friend from foe. The individual combatant would be unlikely to recognise more than a handful of blazons among the dozens, if not hundreds, on a single battlefield, let alone use them to identify their enemies.[107] The system soon

---

[103] Jones, 'Identifying the Warrior', p. 165; Maurice Keen, *Chivalry* (New Haven, CT, 1984), pp. 125–34; Michel Pastoureau, 'L'Apparition des armoiries en Occident: État du problème', *Bibliothèque de l'école des chartes*, 134 (1976), 281–300, at p. 291; Michel Pastoureau, 'La Diffusion de armoiries et les débuts de l'héraldique', in Robert-Henri Bautier (ed.), *La France de Philippe Auguste: Le Temps des mutations* (Paris, 1982), pp. 737–60, at pp. 747–9.

[104] Adrian Ailes, 'The Knight, Heraldry and Armour: The Role of Recognition and the Origins of Heraldry', in Christopher Harper-Bill and Ruth Harvey (eds.) *Medieval Knighthood IV: Papers from the Fifth Strawberry Hill Conference 1990* (Woodbridge, 1992), pp. 1–21, at pp. 14–15; see also Pastoureau, 'L'Apparition', p. 287.

[105] Ailes, 'Knight, Heraldry and Armour', p. 18; Pastoureau, 'La Diffusion', p. 754.

[106] Keen, *Chivalry*, p. 128.

[107] There is some evidence that recognising coats of arms was part of a nobleman's education, certainly in the later Middle Ages. During the famous Scrope v Grosvenor case of 1386, in which two English noble families both claimed the right to a particular coat of arms, a certain Sir Robert Laton, 'fifty two years old, armed thirty two years', was called as a witness for Scrope. He stated that, in addition to the numerous times he had seen the Scropes bearing those specific arms on campaign, his elderly father had 'commanded him to write in a *cédule* all the arms which he had learned from his ancestors, which he knew and remembered belonged to kings, princes, dukes, counts, barons, lords, knights and esquires', which included the Scrope arms. *Cédule* may

became so complex that a new profession, the herald, had to be created to regulate it.[108] Yet the medieval nobility certainly wore their coats of arms into battle. Their function, as Jones and Fergus Cannan have both argued, was not to separate friend from foe but to announce the bearer's presence to both:

> Whilst historians have tended to focus on the dangers of being recognised by your enemies on the battlefield, in cultural terms it was desirable. It gave the warrior the honour of being a target, of gaining greater honour and prestige through feats of arms.[109]

This provided fertile ground for new forms of deception: discarding one's arms or dressing others in them made for an effective disguise.

Identifying these deceptions in the Latin sources is difficult, however, as the chroniclers usually use the highly generic term *arma*, which can mean any sort of military equipment, for 'coats of arms'. In his description of Louis VI of France's siege of the Norman town of Breteuil in 1119, Orderic Vitalis describes how the captain of the Norman garrison, Ralph the Breton, 'hurried from gate to gate, frequently changing his *arma* to avoid recognition'.[110] This ruse proved deadly for an unnamed Flemish knight in the French host: 'He rushed upon the unconquerable Breton in his usual way as if he were a commoner and soon fell, fatally wounded from the blows he gave him'.[111] It is highly unlikely, at this early date, that Orderic was referring to Ralph wearing a coat of arms. It is more probable

---

mean a schedule, a register or any other sort of writing: perhaps a reference to a roll of arms. This evidence should not be taken too far, however. Laton is the only person in the entire deposition to mention a *cédule* of this kind, so this may have been a particular passion or eccentricity of his father's. Most of the other witnesses simply refer to hearing about the Scrope arms from older knights, suggesting a predominantly oral tradition. Nicholas Harris Nicolas, *The Controversy between Sir Ricahrd Scrope and Sir Robert Grosvenor in the Court of Chivalry A.D. MCCCLXXXV – MCCCXC* (2 vols, London, 1832), vol. I, p. 110–11.

[108] For the history and development of the herald, see Richard Barber, 'Heralds and the Court of Chivalry: From Collective Memory to Formal Institutions', in Anthony Musson and Nigel Ramsay (eds.), *Courts of Chivalry and Admiralty in Late Medieval Europe* (Woodbridge, 2018), pp. 15–28; Robert Jones, 'Heraldry and Heralds', in Robert W. Jones and Peter Coss (eds.), *A Companion to Chivalry* (Woodbridge, 2019), pp. 139–59, at pp. 154–7.

[109] Robert W. Jones, *Bloodied Banners: Martial Display on the Medieval Battlefield* (Woodbridge, 2010), p. 27; see also Fergus Cannan, 'The Myths of Medieval Heraldry', *Nottingham Medieval Studies*, 47 (2003), 198–216, at pp. 212–13.

[110] OV, vol. 6, p. 246: 'Insignis Radulfus de porta ad portam discurrebat et arma sepe ne cognoscentur mutabat'.

[111] OV, vol. 6, p. 246–8: 'Inuictum Britonem ut quempiam plebeium solito more occurrit, et mox ab eo letaliter percussus cecidit et coram multis captus post xv dies in carcere Britolii expirauit'.

that Ralph was varying the kind and quality of arms he wore: if he had been wearing little armour, or armour of a poor quality, it would explain why the Fleming mistook him for a poor member of the *plebs*.

Wearing expensive equipment was in itself a significant visual identifier, one that distinguished a member of the knightly class, worthy of capture and ransom, from the common foot soldier, who could be ignored or killed with impunity.[112] We have already observed how discarding one's armour could act as a disguise. In the *Gesta Stephani*, following the rout at Winchester in 1141, the Empress Matilda's supporters are described as follows: 'Indeed, what should I say about the knights and the greatest barons who, when they had cast aside all marks of knighthood [*militandi insigna*], gave false names and fled, on foot and without honour'.[113] As with Ralph the Breton, it is unlikely that *insigna* refers to coats of arms at this early date. It is more likely, particularly combined with the reference to travelling on foot, a reference to the equipment that marked them out as *milites*, such as horse and hauberk, or some sort of field sign or cognizance (see p. 120).

In thirteenth-century sources, however, it is more probable that *arma* refers to a heraldic device.[114] On 1 April 1234, Richard Marshal was killed at a parley on the Curragh Plain in Kildare with his enemies, led by Maurice, justiciar of Ireland. According to Roger of Wendover, a great partisan of Marshal's, the attackers 'gave their arms to knights who were unknown and very strong, whom they had assembled there to kill that innocent man; in this way, desiring to kill him, they would not be seen to have killed him'.[115] During the fighting, Marshal challenged a knight 'to whom Richard de Burgh had given his arms', believing that he was Richard himself.[116] These references may refer to the actual armour and

---

[112] Moffat's study, although concerned with the later Middle Ages, is very instructive on this point: Ralph Moffat, 'The Importance of Being Harnest: Armour, Heraldry and Recognition in the Melee', in Lorna Bleach and Keira Borrill (eds.) *Battle and Bloodshed: The Medieval World at War* (Newcastle upon Tyne, 2013), pp. 5–24.

[113] GS, p. 134: 'Quid loquar de militibus immo et de summis baronibus, qui omnibus militandi abiectis insigniis, pedites et inhonori, nomen suum et fugam mentiebantur'.

[114] The earliest unequivocal use of *arma* to mean 'coat of arms' identified by the compilers of the *Dictionary of Medieval Latin from British Sources* is from the Pipe Rolls, dated to 1237: R. E. Latham and D. R. Howlett, 'arma', *Dictionary of Medieval Latin from British Sources* (3 vols, Oxford, 1975–2013), vol. 1, p. 216.

[115] RW, vol. 4, p. 304: 'Proceres autem Hiberniae, audaciam Marescalli ac probitatem metuentes, arma sua militibus fortissmis tradiderant et ignotis, quos ad hoc conduxerant, ut perimerent innocentem; sic eum occidere cupientes, ut non occidisse viderentur'.

[116] RW, vol. 4, p. 305: 'Indignatus autem, hoc viso, miles quidam ut gigas fortissimus, cui Richardus de Burgo arma sua tradiderat, ut Marescallum occideret, impetum fecit in eum, volens galeam de capite ejus evellere truculenter; quem videns Marescallus existimabat quod esset Richardus de Burgo'.

weaponry but, as they were used to identify (or misidentify) an individual, equally they may refer to coats of arms.

Heraldry gave rise to the peculiarly medieval practice of kings and other important noblemen entering battle wearing another individual's coat of arms or dressing one or more of their bodyguards in identical blazons to misdirect the enemy.[117] At the battle of Courtrai (11 July 1302), for example, the Flemish commander Willem van Jülich dressed his servant, Jan Laminc, in his arms so that he could withdraw from the field and rest without the enemy or his own men becoming aware of it.[118]

The Anonymous of Béthune reports a peculiar example of a nobleman wearing another's arms in their account of the battle of Bouvines (27 July 1214): 'Odo, the duke of Burgundy, wore the coat of arms of the good knight William of Barres, but he bore his own shield. Know that [William] did such feats of arms that people spoke well of him as far away as Syria'. [119] It is unclear why Odo chose to wear William's arms or why he confused matters by carrying his own shield. The two had very different blazons: Odo's seal depicts him with a shield *bendy, a bordure*, while William's shows a shield *lozengy*.[120] Jones has suggested that this was a form of 'Batesian mimicry', similar to an animal evolving to match the appearance of a more dangerous species, with Odo attempting to 'awe his opponents' by adopting the guise of William, a famous warrior and crusader.[121] The real William was also present at Bouvines, fighting in King Philip's division in his capacity as the king's seneschal, so it may be that this stratagem was intended to confuse the enemy, making this fearsome knight appear to be in multiple places at once.[122]

Wearing the arms of a less distinguished individual might make somebody a less tempting target for capture but it brought the risk of being killed

---

[117] This latter ruse appears frequently in the fourteenth century and beyond. John II of France went into battle at Poitiers (19 September 1356) with twenty knights dressed in his arms. Henry V of England made do with only two doppelgangers at Agincourt (25 October 1415): M. Prinet, 'Séance du 15 décembre: Présidence de M. M. Prou, président', *Bulletin de la société nationale des antiquaires de France*, (1909), 363–9, at p. 368.

[118] J. F. Verbruggen, *The Battle of the Golden Spurs: Courtrai, 11 July 1302*, ed. Kelly DeVries, trans. David Richard Ferguson, rev edn (Woodbridge, 2002), pp. 107, 234.

[119] 'Chronique française des rois de France par un anonyme de Béthune', in Léopold Delisle (ed.), *Recueil des historiens des Gaules et de la France* (24 vols, Paris, 1840–1904), vol. 24, pp. 750–76, at p. 769: 'Oedes, li dus de Borgoigne, qui la cote à armer Guillaume des Barres le boen chevalier avoit vestie, mais il portoit son meisme escu. Sachiés qu'il i fist tant d'armes qu'il en fu parlé en bien dusqu'en la terre de Surie'.

[120] Sadly, the seals do not preserve the tinctures: Douët D'Arcq, *Collection de sceaux* (3 vols, Paris, 1863), vol. 1, pp. 337, 467.

[121] Jones, *Bloodied Banners*, p. 27.

[122] Georges Duby, *The Legend of Bouvines: War, Religion and Culture in the Middle Ages*, trans. Catherine Tihanyi (Berkeley, CA, 1990), pp. 24, 40.

out of hand. On 12 September 1213, Peter II of Aragon was killed fighting against the crusading forces of Simon de Montfort at the battle of Muret. All the major chronicles of the Albigensian Crusade mention the battle but only Peter of Les Vaux-de-Cernay, a staunch apologist for Montfort and the crusaders, claims that the king died because he was not recognised:

> in that combat the king of the Aragonese lay dead and many Aragonese with him: for he, a very arrogant man, had stationed himself in the second division, when kings are always accustomed to be in the very rear; moreover, he had changed his arms and had dressed himself in another's arms.[123]

The implication is clear: if the king had conformed to tradition and fought in his proper place, in his own arms, then the crusaders would have recognised him and spared his life.[124] On some occasions, however, the opposite ran true. At the battle of Mons-en-Pévèle (18 August 1304), Philip IV of France only survived a surprise attack on his camp by the Flemish army because the Flemings were 'unable to distinguish him among the fallen because, in the peril of the combat, the aforesaid guards had torn off his coat of arms, which was decorated with his sign, namely lilies, out of fear, so that he would not be recognised by the enemies'.[125]

Heraldic arms made the great and the powerful stand out on the battlefield but, for the purpose of distinguishing friend from foe, medieval combatants appear to have employed a more informal system of field signs or 'cognizances' (OF: *conoissances*). It is often difficult to tell exactly what form these took, especially in early texts. Scholars have tended to interpret the term as another way of describing shield devices.[126] This may have been true in some cases but the term appears to have a broader meaning, one

---

[123] HA, pp. 153–4: 'in quo congressu rex Arragonum occubuit et multi Aragonenses cum eo: ipse enim, utpote superbissimus, in secunda acie se posuerat, cum reges semper esses soleant in extrema; in super arma sua mutaverat armisque se induerat alienis'.

[124] A similar fate befell Manfred of Sicily at Benevento (26 February 1266), Charles I of Hungary (10 November 1330) and Anthony of Brabant at Agincourt (25 October 1415). Prinet, 'Séance', pp. 366–68; Anne Curry (ed.), *The Battle of Agincourt: Sources and Interpretations* (Woodbridge, 2000), p. 174.

[125] AG, p. 71: 'nesciens ipsum inter alios prostratos discernere, eo quod custodes predicti in periculo conflictus pre timore supertunicale suum bellicum, suo signo, scilicet liliorum, decoratum, ne ab hostibus, qui libentius ipsum quam aliquem alium occidissent, agnosceretur, abruperant'.

[126] Ailes, 'Knight, Heraldry and Armour', p. 12; Gerard J. Brault, *Early Blazon: Heraldic Terminology in the Twelfth and Thirteenth Centuries with Special Reference to Arthurian Literature* (Oxford, 1972), pp. 147–8; L. Bouly de Lesdain, 'Etudes historiques sur le XIIe siècle', *Annuaire du conseil heraldique de France*, 20 (1907), 185–244, at p. 196; Victor Shirling, *Die Verteidigungswaffen im altfranzösischen Epos* (Marburg, 1887), p. 21.

that encompassed a variety of signs and marks.[127] Consider Alexander's stratagem to retake Windsor Castle in Chrétien de Troye's *Cligés*:

> 'Let's change our *conuissances*,' he said, 'Let's take the shields and lances from the traitors whom we have killed. Let's go to the castle in this way, so that the traitors inside will believe that we are their men, and whatever they deserve, the gates will be opened for us. And do you know what we'll give them in return? We will kill or capture all of them, if God wills it'.[128]

The shields are part of the disguise but they are given equal standing with the lances, which are presumably painted in specific colours or are decorated with distinctive penons, as necessary *conuissances* to deceive the garrison.

Wace describes the Norman army making *conoissances* on the day of the Battle of Hastings (1066): 'they had all made *conoissances*, that one Norman would know another, that they would not attack each other, that Norman would not kill Norman, nor one Norman strike another'.[129] This was clearly an informal, last-minute act and is unlikely to refer to painting specific devices on shields. Wace makes another illuminating reference to cognizances in his *Roman de Brut*. The British princes Belin and Brenne, having suffered a reverse in a battle against the Romans, prepare their army to make a counterattack: 'They made most of their men, and the best of them, dismount from their horses and ordered and arranged them in the middle of the field on foot. They had broken their lances in two and discarded their *conuissances*'.[130] The lances are presumably broken in order to wield them more effectively on foot but why discard their cognizances? We can assume that Wace did not mean that they dropped their shields, as this would have been suicidal. It is more likely that the act of discarding the cognizances, which marked them out as men worth sparing for ransom, in combination with dismounting to fight on foot,

---

[127] Derived from *connaître*, 'to know', a *conoissance* could be anything that allowed somebody to know another or be known by them. *Anglo-Norman Dictionary: Online Edition*, < http://www.anglo-norman.net/D/conoissance > [Accessed 15 Jun 2018].

[128] Chrétien de Troyes, *Cligés*, ed. Stewart Gregory and Claude Luttrell (Cambridge, 1993), lines 1827–37: '"Chanjons", fet il, "noz conuissances; / Prenons des escuz et des lances / As traïtors qu'ocis avons. / Ensi vers le chastel irons, / Si cuideront li traïtor / Dedanz que nos soiens des lor, / Et quiex que soient les dessertes, / Les portes nos seront overtes. / Et savez quiex nos lor randrons? / Ou morz ou vis toz les prandrons, / Se Damedex le nos consant'.

[129] RdR, vol. 3, lines 7667–98: 'chevaliers orent hauber(n)s blanz, / chauces de fer, helmes luisanz, / escuz as cols, es meins lor lances, / e tuit orent fait conoissances, / que Normant altre coneüst, / qu'entrepresture n'i eüst, / que Normant Normant n'oceïst / ne Normant altre ne ferist'.

[130] Wace, *Roman de Brut: A History of the British*, ed. and trans. Judith Weiss, rev edn (Exeter, 2002), lines 3128–32: 'Le mielz de lur gent e le plus / Descendirent des chevals jus, / En mi le champ furent a pied / Oredeneement e rengied. / Cil unt par mi trenché lur lances, / E guerpies lur conuissances'.

indicated that the Britons intended to fight to the death, expecting no quarter and giving none in return.[131]

Identifying these cognizances in Latin chronicles is more difficult, as the chroniclers rarely mention any use of identifying signs and, when they do, they do not use consistent vocabulary. How, for example, should one understand the following passage from Aelred of Rievaulx's *Battle of the Standard*? Henry, son of David of Scotland, had become trapped behind the English line with his retinue. In order to escape, he proposed they employ a ruse:

> And so, when the *signa* have been thrown down, by which we are distinguished from the rest, let's mingle among our enemies, as if we were pursuing alongside them, until we have gone past all of them to my father's formation, which I see from afar is waiting in strength to withdraw, as is necessary, as soon as we can come there.[132]

Signum can mean banner but, if this is what Aelred meant, why not use the more specific *vexillum*? It is possible that *signum* is being used in a more general sense, referring to some token that distinguished the Scots from the English. Orderic Vitalis's description of the aftermath of the battle of Brémule (20 August 1119), in which Henry I of England defeated Louis VI of France, is less ambiguous: 'Peter of Maule and several other fugitives threw away their cognizances so that they would not be recognized and, having been mixed up with their pursuers, they cunningly shouted the victors' war-cry and proclaimed the greatness of their king Henry with feigned praises'.[133] This ruse combined visual anonymity with the verbal disguise of shouting an enemy war-cry. It was so effective that Roger of Courcy the younger was captured when he unknowingly entered the nearby town of Noyon in the midst of a group of French knights: the only one of the victors to be captured that day.[134]

Occasionally the sources actually describe what these field signs may have looked like. Wace depicts the retinue of Ralph of Taisson, lord of Cinglais, fighting at Val-ès-Dunes (1047) with wimples tied to their lances.[135] At Bouvines (1214), the imperial army adopted the symbol of the

---

[131] Jones, *Bloodied Banners*, pp. 15–16.

[132] RS, p. 198: 'Projectis itaque signis, quibus a ceteris dividimur, ipsis nos hostibus inseramus, quasi insequentes cum ipsis, donec praetergressi cunctos ad paternum cuneum, quem eminus video in suo vigore manentem cedere necessitati, quamtocius veniamus'.

[133] OV, vol. 6, p. 242: 'Petrus de Manlia aliique nonnulli fugientum cognitiones suas ne agnoscerentur proiecerunt, et insectantibus callide mixti signum triumphantium uociferati sunt; atque magnanimitatem Henrici regis suorumque fictis laudibus preconati sunt'.

[134] OV, vol. 6, p. 242.

[135] RdR, vol. 3, lines 3853–6: 'set vint chevaliers out od sei, / tant en aveit en son conrei, / tuit aloient lances levees / e en totes guimples fermees'.

cross: 'They prepared to attack the French, together with the Flemings, with an insatiable hatred, and in order that they could easily recognise one another, they fastened the sign of the cross on pieces of cloth to their the front and back'.[136] Likewise, both sides at Evesham (1265) used a cross for their field sign:

> a single knight and a single squire with him were killed by their allies, because they had not carried their comrades' sign upon their arm, which they had been given. For they were all marked with the sign of a red cross upon both arms, and the other side [Montfort's] were all marked, front and back, with a white cross.[137]

The choice of a cross has obvious crusading overtones, perhaps intended to declare the righteousness of the army's cause and invoke God's blessing on the wearers.[138] One can even draw parallels between these informal field signs and the badges of later periods, such as those Richard II commanded his troops to wear on his expedition into Scotland in 1385:

> Item, that everybody of our party, of whatever estate, condition or nation, should bear a large sign of the arms of St. George on their front and back on peril that, if he is wounded or killed because he does not have it, the one who wounded or killed him will not be punished for it.[139]

A similar ordinance was issued to the Scottish army assembled that same year to repel the English:

> Item, that all the French and Scots should have a sign on their front and back, namely, a white cross of St. Andrew and if his jack is white or his coat is white, he should wear the said white cross on a round or square piece of black cloth.[140]

---

[136] 'Relatio Marchianensis', in *Ex rerum francogallicarum scriptoribus*, MGH, Scriptores, 26 (Hanover, 1882), pp. 390–1, at p. 390: 'Nempe cum Flandrenses odio insatiabili Francigenas persequi prepararent, ut se et suos ad invicem facilius recognoscerent, quedam crucis signacula suis ante et retro panniculis affixerunt'.

[137] FH, vol. 3, p. 6: 'unus miles et unus armiger eo quod signum suorum commilitonum in brachio non portassent, a sociis suis ut fertur interfecti sunt. Namque erant omnes hi rubeo signo in brachiis ambobus cruce signati, ac caeteri partis adversae omnes cruce alba ante et retro insigniti'.

[138] Jones, *Bloodied Banners*, p. 61.

[139] Anne Curry, 'Disciplinary Ordinances for English and Franco-Scottish Armies in 1385: An International Code?', *Journal of Medieval History*, 37 (2011), 269–94, at p. 288: 'Item qe chescun de quel estat condicion ou nacio quil soit issint qil soit de nostre partie porte un signe des armes de Seint George large devant et autre aderer sur peril qe sil naufra ou mort en defaute dycel cely qe le naufra ou tue ne portera nul jeusse pur li'. My thanks to Dr. Trevor Russell Smith for bringing this source to my attention.

[140] Curry, 'Ordinances', p. 292: 'Item que tout home fracois et escot ait un signe devant et derrere cestassavoir une croix blanche saint Andrieu et se son jacque soit blanc ou sa cote blanche il portera la dicte croix blanche en une piece de drap noir ronde ou quaree'.

Conclusions

Establishing identity on the medieval battlefield was a many-layered process. An individual might be identified as somebody of (literal) high or low value by the quality and style of their equipment or by bearing heraldic arms. Announcing one's status through appearance carried great social and cultural value but at the cost of making one an obvious target for capture or even death. Combatants had to balance their desire for renown with the practicalities of fighting safely and effectively, which might entail adopting some form of disguise. When it came to the vital business of distinguishing friend from foe, however, war-cries and simple field signs were employed, which could be easily imitated or cast away if one wished to escape notice.

6

Bribes and Inducements

In 1122, William VI, count of Auvergne, seized the town of Clermont, along with its cathedral. The contemporary French chronicler Suger of St. Denis offers this cryptic statement on how it was accomplished: '[Aimeri, bishop of Clermont], appealing to the lord king, laid before him a tearful complaint on behalf of the Church, that the count of Auvergne had occupied the city and had fortified the Church of the Blessed Mary through the deception of his dean, together with many tyrannical acts'.[1] No other information is provided. Who was this dean? Why did he help William? What was the nature of the *fraus* he committed and how did it help William fortify the cathedral? It is not always possible to tell how and why a stronghold fell, especially when chroniclers use vague terms such as 'fraud' or 'treachery'. Some cases, however, are more explicit and commanders are depicted actively soliciting traitors in the enemy garrison. This was a sound strategy, as it allowed the attackers to take a stronghold quickly, without risking a full-frontal assault. Frontinus dedicated a section of his *Strategemata* to various examples of how to entice members of a garrison to commit treachery ('De eliciendis ad proditionem'):

> Marcus Marcellus, when he had solicited a certain Sosistratus of Syracuse to commit treachery, learned from him that the guards would be more slack on a feast day, when Epicydes was going to provide much wine and food. So, lying in wait for the merry-making (and what followed it), he scaled the walls and, when the sentries had been cut down, he opened the city, famous for noble victories, to the Roman army.[2]

---

[1] SSD, p. 232: 'ad dominum regem confugiens, querelam ecclesie lacrimabilem deponit, comitem Alvernensem civitatem occupasse, ecclesiam Beate Marie episcopalem decani sui fraude multa tirannide munivisse'.

[2] Sextus Julius Frontinus, *Strategemata*, ed. Robert I. Ireland (Leipzig, 1990), p. 73: 'M. Marcellus, cum Syracusanum quendam Sosistratum ad proditionem sollicitasset, ex eo cognouit remissiores custodias fore die festo, quo Epicydes praebiturus esset uini epularumque copiam. Insidiatus igitur hilaritati et (quae eam sequebatur) socordiae munimenta conscendit, uigilibusque caesis aperuit exercitui Romano urbem nobilibus uictoriis claram'.

When discussing siege warfare, medieval chroniclers would sometimes present bribery as the logical alternative to violent assault. This is a variation of the common topos of presenting force and trickery as two potential methods of achieving victory (see Chapter 8). For example, Roger of Wendover described Louis VIII of France's advance to La Rochelle (ruled at that time by Henry III of England) in 1224 as follows: 'In that same year Louis, king of the French, led a grand army to La Rochelle, to conquer the town either by arms or by money'.[3] Baldric of Bourgueil placed this topos into Bohemond of Taranto's mouth, as part of a speech at the siege of Antioch in 1098. As direct assaults had failed, Bohemond tells the other leading crusaders: 'each one of you should try, either by coin, or friendship, or threats, or whatever means you can, to claim this city for yourself'.[4]

The Norman chronicler William of Apulia employed this topos more frequently than most chroniclers, probably due to the frequency with which his subject, Robert Guiscard, employed bribery to acquire strongholds in southern Italy. Describing Guiscard's capture of the Calabrian town of Montepeloso (modern Irsina) in 1068, William wrote: 'because the duke was not strong in arms, he took the *castrum* by craft [...] he beguiled Godfrey, the keeper of that *castrum*, with promises, giving it over to him, and promising that he would give him more things and a stronger *castrum*'.[5] Similarly, when Guiscard bribed a Venetian nobleman to help him enter Dyrrachion (modern Durrës, on the coast of Albania) in 1082, William wrote: 'So the duke took Dyrrachion for himself, and because he was unable to conquer through arms, he subjugated it through craftiness to achieve victory'.[6] He also used the topos in a more general sense, for example when discussing how Guiscard returned to Apulia and Calabria from the Balkans in 1079 to put down a rebellion against his rule:

---

[3] According to Roger, the citizens, despairing of receiving any aid from Henry III of England, accepted Louis's money and surrendered: RW, vol. 2, p. 277: 'Eodem anno rex Francorum Lodowicus duxit exercitum grandem ad Rupellam, ut villam vel armis vel pretio subjugaret'.

[4] BB, p. 55: 'Temptet igitur unusquisque uestrum, patres conscripti, an pecunia, an amicitia, an minis, an quibuslibet ciuitatem hanc sibi uindicare preualebit angariis'. The phrase *patres conscripti* is a traditional form of address to Roman senators, employed in Sallust's *Jugurthine War* and the letters of Cicero and Livy, and was probably used here to emphasise Bohemond's eloquence: BB, p. xxxvii.

[5] WA, p. 156: 'dux quod non evalet armis / Arte capit castrum [...] promissis decipit hujus / Custodem castri Godefridum, dans sibi quaedam, / Pluraque pollicitus castrumque valentius illo'.

[6] WA, p. 230: 'Sic sibi Dirachium dux subdidit, atque quod armis / Vincere non potuit, victoria subiugat artis'.

He overcame them all, either by craft or by arms; some he won over, some he enticed with sweet words, others he broke in battle; cunning and bold, he knew both methods; he seized some castles, others, which could not be obtained by warlike violence, he persuaded to surrender with charming words.[7]

Contemporaries evidently thought that bribery fell under the general category of stratagems, so it is necessary to examine the various methods by which combatants induced their enemies to turn traitor or otherwise act in their interests.

We must be cautious when discussing incidents of bribery, however, as chroniclers sometimes accused castle garrisons of accepting bribes when it appeared that they had surrendered unnecessarily. Contemporaries did not expect garrisons to fight to the death in defence of strongholds. For both practical and ethical reasons, it was accepted that a garrison could surrender without censure if they ran out of supplies or could not reasonably expect to be relieved by a field army. On the other hand, if an attacker was forced to take a stronghold by storm, it was generally understood that the garrison had forfeited any right to clemency: a powerful incentive to come to terms. The garrison was expected to present at least a token resistance, however. Surrendering without a fight could be interpreted as an act of betrayal by the commander, just as if he had let down a ladder for the attackers.[8] In 1136, the rebel Baldwin de Redvers's garrison at Plympton in Devon surrendered to Stephen, king of England, without a fight. Even the author of the *Gesta Stephani*, who was a great partisan of Stephen's, criticised this:

> The knights into whose care Baldwin had given the castle at Plympton despaired of their lord, on account of the king's unconquerable strength, and secretly sent word to the king about giving up the castle and establishing a mutual peace, so that lives would not be placed in danger. They were most weak and fickle in heart, more afraid than was proper.[9]

---

[7] WA, pp. 194–6: 'vel arte vel armis / Omnes exsuperat; monitis quam dulcibus illos / Allicit, hos bello domitat; versutus et audax / Novit utrosque modos; adimit sua castra quibusdam, / Quosdam blanditiis verborum commovet ultro / Tradere, quae nequeunt violento marte parari'.

[8] Maurice Keen, *The Laws of War in the Late Middle Ages* (London, 1965), p. 124; Matthew Strickland, *War and Chivalry: The Conduct and Perception of War in England and Normandy 1066–1217* (Cambridge, 1996), pp. 208–17, 224–9.

[9] GS, pp. 34–6: 'milites Balduini, quibus obseruandi castelli sui de Plintona curam indulserat, propter insuperabilem, quam adesse cum rege audierant, uirtutem, de domino suo desperantes, et ne uitae suae periculum incurrerent, ut inertissimi et inconstantis animi, plus iusto formidantes, de reddendo castello pacisque concordia inter eos statuenda regi occulte miserunt'. William of Newburgh made similar allegations against the count of Aumale when the town surrendered to the count of Flanders in June 1173. WN, vol. 2, p. 210.

William of Tyre presents three possible explanations for the fall of the Cave de Suète (al-Habis Jaldak) to Saladin's nephew, Farrūkh Shāh, in July 1182. Constructed on the east bank of the Jordan in the side of a cliff overlooking the Yarmuk valley, it consisted of three floors of chambers connected by stairways cut into the rock. It had its own water supply, collected in cisterns, and the only way to approach it was by a narrow path that ran along the cliff face.[10] It was considered impregnable, which may explain why William of Tyre devoted so much attention to discussing why it fell. He considered three possibilities in turn. First, that the garrison accepted bribes. Second, that the Muslims tunnelled through the rock to enter the caves from above. Third and finally, what he claimed to be the true cause:

> But afterwards it was discovered that it was officials' fault, those who were in charge of the rest, who caused the fortress to come into the enemies' possession, for the others wanted to resist them, but those who were in authority prevented them from making a defence and afterwards, having opened the fortress to the enemies, joined with them. Also it was said that those who were in charge of that place were Syrians, whom we hold to be effeminate and cowardly, whence the greater fault lies with Fulk [of Tiberias, the castle's lord], who ought to have placed suitable people in charge.[11]

We can see here how stories of blame and recrimination could circulate following the fall of a supposedly invincible stronghold, stories which the chronicler had to judge whether to include in his text. William of Tyre recorded three possible explanations that he had heard for the loss of the Cave de Suète but chose to affirm the one that supported his prejudices about Syrians. Many chroniclers give only a single explanation, hiding the process of evaluation that William presents here. We must be cautious about reading any description of bribery or betrayal as an objective report. More often than not, the explanation conforms to the chronicler's own political or religious leanings.

Chroniclers do not usually specify what precisely was offered as a bribe. Often they simply refer to general 'money' (*pecunia*) or 'bribes' (*munera*). According to the English chronicler Henry of Huntingdon, in 1090 William Rufus gained the castles of Saint-Valéry and Aumale in Normandy by 'giving bribes' (*muneribus datis*) to their garrisons.[12] Robert

---

[10] Hugh Kennedy, *Crusader Castles* (Cambridge, 1994), pp. 52–3.
[11] WT, p. 1029: 'Compertum est autem postmodum quod culpa magistratuum, qui ceteris preerant, municipium ad hostes pervenerit, nam aliis resistere volentibus, ipsi auctoritate qua preminebant inhibebant defensionem et postmodum resignato municipio ad hostes se contulerunt. Dicebantur autem esse qui loco preerant Syri, qui apud nos effeminati et molles habentur, unde maior culpa in predictum refunditur Fulconem, qui tales loco prefecerat tam necessario'.
[12] HH, p. 414. See also GRA, p. 549.

of Torigni claimed that, during the Great Rebellion of 1173 against Henry II of England, the Breton magnate Ralph of Fougères used *pecunia* to take two strongholds.[13] Similarly, the French chronicler Rigord reported that Richard I of England took the castle of Nonancourt, on the Franco-Norman border, in 1196 with *pecunia* while Philip II of France was besieging Aumale: 'the king of England recovered the castle that they call Nonancourt through trickery and betrayal, giving money to the knights who were guarding it'.[14]

It is not clear whether these traitors were paid 'cash in hand' or if the money was to be received at a later date. It might be more accurate to say that they received a *promise* of material reward, should the attackers be victorious. This indicates a process of negotiation between the besiegers and the traitor, one that required a level of mutual trust. Occasionally this is made explicit in the narrative, as in the case of the 'charming words' which Robert Guiscard used to win over the rebel fortresses in Calabria (see p. 125). Describing how William of Arques raised a rebellion against his nephew, William II of Normandy, in 1053, the English chronicler William of Malmesbury wrote: '[his uncle], who was skilled in guile, having given many bribes, having promised more, brought [the castle garrison] over to his side. So having become master of the fortification, he declared war against his lord'.[15] Returning to William of Tyre, he wrote that the governor of the Syrian city Banyas only agreed to abandon his allegiance to Zangī, ruler of Mosul and Aleppo, and surrender to the combined forces of Muʿin al-Dīn of Damascus and Fulk of Jerusalem in June 1140 on the proviso that he would receive an annual payment: 'For it seemed shameful and unseemly that a nobleman and a lord of such a famous city should be driven from his own inheritance, forced to become a beggar'.[16]

Robert Guiscard offered what is surely one of the most lavish bribes of this period in February 1082. Unable to storm Dyrrachion (see p. 124), he bribed one Dominic, a Venetian in Greek service, to admit his men

---

[13] RT, p. 259: 'Radulfus de Fulgeriis, delinitis custodibus pretio et precibus, qui custodire debebant castrum de Cumburc et civitatem Dolensem ad opus regis Anglorum, cepit illas munitiones'.

[14] HPA, pp. 340–2: 'Dum autem rex Philippus ibi moram faceret, rex Anglie, in dolo et sub proditione castellum quod Norencort vocant, data pecunia militibus ipsum custodientibus, recepit'.

[15] GRA, vol. 1, p. 432: 'uerum ille astu quo callebat, multa largiendo, plura pollicendo, in suas partes eosdem traduxit. Munitione igitur potitus, bellum domino suo denuntiauit'. According to the Lanercost chronicle, a man named Peter Spalding betrayed the town of Berwick to the Scots in April 1317 'in return for a large sum of money and the promise of lands' (pro maxima summa pecunia ab eis recepta et terris sibi promissis). Lanercost, pp. 234–5.

[16] WT, p. 689: 'turpe enim videretur et indecens, ut vir nobilis et tam famose urbis dominus propria pulsus hereditate mendicare compelleretur'.

in return for marriage to his niece. The chronicler Geoffrey Malaterra claimed that this arrangement was mainly negotiated through intermediaries, whereas William of Apulia said that Dominic used a 'deserter from Bari' (*perfuga Barinus*) to arrange a face-to-face meeting with Guiscard at a nearby church.[17] Malaterra's account is particularly interesting for the portrayal of Dominic. While Malaterra is clear that the impetus for the betrayal came from Guiscard, he censures Dominic for accepting it: 'But his heart was sick with greed, so that when lust was mixed with promises of avarice, it was easily corrupted, it slipped further down this slope on account of a good and honest proposition'.[18] Note that the proposition – to betray the city in return for marriage into a powerful and influential family – is *bonus honestusque* but the one who was propositioned was motivated by *cupiditas* and *luxuria*. Malaterra appears to be attempting to shift responsibility for a morally dubious affair from Guiscard to Dominic. William of Apulia, by contrast, places the impetus on Dominic, claiming that it was he who contacted Guiscard, on account of his jealously towards his own commander.[19]

Bribery could operate in the opposite direction, with garrisons paying attackers to lift the siege and depart. This does not appear to have occurred in Western Europe, where garrisons were usually attacked by armies from neighbouring polities, which could simply return next year and demand an even greater sum, but there are several notable accounts from Outremer in which autonomous cities secretly paid one element of an attacking force to leave. This should be distinguished from citizens offering tribute in order to 'buy off' a crusading army because it was not negotiated openly, with the entire force, but in secret with a sub-group or individual.[20] Albert of Aachen claims that the citizens of Jabala offered to pay Godfrey of Bouillon's army a sum of money to leave in March 1099 but Godfrey instead demanded their surrender:

> So the citizens and the governor of the city, realising that they could not corrupt the aforesaid princes with money nor any other precious bribes to withdraw their camps, secretly sent messengers to count Raymond [of Saint-Gilles] at Arqah, […] if he should induce the Christian princes to

---

[17] GM, p. 74; WA, p. 230.

[18] GM, p. 74: 'Animus vero cupiditate aeger, ut a promittentibus avaritiae luxuria admiscetur, facile corruptus, a bono honestoque proposito proclivis in deterius dilapsus est'.

[19] WA, p. 230.

[20] For a study of the giving of tribute in Outremer, see Alan V. Murray, 'The Origin of Money-Fiefs in the Latin Kingdom of Jerusalem', in John France (ed.), *Mercenaries and Paid Men: The Mercenary Identity in the Middle Ages. Proceedings of a Conference Held at the University of Wales, Swansea, 7–9th July 2005* (Leiden, 2008), pp. 275–86, at pp. 283–6.

withdraw from the siege by a request or some other craft, he would receive the money which the duke and the others had refused.[21]

Albert claimed that Raymond accepted the money and lured Godfrey and the others away from Jabala by falsely reporting he was about to be attacked by a large army of Turks (see Chapter 2).

William of Tyre wrote a lengthy reflection on why the armies of the Second Crusade failed to take Damascus in July 1148, in which he reported that the citizens had bribed some of the crusaders to recommend shifting the camp to a less advantageous position on the south-east side of the city.[22] William, writing twenty-five years after the events described, claimed to have interviewed those who could still remember the siege in order to determine who was responsible for giving this treacherous advice. Some said that certain noblemen from the kingdom of Jerusalem had conspired with the citizens because they resented the efforts made by Thierry, count of Flanders, to claim lordship over the city once it had fallen. Others said that it was Raymond, prince of Antioch, who wished to take revenge on Louis VII of France, who had refused to help him but chosen to travel south to Jerusalem, and still others said that the traitors were never identified.[23] Contemporary German chroniclers, such as Gerhoh of Reichersberg, blamed Baldwin III of Jerusalem, claiming he abandoned the crusaders, or even the Knights Templar.[24] Modern scholars, drawing on the accounts of Ibn al-Qalānisī and Ibn al-Athīr, now argue that the Christians shifted their attack from the heavily defended western approach to the city after encountering heavy resistance and, believing that a relief force was approaching from Aleppo, wagered that they could storm the city more quickly from the south-east.[25] The accusations of bribery and treachery are indicative of later attempts to explain the failure of the siege and to find a scapegoat. As with his account of the siege of the Cave de Suète, William of Tyre's report is more valuable for the insight it provides

---

[21] AA, p. 380: 'Intelligentes ergo ciues et urbis magistratus quoniam non pecunia nec aliquibus preciosis muneribus corrumpi possent prefati principes ut castra amouerent, nuncios clam ad Arcahs comiti Reimundo, factis et potentia apud primores gentilium diffamato, miserunt, ut pecuniam a duce et ceteris refutatam acciperet, quatenus ab obsidione Christianos principes prece aut aliqua arte recedere suaderet'.

[22] WT, p. 766: 'tota enim sollicitudine in argumenta varia se attollentes, quibusdam de principibus nostris, promissa et collata infinite quantitatis pecunia ut eorum studio et opera obsidio solveretur, ut Iude proditoris officio fungerentur persuaserunt'.

[23] WT, pp. 768–9.

[24] A. J. Forey, 'The Failure of the Siege of Damascus in 1148', *Journal of Medieval History*, 10 (1984), 13–23, at p. 14.

[25] G. A. Loud, 'Some Reflections on the Failure of the Second Crusade', *Crusades*, 4 (2005), 1–14, at p. 14; Jonathan Phillips, *The Second Crusade: Extending the Frontiers of Christendom* (New Haven, CT, 2007), pp. 221–6.

into his historical method and contemporary rumours about the siege of Damascus than for what it tells about the events of 1148.

Money and power were not the only inducements that an attacker could use to persuade an enemy to come over to their side. Religion could also be a powerful motivator. In 1094, prompted by rumours that his brother-in-law Roger Borsa, the duke of Apulia, had died, the Norman baron William Grandmesnil seized a number of Calabrian strongholds for himself. Borsa, together with Bohemond of Taranto, moved swiftly to put down Grandmesnil's rebellion. They were able to induce the town of Rossano to surrender (although not the citadel, which was held by men loyal to Grandmesnil) with promises to replace the Latin archbishop had imposed upon them the year prior.[26] The Greek citizens were clearly shrewd enough to exploit the conflict between their Norman rulers to their own advantage.

Geoffrey Malaterra relates an unusual account of a Christian leader persuading a Muslim commander to both betray his stronghold and convert to Christianity. In 1086, the Norman warlord Roger of Sicily sought to add the Sicilian town of Castrogiovanni to his holdings. The governor, Chamut:

> Having learned about the experience of others, knowing that the count was never frustrated in anything he set out to do, since fortune favoured him, he was also somewhat inspired, silently, within his breast, to convert to the faith. He secretly arranged that, when the count came before the *castrum* with his army, he and his household would be received, together with all his belongings, when he went over to his side.[27]

The qualifying adverb 'somewhat' (*aliquantulum*) suggests that Malaterra may have doubted the sincerity of Chamut's conversion. Nevertheless, he reported that, having settled in Calabria (he feared reprisals from the citizens whom he had betrayed), Chamut remained Roger's loyal subject.[28]

Probably the most famous medieval example of an attacker inducing somebody to betray their stronghold occurred in June 1098, at the siege of Antioch. It was the incident that enabled the armies of the First Crusade to take the city after an ineffective blockade that had lasted for nine months, opening the way to Jerusalem. As a result, every chronicle of the First Crusade mentions it, although there is great variation in even the basic details. The *Gesta Francorum* gives what is probably the plainest account:

---

[26] GM, p. 100.

[27] GM, p. 88: 'Porro ille, cognoscens, experimento de aliis sumpto, comitem ad quodcumque intenderet, fortuna favente, nihil furstra niti, aliquantulum etiam de conversione ad fidem tacito sub pectore inspiratus, clam suos agit, ut, statuto termino, comes, cum suo exercitu ante castrum veniens, ipsum cum omni suppellectili sua ad se transfugientem suscipiat'.

[28] GM, p. 88.

There was a certain emir of Turkish race named Pirrus, who had entered into a very close friendship with Bohemond. Bohemond often urged him, having sent one messenger after another to him, to receive him within the city in the most friendly manner; he promised him the freedom of the Christian religion, and committed to make him wealthy with much honour. [Pirrus] agreed to his words and promises, saying: 'I guard three towers, and I gladly promise them to him, and I will receive him into them at whatever hour he wishes'.[29]

According to John France, Bohemond may have made contact with Pirrus during an extended truce that took place between the crusaders and the garrison in the spring, which was reported in a letter of Anselm, bishop of Ribemont, but is not recorded in any of the surviving chronicles.[30] Having made this arrangement, Bohemond then used his potential strategic coup to persuade the other leading crusaders to turn the city over to him, should he manage to capture it: a violation of their standing agreement with the Byzantine emperor to give any captured cities to him. The actual attack took place on the evening of 2 June, after the main crusader force had made a show of withdrawing, as if going to forage for supplies. Bohemond led a small force to the foot of the tower which Pirrus guarded, climbed the wall and took control of the city, although the citadel would remain in Turkish hands until the crusaders' victory over the army of Karbughā on 28 June.[31]

The *Gesta Francorum* reports Bohemond's approaches to Pirrus in a straightforward manner. Pirrus would betray the city and convert to Christianity, in return for which he would receive both wealth and honour. Joshua Birk has suggested that the *Gesta*'s author, who was probably a Norman from southern Italy who had served in Bohemond's following, was not unduly troubled by this agreement, as similar arrangements were well-known in Italy and Sicily (see p. 124).[32] By contrast, the other chroniclers of the crusade, who were mostly monks from northern France with little

---

[29] GF, p. 44: 'Erat quidam ammiratus de genere Turcorum cui nomen Pirus, qui maximam amicitiam receperat cum Boamundo. Hunc sepe Boamundus pulsabat nuntiis adinuicem missis, quo eum infra ciuitatem amicissime reciperet; eique christianitatem liberius promittebat, et eum se diuitem facturum cum multo honore mandabat. Consensit ille dictis et promissionibus dicens: "Tres turres custodio, eique libenter ipsas promitto, et quacunque hora voluerit in eas eum recolligam"'.

[30] John France, 'The Fall of Antioch during the First Crusade', in Michel Balard, Benjamin Z. Kedar and Jonathan Riley-Smith (eds.), *Dei gesta per Francos: Etudes sur les croisades dédiées à Jean Richard* (Aldershot, 2001), pp. 13–20, at pp. 17–19.

[31] For a complete study of this incident, see Yuval Noah Harari, *Special Operations in the Age of Chivalry 1100–1550* (Woodbridge, 2007), pp. 53–73.

[32] Joshua C. Birk, 'The Betrayal of Antioch: Narratives of Conversion and Conquest during the First Crusade', *Journal of Medieval and Early Modern Studies*, 41 (2011), 463–86, at p. 464.

to no contact with Muslims, were more troubled by Pirrus's easy conversion and Bohemond's use of bribery to achieve a holy goal.[33] To make the historical events conform to the theological framework which they had constructed for their narrative, Pirrus's treachery was portrayed as a product of divine inspiration.[34] Fulcher of Chartres introduces his account of the fall of Antioch with the phrase: 'So hear about an act of fraud and yet not fraud'.[35] In Fulcher's text, Pirrus received three visions from God, urging him to surrender the city to the crusaders. Here the agency is ascribed to God, with Bohemond being an almost passive recipient of God's gift in Pirrus.[36] Robert the Monk retained Bohemond's central role but, instead of a simple act of bribery, their relationship becomes an extended act of evangelism on Bohemond's part, as he persuades Pirrus of the truth of the Christian faith and its inevitable triumph over Islam.[37] Guibert of Nogent, however, claimed that Pirrus's conversion was short lived and that he soon betrayed the Franks:

> Thereupon, when he had utterly deserted the Christians, he resumed the luxurious and impure living of the Gentiles that he had followed of old. Nor was this any shame to him: for Pyrrus is the Greek for the Latin *Rufus* and it is well known that the unfaithful are marked by their red hair, so it is proven that this man did not stray far from his line.[38]

There is a possibility that Pirrus was in fact an Armenian in Turkish service who had nominally converted to Islam and used the siege as an opportunity to aid his co-religionists but this is doubtful. The only Western chronicler who calls Pirrus an Armenian is Ralph of Caen, who was writing much later than the authors discussed above.[39] The Damascene chronicler Ibn al-Qalānisī identifies him as an Armenian serving Yāghī Siyān as an armourer but this may be an attempt by al-Qalānisī to shift the blame for

---

[33] Slitt has explored the social anxieties raised by an apparent friendship between a crusader and a Muslim and the strategies the chroniclers employed to minimise it in their narratives, either by elevating Pirrus's social status or emphasising Bohemond's spiritual and military superiority: Rebecca L. Slitt, 'Justifying Cross-Cultural Friendship: Bohemond, Firuz, and the Fall of Antioch', *Viator*, 38 (2007), 339–49.

[34] Levine has performed a thorough rhetorical study of the different accounts of Pirrus's treachery: Robert Levine, 'The Pious Traitor: Rhetorical Reinventions of the Fall of Antioch', *Mittellateinisches Jahrbuch*, 33 (1998), 59–80.

[35] FC, p. 231: 'Audite ergo fraudem et non fraudem'.

[36] FC, pp. 230–1.

[37] RM, pp. 796–801.

[38] GN, p. 251: 'Ibi prorsus Christianitate deserta, veteris luxuriae et gentilitatis inquinamenta resumpsit. Nec id iniuria: si enim Pyrrus grece "rufus" est latine et infidelitatis nota rufis inuritur, isdem ergo a sua minime linea exorbitasse probatur'.

[39] GT, pp. 59–60.

the city's fall away from his own people.[40] By contrast, Ibn al-Athīr simply describes him as 'an armourer' who was guarding one of the towers, with no mention of his ethnicity or religion.[41]

When faced with the formidable task of taking a medieval stronghold, it is little surprise that commanders would seek to use every method available to avoid having to make a direct assault, including resorting to bribery. While chronicle accounts of bribery are suspect, often reflecting the authors' prejudices and the accusations that inevitably circulated in the aftermath of a defeat, there is sufficient evidence to suggest that such inducements were an effective, if morally dubious, means of acquiring strongholds without violence. Avoiding violence in this way could even be presented as a positive attribute by a sympathetic chronicler, such as William of Apulia, who could claim it demonstrated ingenuity and political acumen. We can see a similar process at work when studying how oaths were used to regulate siege warfare and incidents in which combatants were believed to have twisted or broken the terms they had sworn to uphold.

---

[40] H. A. R. Gibb (trans.), *The Damascus Chronicle of the Crusades: Extracted and Translated from the Chronicle of Ibn Al-Qalānisī* (London, 1932), pp. 44–5.
[41] Ibn al-Athīr, *Chronicle for the Crusading Period from al-Kamil fi'l-ta'rikh*, trans. D. S. Richards (3 vols, Aldershot, 2006–8), vol. 1, pp. 14–15.

7

Oaths and Truces

Despite Christ's injunction to his disciples to refrain from swearing oaths, oaths and oath-taking were a fundamental element of medieval Christian culture.[1] Oaths 'served as a method of proof and a guarantee of truth in legal process and social life', whether this was the truth of a statement, such as the testimony of a witness in court, or the truth of a promise to undertake some course of action, such as wedding vows.[2] The medieval aristocracy, both lay people and clergy, was acutely aware of the importance of oaths. Vassals swore an oath of homage to their lord, monks swore an oath of obedience to their abbot and clerics to their superiors in the Church hierarchy.[3]

The most common Latin words for oath were *iusiurandum* and *iuramentum*, deriving from *ius* (right or law), which indicate their legal nature, and *sacramentum*, from *sacrum* (sacred), indicates their connection with the spiritual and divine.[4] Canon lawyers were unanimous that oaths fell under 'natural' or divine law, as the violation of an oath was a crime against God, who was invoked as a witness to its content.[5] Oath-taking rituals frequently involved the swearer making physical contact with a scared object, such as a Gospel book or relic.[6] Contemporaries made a distinction between this kind of solemn oath, which invoked the divine,

---

[1] Matthew 5. 33–7.
[2] Robert E. Bjork (ed.), *Oxford Dictionary of the Middle Ages* (4 vols, Oxford, 2010), vol. 3, p. 1220.
[3] Kenneth Pennington, 'Feudal Oath of Fidelity and Homage', in Kenneth Pennington and Melodie Harris Eichbauer (eds.), *Law as Profession and Practice in Medieval Europe* (Farnham, 2011), pp. 93–116, at pp. 105–6.
[4] Joseph R. Strayer (ed.), *Dictionary of the Middle Ages* (13 vols, New York, 1982–9), vol. 9, p. 207.
[5] Lisa Jefferson, *Oaths, Vows and Promises in the First Part of the French Prose Lancelot Romance* (Bern, 1993), p. 29.
[6] Jenny Benham, *Peacemaking in the Middle Ages: Principles and Practice* (Manchester, 2011), p. 150.

and other promises.[7] There was also powerful social pressure on people to keep their oaths: oath-taking often formed part of public rituals and witnesses were expected to ensure that its terms were adhered to. An oath-breaker would lose face before their peers and be ostracised from normal social relations, as one who could not be trusted to keep their word.[8]

In the context of medieval warfare, combatants would make agreements with their opponents, usually to observe a truce, suspending hostilities for a given period for a parley or other reason. This was a generally accepted custom, similar to the granting of a conditional respite to a garrison or surrendering a stronghold when there was no prospect of mounting an adequate defence. It can be difficult to determine precisely what was said in a given situation and what oaths, if any, were sworn. These were verbal, ad hoc arrangements, made between the commanders of the two forces. When chroniclers explicitly state that oaths were sworn, it was usually to criticise the person who subsequently broke an agreement: not only were they dishonest, they were sacrilegious.

It is important to stress that these agreements were customs, not laws: there were no authoritative texts that specified that combatants should behave in this way. There was no formal medieval 'law of war'. Transnational 'courts of chivalry', where individual knights might seek redress for offences committed against the 'law of arms', would not develop until the mid-fourteenth century.[9] In the period under discussion, the process was governed solely by the values of honour and shame: in theory, both sides sought to protect their reputation by maintaining the agreement and risked earning shame if they failed. Modern readers may scoff at this, and there are many examples of individuals abusing the custom, as shall be discussed below, but there is evidence that it was taken very seriously. As Fredric Cheyette has demonstrated, the distinction between 'laws' and 'customs', between stated rules and observed practice, was not so great in the West during this period as it would become in later centuries.[10] Studying the resolution of tenure disputes in twelfth- and early thirteenth-century France, Cheyette showed how arbitrators were appointed, not

---

[7] Jefferson, *Oaths, Vows and Promises*, p. 30.
[8] Björn Weiler, 'Knighting, Homage and the Meaning of Ritual', *Viator*, 37 (2006), 275–300, at pp. 276–7.
[9] Yvonne Friedman, 'Did Laws of War Exist in the Crusader Kingdom of Jerusalem?', in Yitzhak Hen (ed.), *De Sion exibit lex et verbum domini de Hierusalem: Essays on Medieval Law, Liturgy, and Literature in Honour of Amnon Linder* (Turnhout, 2001), pp. 81–103, at p. 82; Maurice Keen, *The Laws of War in the Late Middle Ages* (London, 1965), pp. 23–59; Matthew Strickland, *War and Chivalry: The Conduct and Perception of War in England and Normandy 1066–1217* (Cambridge, 1996), pp. 46–7.
[10] Fredric L. Cheyette, 'Giving Each his Due', in Lester K. Little and Barbara H. Rosenwein (eds.), *Debating the Middle Ages: Issues and Readings* (Oxford, 1998), pp. 170–9, at p. 171.

to make settlements according to objective case law, but to resolve the dispute so that neither side unduly lost face. This was possible because '[there existed] a social group whose members rubbed each other often enough for their pressure to be effective and the ritual to perform its appointed task'.[11]

In a similar way, fear of losing status in the eyes of their peers could affect the behaviour of medieval combatants. According to the English chronicler Richard of Devizes, when Richard I of England rallied his men for an attack on Messina in October 1190, he laid down punishments for those who fled: 'This law is to be kept without remission: the foot soldier who flees on his foot shall lose that foot; the knight will be stripped of his belt'.[12] It is noteworthy that a knight losing his *cingulum*, the symbol of his social status and honour, was considered comparable to crippling a foot soldier. Consider also William of Malmesbury's account of the death of Harold Godwinson at Hastings. One of William the Conqueror's knights struck Harold's corpse in the thigh: 'because of this he was branded with disgrace by William, because he had done this ignoble and shameful thing, he was banished from the *militia*'.[13] While this incident is almost certainly apocryphal, it is a valuable insight into the aristocratic culture of Malmesbury's day, a generation before Richard I's: the shame of losing one's status as a knight was evidently considered a severe punishment.

There was also a practical dimension to these customs. Strickland has noted that garrisons that were granted conditional respites were rarely actually relieved: besiegers only allowed them to seek help when they felt confident that no help would be forthcoming.[14] Regarding the observation of periods of truce, this also had pragmatic advantages: 'If safe conduct during parleys was consistently violated, both parties ran the risk of rendering unworkable the very mechanisms by which warfare might be postponed or brought to a conclusion'.[15] Nevertheless, we should not discount the very real role that honour and the avoidance of public shame played in regulating warfare. Consider Philip II of France's violent reaction when he learned that Richard I of England was assaulting the Palestinian city of Acre in 1191 while he was conducting negotiations with representatives from the garrison, to whom he had given a pledge of safe

---

[11] Cheyette, 'Giving Each his Due', p. 176.

[12] Richard of Devizes, 'De rebus gestis Ricardi primi', in Richard Howlett (ed.), *Chronicles of the Reigns of Stephen, Henry II and Richard I*, RS, 82 (4 vols, London, 1884–9), vol. 3, pp. 381–454, at p. 399: 'Sit lex servata sine remedio: pedes pleno pede fugiens, pedem perdat; miles privetur cingulo'.

[13] GRA, p. 456: 'unde a Willelmo ignominiae notatus, quod rem ignauam et pudendam fecisset, militia pulsus est'.

[14] Strickland, *War and Chivalry*, p. 210.

[15] Strickland, *War and Chivalry*, p. 49.

conduct: 'And the king, on account of his anger, ordered his men to take up arms to go and attack the king of England. And he had even laced up his chausses, when the worthy men of the army intervened to sooth his anger'.[16] Richard had humiliated Philip before the garrison of Acre by ignoring his safe conduct. He had made him appear weak, unable to command respect among his allies and, even worse, untrustworthy, liable to break any future agreement. Hence Philip's angry and impulsive recourse to violence in order to reassert his dominance over Richard and to avenge the insult to his honour.

Geoffrey de Villehardouin reported a similar incident during negotiations between Henry of Hainault, regent of the Latin Empire of Constantinople, and the citizens of Apros (near modern Kermeyan, Turkey) in 1205: 'While they were seeking an agreement in one place, members of the host were entering in another; Henry, the regent of the empire and those who were talking in that place did not know a thing about it, and they were very upset about it'.[17] In both incidents, the violation of the truce provoked anger. Not only did it damage a commander's reputation as a man of honour, it also risked undermining the conventions of siege warfare. If the enemy came to believe that they could not be trusted, then they would be more likely to fight to the death in future encounters, making it significantly more difficult to take other strongholds.

While this chapter will necessarily focus on times when people *broke* their word, there are a few incidents that portray individuals sacrificing a tactical or strategic advantage in the name of honour. In 1296, Edward I of England laid siege to Edinburgh Castle. According to the Lanercost chronicler, a certain Welshman named Lewyn was given letters to deliver to London but instead brought them to the (unnamed) Scottish constable, hoping to be rewarded:

> But whereas others wanted the mysteries contained within the letters to be disclosed, he who was in charge prevented it and immediately, standing in a high place, cried loudly to those passing by that they should make it known in the king's court that there was a traitor who was inciting those within the castle to perform an act of deceit, which he would not agree to for any reason contrary to *fides*.[18]

---

[16] LE, pp. 123–5: 'Et le rei meismes, dou coros que il ot, comanda a ses homes que il se deussent armer por aler assaillir le roi d'Engleterre. Et li meismes avoit ja laciees ses chauces, se les proudeshomes de l'ost nen i fussent survenus, qui le rapaisserent de sa ire'.

[17] GV, vol. 2, p. 200: 'Endementiers que il queroient plait d'une part, cil de l'ost entroient de l'autre part; si que Henris li balz de l'empire et cil qui parloient del plait n'en sorent mot, ainz lor en pesa mult'.

[18] Lanercost, p. 178: 'Cum vero caeteri vellent igitur sacramenta detegi inhibuit qui praeerat, et statim in eminenti loco stans acclamavit fortiter transeuntes quatinus

The constable returned the letters together with the unfortunate Lewyn, who was drawn and hanged as a traitor. Edward was reportedly so moved by the constable's gesture that he ordered that there should be no further bombardment of the castle and agreed to allow the garrison to seek aid from John Balliol, king of Scotland.

It is not clear in what sense the chronicler is using *fides*. It may mean something like 'good faith' or 'trustworthiness', suggesting that the constable considered cooperating with a traitor to be unworthy of a man of honour, or it may literally mean 'faith', suggesting he regarded it as an impious act, or both together. The use of *sacramenta* to describe the letters, which the other defenders wanted to 'disclose', does suggest that the chronicler saw Lewyn's actions as sacrilegious. He appears to have seen the incident as instructive, introducing it as follows: 'On the Feast of St. Barnabas, a memorable thing happened concerning the treacherous character of those called Welshmen', and concluding with: 'I inserted this story here so that the wise may avoid friendship with dishonest people'.[19]

Another incident in which a commander explicitly refused to break a promise occurred at Apamea, Syria in 1106. A man, whom Albert of Aachen calls Botherus, murdered the city's ruler, Kahalf ibn Mulā'ib, and invited Riwān, ruler of Aleppo, to take possession of the town.[20] The Christian citizens of Apamea, together with the sons of Ibn Mulā'ib, appealed to Tancred, prince of Galilee and at that time regent of Antioch, for protection. After a long siege, Tancred negotiated a surrender, together with an agreement to spare Botherus. Ibn Mulā'ib's sons were, understandably, furious and demanded Botherus's death:

> Tancred answered them thus, in all mildness: 'I made a pledge to this man, whom I know very well is perverse and false. It is not the custom of Christians to violate faith and truth but to keep them with all people, and we grant this man his life, together with the safety of his limbs'.[21]

Tancred consoled them by explaining he had only guaranteed Botherus's safety: his fellow conspirators were not protected and the sons could take their revenge on them as they wished. This speech may be ironic, given

---

notum facerent in curia regis proditorem suum eos qui deintus erant sollicitare de fraude, cui nulla ratione contra fidem vellet assensum praebere'.

[19] Lanercost, pp. 177–9: 'In festo Sancti Barabae apostli accidit memorabile pro Walensium tergiversatione nominandum [...] Hoc exemplum hic inserui ut sapiens subterfugiat familiaritatem fraudaulenti'.

[20] This 'Botherus' may have been Abū Tāhir al-Saïgh, the leader of the Assassins of Aleppo, or a Persian goldsmith named Abū Tāhir: AA, p. 735 n. 21.

[21] AA, p. 740: 'Quibus Tancradus in omni mansuetudine sic respondit: "Fidem quam promisisti isti, quem satis peruersum scio ac periurum, non Christiani moris est uiolare, sed nostrum est omni populo fidem et ueritatem seruare, et ideo huic concedimus uitam cum salute menbrorum"'.

Tancred's general reputation for ruthlessness and sharp practice. There is evidence to suggest that his treatment of Botherus was not a display of pure magnanimity: according to the Damascene chronicler Ibn al-Qalānisī, Botherus was required to pay Tancred a substantial ransom for his safety.[22]

Periods of negotiation were regarded as part of a truce: military activity was to be suspended and messengers were free to go between the belligerent parties unharmed. This was not always adhered to. On 23 July 1195, Philip II of France and Richard I of England agreed to a truce, during which Philip would hold all the lands in Normandy he occupied at that time, while the two sides attempted to negotiate a lasting peace. Philip, realising that he would be unable to hold many of the castles if the fighting should resume, preferred to demolish them rather than allow them to return to Richard intact.[23] The Anglo-Normans considered this to be a violation of the truce, at least according to the *History of William Marshal*. Philip and Richard had met for another round of negotiations at the castle of Vaudreuil: 'They held talks but the French behaved wickedly: while the kings were talking about peace, they continuously undermined the castle until it fell down; they performed an act of cowardly treason'.[24]

Henry III of England was accused of employing a similar strategy at the siege of Northampton, which was held against him by supporters of Simon de Montfort, in April 1264. The English chronicler Walter of Guisborough reported that, while the two sides were negotiating on one side of the town, a royalist force led by one Philip Basset was secretly breaking down another section of wall near St. Andrew's monastery, claiming: 'This trick was ascribed to the foreign monks themselves because they prepared an entrance for the invaders'.[25] These accusations against the foreign Cluniacs of St. Andrew's are in keeping with the nativist sentiments of the period and the barons' complaints about foreign influence at the royal court. Thomas Wykes, one of the few royalist chroniclers of this conflict, records that the royalists breached the wall but makes no mention of the negotiations, focusing instead on the foolish actions of Simon de Montfort the younger, who was thrown from his horse while riding to oppose the attackers.[26]

One way combatants could exploit the custom of the truce was by deliberately delaying or drawing out the negotiations to their own advantage.

---

[22] H. A. R. Gibb (trans.), *The Damascus Chronicle of the Crusades: Extracted and Translated from the Chronicle of Ibn Al-Qalānisī* (London, 1932), p. 73.
[23] John Gillingham, *Richard the Lionheart*, 2nd edn (London, 1989), pp. 253–4.
[24] HWM, lines 10537–48: 'Tant firent qu'un parlement pristrent, / Mes Franceis laidement mespristrent: / Dementiers que de pais parloent / Li rei, e il toz dis minoent / Le chastel tant qu'il l'abatirent; / Coarde traïson i firent'.
[25] WG, pp. 189–90: 'Imputatus est etiam dolus ipsis monachis alienigenis quod introeuntibus introitum preparabant'.
[26] TW, p. 144.

In September 1097, a crusading army under Tancred laid siege to the Cilician city of Tarsos. The Turkish garrison initially agreed to receive Tancred's banner, which they flew over their walls as a sign that they had submitted to his authority and that they should not be attacked by other crusaders. While Tancred remained encamped before the city, Baldwin of Boulogne approached with his army. The garrison, thinking that it was a Turkish force coming to their relief, began to taunt Tancred and his men from the walls:

> See! Our troops are hastening to aid us. We are not in your power, as you thought, but our hand and our power shall surely crush you today. This is the reason we came to this agreement with you for no purpose. Now you can be sure that you were deceived. We did this for no other reason than to keep you in your camps, as we were waiting for help from the divisions you now see, to destroy you and your men.[27]

When the Turks realised their error, they quickly threw down Tancred's banner and accepted Baldwin's protection instead, as he possessed the stronger force. Tancred, who was unwilling to fight Baldwin, withdrew to Adana.

In 1152 John Marshal, a partisan of the Empress Matilda, was besieged at Newbury by Stephen, king of England. John negotiated a truce with the king, giving his son William to him as a hostage (see Chapter 1). John had told Stephen that he would use the truce to request relief from Matilda but instead used the time to strengthen his defences: 'The child was in danger; the king knew very well that he had been deceived but he waited until the set time when [Marshal] would have to surrender the castle; he would surrender nothing: he would have to take it with the troops he had assembled'.[28] Stephen's behaviour may seem naive but it is in keeping with his depiction in other sources as generous and honourable, even when it ran contrary to his own immediate interests.[29] It is not clear whether the poet expected his audience to approve of John's deceitful behaviour here or to condemn it. It may be that we are simply meant to worry about the consequences for the young Marshal, caught in a conflict between two ruthless adults.

---

[27] AA, p. 146: 'Ecce manus nobis auxiliari properantium. Nos non in tua ut estimabas, sed tu tuique in manu et uirtute nostra hodie conterendi estis. Quapropter te hoc in foedere quod frustra pepigimus, iam deceptum credas. Nec aliam ob causam te morari in castris fecimus, nisi quia spem auxilii in hiis quas uides aciebus in tuam tuorumque perditionem prestolabamur'.

[28] HWM, lines 493–508: 'Li emfes fu an aventure; / Bien s'ert li reis aperceü / K'il aveit esté deceü; / Mais li terme fu atenduz / Que li deveit estre renduz / Li chastels; naien fu del rendre: / A ce ku'il out l'en convint prendre'.

[29] For example, his gift of funds to Henry of Anjou in 1147 after he found himself unable to pay his retinue: GS, p. 207.

Jordan Fantosme, a twelfth-century chronicler writing for the court of Henry II of England, presented an incident in which a combatant negotiated with intent to deceive in an unambiguously positive light. In September 1173, Robert III, earl of Leicester, landed in Norfolk with an army of Flemings in support of Henry the Young King's rebellion against his father. Humphrey III de Bohun, the royal constable, was at that time in Northumbria campaigning against William I of Scotland, who had invaded England earlier that year. It was Richard de Lucy, the justiciar of England, who suggested that the English barons negotiate a truce with the Scots to allow themselves time to march south and confront Leicester. Here is Bohun's response, according to Fantosme:

> Sir Richard de Lucy, now your age will be apparent. Be swift, if you are the wise man it is said you are. Go to the king of Scotland and conceal this danger from him. If he hears this news, he will be much emboldened that the earl has arrived and crossed the Channel. He will not grant your truce, unless he has madness in his heart. I will go back; it will be to their danger. If God wills it, I will put an end to this outrage.[30]

Fantosme concludes by stating that Lucy 'acted with good sense' (*senê*), acquiring everything he wanted from William of Scotland. Rather than being criticised, this piece of shrewd diplomacy is praised by the poet as a demonstration of the positive qualities: *sage* and *sens*.

Roger of Howden recorded an illuminating example of how an unscrupulous commander could adhere to the letter of an agreement while disregarding its spirit. In July 1173, Louis VII of France and Henry the Young King laid siege to the Norman town of Verneuil, as part of their campaign against Henry II of England. After a month, the town had run out of supplies and the citizens asked that they be allowed to send for help. Louis agreed, swearing that, if no relief had arrived by St. Lawrence's Day (10 August), he would enter the town without doing any violence to the inhabitants. The citizens gave hostages as sureties for their surrender, then sent word to Henry II. Henry arrived in the vicinity of Verneuil on 9 August and drew up his army for battle. Louis sent a delegation, made up of the archbishop of Sens and the counts of Troyes and Blois, and agreed to negotiate the next morning.[31] Instead, Louis entered the town that same evening, seized the burgesses and their cattle, set fire to the buildings and then retreated with his plunder. Howden is very clear that Louis and the

---

[30] JF, lines 818–25: 'Sire Richard de Luci, or parra voste age / E vus seiez en haste, si cum l'um dit, tant sage. / Alez al rei d'Escoce, celez lui cest damage. / S'il set ceste novele, mult iert de fier curage / Ke li cuens seit arivez e venuz a passage, / Ne vus durrad sa triewe, s'il n'ad el cuer la rage. / Jo m'en irrai ariere; ço iert pur sun damage. / Si Deus le volt e gree, jo desfrai l'utrage'.

[31] HowChr, vol. 2, pp. 49–50.

French magnates had sworn an oath to the townsfolk: '*juraverunt eis*'.[32] He also made sure to frame his description of the sack of Verneuil within the language of sacred law: 'But this did not prevent his outrage, he transgressed the sacred oaths which he had made to the burgesses. For he did not return their hostages, nor keep the peace, as he promised'.[33]

Louis may have felt justified in his actions, however. He had agreed to allow the town to summon help, which had arrived, meaning that his oath had been fulfilled and, with the resumption of hostilities, he was no longer bound to spare the burgesses or their possessions. He did break his agreement to meet with Henry the next morning but this does not appear to have been affirmed with an oath, so he may not have felt bound to observe it in the same way: Howden uses the generic verb *capere* for the agreement relating to the *colloquium*, rather than the specific *jurare*, which he used for the agreement made between Louis and the town.

The above examples are all somewhat ambiguous: one party entered into an agreement with ulterior motives but they at least made a show of adhering to the agreed terms. There are other incidents in which combatants simply disregarded agreements in order to surprise or otherwise gain an advantage over their opponent. Following his victory over the Latins at Adrianople (14–15 April 1205), Kalojan, king of Bulgaria and Vlachia, laid siege to their castle at Serres in Macedonia. The garrison agreed to surrender and Kalojan 'had twenty five of his most noble men who were present swear an oath that he would escort them safely, with all their horses and arms, to Salonika or Constantinople or into Hungary, wherever they wanted'.[34] According to the crusader-chronicler Geoffrey Villehardouin, the garrison camped before the castle for three days, waiting to depart, before Kalojan's men suddenly fell upon them, despoiled them and took them back to Vlachia as prisoners.[35] While it is possible to interpret this as an instance in which Western European culture came into conflict with a culture that did not necessarily hold oaths and agreements in the same reverence (see Chapter 9), there are also examples of Westerners willing to violate sworn agreements. Roger of Wendover recorded that, in 1233, Henry III of England laid siege to a certain castle in Wales ('whose name I do not remember') belonging to the rebel earl of Pembroke, Richard Marshal. The king, realising that he did not have sufficient supplies to

---

[32] HowChr, vol. 2, p. 49.

[33] HowChr, vol. 2, p. 50: 'Sed ipse non ausus eam retinere, transgressus est sacramenta quae ipse burgensibus fecerat. Ipse namque obsides eorum non reddidit, nec pacem, quam promiserat, servavit'.

[34] GV, p. 202: 'Et Johannis lot fist jurer a.xxv. des plus halz homes que il avoit que il les conduroit salvement a toz lor chevaus et a totes lor armes a Salenique ou en Costantinople ou en Hongrie, lequel que il voldroient des trois'.

[35] GV, p. 204.

maintain the siege, sent a delegation to Richard 'and acquired from him an agreement that he would surrender the castle to him, on account of the king's honour, lest it seem that he had besieged the castle in vain'. Henry promised to restore the castle to Richard in fifteen days, in addition to satisfying his political grievances.[36] We see here again the importance of shame as a motivation for political and military decision making. Wendover says that Henry was 'ashamed that he had come [to the siege]' and appealed to Richard on the grounds of honour, lest he appear to have acted in vain or foolishly (*inaniter*) and lose face before his subjects. Richard agreed but, perhaps unsurprisingly, Henry refused to return the castle after the agreed time had elapsed and Richard was forced to lay siege to his own castle to retake it. Presumably Henry calculated that the shame of failing to take a castle would have been more damaging than that of breaking an agreement with a rebel.

Gerald of Wales produced an elaborate, if not entirely trustworthy, account of the siege of Wexford castle in 1171, claiming that it was taken by deceit. The men of Wexford and Uí Chennselaig had joined forces to assault the Cambro-Norman garrison there, while a force of Dubliners and Norwegians attacked Dublin. According to Gerald, as the Irish could not take the castle by force, 'they assembled the weapons "guile" and "invention", according to their custom of deceit'.[37] A delegation of clerics, led by the bishops of Kildare and Ferns, processed sent to the castle ditch, where its members swore on relics that Dublin had fallen, the other Cambro-Normans were dead and that armies from Connaught and Leinster were approaching to join the siege.[38] They also promised to allow the garrison to go free and return safely to Wales. The garrison believed them but were immediately killed or captured when they left the castle.[39]

This incident is of dubious historicity. Sources for the Anglo-Norman invasion of Ireland are scarce but the other major narrative text, *The Song of Dermot*, says only that fitz Gilbert's 'men were all betrayed'.[40] Furthermore, Gerald's prejudices against the Irish and especially their bishops are well-documented in his *Topography*. While he acknowledged that the Irish clergy were chaste and faithful, he criticised their bishops for their idle-

---

[36] RW, vol. 4, p. 273: 'unde, missis quibusdam episcopis ad comitem Marescallum, exegit ab eo, quatenus propter honorem ipsius regis, ne videretur castellum inaniter obsedisse, illud sibi tali conventione redderet, ut infra dies quindecim illud integrum ipsi restitueret Marescallo, atque omnia, quae in regno erant corrigenda, interim per consilium episcoporum, qui super his fidejussores fuerant, emendaret'.

[37] EH, p. 84: 'ad consueta fallacie tela figmentaque dolosa concurrunt'.

[38] The bishop of Kildare was Malachias Ua Briain. The identity of the bishop of Ferns at this time is uncertain but he may have been Joseph Ua hAedha [sic]. Regardless, they were both native Irish: EH, p. 308 n. 130.

[39] EH, p. 85.

[40] Dermot, line 1776: 'Sa gent unt trestut traïz'.

ness, failure to preach and to correct their people's errors.[41] Nevertheless, his description of the siege is useful as an example of the kind of action that Gerald and his contemporaries found despicable: a deliberate falsehood, sworn under oath on holy relics.

Walter of Guisborough records an unusual agreement that occurred prior to the battle of Methven (19 June 1306). Robert Bruce's army was drawn up before Perth and challenged the English garrison to fight or surrender:

> But, seeing that they were fewer in number [than the Scots], they answered him cautiously that they ought not to come out at that time but would gladly fight with him at dawn tomorrow, since today was a feast day. For it was the first Sunday after the Feast of the Nativity of the Blessed John the Baptist.[42]

Bruce, whom Guisborough describes as 'too credulous' (*nimis credulus*), withdrew and made camp nearby at Methven. The garrison then sallied out in the evening and slaughtered the unarmed and unsuspecting Scots. Both Nicholas of Trivet and John Barbour refer to the English agreeing to give battle the next morning before attacking at dusk but neither claim that they used a feast day as an excuse.[43] It is unusual for an English chronicler to include a detail that cast his fellow countrymen in such a negative light, when the fiercely patriotic Barbour did not. Guisborough may have had access to different sources to Trivet and Barbour or he may have felt special partiality to Bruce, whose ancestor and namesake had founded his priory, St. Mary's of Guisborough, and whose family had remained its patrons.[44]

One of the most explicit examples of a combatant breaking a truce is recorded in William of Newburgh's *Historia rerum Anglicarum*. In July 1174, having decided against invading England via Boulogne, Philip I of Flanders and Henry the Young King joined with Louis VII of France to lay siege to the Norman city of Rouen. Due to the city's location on the Seine, the besiegers were unable to blockade it effectively, so instead kept up a continuous assault, day and night, in an attempt to breach the walls. After nineteen days of fighting, Louis granted the citizens a day's truce to honour the Feast of St. Lawrence (10 August): 'The king of the French, on account of his especial reverence for the martyr, whom he was accustomed

---

[41] Gerald of Wales, 'Topographia Hibernica', in J. S. Brewer (ed.), *Opera*, RS, 21 (8 vols, London, 1861–91), vol. 5, pp. 3–206, at pp. 172–7.

[42] WG, p. 367: 'At illi videntes se numero pauciores responderunt ei caute quod non egrederentur tunc sed die crastina pugnarent cum eo libenter quia dies festus erat. Erat enim dies dominica proxima post festum Natiuitatis beati Johannis baptiste'.

[43] Bruce, Book 2, lines 301–4; NT, pp. 409–10.

[44] G. W. S. Barrow, *Robert Bruce and the Community of the Realm of Scotland*, 4th edn (London, 2005), pp. 29–30.

to particularly and devoutly venerate, solemnly decreed a rest be granted to the citizens on his day'.[45] Note how William's language emphasises the sacred character of the truce: *reuerentia, deuotius, sollemniter*. The citizens used the day's truce to sing and dance upon the walls, while their young knights went and jousted on the far river bank in sight of Louis's army 'to irritate the enemy'.[46] This proved too much for Louis's counsellors (note again the importance of shame) who came to him, led by Philip of Flanders, and advised him to attack while the citizens were unprepared. Louis initially rejected the plan but was persuaded:

> 'God forbid!' said the king, 'God forbid the royal honour be blackened by me with this stain; for you know this rest was granted to the citizens by me out of reverence for this day of the most blessed Lawrence'. Then all the noblemen who were present reproached him for his softness with bold familiarity, saying: 'Trickery or force, who would ask which in the case of an enemy?'[47]

The last phrase is a quotation from the *Aeneid*, where it is spoken by the Trojan warrior Coroebus, who instructs his men to strip the dead Greeks of their armour and put it on as a disguise.[48] It was well-known in the central Middle Ages and variations appear in a number of chronicles, where it is attached to incidents of military deception (see Chapter 8). While it is highly unlikely that the French and Flemish nobles were quoting classical verse at the siege of Rouen, its appearance here suggests the kind of arguments that William of Newburgh thought were plausible for people to make in these circumstances: a medieval equivalent to 'all is fair in love and war'.

The plan was put into effect: an assault party was arranged in whispers, without the usual trumpets or proclamations. This unusual silence and activity in the camp was noticed by a Norman cleric who was taking the sun on a church tower and who raised the alarm before the besiegers could scale the wall. After some hard fighting, the attackers were driven back.[49] William reports that Louis subsequently attempted to blame Philip of Flanders for breaking the truce: 'The king poured the blame back onto the

---

[45] WN, vol. 2, p. 146: 'Rex autem Francorum pro eiusdem praecipui martyris reuerentia, quem specialiter et deuotius consueuerat uenerari, requiem ipso die ciuitati indultam iussit sollemniter praeconari'.

[46] WN, vol. 2, p. 146.

[47] WN, vol. 2, p. 148: '"Absit", inquit rex, "absit a me honestatem regiam hac macula denigrare; nosti enim me pro reuerentia beatissimi Laurentii diei huius requiem indulsisse ciuitati". Tunc universis qui aderat proceribus familiari ausu mollitiem improperantibus et dicentibus "dolus an virtus, quis in hoste requirat?"'.

[48] P. Vergilius Maro, *Aeneid*, ed. Gian Biagio Conte (Berlin, 2009), Book 2, lines 386–91.

[49] WN, vol. 2, p. 151.

count of Flanders, but nevertheless the stain of such a disgraceful transgression stuck more to the king's character'.[50] It is an evocative metaphor, picturing shame as something smelly and sticky that Louis attempted to pour away, only for it to splash back and cling to him instead.

It is a dramatic, colourful story but there are good reasons to question its historicity. Firstly, while the siege of Rouen is described in numerous contemporary chroniclers, William of Newburgh is the only one to mention the truce.[51] More significant are the striking parallels between this incident and Roger of Howden's account of the siege of Verneuil in 1173 (see p. 141). Both accounts involve Louis making a truce with the citizens of a Norman town that he subsequently broke. Crucially, Roger says that Louis's truce with the citizens ended on St. Lawrence's Day. It seems highly implausible that he would make and break a truce on the same day, two years in a row. William does describe the siege of Verneuil but makes no reference to a truce, saying only that Louis fled in the night rather than give battle.[52] While it is always problematic to argue for one chronicler's version of events over another, Roger's account should probably be preferred as he was closer to the events he described, having been a clerk in Henry II's household.[53] At the very least, it is clear that stories were circulating about Louis's shameful conduct during the Great Rebellion of 1173–4, which were somehow connected to St. Lawrence's Day.

One of the unusual features of William of Newburgh's account is that it presents the combatants' rationale for breaking an agreement. Such descriptions are rare but do offer a possible insight into what contemporaries thought about such breaches. The *Gesta Stephani* presents one such incident that allegedly occurred at the town of Bath in 1138. Bath had remained loyal to King Stephen but the citizens of Bristol had joined Robert, earl of Gloucester, in rebellion against him. Gilbert de Lacy, a member of Robert's household, and Geoffrey Talbot, Gilbert's cousin, were leading a force of Bristolians to reconnoitre Bath for a possible attack when they unexpectedly encountered an enemy patrol. Lacy escaped but Talbot was captured and imprisoned within Bath:

> Nevertheless they did not despair because of this but, having been resolutely revived, and rousing one another, and plotting together to liberate Talbot, they made for Bath, and, when the bishop [of Bath, Robert Lewes] had been summoned under a pledge and oath, they promised to let him come out and go back, free and unharmed. At length the bishop, like 'an

---

[50] WN, vol. 2, p. 150: 'Rex in Flandrensem comitem culpam refudit, sed personae regiae tam foedae praeuaricationis macula plus adhaesit'.

[51] HowChr, vol. 2, pp. 64–6; RD, vol. 2, pp. 386–7; RT, p. 265.

[52] WN, vol. 2, p. 125.

[53] Antonia Gransden, *Historical Writing in England* (2 vols, London, 1974–82), vol. 1, pp. 226–8.

innocent who believes every word' [Proverbs 14. 15], like another Jacob 'who lived simply in the house' [Genesis 25. 27], was joyfully (yet cunningly) received by the impious.[54]

The description of the bishop as an *innocens* was not a compliment: the author of the *Gesta* would have expected his readers to know the complete quotation from Proverbs: 'The innocent person believes every word; the astute person considers their steps'.[55] As soon as he left the safety of the city, the bishop was captured, forcing the citizens to exchange Talbot for his safe release. Once this had been arranged, the bishop began to berate the Bristolians for breaking their oath, demanding 'they fulfil the pledge which they had undertaken, to ask where on earth was their oath, and to charge them with having profaned both, nor would they prosper in their other deeds, since reverence and decency had been let slip, they appeared to have offended God by this act'.[56] Again the sacred dimension of an oath is emphasised through the choice of vocabulary: the Bristolians did not merely break their word, they 'profaned it', and in doing so offended God. The Bristolians' response is illuminating, as it appears to agree with the author's own opinion of the too-credulous bishop:

> they asserted that they had neither made an oath to him nor agreed a pledge, since it was surely reckoned by all wise people that perjurers ought to not swear oaths nor could those without faith give a pledge to anybody. They said this to him to accuse the bishop of ignorance, who too readily believed men who were very great perjurers and liars.[57]

The author of the *Gesta* did not intend to justify the deception but he clearly believed the bishop should have been more prudent. The Bristolians were known perjurers (likely a reference to their rebellion against the king, to whom the author of the *Gesta* was generally sympathetic) and

---

[54] GS, p. 60: 'Nec tamen illi ob hoc desperati, sed constantius animati, seque in inuicem cohortantes, et ad eum liberandum unanimiter conspirantes Battam petierunt, accersitoque praesule sub fide et iureiurando, liberam ei et indemnem egressionem saluamque reditionem spoponderunt. Episcopus tandem, ut innocens qui credit omni uerbo, ut alter Iacob qui simpliciter habitabat in domo, dolose ab impiis laetanter suscipitur'.
[55] Proverbs 14. 15: 'Innocens credit omni verbo; astutus considerat gressus suos'.
[56] GS, pp. 60–2: 'coepit episcopus pastorali tunc demum utens auctoritate fidem repromissam reposcere, iuramenti sacramentum ubinam esset requirere, utrorumque uiolatores eos astruere, nec prospere eis aliis in factis succedere, qui, reuerentia et pudore amisso, Deum uidebantur propter hoc offendisse'.
[57] GS, pp. 60–2: 'Haec episcopo prosequente, asserebant nec iuramentum ei fecisse, nec fidem pepigisse, cum omni sane sapienti ratum sit, nec periuros iurare debere, nec qui fide carent fidem alicui posse donare. Quae ideo dicebant, ut episcopum de ignorantia notarent, qui nimium nimiumque periuris et perfidis plus iusto credebat'.

apparently quite unashamed about it. The bishop should have taken this into account and not trusted their offer of safe conduct.

A similar rationale is presented in Galbert of Bruges's chronicle, a text contemporary with the *Gesta Stephani*. In his account of how members of the Erembald clan were besieged in Bruges castle in March 1127 following their murder of Charles, count of Flanders, Galbert described the negotiations that took place between the two sides:

> But the princes did not care what they promised to the besieged or how many oaths they swore as long as they could extort money and the good count's treasure from them. And it was right for them to act in this way, accepting the count's treasure and many more gifts from the besieged, seeing that they were not obliged to respect any faith or any oath to those most impious serfs who had betrayed their legitimate and natural lord.[58]

While he does not explicitly condemn them, it is likely that Galbert is mocking the besiegers and their justifications here. He was certainly not naive enough to believe that they were all fighting out of devotion to the memory of 'the good count'. He was very frank elsewhere in his chronicle about the mixture of motives that brought people to the siege. See, for example, his description of the final assault on the castle keep:

> [the attackers] revived their spirits, holding before their heart's eyes how they might die an excellent death for their lord and land and how, when they had conquered, they might win an honourable victory, and how those wicked and criminal traitors had made Christ's temple into a den of thieves, and (which seems more likely), how they might throw themselves upon the besieged to greedily and eagerly plunder the lord count's treasure and money and for that reason alone they hastened there.[59]

That the besiegers received treasure from the castle garrison is confirmed by the proceedings of an inquest, held after the siege by William Clito, the titular count of Flanders: 'The castellan of Ghent [Wenemar II] was attainted because he had divided the count's wealth with Robert the Boy, who was recognised for the same thing before the count and all the barons

---

[58] GB, pp. 72–3: 'At principes non curabant quid obsessis promitterent et quanta juramenta facerent, solummodo ut pecuniam et thesaurum boni comitis ab eis extorquerent. Et jure quidem sic fecerunt, accipientes ab obsessis thesaurum comitis et insuper donaria multa, quandoquidem nulla fides et juramenta nulla illis debebant observare qui legitimum et naturalem dominum suum impiissimi servi tradiderant'.

[59] GB, p. 116: 'jam animos revocaverant suos, prae oculis cordis habentes quam egregie pro patre et patria moriendum foret et quam honesta victoria vincentibus praeposita esset, quamque scelesti et facinorosi fuissent traditores illi qui de templo Christi speluncam sibi fecissent, et, quod magis videbantur, quam avide et cupide propter thesauri et pecuniae domini consulis rapinam irruerent super obsessos ipsi et idcirco solummodo festinabant'.

of the land of Flanders'.[60] Robert the Boy was the nephew of Haket, the castellan of Bruges, and was executed after the siege on the orders of Louis VI of France. Although he was attainted, Wenemar appears to have escaped any punishment for his behaviour: he remained castellan of Ghent throughout the civil war and beyond, attending the court of the eventual victor, Thierry of Alsace, in 1128.[61]

Returning to Galbert's text, it is notable that the besiegers used a similar justification to the Bristolians who captured the bishop of Bath in the *Gesta Stephani*: a known oath-breaker could not be expected to abide by an agreement, so the besiegers were not bound to observe any agreement made with the garrison. The Erembalds' rebellion and murder of their lord had violated legal and social norms to such an extent that it placed them outside the customs that governed social interaction. The *Gesta* says that the Bristolians used this as a defence, justifying their deceit by shifting the blame onto the bishop, who should have known better than to trust them, whereas Wenemar and his allies seem to have regarded the usual compulsions of honour to have been suspended for the purpose of this conflict. Consider also how the surviving members of the garrison were executed:

> When this had been arranged, the king and the count sent guards to the prison, who cunningly called out first Wulfic Cnop, the brother of the provost Bertulf, and those who had been sent under this pretence lied to the prisoners, saying that the king would act mercifully towards them. So, in the hope of mercy, they came out from the prison without delay'.[62]

One by one the prisoners were called out, expecting clemency, only to be thrown to their death from the top of the keep.[63]

---

[60] Walter of Thérouanne, *Vita Karoli comitis Flandrie et Vita domi Ioannis Morinensis episcopi*, ed. Jeff Rider (Turnhout, 2006), p. 442: 'Li chastelains de Gant fu atains que il ot partie de la pechune le conte par Robiert l'Enfant, laquel chose il meismes reconnut pardevant le conte et auchuns des barons de la terre de Flandres'.

[61] E. Warlop, *The Flemish Nobility before 1300* (2 vols, Kortrijk, 1975), vol. 1, p. 829.

[62] GB, p. 132: 'Quo praeordinato, misit rex et comes speculatores ad carcerem qui callide evocarent primum Wulfricum Cnop, fratrem praepositi Bertulfi, et sub dissimulatione qui missi fuerant mentiebantur carceratis quod rex misericorditer acturus foret cum ipsis. Sub illa ergo misericordiae spe, sine dilatione e carcere egressi sunt'.

[63] Ambroise, author of an account of the Third Crusade in Old French verse, presented another example of this rationale in an anecdote about a duel between a 'Parthian' and a Welsh archer. The 'Parthian' proposed that they take it in turn to stand and shoot arrows at one another. The Welshman agreed. The 'Parthian' took the first shot and missed. He then insisted that he be allowed to shoot a second arrow, after which the Welshman would be able to shoot two in return. The Welshman agreed to this, only to shoot the 'Parthian' dead before he could draw his bow, declaring: 'You did not hold to the agreement, so nor did I, by St. Denis!'. Amb, lines 3763–4: 'Covenant ne tenis / Ne jo a tei, par Sein Denis'. See also IP, pp. 108–9.

When Muslim ruler Saladin released Guy of Lusignan, former king of Jerusalem, in May 1188, over a year after his capture at the battle of Hattin, it was on the condition that Guy swear an oath that he would abdicate the throne of Jerusalem and not lead any armies against Saladin. Guy went to Tripoli where, according to the English chronicle the *Itinerarium Peregrinorum*, the assembled clergy declared that the oath was invalid because Guy had been forced to swear it under duress. The author then adds the following reflection: 'This was certainly a worthy decision because craft deceived craft, because the tyrant's perfidy was cheated by his own example; for one who is slippery in making promises invites equal inconstancy in giving promises'.[64] Although the phrasing is different, the sentiment is the same: Saladin's past behaviour had removed the Christians' obligation to observe their promises to him. It is possible that a similar rationale lay behind the other breaches of faith analysed elsewhere in this chapter: the deceivers considered themselves no longer bound to keep their word with an enemy because of their actual or alleged crimes.

To conclude, the conduct of medieval combatants was governed by a complex and imprecise series of customs that were enforced, not by legal courts, but by the court of public opinion. Honour and shame were powerful motivators for the proud warrior aristocracy who typically led the armies of the medieval West, albeit ones that could conflict with the dictates of military necessity. While there are examples of individuals holding to their word, even at personal cost, there are just as many examples of people breaking or bending customary practice in order to gain an advantage over their enemy. Occasionally, the chroniclers even record the excuses that they may have used to justify these violations: justifications that appealed to the faithlessness of the enemy or the need to achieve victory any cost.

---

[64] IP, p. 59: 'Dignum sane quod ars artem deluderet, quod tyranni perfidia suo fraudaretur exemplo; nam promissor lubricus parem promittentis levitatem invitat'.

8

The Language of Deception

It can be very difficult to identify the beliefs and attitudes of a long-dead society. The writings of moralists and law-makers may only represent an ideal: a prescriptive view of morality had little relation to how the majority actually thought and behaved. It is even harder to discern the attitudes of medieval combatants, as most of our sources were written by non-combatants. The closest we can get is to declare that this was how our authors *thought* combatants should behave and that, perhaps, those who actually waged these wars agreed with them.

Astute Heroes and Deceitful Villains: Case Studies in the Language of Deception

To determine whether medieval chroniclers thought military deceptions were licit or illicit, we can analyse the vocabulary they used to describe acts of deceit. Just as modern English possesses numerous synonyms for deception and trickery, such as craft, cunning, subtlety, ingenuity and guile, each with their own particular connotations, medieval chroniclers employed a range of words when writing about deception: *callidus, ingenium, ars, uafer, dolus, fraus*. The following section is made up of three case studies based on chronicles that are rich in the language of deception and representative of broader trends in contemporary narratives. Each study analyses the terms that the chronicler used for tricks and stratagems and how these terms were used to present these acts as licit or illicit. One could write an analysis of individual word use across a broad corpus of sources but such a study would not present these terms in their proper context, as well as being tedious to read.

Orderic Vitalis

The *Ecclesiastical History* of Orderic Vitalis (d. c. 1142), a monk of Saint-Évroul in Normandy, is one of the most detailed sources for Anglo-

Norman affairs during the late eleventh and early twelfth century.[1] It is replete with accounts of warfare, from the greatest campaigns of the day to highly localised conflicts fought in the vicinity of Saint-Évroul. The breadth and the variety of the military narratives contained within the *Historia* make it an ideal case study for the language of military deception in the central Middle Ages.

One of the great villains of Orderic's narrative is Robert of Bellême (c. 1057–c. 1131), son and heir to Roger of Montgomery, the first earl of Shrewsbury (d. 1094). Robert's principal continental holdings were in the Hiémois region of north-eastern France, just north Saint-Évroul. He held land from no less than three major princes: the counts of Maine, the dukes of Normandy and the kings of France. Robert's career was spent fighting to both expand and to 'preserve the integrity of his far-flung family lands' against his neighbours' encroachments, alternatively siding with and against the dukes of Normandy as seemed expedient.[2] Although he was an active and talented soldier, he proved to be a poor politician and ended his days as a prisoner of Henry I of England, having backed Henry's elder brother, Robert Curthose, in their conflict for the duchy of Normandy. In the course of his various wars in and around the Hiémois, Robert annexed church lands, constructed castles on church property and compelled local monasteries, including Saint-Évroul, to provide him with both manpower and financial support, all of which earned him the ire of Orderic, Saint-Évroul's resident historian.[3] While Kathleen Thompson has done much to rehabilitate Robert's reputation by placing his career in its historical context, Orderic presents him as nothing less than evil incarnate: a sadistic, treacherous blasphemer, intent on stirring up rebellion against the dukes of Normandy purely for personal gain. According to Thompson, Robert's function in the *Historia*'s narrative is to serve as 'the opposition, the negative force with which the ruler [of Normandy] must contend'.[4]

One of Robert of Bellême's defining characteristics, in Orderic's account, was his propensity for treachery and his mastery of deceitful tactics in warfare. Consider Orderic's initial description of Robert and his character:

---

[1] For an introduction to Orderic and his chronicle, see Marjorie Chibnall, *The World of Orderic Vitalis* (Oxford, 1984); Charles C. Rozier, Daniel Roach, Giles E. M. Gasper and Elisabeth van Houts (eds.), *Orderic Vitalis: Life, Works and Interpretations* (Woodbridge, 2016).

[2] Kathleen Thompson, 'Robert of Bellême Reconsidered', in Marjorie Chibnall (ed.), *Anglo-Norman Studies XIII: Proceedings of the Battle Conference, 1990* (Woodbridge, 1991), pp. 263–86, at p. 266.

[3] Kathleen Thompson, 'Orderic Vitalis and Robert of Bellême', *Journal of Medieval History*, 20 (1994), 133–41, at p. 135.

[4] Thompson, 'Orderic Vitalis', p. 140.

He prevented many from helping and serving [Robert Curthose] by cunningly hanging back from aiding him; and he diminished the duke's domain, that his ancestors had held and who had greatly enlarged it. For he was subtle in character, cunning and shifty, great and strong in body, bold and powerful in arms, eloquent and excessively cruel, greedy and insatiable in lust. A perceptive deviser of savage works, an inventor of structures, and suffered the heaviest labours in the exertions of the world. An ingenious artificer in raising up structures, machines and other tall works and a inexorable butcher in torturing men.[5]

Orderic uses a variety of epithets related to Robert's deceitful nature: *subtilis, dolosus, versipellis*. His plan to draw support away from Robert Curthose was *callidus* (cunning), a term that will be particularly important in the following discussion. Orderic also connects Robert's cunning personality with his talent for building and utilising war machines: he is *perspicax* and *ingeniosus*, both adjectives with associations of cleverness and mental acuity.[6] Compare Orderic's description of Robert's actions at the siege of Courcy, in Normandy in January 1091: 'But for three weeks Robert assailed the enemies with every possible trick and act of violence; and he harassed the town with diverse machines'.[7] Robert's attacks on the garrison consisted of both *doli* and *machinationes*, although the latter could also be a synonym for tricks and devices, further illustrating the close link between Robert's cunning and his siegecraft.[8]

Orderic employed further negative adjectives for Robert when describing his attempt to capture the castle at Saint-Céneri by surprise. This took place shortly after the siege of Bréval in 1092: Philip I of France and Robert Curthose had joined with William of Breteuil to subjugate William's vassal, Ascelin Goel. Ascelin surrendered but, according to Orderic, Robert of Bellême, who had been in command of the siege engines, was angered that he had not been invited to participate in the negotiations. Consequently, he sought to use the confused political situation to seize Saint-Céneri, which had previously belonged to his family but had been given to one Robert Giroie by Robert Curthose in 1088:

---

[5] OV, vol. 4, p. 158: 'Multos ab auxilio eius et famulatu callidis tergiuersationibus auertit; et dominium ducis quod antecessores eius possederant et copiose auxerant imminuit. Erat enim ingenio subtilis, dolosus et uersipellis, corpore magnus et fortis, audax et potens in armis, eloquens nimiumque crudelis, auaricia et libidine inexplebilis. Perspicax seuorum commentor operum, et in exercitiis mundi grauissimorum patiens laborum. In extruendis aedificis et machinis aliisque arduis operibus ingeniosus artifex; et in torquendis hominibus inexorabilis carnifex'.
[6] Charlton T. Lewis and Charles Short, *A Latin Dictionary* (Oxford, 1879), p. 950, 1356.
[7] OV, vol. 4, p. 233: 'Robertus uero per tres septimanas dolis et uiribus in hostes omnimodis surrexit; et diuersis machinationibus municipium infestauit'.
[8] Lewis and Short, *Latin Dictionary*, p. 1092.

> And then the aforesaid knight [i.e. Robert of Bellême] learned that an agreement had been made between the warring parties; he assembled his troops at once. Not revealing to anybody the deceit that was in his heart, he swiftly returned, rushing to fall upon Robert Giroie at Saint-Céneri while he was unprepared. But the citizens had come out, believing Robert [of Bellême] was with the duke in the general expedition; and they were wandering here and there through the fields, untroubled, as it pleased them. And when the sly deceiver suddenly rushed up with his forces, he was pressing hard to enter the town and to place the occupants under his rule.[9]

In the event, Robert of Bellême's surprise attack failed, as Robert of Giroie was able to rush ahead and shut the castle gates in his face. Once again, Orderic uses clearly negative language to describe Robert of Bellême's actions: his scheme was a *fraus* and he was a *vafer insidiator*.

When describing other incidents of military deception, however, Orderic was capable of expressing admiration and would even employ the same vocabulary that he used for the villainous Robert of Bellême. Consider his description of Bernard the Dane, one of the co-regents of Normandy during the minority of Duke Richard I. Following the death of Richard's father, William Longsword, in 942, Louis IV of France had ceded the Norman regions of Exmes, Bayeux and the Cotentin to Hugh, count of Orléans. In 946, Louis and Hugh invaded the duchy in response to a rebellion, centred around Bayeux. Orderic describes how Bernard, realising that the Normans were too weak to resist by force of arms, sought to turn the king against Hugh:

> He was anxious because he cunningly observed that he alone, with the strength of Normandy, would be unable to hold back such strong princes by fighting and so, having a sharp-sighted nature, he cleverly busied himself as to how he might drive the crisis that was set before him away from himself and his people.[10]

Orderic employs the same vocabulary, *perspicax* (keen) and *callide* (cunningly), that he would later apply to Robert of Bellême, to describe Bernard's assessment of his situation. In this context, we might prefer to read *callide* in its broader sense of 'skilfully' or 'with expertise' but it is surely significant that Orderic could use the same word to describe both

---

[9] OV, vol. 4, p. 292: 'Denique prefatus miles ut concordiam inter discordes factam cognouit; cuneos suos protinus conuocauit, nullique fraudem sui cordis detegens festinanter remeauit, ac ad sactum Serenicum super Robertum Geroianum ex improuiso conuolauit. Municipes autem Robertum in expeditione generali cum duce putantes exierant; et sparsim per agros securi pro libitu suo discurrebant. Cumque uafer insidiator cum copiis suis repente irrueret, et oppidum ingredi castellanosque sibi subire satageret'.

[10] OV, vol. 3, p. 310: 'anxius quod tam robustos principes solus cum Normannicis uiribus bellando sustinere non posset callide perspexit, et perspicax ingenium qualiter anceps discrimen a se et a suis abigeret sollerter apponens exercuit'.

an act of rebellion and a patriotic defence of the duchy.[11] Orderic uses the adverb again to describe how Bernard persuaded Louis to change his mind by insinuating about the court that Hugh of Orléans was unworthy to possess Norman land: 'And when one day, after lunch, the king sat in the main hall, so that he could cheerfully discuss the business of the kingdom with those sitting with him, the clever Bernard cunningly [*callide*] put forward untrustworthy speeches to many people'.[12]

Orderic also used *callidus* in its positive sense in a military context. The early sections of the *Historia* include a history of Saint-Évroul's foundation and its benefactors, the Giroie family, named for their patriarch, Giroie, son of Arnold the Fat of Courceraut.[13] Here is Orderic's summary of the character of Giroie's seven sons: 'For all these brothers were active and bountiful, cunning [*callidi*] and nimble in war; terrible towards enemies yet pleasant and courteous to friends'.[14] The sons of Giroie were no paragons of virtue: they murdered Gilbert, count of Brionne, in c. 1041, although Orderic did not criticise them for this in the *Historia*.[15] Since we know that Orderic was consciously presenting the Giroie brothers in a positive way here, it is significant that he chose to list *callidus* as one of their defining qualities, alongside their vigour, generosity and courtesy.

Orderic was also happy to depict his heroes employing deceitful tactics. We have already discussed Orderic's description of the valiant Ralph the Breton changing his arms to avoid being recognised while defending Breteuil against the French in 1119 (see Chapter 5). In a brief character sketch of Herbert I, count of Maine (1015–32), Orderic wrote admiringly of his raids into Anjou:

> [he] earned from the common people (but not in Latin) the nickname of 'Wake-Dog' on account of his remarkable valour. For, after the death of his father, Hugh [III], whom the elder Fulk [III of Anjou] had violently conquered, raising arms against the same man, he often conducted nocturnal expeditions and terrified the men and dogs of Anjou in that city or in their fortified towns and compelled the terror-struck [citizens] to keep watch for his dreadful assaults.[16]

---

[11] Lewis and Short, *Latin Dictionary*, p. 270.

[12] OV, vol. 3, p. 310: 'Cumque rex quadam die post prandium in aula principali resedisset, et cum assidentibus sibi letus negotia regni tractasset; sollers Bernardus ambiguam plurimis locutionem callide promouet'.

[13] OV, vol. 1, pp. 6–8.

[14] OV, vol. 2, p. 24: 'Omnes enim isti fratres fuerunt strenui et dapsiles, in militia callidi et agiles; hostibus terribiles, sociisque blandi et affabiles'.

[15] He did, however, call it an 'evil and cruel deed' when making interpolations in William of Jumièges's *Gesta Normannorum Ducum*: OV, vol. 2, p. 24 n. 3.

[16] OV, vol. 2, p. 304: 'et uulgo sed parum latine cognominari Euigilans-canem pro ingenti probitate promeruit. Nam post mortem Hugonis patris sui quem Fulco senior sibi uiolenter subiugarat, in eundem arma leuans nocturnas expeditiones crebro agebat;

Instead of regarding Herbert's night raids as evidence that he was unwilling or unable to fight openly against the Angevins, Orderic claims that they were a manifestation of Herbert's 'remarkable valour' (*ingens probitas*). It appears to have amused Orderic to picture the Angevins, inveterate enemies of the Norman dukes, sitting in the dark, quaking with fear at Herbert's approach.

Orderic uses a rich and varied vocabulary to describe incidents of deception in his *Historia* but it is the intersection of 'positive' and 'negative' incidents that is most illuminating. In particular, Orderic's use of *callidus* and its derivatives suggest that he (and presumably his audience) did not consider 'cunning' to be an inherently negative quality. When it was employed for evil ends, as in the case of Robert of Bellême, then it was contemptible but it could also be used in a worthy cause, as in the cases of Herbert Wake-Dog or Bernard the Dane.

Walter the Chancellor

While Orderic's *Historia* is valuable for the breadth and diversity of the conflicts it records, Walter the Chancellor's *Bella Antiochena* is useful because it focuses on a single conflict: the wars between the principality of Antioch and the neighbouring Turkish powers, in particular Roger of Salerno's disastrous campaign of 1119 that led to his death at the Field of Blood. As chancellor of the principality, Walter was an eyewitness to many of the events he recorded and was probably present at the Field of Blood itself. While he portrays the Turkish ruler Īlghāzī as a bloodthirsty tyrant, Walter's general attitude towards the Turks is more equivocal and seems to reflect a grudging admiration among the Franks for their martial ability (see p. 179). Nonetheless, he typically uses negative epithets for incidents involving Turkish deceit, reserving more positive terms for descriptions of Frankish tactics.

In February 1115, Bursuq ibn Bursuq of Hamadān, a general in the service of the Saljūq sultan Muhammad Tapar (1105–18), crossed the Euphrates with an army and moved to occupy Aleppo. A hasty alliance was formed between the Frankish settlers and the independent Turkish warlords of Syria to oppose him.[17] Following an unsuccessful attack on Roger of Salerno's camp at Apamea, Bursuq withdrew and pretended to disband his forces:

> So Bursuq, a commander of deceitful cunning, withdrawing, pretended to flee and, as if wishing to return to his homeland, concealed his wickedness for the moment by dividing his troops throughout the lands of Shaizar

---

et Andegauenses homines et canes in ipsa urbe uel in munitioribus oppidis terrebat, et horrendis assultibus pauidos uigilare cogebat'.

[17] For an account of the campaign see Nicholas Morton, *The Field of Blood: The Battle for Aleppo and the Remaking of the Medieval Middle East* (New York, 2018), pp. 64–7.

[south of Apamea, on the Orontes river], so that, when our men withdrew and separated, he would be better able to destroy our coastal cities in safety.[18]

Walter calls Bursuq a man of *dolosa calliditas* (deceitful cunning) and his stratagem an act of *nequitia* (wickedness). His description of the Turks' reconnaissance of the Frankish camp at the Field of Blood in 1119 is similar:

> And so those men of deceitful cunning, to conceal what they were planning, namely to attack us unexpectedly, their divisions having been arranged and those who were better prepared having been sent forward, came as if intending to besiege Cerepus [al-Atharib, ten miles to the south-east], which had been observed, so that they would see and be seen [by the Franks].[19]

Once again, he characterises the Turks as *dolosa callditas*, whose 'cunning' is manifested in a strategic manoeuvre, intended to conceal their true intentions from the Franks.

Walter the Chancellor was not entirely against cunning tactics, however. He is at pains to defend Roger of Salerno's decision to remain in camp and delay fighting against Bursuq at Apamea in 1115, when many of his army wanted to sally out and fight immediately:

> And some of our people reckoned that this was done because of cowardice, but several people of greater ingenuity concluded that this was done according to the prince's design, that, when a suitable time had been identified, they would be stronger to attack the Turks, not when their enemies suggested nor because of our presumed strength but because of the provident direction and proven ingenuity of Roger and the king [Baldwin I of Jerusalem], who was very close. For, as has been proven, a small number of fighters with boldness and ingenuity are often stronger in battle than a senseless and vacillating multitude of armed men.[20]

Walter emphasises Roger's prudence and generalship, which were a product of his *ingenium*. This word has connotations of innate cleverness, talent

---

[18] WC, p. 70: 'Burso igitur, dux dolosae calliditatis, retrocedens fugam simulat et quasi repatriare uolens per partes Sisarae diuortia faciendo ad tempus suam occultauit nequitiam, ut nostris retrocessis ac separatris nostra ualerent tutius diruere maritima municipia'.

[19] WC, p. 81: 'Ipsi itaque dolosae calliditatis uiri, ut dissimularent quod moliebantur, uidelicet ex insperato nos inuadere, palam ordinatis aciebus habilioribusque praeludio iam praemissis, quasi obsessuri Cerepum spectatum ueniunt, ab hoc utique ut spectent et spectentur'.

[20] WC, p. 69: 'Quidam etiam nostrorum id facti timiditati reputant, nonnulli autem capacioris ingenii hoc fieri de principis industria coniiciunt, ut, explorato congrui temporis articulo, non admonitione hostium nec praesumptione uirium, sed sui regisque in proximo aduenientis dispositione prouida ingenioque experienti eos inpetere praeualeant. Saepius enim, ut expertum est, praualet in bello cum audacia et ingenio pugnatorum paucitas, quam infrunita et uacillans armatorum multitudo'.

and genius, and is the root of the modern English 'ingenuity'.[21] According to Walter, this quality, when employed in conjunction with *audacia*, could enable a smaller army to defeat a larger but less astute enemy. Roger of Salerno's strategy at Apamea was a product of *ingenium* but Bursuq's counter-manoeuvre received the more negative labels *dolosus* and *callidus*: a noteworthy example of a Christian chronicler's double-standard when depicting Frankish-Muslim conflicts.

In the aftermath of the massacre at the Field of Blood, Rainald Mazoir, lord of Marqab and constable of Antioch, retreated to a nearby tower, where he was briefly besieged by Īlghāzī. Walter describes Rainald as acting with *astutia*, a synonym for cleverness or cunning with both positive and negative connotations, for negotiating a surrender with Īlghāzī:

> Nevertheless, protected by astuteness, he spoke cautiously, as if he was able to defend himself in the tower. For he said to the triumphant Īlghāzī: 'I will by no means hand myself over to you unless you first promise me, with a pledge and a scared oath according to your law, the safety of your protection and help to escape'.[22]

This was clearly a deception: Rainald was unable to hold the tower yet negotiated 'as if' (*quasi*) he was able. Yet Walter does not criticise Rainald for deceiving Īlghāzī or for surrendering: his ire is reserved for those who fled the field entirely. Rainald's decision proved very shrewd, as Īlghāzī accepted his surrender and kept his promise to release Rainald after a month's imprisonment. Rainald remained a major figure at the Antiochene court and was appointed regent of the principality by Fulk of Jerusalem in 1132, following the deposition of Alice of Jerusalem, widow of the former prince Bohemond II. This may indicate why Walter credited him with *astutia* for his actions after the Field of Blood. It would have been impolitic to accuse such a senior official of cowardice or treachery.

Like Orderic, Walter the Chancellor describes acts of cunning and deceit in both positive and negative ways. He uses *callidus* exclusively to describe the Turks while using more general terms such as *ingenium* and *astutia* for Christian stratagems. As will be discussed below, however, Walter was more nuanced in his attitudes than this survey may suggest and also credited the Turks with employing *ingenium*.

---

[21] Lewis and Short, *Latin Dictionary*, p. 950.
[22] WC, p. 89: 'Astutia tamen praemunitus, quasi se in turre defendere posset, caute locutus est; ait enim triumphanti: me nequaquam tibi reddam, nisi te prius fide et sacramento tuae legis mihi adseras praesentis tutelae patrocinium et euadendi subsidium'.

William of Apulia

The Latin verse poem celebrating the life of eleventh-century Norman adventurer Robert Guiscard is particularly rich in vocabulary of trickery and deceit, as befits the story of a man whose cognomen means 'the Wily'. Dedicated to (and presumably commissioned by) Guiscard's son and heir, Roger Borsa, the *Gesta Roberti Wiscardi* was composed by the otherwise unknown William of Apulia and is a key example of a medieval author attempting to turn a morally dubious subject into something laudable.[23] William's preferred term when describing Guiscard's 'wiliness' is *ars*, a word with connotations of skill, artifice and the practical application of knowledge.[24] Describing Guiscard's character, William wrote: 'He seized the palm of victory either by craft [*ars*] or by arms, he considered both in the same manner, because a cunning mind often accomplishes what violence cannot'.[25] Regarding Guiscard's attempt to bribe the keeper of Montepeloso in 1064, he wrote: 'because the duke did not prevail through arms, he took the *castrum* through craft [*ars*]'.[26] The capture of Dyracchion through bribery and his infiltration of an unnamed castrum using the 'fake corpse' ruse were both described as products of *ars*.[27] As discussed in Chapter 6, Guiscard's suppression of a revolt in his Italian lands in 1079 was summarised with the phrase: 'he overcame them all, either by craft [*ars*] or arms'.[28]

William of Apulia also uses *ars* in its broader sense, for skilfulness or craft in other matters. In a curious story, set just after the capture of Bari in 1071, William describes how Guiscard organised the capture of a 'great fish' (presumably a species of whale) that had come near to shore, using weighted nets: 'The prudence of the duke captured this [fish] through various *artes*'.[29] In a similar incident, he described how Guiscard constructed a dam to raise the level of the river Glykys in western Greece and refloat his fleet in the winter of 1084–5:

---

[23] For more information on William of Apulia, see Paul Brown, 'The *Gesta Roberti Wiscardi*: A Byzantine History?', *Journal of Medieval History*, 37 (2011), 162–79; Peter Frankopan, 'Turning Latin into Greek: Anna Komnene and the *Gesta Roberti Wiscardi*', *Journal of Medieval History*, 39 (2013), 80–99; Graham Loud, *The Age of Robert Guiscard: Southern Italy and the Norman Conquest* (London, 2000), p. 5.

[24] Lewis and Short, *Latin Dictionary*, p. 166.

[25] WA, p. 148: 'Si contingebat sibi palma vel arte vel armis, / Aeque ducebat, quia quod violentia saepe / Non explere potest, explet versutia mentis'.

[26] WA, p. 156: 'dux quod non evalet armis / Arte capit castrum'.

[27] WA, pp. 150, 230.

[28] WA, p. 194: 'vel arte vel armis / Omnes exsuperat'.

[29] WA, p. 172: 'Per varias artes ducis hunc prudentia cepit'.

The duke, who made the difficult task easy through craft [*ars*], when he learned the river needed its usual flow, for a small amount of water flowed through a narrow channel, he directed that many posts be brought and set up on either bank, joined together with branches, and he made fascines from many branches which he had cut, and filled them with sand from above.[30]

As with Orderic Vitalis's description of Robert of Bellême, William of Apulia's use of *ars* in different contexts indicates an intellectual connection between 'cunning' and more general skilfulness or intelligence, a connection reflected in the different possible meanings of the modern English word 'craft'.

William used other terms for Guiscard's 'cunning', albeit less frequently. For example, here is William's explanation for Guiscard's cognomen: 'He was nicknamed "Guiscard" because neither Cicero nor the wily Ulysses were of such cunning [*calliditas*]'.[31] The comparison with Ulysses, the man who devised the Trojan Horse, seems fitting but the connection with Cicero is more puzzling. It may indicate a connection between 'craft' and eloquence: Guiscard's *ars* was manifested in 'sweet words'.[32] Compare Ralph of Caen's description of his teacher and patron, Arnulf of Chocques, who challenged Tancred concerning his plundering of the Temple Mount in 1099: 'Since he had been stung by Arnulf's darts, as of a second Ulysses, eloquence provoked him [to take action]'.[33] Geoffrey Malaterra also connected a propensity for deceit with rhetoric in his description of the Norman people:

> They are a most astute people, vengeful of injuries, despising their ancestral fields in the hope of winning more elsewhere, greedy for profit and domination, pretenders and dissemblers in everything, holding a certain balance between liberality and avarice [...] These people know how to flatter, being so devoted to the study of eloquence that you should even attend to their boys as if they were rhetoricians.[34]

---

[30] WA, p. 248: 'Dux, qui difficilem facilem facit arte laborem, / dum fluvium solitis cognovit egere fluentis, / namque meatus aquae brevis arta fauce fluebat, / multos afferri palos et ab amnis utraque / Margine configi connexos vimine iussit, / Et multis multa praecisis arbore ramis / Composuit crates, et arenis desuper implet'.

[31] WA, p. 138: 'Cognomen Guiscardus erat, quia calliditatis / Non Cicero tantae fuit aut versutus Ulixes'.

[32] WA, pp. 194–6.

[33] GT, p. 111: 'Quibus armata iaculis Arnulfi, quasi alterius Vlixis, facundia uirum prouocat'.

[34] GM, p. 10: 'Est quippe gens astutissima, injuriarum ultrix, spe alias plus lucrandi patrios agros vilipendens, quaestus et dominationis avida, cuiuslibet rei simulatrix ac dissimulatrix, inter largitatem et avaritiam quoddam medium habens [...] Gens adulari sciens, eloquentiae studiis inserviens in tantum, ut etiam et ipsos pueros quasi rhetores attendas'.

Describing how the Byzantine emperor Constantine IX dispatched Argyros, the Lombard ruler of Bari, to try and persuade the Normans to leave Italy and go to fight for the empire in the Near East, William of Apulia depicted the Norman 'cunning' (*callidus*) outwitting that of the Greeks:

> He summoned the Frankish counts and promised to give them lots of money if, having left Latius [Italy], they would cross over to Argos [Greece], which was engaged in grave struggles with the Persians and, swearing an oath, he promised that they would be joyfully received by him who rules the empire, and promised that they would be enriched with great wealth. The Greeks' cunning promise was not hidden from the [Norman] people's cunning.[35]

William describes non-Norman trickery in both positive and negative ways. He generally portrays Alexios Komnenos as a 'worthy foe' of Robert Guiscard, including in matters of cunning. Describing how Alexios made his name as a general under Michael VII and Nikephoros III, he wrote: 'In this way the victorious Alexios, active and careful, overcame the empire's many enemies by arms and craft [*ars*]'.[36] He also used negative language for Greek deceit. When Guiscard launched his first campaign in the Balkans, William claimed that he had cultivated a friendship with the governor of Dyrrachion, George Monomachatos.[37] Unfortunately for Guiscard, Alexios removed Monomachatos once he had seized the imperial throne and replaced him with his own brother-in-law, George Palaiologos, forcing Guiscard to lay siege to a city that he had hoped would be open to him.[38] William claimed Monomachatos's fall was accomplished through 'trickery' (*fraus*) but gives no further details: 'Palaiologos brought many Greeks to Dyracchion and George was driven out through trickery'.[39]

One of William of Apulia's strangest references to deception occurs just before Guiscard's battle with Alexios Komnenos outside Dyracchion (18 October 1081). Alexios's army had been spotted and some of Guiscard's men advocated leaving their siege camp in front of the city to give battle. Guiscard's response is surprising, to say the least: 'The duke replied that

---

[35] WA, p. 134: 'Francorum comites vocat, et se magna daturum / Munera promittit, / si transgrediantur ad Argos, / Dimisso Latio, grave qui certamen habebant / Cum Persis, et eos iurans promittit ab illo / Qui regit imperium gratanter suscipiendos, / Et magnis opibus ditandos affore spondit. / Callida Graecorum promissio calliditatem / Non latuit gentis Latium superare volentis'.

[36] WA, p. 20: 'Impiger et cautus sic victor Alexius hostes / Imperii multos armis superavit et arte'.

[37] Anna Komnene also says that Monomachatus received bribes from Guiscard: Anna Komnene, *The Alexiad*, trans. E. R. A. Sewter (London, 1969), pp. 125–6.

[38] Georgios Theotokis, *The Norman Campaigns in the Balkans 1081–1108* (Woodbridge, 2014), p. 146.

[39] WA, p. 216: 'multos Paliologus Argos / Diarchium duxit, pulsusque Georgius urbe / Fraude fuit'.

it was better not to leave the well-supplied camps until the imperial army was closer and he announced that it was unnecessary for a trick [*ars*] to be sought in order to gain victory, since victory is given to nobody unless it comes from heaven'.[40] It is striking indeed to find Guiscard, a man renowned for his stratagems, piously advising his men that they should trust in heaven alone, especially in a chronicle that records how useful *ars* had been to Guiscard throughout his career. Emily Albu has suggested that this statement is deliberately ironic, either by Guiscard himself or William of Apulia.[41] This is corroborated in the next passage, in which William emphasises Guiscard's prudent and circumspect preparations for the battle:

> Although he knew that he had excellent horsemen with him, nevertheless he did not want to be reckless in any undertaking. He had been told that an innumerable people were approaching but it had not yet been made known to him what kind of men they were; for which reason the clever duke wisely arrayed all his men in advance, and arranged everything that had to be prepared.[42]

William Apulia's *Gesta* is an illuminating example of how a medieval author could use language to frame deceptive behaviour in a positive manner. Rather than employing explicit terms such as *dolus* or *callidus* William preferred to speak of Guiscard's behaviour as *ars*, with its associations of skill and craft. This 'craftiness' was demonstrated not only in his clever stratagems but also in his prudent generalship and engineering skill, a theme shared by other medieval chronicles (see 163–6).

As we have seen, medieval chroniclers drew up a wide range of vocabulary when discussing acts of military deception. While some terms, such as *fraus* and *dolus*, appear to have had largely negative connotations, many were more ambiguous, like *callidus* or *ars*. These terms, associated with ideas of skilfulness and practical knowledge, suggest that trickery and ruses were not seen as inherently illicit but could be viewed positively, as demonstrations of intelligence and good generalship. The close relationship between terms for cunning and the language of siege warfare reinforces this idea.

---

[40] WA, p. 222: 'Esse refert melius dux, non abscedere castris, / Copia dum propius conspecta sit imperialis, / Et frustra quaeri vincendi praedicat artem, / Cum nisi de coelo nulli victoria detur'.

[41] Emily Albu, *The Normans in Their Histories: Propaganda, Myth, and Subversion* (Woodbridge, 2001), p. 143.

[42] WA, pp. 222–4: 'Is licet egregios equites sibi sciret adesse, / Nil ineundo tamen temerarius esse volebat. / Congressura quidem gens innumerabilis esse / Dicebatur ei, nec adhuc natura virorum / Nota sibi fuerat; catus unde sagaciter omnes / Ordinat ante suos, et quaeque paranda coaptat'.

Machines or Machinations?: The Language of Trickery and Siege Craft

While certain elements of medieval siege warfare have been studied in considerable depth, such as the evolution of counter-weight artillery, the role played by specialist engineers and sappers, and the development of gunpowder, modern scholars have yet to adequately analyse the connection between the language of 'siege craft' and the language of deception in contemporary narratives.[43] In many instances, the vocabulary is identical and it can be difficult to tell whether an author is referring to combatants assaulting a stronghold with stratagems or siege engines. The modern English 'engineer' is derived from the Anglo-Norman *engin* (itself ultimately derived from the Latin *ingenium*), which could mean a machine, a ruse or any general skill: an engineer was one who created *engin*.[44] While there is insufficient space here to treat this topic as fully as it deserves, a brief chronological survey of representative examples will demonstrate the linguistic connection between siege warfare and stratagems in medieval narratives. This is indicative of more general attitudes towards military deceptions: they could be viewed as products of intelligence and skill, without any particular ethical connotations.

Consider Orderic Vitalis's description of Robert Curthose's siege of Brionne in June 1090: 'The cunning besiegers heated the iron [heads] of their missiles in a smith's furnace, which had been hurriedly built', which they proceeded to shoot into the castle's wooden roof. As it had been a very hot and dry summer, 'a great fire was quickly kindled; and it grew exceedingly strong, since the defenders of the castle were fighting vigorously and were unaware of the trick, until the fire had advanced directly over their heads'.[45] It is curious that Orderic should call this a trick (*dolus*): there is no deception here, unless it is that the garrison were unaware that their roof had been set on fire. It is likely that he is using *dolus* in a sense closer to 'stratagem', a product of the attackers' cunning (*callidi*), which was employed instead of a direct attack.

Robert the Monk describes the leaders of the First Crusade making a similar decision when they arrived before Antioch in October 1097: 'the

---

[43] Purton acknowledges this link but does not explore its implications: Peter Purton, *The Medieval Military Engineer: From the Roman Empire to the Sixteenth Century* (Woodbridge, 2018), pp. 16–19.

[44] 'engine, n.', *OED Online*, <http://www.oed.com/view/Entry/62223> [accessed 18 October 2018].

[45] OV, vol. 4, p. 208: 'Callidi enim obsessores in fabrili fornace quae in promptu structa fuerat ferrum missilium calefaciebant [...] Inde magnus ignis celeriter confotus est; et defensoribus oppidi ualide pugnantibus dolumque nescientibus nimis confortatus est, donec flamma super capita eorum extimplo progressa est'.

princes devised a plan, for they would fight against the city with ingenuity, not force; with craft, not force of arms; with machines, not warlike combats'.[46] A coherent English translation cannot accurately convey Robert's wordplay here, particularly the contrast between *ars* and *Mars* in the final phrase. Note that this passage does not refer to Bohemond's act of bribery or any other act of deception. It is followed by this sentence, clearly connected to the previous by the conjunction *igitur*: 'So first they built a bridge over the river, so that they could cross the river easily, as often as they needed'. The consequence of the princes choosing *ingenium*, *ars* and *machinamentum* over brute force was a feat of engineering, not a ruse.

The *Gesta Stephani*, with its numerous accounts of sieges, is particularly rich in examples of this kind of language. Describing Stephen of England's siege of Exeter Castle in 1136, the anonymous chronicler wrote: '[The garrison], from their side, strongly and unhesitatingly opposed all his machines, which the ingenuity of many craftsmen had laboured upon, caring for nothing: so, as both sides were fighting vigorously and ingeniously, their great struggle became one of prudence and speed'.[47] Later, when the castle well dried up, the chronicler describes the dire straits members of the garrison were reduced to: 'Also, they always ran to extinguish with wine the fire and torches that the king's craftsmen were prudently and craftily throwing inside, which were intended to scorch their machines or burn down their buildings'.[48] Describing the Empress Matilda's assault upon Henry, bishop of Winchester's castle in 1141, the chronicler wrote: 'Because, while they were pressing to the obtain the bishop's castle by craft and ingenuity, those who were shut up inside, since they had thrown out fires, reduced the greater part of the city to ashes, including two abbeys'.[49] Likewise, the *Itinerarium Peregrinorum*, describes Richard I of England contemplating how to assault Acre in the following terms: 'He considered

---

[46] RM, p. 775: 'consilium inierunt principes quod contra eam pugnarent non virtute, sed ingenio; arte, non Marte; machinamento, non conflictu bellico. Prius igitur pontem supra flumen statuerunt, ut expeditius flumen transirent, quotiens transeundi necesse haberent'.

[47] GS, p. 34: 'Illi e contra fortiter et promptissime refragantes, omnia eius machinamenta, in quibus plurimum artificum desudarat ingenium, nihili pendebant: ita ut strenue et ingeniose utrisque decertantibus, magnum eorum fieret prudentiae et uelocitatis certamen'.

[48] GS, p. 40: 'Igni quoque et facibus, quos ad machinas eorum ustulandas, uel ad domos consumendas, regis artifices prudenter et artice immittebant, cum uino semper extincturi occurrebant'.

[49] GS, p. 130: 'quia dum illi ad episcopi obtinendum castellum arte et ingenio contendebant, qui intus recludebantur ignibus foras emissis maiorem ciutatis partem, sed et duas abbatias, in fauillas penitus redegerunt'.

many things with careful attention: by what attack, by what craft [*ars*], with what machines the city might be captured more easily'.[50]

The vernacular chronicles do not provide as many examples of this topos as the Latin but there does appear to have been a similar connection between ideas of engineering, skilfulness and trickery. For instance, in his *Roman de Brut*, Wace described Brutus and his followers retreating to their castle at Sparatin, where they were besieged by Pandrasus, king of Greece: 'When the king saw that it was no use, that he could not take it by assault nor by any *engine* that he could fashion, he withdrew and menaced them'.[51] Geoffrey de Villehardouin, recalling the siege of Constantinople in July 1203, described how the besiegers 'thought of a very good *engin*: they surrounded the whole host with a fine palisade and fine timberwork and a fine barrier; and so they were much stronger and more secure inside'.[52] The connection also appears in Old Scots. In Barbour's *Bruce*, *sutelté* is used to describe the specialist skills of John Crab, a Flemish engineer recruited by the Scots for the siege of Berwick in 1319, and the skills of the silversmith who made the casket that held Robert Bruce's embalmed heart.[53] It is also applied to stealthy and deceitful tactics. When James Douglas needed to take Roxburgh castle in February 1315, Barbour wrote that he 'set all his wit for to pruchas / How Roxburch throu sutelté / Or ony craft mycht wonnyn be'.[54] Likewise, Thomas Randolph, earl of Moray, when ordered to seize Edinburgh Castle in March 1314, is pictured seeking: 'sum sutelte or wile to get / Quharthrou the castell have mycht he'.[55]

The fact that chroniclers could use the same vocabulary to describe a ruse and a siege-engine indicates that, not only were both considered products of intelligence and skill, but that terms such as *ars* and *ingenium* in a military context did not necessarily carry any ethical overtones. Nobody would argue that catapults or siege towers were an illicit or dishonourable method of fighting: they were simply practical alternatives to brute force and hand-to-hand assaults. This disjunction between force and trickery,

---

[50] IP, p. 211: 'Multa quidem meditabatur sollicitudine, qua instantia, quo artificio, quibus machinis civitas expeditiori comprehenderetur compendio'. The chronicler has expanded on Ambroise here, who does not specify what methods Richard considered when planning the siege: Amb, lines 2347–50: 'Le rei Richart vint a ses tentes / E mist paine e granz ententes / Coment Acre sereit comquise / E com el sereit plus tost prise'.
[51] RdB, lines 337–40: 'Kant veit li reis que ne li valt / Que nes puet prendre par assalt / Ne par nul engine ke li face, / Trait sei en sus e sis menace'.
[52] GV, vol. 1, p. 168: 'Lors se porpenserent de un mult bon engin: qui il fermerent tote l'ost de bones lices et de bons merriens et bones barres; et si en furent mult plus fort et plus seür'.
[53] Bruce, Book 17, line 240; 20, line 315.
[54] Bruce, Book 10, lines 360–2.
[55] Bruce, Book 10, lines 538–42.

strength and shrewdness, was a common Latin topos and one that can be observed throughout chronicle narratives of this period.

'By Hook or By Crook, We Will': The Disjunction of Force and Trickery

The grammatical term 'disjunction' refers to 'a statement or condition of affairs involving a choice between two or more statements or courses; an alternative'.[56] For example, one might say: 'You can get to London by car or by train'. Here, the two modes of transport are in disjunction with one another: they are offered as equally valid alternative methods for reaching London. In Latin this idea is commonly expressed through the use of the conjunctions *an* and *vel*.[57] A number of medieval chroniclers present the ideas of force and trickery in disjunction with one another: as two means of achieving a military objective. One of the most famous occurrences of this topos can be found Vergil's *Aeneid*, in which the Trojan warrior Coroebus declares: 'Trickery or strength, who asks which in the case of an enemy?' when urging his fellow warriors to dress in Greek armour as a disguise.[58] We have already seen how William of Newburgh placed this quotation into the mouths of Louis VII's advisors at the siege of Rouen (see Chapter 7). It was also employed by Ralph of Caen when he described how Raymond of Saint-Gilles sought to revenge himself upon Bohemond. Bohemond had insulted Raymond by suggesting that the Holy Lance, which had been discovered by one of Raymond's followers during the siege of Antioch, was a fake:

> Therefore Raymond searches for vengeance in a thousand arts, in a thousand ways, having been wounded by the sharp darts of Bohemond's arguments; so he is clearly separating himself from the Guiscardian's insults without delay. 'May I avenge myself or die first! If opposing him openly will not suffice, I must oppose him secretly. Where the lance does not prevail, the dagger may. "Trickery or force, who asks which in the case of an enemy?"'[59]

---

[56] 'disjunction, adj. and n.', *OED Online* <www.oed.com/view/Entry/54659> [accessed 19 October 2018].

[57] Lewis and Short, *Latin Dictionary*, p. 1963.

[58] P. Vergilius Maro, *Aeneid*, ed. Gian Biagio Conte (Berlin, 2009), Book 2, line 390: 'dolus an uirtus, quis in hoste requirat?'.

[59] GT, p. 88: 'Igitur Raimundus, acutis Boamundi argumentorum spiculis sauciatus, mille artibus, mille semitis uindictam inuestigat; ita secum sine medio disiungens Wiscardidae contumelias: "Aut premoriar aut ulciscar! Si palam occursus non suppetit, suppetat occultus; ubi non ualet lancea, ualeat sica: 'Dolus an uirtus, quis in hoste requirat?'"'.

Gerald of Wales employed the quote in his *Topography* as part of a lengthy diatribe on the treacherous character of the Irish (see p. 186–8):

> So their craft is to be feared more than their strength in arms; their peace more than their strife; their sweetness more than their gall; their malice more than their military; their treachery more than their expeditions; their counterfeit friendship more than their contemptible enmity. For this is their opinion: 'Trickery or strength, who asks which in the case of an enemy?' and this is their custom: 'Neither strong in battle nor faithful in peace'.[60]

None of these authors employed the quote to praise their subjects. William attributed it to dishonourable counsellors, Gerald to a faithless people and Ralph to a crusader whom he portrayed as an avaricious enemy of Bohemond. However, this does not reflect the original context of the quote (Coroebus is a heroic figure in the *Aeneid*) nor the more general use of disjunction between force and trickery in medieval narratives. For instance, Geoffrey Malaterra used a similar quote (taken from fourth-century poet Prudentius's *Psychomachia*) to describe how Roger I of Sicily formulated a stratagem to evade the Muslim fleet that was guarding the straits of Messina in May 1061:

> And so count Roger, seeing the enemy was opposing his army on the far side of the straits and not moving, turned to cunning devices, as he was accustomed to do. It was as if he had read: 'What does it matter whether the palm of victory is won by arms or tricks?'.[61]

Even Gerald of Wales was capable of giving the topos a positive connotation. Describing how the forces of Diarmait Mac Murchada and Robert fitz Stephen advanced to make a second assault on Wexford in May 1169 (the first had been driven back by the garrison), he wrote: 'they advanced to the assault more prudently and better prepared, and supported by ingenuity as much as by the aid of force, relying upon craft as much as force of arms'.[62] Gerald does not elaborate what form their *ingenium* or *ars* took: he simply relates that the garrison negotiated a surrender when they saw the army approaching. Regardless, this passage is indicative of Gerald's

---

[60] Gerald of Wales, 'Topographia Hibernica', in J. S. Brewer (ed.), *Opera*, RS, 21 (8 vols, London, 1861–91), vol. 5, pp. 3–206, at pp. 165–6: 'Est igitur longe fortius timenda eorum ars, quam Mars; eorum pax, quam fax; eorum mel, quam fel; malitia quam militia; proditio quam expeditio; amicitia defucata, quam inimicitia despicata. Haec enim horum sententia; "Dolus, an virtus; quis in hoste requirat?" Hi mores: "Nec in bello fortes, nec in pace fideles"'.
[61] GM, p. 32: 'Comes itaque Rogerius, videns hostes ex altera ripa contra suum exercitum adjacere et nusquam promoveri, ad callida argumenta, ut solitus erat ac si legisset: "Quid refert? Armis contingat palma dolisve"'. For the original, see Aurelius Prudentius Clemens, *Carmina*, ed. Maurice P. Cunningham (Turnholt, 1966), p. 169.
[62] EH, p. 34: 'consultius et instructius ad insultum procedentes, et tam ingenii quam virium ope suffulti, tam arte scilicet quam marte confisi'.

attitude towards deception: when describing his relatives, the Cambro-Normans, employing *ars*, it was prudent and virtuous. When it was used by the Irish, it was treacherous.

The topos of presenting the disjunction between force and trickery was often used to emphasise the strength of a particular stronghold. For example, William of Poitiers's description of the castle at Mayenne in Normandy, which was held against William the Conqueror in 1063: 'The castle could not be assailed by any force, any ingenuity or any human craft on one side because a rapid and rocky river flowed past'.[63] It was used in the description of London in the *Carmen de Hastingae*: 'Protected on the left by walls, on the right by the river, it does not fear enemies nor is it afraid to be captured by craft'.[64] Albert of Aachen wrote that Antioch, 'sited upon the mountains, can be conquered by neither craft nor force'.[65]

It could also be employed as a general summary of military strategy. Fulcher of Chartres used the topos to describe Baldwin of Bouillon's conquests in Upper Mesopotamia during the crusade: 'Therefore trusting in the Lord and in his own valour, he gathered a few knights with him and set out to the river Euphrates and there seized many castles, as much by force as ingenuity'.[66] The twelfth-century courtier Walter Map, recalling the story of an anonymous monk of Cluny who resumed his former life as a knight in order to defend his family's lands, used the topos to describe the monk's success: 'He raged upon his enemies in swift assaults, he frequently assailed them and bravely pursued them for a long time, whence it happened that he often defeated those who he found were unequal to him in cleverness or strength'.[67]

Walter the Chancellor, imagining a council between Ïlghāzī and his nobles following the Field of Blood, depicted Ïlghāzī using the topos to persuade his men that they should ransom their prisoners back to Baldwin

---

[63] WP, pp. 65–6: 'Huius castri latus alterum, quod alluitur scopuloso rapidoque flumine (nam supra Meduanae ripam in praerupta montis rupe situm est) id nulla ui, nullo ingenio uel arte humana attentari potest'.

[64] CDH, p. 38: 'Vrbs est ampla nimis, peruersis plena colonis, / Et regni reliquis dicior est opibus. / A leua muris, a dextra flumine tuta, / Hostes nec metuit nec pauet arte capi'.

[65] AA, p. 284: 'Hec enim arx et palatium in montanis situm nulla arte, nulla ui superari potest'.

[66] FC, p. 208: 'Itaque confidens in Domino et in valore suo, collegit secum milites paucos profectusque est versus Euphraten fluvium et comprehendit ibi plurima castra tam vi quam ingenio'.

[67] Walter Map, *De nugis curialium: Courtiers trifles*, ed. and trans. M. R. James, rev. C. N. L. Brooke and R. A. B. Mynors, rev edn (Oxford, 1983), p. 340: 'Conuocatis ergo suis et alienis quoscunque potuit, in latentes et prestolantes quid fiat, insurgit rapidisque furit in hostes irrupcionibus, frequenter assilit et in instancia perdurat fortiter, unde fit ut sepe conficiat quos impares inuenit astucie uel fortitudinis'.

II of Jerusalem in exchange for the strategically vital castle at 'Azaz: 'For surely, believe my words, while [the king] lives, we will be unable to reclaim this castle or the land which has been under his authority, either by force or ingenuity'.[68] William of Malmesbury used the topos to describe the Normans:

> But the Normans, as we should say something about them, were, and still are, well-dressed to a fault, and delicate regarding their food, but on this side of any excess. Since they are a people accustomed to war, and almost unable to live without battle, they actively run to engage their enemy, and where strength has not succeeded, they corrupt them with trickery and wealth.[69]

As with the language of siege craft, there are fewer examples of this topos in the vernacular chronicles but it is present. Describing Robert Bruce's night escalade against Perth in 1313, John Barbour declared that since 'the toun wes hard to ta / With opyn saw strenth or mycht / Tharfor he tocht to wyrk with slycht [cunning]'.[70] Similarly, when describing James Douglas's return to Douglasdale in 1307 to reclaim his heritage, Barbour noted: 'he wes wys / And saw he mycht on nakyn wys / Werray his fa with evyn mycht / Tharfor he thocht to wyrk with slycht'.[71]

In the *Roman de Brut*, King Vortigern is advised by his counsellors to construct an impregnable tower: 'His counsellors advised him to build such a tower that it could never be taken by force nor conquered by an *engine* of man'.[72] Earlier in the narrative, Wace described Brutus planning to relieve his garrison at Sparatin, which was under siege by Pandrasus of Greece (see p. 165). His description elaborates on the topos:

> Brutus was much preoccupied with how he might rescue his men; he considered what he might do, by what *engine* he might deliver them; he needed to find an *engine*, for he did not have the strength to oppose such a host. One must use trickery and *engine* to destroy one's enemy, and to rescue one's friends one must enter great danger'.[73]

---

[68] WC, p. 109: 'Eo etenim uiuente, puta dictum, nos nullatenus illud castrum, sed nec quidquam terrae suae dominationi subditae, nisi ui aut ingenio posse rehabere'.

[69] GRA, p. 461: 'Porro Normanni, ut de eis quoque dicamus, erant tunc, et sunt adhuc, uestibus ad inuidiam culti, cibis citra ullam nimietatem delicati. Gens militiae assueta et sine bello pene uiuere nescia, in hostem impigre procurrere, et ubi uires non successissent, non minus dolo et pecunia corrumpere'.

[70] Bruce, Book 9, lines 350–2.

[71] Bruce, Book 5, lines 267–70.

[72] RdB, lines 7319–22: 'Loé li unt si cunseilier / Que tel tur face edifier / Que ja par force ne seit prise / Ne par engine d'ome conquise'.

[73] RdB, lines 357–66: 'Brutus fu forment curius / Coment li suen fussent rescus; / Purpensa sei que il fereit, / Par quell engine les secoreit; / Engieng quere li estuveit, / Kar vers tel ost force n'aveit. / Boisdie e engine deit l'en faire / Pur destrure son adversaire, / E pur ses amis delivrer / Deit l'en en grant peril entrer'.

Brutus lures the guards away from Pandrasus's camp with false reports that Pandrasus's brother is stranded in the woods, in need of rescue, before proceeding to assault the unguarded camp under cover of darkness.

Conclusions

Medieval chroniclers were not careless with their words. They wrote to the best of their ability in order to record important events, to edify and entertain their readers and to demonstrate their own skill as writers. By carefully studying the vocabulary they selected to describe incidents of military deception, we can gain an insight into their thoughts and attitudes. The fact that authors chose to use similar language to describe the deceitful actions of both their heroes and villains suggests that the act of deception was not, in itself, held to be wholly reprehensible. It could even be admirable, a demonstration of boldness, prudence and intelligence. The phrase 'by force or trickery', repeated not only in Latin but also in French and Scots texts, further indicates that deceit was considered one of several, equally valid, options open to a commander. Indeed, in certain circumstances, it may have been the most appropriate means to an end. Medieval authors seem to have taken this for granted, as it is very rare to find explicit discussions on the morality of deceiving an enemy in time of war. Lawyers and theologians were more concerned about the justice of particular conflicts, or the concept of war itself, than the dirty business of fighting. As we shall see in our final chapter, when chroniclers do explicitly discuss military deceptions, it usually indicates an anxiety to justify the subject's conduct and the general righteousness of their cause.

9

The Morality of Deception

Chroniclers appear to have assumed that their audience would know what was and was not licit behaviour in war. Beyond the legal texts that attempted to establish a theological framework for warfare, discussions about the legitimacy of deception usually occur when an author wishes to justify or defend their subject's behaviour or when discussing the cultural or religious 'other': those groups that were perceived to fight and behave contrary to Western European norms and were often labelled as habitually treacherous. Studying what Western chroniclers considered abnormal in 'the other' is another way of trying to understand what they believed to be acceptable behaviour.

Jus in Bello: Military Deceptions in Theology and Canon Law

Philosophical, ethical and theological anxieties about warfare are as old as war itself. When is it morally right to go to war? Who has the right to start or end a war? How should people act in war? Is there any way to limit its horrors? According to James Turner Johnson, in classic Western philosophy the definition of a 'just war' is typically divided into two parts. First, *jus ad bellum*: a just war must be declared by the proper authorities and for legitimate reasons. Second, *jus in bello*: a just war must be conducted in the right way, for example by refraining from doing harm to non-combatants or by showing clemency to enemy prisoners.[1] Until the fourteenth century, medieval theologians and canonists had remarkably little to say about *jus in bello* and practically nothing about the legitimacy of particular tactics. Their primary concern was to demonstrate that it was legitimate for Christians to wage war and to determine who had the

---

[1] James Turner Johnson, *Ideology, Reason, and the Limitation of War: Religious and Secular Concepts 1200–1740* (Princeton, NJ, 1975), p. 26.

authority to declare war.[2] This is only to be expected. The clerics and lawyers who wrote these texts had little first-hand experience of war and were not overly concerned with the niceties of military tactics.

The basis for all theological and canonical writing on stratagems in the Middle Ages was Augustine's *Quaestionum in Heptateuchum libri vii*, specifically his reflections on Joshua 7. In this passage, God commands Joshua and the Israelites to lay an ambush for the Canaanite citizens of Ai (as discussed in Chapter 3). Augustine attempted to resolve the seeming paradox of a righteous God and His people employing a deception:

> Because God, speaking to Joshua, bids him set ambushes in their rear (that is, warriors lying in wait to ambush the enemies), we are cautioned that this is not done unjustly by those who are waging a just war, as no just person ought to think chiefly on these things unless he is undertaking a just war, which it is right to fight in, for it is not right to do so in all wars. But when a just person has undertaken a just war, whether he conquers in open battle or by ambushes, it is no concern to justice.[3]

Although he is talking about a specific incident, Augustine is clearly using *insidia* here in its broad sense to cover all kinds of stratagem (see Chapter 3). Augustine's conclusion would be repeated by future thinkers: so long as the war is just, then it does not matter how it is fought. The real problem is establishing what constitutes a just war. The Israelites were clearly fighting a just war because they had been commanded to fight by God but what were Christians to do in the absence of a clear divine mandate? Augustine offered what he considered to be the common definition of a just war: 'just wars are accustomed to be defined as those which avenge wrongs, if any people or city has failed either to punish what was wickedly done by its own people or to return that which was stolen through said wrongs, it ought to be assailed in war'.[4] As this definition does not specify what kind of *injuria* would justify war, it could conceivably be adopted by any aggrieved party to claim that their cause was just.

Augustine's writings on just war were hugely influential. Gratian, the twelfth-century Bolognese canonist, whom Johnson described as under-

---

[2] James Turner Johnson, *Just War Tradition and the Restraint of War: A Moral and Historical Inquiry* (Princeton, NJ, 1981), p. 123.

[3] Augustine, *Quaestionum in Heptateuchum libri* VII, ed. Joseph Zycha (Vienna, 1985), p. 428: 'Quod deus iubet loquens ad Iesum, ut constituat sibi retrorsus insidias, id est insidiantes bellatores ad insidiandum hostibus, hinc admonemur non iniuste fieri ab his qui iustum bellum gerunt, ut nihil homo iustus praecipue cogitare debeat in his rebus, nisi ut iustum bellum suscipiat, cui bellare fas est; non enim omnibus fas est. cum autem iustum bellum susceperit, utrum aperta pugna, utrum insidiis uincat, nihil ad iustitiam interest'.

[4] Augustine, *Quaestionum*, p. 429: 'Iusta autem bella ea definiri solent quae ulciscuntur iniurias, si qua gens uel ciuitas, quae bello petenda est, uel uindicare neglexerit quod a suis inprobe factum est uel reddere quod per iniurias ablatum est'.

taking the first 'comprehensive and continuing inquiry initiated into just moral and legal limits to war' in the West, repeated Augustine verbatim on the subject of stratagems.[5] The passage in question appears in Part 2, *Causa* 23 of the *Decretum*, which is presented as a series of questions discussing whether it was licit for a group of (hypothetical) bishops to wage war against heretics in defence of the faithful: 'the bishops, having received these apostolic commands, when knights had been assembled, began to fight against the heretics openly and through ambushes'.[6] *Questio* 1 establishes whether it was a sin for the bishops to fight. *Questio* 2 discusses what constitutes a 'just war' ('Quid sit justum bellum?') and whether one may employ ambushes in such a conflict. Gratian's answer is to quote Augustine.[7] He goes on to quote Augustine's definition of a just war as one 'that avenges wrongs', followed by a discussion that establishes what 'wrongs' heretics commit against Catholics, confirming that the hypothetical bishops were indeed fighting a just war.

Thomas Aquinas (c. 1224–74) offered a fuller discussion of the morality of stratagems in his *Summa Theologia*, although he still deferred to Augustine. Aquinas's writings reveal an interest in both the morality and conduct of war, perhaps because, as Gregory Reichberg has suggested, he was the son of a minor Italian nobleman and was conscious of his family's knightly background.[8] The discussion on ambushes is found in Question 40, Article 3 of the *Summa*, under the heading: 'Whether it is licit to use ambushes in warfare'.[9] Aquinas begins by presenting three possible objections to the use of *insidia*. First, that deception appears to violate God's command in Deuteronomy 16: 'seek what is just in a just way'.[10] Second, that one ought to keep faith with enemies, as Augustine wrote in his *Letters to Boniface*. Third, that Christ had commanded, 'Do to others as you would have them do to you', and, 'since nobody would

---

[5] Johnson, *Just War*, p. 121.
[6] Gratian, 'Decretum', in Emil Ludwig Richter (ed.), *Corpus iuris canonici*, rev. Emil Friedberg (2 vols, Graz, 1955), vol. 1, pp. 1–1467, at p. 889: 'Episcopi, hec mandata Apostolica accipientes, conuocatis militibus aperte et per insidias contra hereticos pugnare ceperunt'.
[7] Gratian, 'Decretum', vol. 1, p. 894: 'Dominus Deus noster iubet ad Iesum Naue, ut constituat sibi retrorsum insidias, id est insidiantes bellatores ad insidiandum hostibus. Hinc admonemur, hoc non iniuste fieri ab his, qui iustum bellum gerunt, ut nichil iustus precipue cogitet in his rebus, nisi ut bellum suscipiat cui bellare fas est. Non enim fas est omnibus. Cum autem iustum bellum susceperit, utrum aperte pugnet, an ex insidiis, nichil ad iusticiam interest'.
[8] Gregory M. Reichberg, *Thomas Aquinas on War and Peace* (Cambridge, 2017), pp. 11–12.
[9] Thomas Aquinas, *Summa theologiae*, ed. and trans. Thomas Gilby and others (61 vols, London, 1964–81), vol. 35, p. 88: 'Utrum sit licitum in bellis uti insidiis'.
[10] Aquinas, *Summa*, vol. 35, p. 88: 'juste quod justum est exequeris'.

want to have ambushes or deceptions prepared for them, it appears that nobody should conduct wars using ambushes'.[11]

Aquinas then presents the counter-arguments to these points. First, he repeats Augustine's conclusion, based on Joshua 7: 'When one has undertaken a just war, whether one fights openly or from ambush, it is of no interest to justice'.[12] He then breaks with Gratian by differentiating between two kinds of deception:

> One way a person may be deceived, in which a person is told a falsehood or a promise is not kept. And that is always illicit. And nobody should deceive enemies in this way: for there are certain laws of war and agreements ought to be kept even between enemies, as Ambrose says.[13]

This is a reference to *De officiis*, a text on Christian duty and morality by Ambrose (c. 340–97), archbishop of Milan, which was itself based on Cicero's work of the same title. Discussing the importance of justice, Ambrose wrote: '[Justice] is even preserved with enemies as, if a place or day has been agreed upon for battle with an enemy, it is thought to be against justice to arrive early at either the place or the time'.[14] The idea that agreements should be honoured even between enemies was clearly current in the Middle Ages, as detailed in Chapter 7, although probably not because contemporaries were familiar with either Ambrose or Cicero.

Aquinas argues that there is another, acceptable, form of deception, in which a person conceals their plans or intentions from another. He justifies this using Scripture, saying: 'many things in holy teaching ought to be hidden, most of all from infidels, lest they ridicule them, according to this saying, "Do not give what is holy to dogs" [Matthew 7. 6]'.[15] He also appeals to classical authority, citing Frontinus:

---

[11] Aquinas, *Summa*, vol. 35, p. 90: '*Quae vultis ut faciant vobis homines, et vos facite illis*: et hoc est observandum ad omnes proximos. Inimici autem sunt proximi. Cum ergo nullus sibi velit insidias vel fraudes parari, videtur quod nullus ex insidiis debeat gerere bella'.
[12] Aquinas, *Summa*, vol. 35, p. 90: 'Cum justum bellum suscipitur, utrum aperte pugnet aliquis an ex insidiis, nihil ad justitiam interest [sic]'.
[13] Aquinas, *Summa*, vol. 35, p. 90: 'Uno modo, ex eo quod ei dicitur falsum, vel non servatur promissum. Et istud semper est illicitum. Et hoc modo nullus debet hostes fallere: sunt enim quaedam jura bellorum et foedera etiam inter ipsos hostes servanda, ut Ambrosius dicit'.
[14] Ambrose, *De officiis*, ed. and trans. Ivor J. Davidson (2 vols, Oxford, 2001), vol. 1, p. 196: 'Quanta autem iustitia sit ex hoc intellegi potest quod nec locis nec personis nec temporibus excipitur, quae etiam hostibus reservatur, ut, si constitutus sit cum hoste aut locus aut dies proelio, adversus iustitiam putetur aut loco praevenire aut tempore'.
[15] Aquinas, *Summa*, vol. 35, p. 90: 'quia etiam in doctrina sacra multa sunt occultanda, maxime infidelibus, ne irrideant, secundum illud, Nolite sanctum dare canibus'.

it is set down in all other writings on military matters concerning the need to conceal one's plans so that they do not reach enemies; as it is revealed in Frontinus's book, *Strategemata*. And such concealment relates to the planning of ambushes, which it is licit to use in just wars.[16]

Finally, he states that it is simply unreasonable to expect others not to conceal things from you: 'Nor should ambushes properly be called deceptions [*fraudes*]; they are neither incompatible with justice, nor an orderly will: for the will would be disordered indeed if somebody wanted nothing to be concealed from them by others'.[17] This last point is particularly relevant to the discussion below on the vocabulary used in chronicles to describe acts of trickery. Aquinas acknowledges that an *insidia* is an act of deception but he carefully distinguishes it from other, illicit forms of deception that would fall under the category *fraus*. As we shall see, chroniclers could use similar semantic tricks to distinguish admirable instances of deceit (craft, prudence, skilfulness) from contemptible ones (treachery, treason, fraud).

While it is highly unlikely that many (if any) medieval combatants were familiar with Augustine or Aquinas's views on the ethics of stratagems, clerical and monastic chroniclers may have read their work. Even if canonists' pronouncements had little bearing on *how* war was fought, they may have influenced how contemporaries wrote *about* war. As will become clear below, chroniclers' descriptions of military ruses were influenced by their attitude towards the combatants and their cause, more than by the actual tricks used. If the chronicler considered the cause to be just then they would (usually) portray the ruse as legitimate. If they did not, they would portray a similar act as illegitimate or immoral.

Valour, Sloth and *Playne Fechtyng*: Justifying Trickery in Chronicles

Chroniclers seem to have assumed that their readers would share their assumptions about what constituted acceptable behaviour and reflected these assumptions, perhaps unconsciously, in their choice of vocabulary. This is why it is so important to analyse the language of medieval military narratives. There are, however, a handful of passages in which chroniclers explicitly justified the use of trickery in war. The tone is generally defen-

---

[16] Aquinas, *Summa*, vol. 35, p. 90: 'inter cetera documenta rei militaris hoc praecipue ponitur de occultandis consiliis ne ad hostes perveniant; ut patet in libro Strategematum Frontini. Et talis occultatio pertinet ad rationem insidiarum quibus licitum est uti in bellis justis'.
[17] Aquinas, *Summa*, vol. 35, p. 90: 'Nec proprie hujusmodi insidiae vocantur fraudes; nec justitiae repugnant, nec ordinatae voluntati: esset enim inordinata voluntas si aliquis vellet nihil sibi ab aliis occultari'.

sive, suggesting that the authors felt some unease about the subject. This reflects the ambiguity surrounding attitudes to trickery, seen in the study of vocabulary in the previous chapter: neither inherently licit or illicit, it could be portrayed as either, depending on the context.

The French chronicler William the Breton, chaplain to Philip II of France, recorded a colourful anecdote about a military ruse in his *Gesta Philippi*. In February 1214, King John of England landed at La Rochelle to begin his reconquest of Poitou, which he had lost to Philip of France in 1204. After some initial successes, on 19 June he laid siege to the castle at Roche-au-Moine, which was sited on the Loire. William the Breton introduced his story as follows:

> And so, when the siege had been laid, and the petrariae and other war machines erected, John began to attack the castle in a remarkable fashion. But those who were besieged defended themselves no less strenuously. I cannot keep silent about one who happened to be there among those valiant people.[18]

William recalled that a crossbowman from John's army had taken to walking about in front of the castle walls, shooting at the defenders while protected by a large shield carried by his servant: 'So one day a crossbowman from the castle, who was infuriated, used an admirable new trick and between enemies it should not to be reproached, as it is said: "trickery or strength, who asks which in regards to the enemy?"'.[19] The crossbowman from the castle attached a rope to a bolt, shot it into his enemy's shield, then pulled it so that the servant fell into a ditch, leaving his master exposed. William called this a *nova fraus admirabilis* (an admirable new trick). Although *fraus* generally has negative connotations, and could be translated here as 'deceit', there is nothing deceptive in the defender's actions: he simply found a clever way to remove his enemy's defences. This, combined with the quotation from Vergil that refers to *doli*, suggests William used *fraus* here in a sense that is more akin to 'trick' than 'fraud'. Whether this incident occurred exactly as written is less important than the fact that William chose to record it at all. He clearly thought it was an interesting tale that his readers would want to hear. Moreover, he called it *admirabilis*, a specific example of the garrison's general *probitas* (valour, prowess). If some of his readers wished to

---

[18] GPA, p. 261: 'Facta itaque obsidione, erectis petrariis et aliis machinis bellicis, cepit rex Johannes castrum mirabiliter expugnare. Obsessi autem non minus strenue se defendebant, inter quorum probitates illud quod ibidem contigit reticere non possum'.
[19] GPA, pp. 261–2: 'Quidam ergo arcubalistarius de castro indignatus, quadam die, nova fraude admirabili et inter hostes non culpanda usus est, juxta illud: "dolus an virtus quis in hoste requirat?"'.

criticise the crossbowman, then William could present a famous classical justification for the use of 'trickery' against enemies.

The anonymous author of the *Annales Gandenses* (likely a Franciscan friar from Ghent) explicitly refutes an accusation of treachery levelled against the citizens of Bruges.[20] In 1302 the citizens of Bruges rebelled against French rule at the instigation of Willem van Jülich, a relative and representative of Guy de Namur, son and heir to the last count of Flanders. James of Saint-Pol, the French governor of Flanders, moved against Bruges with an army. Willem, the ringleader, fled, leading to widespread panic in the city. On 16 May James agreed that offenders from the city commune were free to leave before he arrived. Many did and the French entered Bruges the following day. The citizens who had remained in the city then sent word to those who had left, saying that they could now return and take the French by surprise. This was particularly easy because the French had slighted the city's fortifications following a riot the previous year. The Flemings attacked at the dawn on the morning of 18 May.[21] The chronicler records that they used a password, a literal shibboleth, to distinguish themselves from the French in the confusion. The Flemings shouted *scilt*, which they pronounced with an aspiration (*sh-ilt*) but which the French were incapable of pronouncing correctly.[22] The attack was so successful that James of Saint-Pol was forced to flee the city, abandoning all his possessions. Fifteen hundred French were slain and a further hundred were taken captive. It is at this point in his narrative that the chronicler defends the Flemings for their actions:

> The French say that their men were vanquished and slain in this conflict by treachery; but it is certain, so far as I was able to find by diligent investigation, if there was any treachery, few were guilty; and indeed, I found no sure proof of this. The blame should rather be laid upon their own men who, without due care and prudence, entered a town which was not well fortified, though around and near it there were so many of their capital enemies, strong, well-armed and almost desperate.[23]

This passage captures the essence of the Franco-Flemish conflict. To the French, the Flemings were subjects of Philip IV of France and James of

---

[20] AG, p. xi.
[21] J. F. Verbruggen, *The Battle of the Golden Spurs: Courtrai, 11 July 1302*, ed. Kelly DeVries, trans. David Richard Ferguson, rev edn (Woodbridge, 2002), pp. 22–5.
[22] AG, p. 24.
[23] AG, p. 24: 'Dicunt Franci, suos in hac pugna proditiose fuisse victos et occisos; sed certe, sicut ego diligentius potui investigare, si aliqua ibi proditio fuit, tunc pauci ipsius erant conscii, non tamen hoc certitudinaliter inveni; imo potius debent hoc suis imputare, qui minus caute et prudenter villam non bene munitam intraverunt, tot existentibus circa et juxta eam inimicis suis capitalibus, fortibus et bene armatis et quasi desperatis'.

Saint Pol the royal governor. To attack him and his men in this manner constituted treason (*proditio*): the Flemings were rebels against their rightful lord and king. To the Flemings, however, the French were foreigners who had invaded Flanders and imposed their rule on a free people. They were not rebels but patriots, fighting for their independence. This view is clearly shared by the author of the *Annales*, as he criticises the French for their complacency and lack of prudence. It was the responsibility of the French to protect themselves appropriately, as they were surrounded by their enemies.

The legitimacy of using trickery in war is discussed by John Barbour in several passage of *The Bruce*, suggesting a certain anxiety about the guerrilla-style tactics employed by the Scots during the First War of Independence (1296–1328). In the spring of 1306, Robert Bruce attacked the forces of Henry Percy, one of the senior English commanders in Scotland, by night while they were billeted in a village near Turnberry in Ayrshire. Barbour places a speech into Bruce's mouth that justifies the attack: 'Repruff tharoff na man sall / For werrayour na fors suld ma / Quhether he mycht ourcum his fa / Throu strenth or throu sutelté, / Bot that guy faith ay haldyn be'.[24] This statement is notable for a number of reasons. Its sentiment, that a combatant could fight with either force or cunning so long as he does not break 'good faith' with anybody, is very close to Aquinas's conclusions on the use of *insidia* in war (see p. 173). As a cleric, Barbour would likely have been familiar with the *Summa Theologiae* and may have deliberately inserted this scholarly justification of 'sutelté' into his text to excuse Bruce's morally suspect behaviour. That being said, *The Bruce* is significant for being the first surviving work of literature written in Old Scots. It was commissioned by Robert II of Scotland, Bruce's grandson, who paid Barbour an annual pension for its composition.[25] It is a work of vernacular literature, intended to be declaimed in a royal court. The sentiments expressed here may owe less to canon law than to the social mores and conventions of a late fourteenth-century court, populated by fighting men who appreciated the value of a wily stratagem.

Twice in the poem, Bruce is upbraided by others for his use of stealthy or deceitful tactics. In the first such incident Aymer de Valence, earl of Pembroke, challenges Bruce to a pitched battle at Loudon Hill (10 May 1307): 'And giff that he wald mey him that / He said his worschip suld be mar, / And mar be turnyt in nobillay, / To wyn him in the playne away / With hard dintis in evyn fechtyng / Then to do fer mar with skulking'.[26] Barbour declares that Aymer 'spak [...] heyley' in issuing this challenge.

---

[24] Bruce, Book 5, lines 84–8.
[25] Bruce, p. 3.
[26] Bruce, Book 8, lines 135–40.

Bruce reacts angrily and accepts at once. At Loudon Hill, Bruce defeated Aymer, marking his first major victory since being driven into exile after the battle of Methven in June the previous year. This haughty challenge, followed by a crushing defeat at the hands of the Scottish patriots, suggests that Barbour did not expect his audience to agree with Aymer's suggestion that Bruce had merely been 'skulking'.

In the second incident, Bruce is criticised by his own nephew, Thomas Randolph, earl of Moray. Randolph had initially supported Bruce's claim to the throne but shifted his allegiance to Edward I of England after being captured at Methven. In the summer of 1308 Randolph was captured again, this time by James Douglas, and sent to Bruce. According to Barbour, Bruce demanded Randolph be reconciled with him. Randolph answered: 'Ye chasty me, bot ye / Aucht bettre chastyt for to be, / For sense ye werrayit the king / Off Ingland, in playne fechtyng / Ye suld pres to derenyhe rycht / And nocht with cowardy na with slycht'.[27] Bruce responds that it might come to 'playne fechtyng' soon enough. He does not explicitly defend his use of 'slycht' but he rebukes Randolph for the tone of his address: 'Bot sen thou spekys sa rudly / It is gret skyll men chasty / Thai proud wordis till that thou knaw / The rycht and bow as thou aw'.[28] As with Aymer de Valence, the accusation against Bruce is attributed to pride and arrogance, not wisdom or chivalrous virtue. It is telling that, later in the poem, when Randolph is given the task of seizing Edinburgh Castle for Bruce, Barbour says he considered how to achieve it through 'sum sutelte or wile'.[29] Even if Randolph is expressing a contemporary opinion that 'slycht' was a cowardly way to fight, he changed his mind after returning to Bruce's party.

Twelfth-century chronicler of Outremer Walter the Chancellor presents a particularly revealing description of trickery. Recounting Īlghāzī's feigned march on al-Atharib in 1119, which Walter interpreted as a cover for a reconnaissance of Roger of Salerno's camp at the Field of Blood (see p. 157), Walter described the Turks feigning flight when confronted:

> But the Turks' strength was deliberately hidden in order that, by these signs, they might be able to draw our men far from the camps. This action is often considered by many warriors since, for the sake of the dishonest action, the observers are kept safe, though it may often be heartily approved because of the cleverness of the *ingenium*.[30]

---

[27] Bruce, Book 9, lines 747–52.
[28] Bruce, Book 9, lines 755–8.
[29] Bruce, Book 10, line 540.
[30] WC, p. 81: 'Sed res erat tecta fraude ex industria, ut his indiciis remotius a castris nostros extrahere potuissent. Quod factum saepe a pluribus bellatorum cautis inspectoribus pro inprobitate reputatur, licet multotiens ex astutiae ingenio id fieri csomprobetur'. My sincere thanks to Dr. William Flynn for his help with this passage.

The Latin here is somewhat opaque, especially in the crucial final sentence. Walter had previously stated that this Turkish force had been sent towards al-Atharib *ut spectent et spectentur* (in order to see and be seen) i.e. so that they could observe the Franks and, in doing so, deceive them by appearing to move away from the Field of Blood.[31] This helps to explain the otherwise confusing reference to *inspectores* (observers) in the last sentence. Walter is commenting on whether feigning flight should be considered a licit tactic. Combatants often consider using it, despite being an act of *inprobitas* (dishonesty, wickedness), because it keeps the decoy force, the *inspectores* who were sent out 'to see and be seen' (*spectare*), safe from harm. Walter then opines that, in fact, such a stratagem (*ingenium*) should be 'heartily recommended' (*comprobetur*) because it demonstrates cleverness (*astutia*). This is a rare insight into what must have been a current debate among Walter's contemporaries, as evidenced by his use of the present tense. The act of feigning flight was dishonest. Some would even call it wicked. Others, however, defended it, not only because it was useful but because it was an admirable display of intelligence.

As stated above, explicit justifications for acts of trickery are unusual in medieval chronicles. Scholars are left to judge whether or not the author approved of a certain tactic by examining the vocabulary they employed to describe it. On the rare occasions when we do see explicit discussions on the morality of trickery, they concur with other evidence already cited. Deception could be portrayed as something negative, cowardly or immoral, hence the defensive tone in some of the passages discussed above. On the other hand, a clever deception, employed against an enemy in a time of open war, could be admirable: a demonstration of the valour and cleverness that society lauded in their fighting men. As Walter the Chancellor demonstrates, this admiration was not necessarily confined to Western Europeans but could even extend to the cultural or religious 'other'.

The Treacherous 'Other': Trickery as Practiced by Non-Normative Enemies

Western authors often identified a group's conduct in warfare, and how it differed from Western norms, as a key signifier of their 'otherness'. Some were thought to be more violent, others more cowardly than Westerners. Some fought in unconventional ways that confounded or impressed chroniclers. Whether or not these differences were as pronounced as our sources claim is less important for this present study than what they reveal about Westerners' self-image and their attitudes towards military deception.

---

[31] WC, p. 81.

The groups under discussion here differed either linguistically, culturally, religiously or politically from the Francophone West. It is tempting to label these as ethnic or national differences but modern concepts of ethnicity and nationhood do not map easily onto the Middle Ages.[32] The most common Latin terms for a cultural-ethnic group in this period were *gens* and *natio*. What was believed to unite a *gens* could vary from place to place. Some, such as the Normans or the Lombards, claimed common descent from a single kin group who were believed to have emigrated from the remote east or north (Troy was a popular genesis point) and settled in Europe.[33] In other cases, religion was the unifying factor. Authors could talk of a Catholic *gens* or a pagan *natio*. Hirokazu Tsurushima has described how Bede conceived of the English, the *gens Anglus*, as united, not by a common language or political allegiance, encompassing as it did Saxons, Jutes and Angles, but by a shared religious identity: they were all Christians under the authority of the archbishop of Canterbury, observing the Roman rite.[34] In other circumstances, a *natio* could be made up of different *gens* whose unity was expressed in allegiance to a common ruler, as in the case of Scotland (see p. 188) or Anglo-Norman England, where kings would address charters to their French, English and Flemish subjects.[35]

To be a member of a *gens* was to share certain common features. These could include language, customs, laws and traditions. Particularly important for this study was the idea of shared characteristics: that members of a *gens* shared inherent personality traits and behaviours. Some authors ascribed these to geographical determinism: the belief, ultimately derived from ancient Greek and Roman theories, that a region's climate could affect the humoral balance of its inhabitants and therefore their essential character.[36] Some authors, such as Gerald of Wales (see p. 183) portrayed

---

[32] See Patrick J. Geary, *The Myth of Nations: The Medieval Origins of Europe* (Princeton, NJ, 2002); Lesley Johnson, 'Imagining Communities: Medieval and Modern', in Simon Forde, Lesley Johnson, and Alan V. Murray (eds.), *Concepts of National Identity in the Middle Ages* (Leeds, 1995), pp. 1–20; Alan V. Murray, 'Ethnic Identity in the Crusader States: The Frankish Race and the Settlement of Outremer', in Simon Forde, Lesley Johnson, and Alan V. Murray (eds.), *Concepts of National Identity in the Middle Ages* (Leeds, 1995), pp. 59–74; Susan Reynolds, *Kingdoms and Communities in Western Europe, 900–1300*, 2nd edn (Oxford, 1997), pp. 253–6.

[33] Peter Hoppenbrouwers, 'Such Stuff as Peoples Are Made On: Ethnogenesis and the Construction of Nationhood in Medieval Europe', *The Medieval History Journal*, 9 (2006), 195–242.

[34] Hirokazu Tsurushima, 'What Do We Mean by "Nations" in Early Medieval Britain?', in Hirokazu Tsurushima (ed.), *Nations in Medieval Britain* (Donington, 2010), pp. 1–18, at p. 8.

[35] Robert Bartlett, 'Medieval and Modern Concepts of Race and Ethnicity', *Journal of Medieval and Early Modern Studies*, 3 (2001), 39–56, at pp. 47–9.

[36] Bartlett, 'Medieval and Modern Concepts of Race', p. 46.

the social customs of a group as actually influencing the biological and mental characteristics of its members: children born into a culture with certain (usually bad) customs would inherit the associated qualities.[37] The character of a particular *gens* was also thought to influence, and be reflected in, its military culture: how they fought, whether they were brave or hardy or cunning in the face of danger.

Stephen Morillo has done important work in highlighting the unique challenges faced when two distinct military cultures encounter one another on the battlefield. In his typology of 'transcultural wars', Morillo identified three types of war. 'Intracultural wars' are those fought between two parties who live and operate within the same cultural framework, such as the Anglo-Normans and the French in twelfth-century Europe.[38] Next is 'intercultural war', conflicts between two distinct cultures, leading to what Morillo terms 'mutual incomprehension', such as the first encounters between Western Europeans and the Mongols.[39] When a military culture, such as Western Europe, that customarily took prisoners, for example, came into conflict with a head-taking culture, such as the Galwegians of south-western Scotland, then the 'mutual incomprehension' could lead the former to view the latter as a savage, barbaric or morally depraved. Finally there are 'subcultural wars', in which a dominant social or political group wages war against a minority group who, although existing within the same broader culture, is nevertheless perceived to be 'other' for some reason. An example would be medieval noblemen waging war against a peasant's revolt: although all the participants are Latin Christians, the nobility would not consider the commoners to be part of the same cultural group as themselves.[40] Morillo's typology is very helpful for analysing the following conflicts, although he does overstate the cultural distinction between Franks and Turks when he states that the Franks considered the feigned flight 'cowardly'.[41] Western Europeans knew and employed the feigned flight before the crusades and occasionally employed it *against* Muslim forces (see Chapter 4). Like any typology, the boundaries between the categories are fluid. In some of the instances discussed below, the conflicts could be understood as both intercultural and subcultural, as the

---

[37] Robert Bartlett, *Gerald of Wales: A Voice of the Middle Ages* (Stroud, 2006), pp. 156–7; Owain Nash, 'Elements of Identity: Gerald, the Humours and National Characteristics', in Georgia Henley and A. Joseph McMullen (eds.), *Gerald of Wales: New Perspectives on a Medieval Writer* (Cardiff, 2018), pp. 203–20, at pp. 210–11.

[38] Stephen Morillo, 'A General Typology of Transcultural Wars - The Early Middle Ages and Beyond', in Hans-Henning Kortüm (ed.), *Transcultural Wars from the Middle Ages to the 21st Century* (Berlin, 2006), pp. 29–42 at pp. 31–3.

[39] Morillo, 'Transcultural Wars', pp. 33–6.

[40] Morillo, 'Transcultural Wars', pp. 36–41.

[41] Morillo, 'Transcultural Wars', p. 31.

politically dominant Anglo-Normans fought against *gentes* who may have perceived the conflict as a legitimate war of independence.

Welsh

The Welsh were distinguished from their Anglo-Norman neighbours by their language, dress, culture and method of fighting. This, at least, was how Gerald of Wales depicted them in his *Descriptio Kambriae*:

> For you see, the Flemings, Normans, *cotoreaux* and Brabanters, although they may be excellent knights in their own lands, and highly trained in arms, nevertheless warfare in Wales, just as in Ireland, is recognized to be different to that in Gaul. For there they seek level places, here rough terrain; there open fields, here woodland; there arms are honourable, here they are onerous; there one conquers through steadiness, here through agility; there knights are captured, here they are decapitated; there they are ransomed, here they are run through.[42]

This description has formed the basis of many modern descriptions of Anglo-Welsh conflict in the central Middle Ages. The Welsh, unable to confront the more heavily armed invaders in the open, resorted to guerrilla-style tactics, operating in wooded and mountainous terrain where heavy cavalry could not operate.[43] This picture is somewhat misleading, however. Sean Davies, drawing on contemporary Welsh language sources, has demonstrated that the Welsh social elite, at least, fought in a very similar manner to the Anglo-Normans: mounted, in mail and carrying a lance and shield.[44] Nor were the Welsh incapable of fighting pitched battles: in the right circumstances, Welsh armies could and did defeat Anglo-Norman armies in the open, for example at Cardigan in 1136 and Radnor in 1196.[45]

Gerald's description of Welsh military tactics was intended to strengthen his argument that the Angevin kings of England should favour Cambro-Norman marcher lords and his own relatives in particular. Gerald argued that only the marchers (whom he described as a *gens*, distinct from both the English and the Welsh) had the requisite character and experience

---

[42] DK, p. 220: 'Flandrenses quippe, Normanni, Coterelli, et Bragmanni, quanquam suis in terris milites egregii sint, et armis instructissimi, Gallica tmane militia multum a Kambrica, sicut ab Hybernica, distare dignoscitur. Ibi namque plana petuntur, hic aspera; ibi campestria, hic silvestria; ibi arma honori, hic oneri; ibi stabilitate vincitur, hic agilitate; ibi capiuntur milites, hic decapitantur; ibi redimuntur, hic perimuntur'.

[43] John Gillingham, 'Conquering the Barbarians: War and Chivalry in Twelfth-Century Britain', *Haskins Society Journal*, 4 (1992), 67–84, at p. 75; William Randolph Jones, 'England against the Celtic Fringe: A Study in Cultural Stereotypes', *Journal of World History*, 13 (1971), 155–71, at p. 162.

[44] Sean Davies, *War and Society in Medieval Wales 633–1283: Welsh Military Institutions* (Cardiff, 2004), pp. 157–76.

[45] Davies, *War and Society*, pp. 125–35.

necessary to continue the conquest of Ireland and subjugate the Welsh.[46] 'They began the invasions into both Ireland and Wales with great force: and only with such men can the conquests be completed, or not at all'.[47] This is not to say that Gerald's claims were entirely baseless. Other contemporary chronicles refer to the Welsh retreating into difficult terrain to escape the Anglo-Normans, or using their knowledge of the landscape to launch ambushes.[48] John of Salisbury complained that England was at the mercy of raiding parties based in Snowdonia because Anglo-Norman knights were unwilling and unable to pursue them into the mountains in their heavy armour.[49] Gerald remains our most detailed source for Welsh warfare in this period but scholars must use him with caution and an awareness that his descriptions are likely exaggerated for political and rhetorical effect.

When discussing the native Welsh use of trickery in war, Gerald expresses appreciation, even admiration for their abilities: 'And if perhaps they do not prevail in open encounters and appointed battle, at least they weary their enemy with ambushes and nocturnal assaults'.[50] He dignifies their tactics with comparison to the ancient Parthians: 'Without a doubt, their courageous virility is more apparent in fleeing and weakening their enemies, frequently turning back, and fighting back like Parthians, shooting arrows backwards while fleeing'.[51]

Gerald certainly enjoyed recounting stories of particularly daring stratagems. In the *Itinerarium Kambriae* he described how, in 1182, the sons of Seisyll ap Dynfnwall took revenge on the garrison of Abergavenny castle for their father's murder by scaling the walls at night. One of the Welshmen, Seisyll, son of Eudas, even went so far as to tell the castle constable where they would enter the day before the attack 'as if he were warning him, nevertheless more as a joke and as laughter than seriously'.[52] The Welsh seized the constable and his family before burning the castle to the ground, leading Gerald to conclude: 'according to the just judgement of God, the offence was punished in the same place where it was

---

[46] Bartlett, *Gerald of Wales*, p. 153.

[47] DK, p. 220: 'Talibus tam Hybernia quam Kambria viris initium habuit expugnationis: talibus quoque, vel nullis, consummabilis finem habitura conquisitionis'.

[48] See GRH, vol. 2, pp. 74–5; GS, pp. 15–17; RdB, lines 7719–22; RT, p. 265; RW, vol. 4, p. 222; WN, vol. 2, pp. 25, 153.

[49] John of Salisbury, *Policraticus*, ed. Clemens C. I. Webb (2 vols, New York, 1979), vol. 2, p. 598.

[50] DK, p. 210: 'Et si apertis congressibus, belloque indicto forte non praevalet, insidiis saltem et nocturnis irruptionibus hostem gravat'.

[51] DK, p. 210: 'In fuga nimirum et confectione crebro revertens, et tanquam Parthicis a tergo sagittis fugiendo repugnans, animosa virilitas magis apparet'.

[52] IK, p. 49: 'quasi praemuniendo, sub risu tamen et ludicro magis quam serio'.

committed'.[53] When describing the death of the Anglo-Norman nobleman Richard de Clare in an ambush near Cardigan in 1136, Gerald offered no criticism of the Welsh but instead blamed Richard for being imprudent. Not only did he ignore the advice of Brian de Wallingford, who knew the territory, not to enter the forest: 'he had a minstrel go before him, and a singer, answering to a refrain with notes on a harp'.[54] Gerald used the story of Richard's folly to offer a moral lesson for his readers:

> Therefore from various events it is well known that the incautious person is always too stubborn, and ignores his men. For fear teaches you to provide for the future and directs the diligent person into success: but recklessness assuredly approaches unawares to cast you down, and thoughtless temerity is unwilling to await the counsel of a guide.[55]

Gerald barely comments on the role played by the Welsh in this anecdote. He seems to have regarded it as inevitable that they would be lying in ambush in a forest. It was Richard de Clare's responsibility as a leader to listen to good advice and demonstrate sufficient foresight to avoid them.

When describing the character of the Welsh *gens*, Gerald claimed that they were a 'treacherous' people. This does not appear to be related to their conduct in warfare, however, but to the keeping of oaths and promises: 'An oath is nothing to them; they have reverence for neither faith nor truth. [...] they do not consider that which is inviolable to other peoples a solemn or necessary matter but a joke. They are accustomed to freely discard a pledge'.[56] This disregard for oaths would have been particularly offensive to Anglo-Norman aristocrats. Whether the Welsh really regarded all promises so lightly is another matter. Part of this may be attributable to the fragmented political geography of Wales. Even if the conquerors made an agreement with a particular prince or princes, these princes may not have actually had authority to speak for other rulers or groups, giving the impression that they had negotiated in bad faith.[57] There is also the possibility that, because they thought of themselves as fighting for their inde-

---

[53] IK, p. 51: 'justo Dei judicio, eo quo delictum est loco perpetratum, poena delicti ex parte secuta'.

[54] IK, p. 47: 'ex nimia quoque securitatis praesumptione, fidicinem praevium habens, et praecentorem, cantilenae notulis alternatim in fidicula respondentem'.

[55] IK, p. 48: 'Ex variis itaque patet rerum eventibus, quoniam incauta est semper nimia praesumptio, et sui negligens. Timor enim prospicere futuris admonet, et diligentiam docet in prosperis: audacia vero praecipitanter obrepit, et inconsulta temeritas nescit consilium ducis exspectare'.

[56] DK, p. 206: 'Nullum eis jusjurandum; nulla fidei, nulla veritatis reverentia. Adeo namque fidei foedus, aliis inviolabile gentibus, parvipendere solent, ut non in seriis solum et necessariis, verum in ludicris, omnique fere verbo firmando, dextrae manus ut mos est porrectione, signo usuali dato, fidem gratis effundere consueverint'.

[57] Bartlett, *Gerald of Wales*, p. 137.

pendence against a foreign enemy, they may have felt that they were not obliged to keep promises made to their oppressors. Contemporaries were unanimous in the belief that an oath made under duress was not valid. It is likely that the Welshmen who swore fidelity or to keep the peace at the point of an Anglo-Norman lance considered themselves under significant duress. As Davies has observed in relation to the excessive violence employed in Anglo-Welsh conflicts, in comparison to Continental warfare: 'Wales remained a land of conquest. War was more brutal here than in Anglo-French clashes because there was more to fight for'.[58]

Irish
Studies of Anglo-Norman attitudes to the Irish in this period are inevitably bound up with attitudes to the Welsh because Gerald of Wales is our best source for both. While Gerald was capable of nuance in his attitude to the native Welsh, acknowledging both their virtues and their vices, he was almost unequivocally hostile to the Irish and every aspect of their culture, including their military traditions. This was not a prejudice of Gerald's alone. There was growing hostility towards the Irish in clerical circles in Western Europe throughout the twelfth century, as Ireland had not been affected by the reform movement that was reshaping the rest of the Latin church. In his biography of his friend Malachy of Armagh (d. 1148), Bernard of Clairvaux portrayed Ireland as a barbarous and semi-pagan land that had resisted the saintly Malachy's attempts at reform.[59] In 1155, John of Salisbury, bishop of Chartres, helped to sway papal opinion against the Irish Church during a mission to the papal curia at Benevento. This led to the publication of the bull *Laudibiliter*, which granted the entirety of Ireland to Henry II of England as a hereditary fief.[60] Although Gerald of Wales did visit Ireland in 1183 and 1185, his depiction of the Irish in the *Expugnatio Hibernica* and *Topographia Hibernica* was influenced by an established tradition that depicted the Irish as savages in need of moral reform.[61]

According to Gerald's *Topographia*, the Irish demonstrated their want of civilisation in their long hair and beards, their custom of riding without stirrups and the fact they did not cultivate crops but lived as pastoralists. They were characterised as 'backward', a common topos among contem-

---

[58] Davies, *War and Society*, p. 238.
[59] F. X. Martin, 'Diarmait Mac Murchada and the Coming of the Anglo-Normans', in Art Cosgrove (ed.), *A New History of Ireland: II Medieval Ireland 1169–1534* (Oxford, 1987), pp. 43–66, at p. 60.
[60] Martin, 'Diarmait Mac Murchada', pp. 57–9.
[61] See also Anthony Perron, 'The Face of the "Pagan": Portraits of Religious Deviance on the Medieval Periphery', *Journal of the Historical Society*, 9 (2009), 467–92, at pp. 470–6.

porary writers for a variety of 'barbarian' *gentes* who were perceived as having failed to evolve into a sophisticated, civilised society.[62] Asa Mittman has identified how Gerald's description on Ireland as a land of miracles, akin to the marvellous and mysterious East, contributed to the idea of the Irish as the 'other'.[63] All of which added further weight to Gerald's argument for the need to continue the conquest of Ireland, to civilise the barbaric Irish and bring them into line with the rest of Christendom.

When describing Irish warfare, Gerald wrote: 'they go to battle naked and unarmed. For they hold arms to be a burden; indeed, they regard those who fight unarmed as brave and honourable'.[64] It is not certain whether 'naked' should be understood literally or figuratively here. Gerald may be drawing on the classical stereotype of the naked barbarian or he may be using *nudus* as a synonym for *inermus*: a man who goes into battle without armour is effectively (but not literally) naked. Like his descriptions of the Welsh, Gerald may have been exaggerating for effect. As Marie Therese Flanagan has shown, the pre-Norman Irish kingdoms were capable of sophisticated military operations, fielding substantial armies, conducting siege warfare and their nobility, at least, fought as armoured cavalry.[65] This would seem to discredit Gerald's assertion that the Irish learned the art of war from their encounters with the Anglo-Normans: '[they] were gradually taught and accustomed to be equally proficient with arrows and arms, and also through mutual and frequent warlike conflicts with our men, and many successes, were instructed in both the stratagems and devices of Mars'.[66] This passage, part of the concluding remarks of the *Expugnatio*, is very similar to Gerald's statement regarding the differences between continental and Welsh warfare (which he also reproduced in the *Expugnatio*). Gerald castigated those who had been left responsible for completing the conquest, begun so successfully by Gerald's relatives, because they had allowed the Irish time to develop a more effective art of war. He declared that the Irish would only be completely subdued if

---

[62] Bartlett, *Gerald of Wales*, pp. 131–9; W. R. Jones, 'England against the Celtic Fringe', pp. 163–5; W. R. Jones, 'The Image of the Barbarian in Medieval Europe', *Comparative Studies in Society and History*, 13 (1971), 376–407, at pp. 394–7.
[63] Asa Simon Mittman, 'The Other Close at Hand: Gerald of Wales and the "Marvels of the West"', in Bettina Bildhauer and Robert Mills, *The Monstrous Middle Ages* (Cardiff, 2003), pp. 97–112.
[64] TH, p. 150: 'Praeterea, nudi et inermes ad bella procedunt. Habent enim arma pro onere; inermes vero dimicare pro audacia reputant et honore'.
[65] Marie Therese Flanagan, 'Irish and Anglo-Norman Warfare in Twelfth-Century Ireland', in Thomas Bartlett and Keith Jeffery (eds.), *A Military History of Ireland* (Cambridge, 1996), pp. 52–75.
[66] EH, p. 230: 'usu pariter et exercicio sagittis et armis paulatim edocta et assueta, necnon et marciis tam insidiis quam cautelis per mutuos et crebros cum nostris belli conflictus et successus plurimos instructa'.

the crown was to appoint Welsh marchers to key lordships.[67] As such, it probably tells us more about Gerald's ambitions for his relatives than the development of Irish military practice. Nevertheless, it is noteworthy that he chose to include the use of 'ambushes' (*insidiae*) alongside 'arrows and other arms' as fundamental aspects of warfare, yet another example of the disjunction between cunning and force in medieval thought.

Gerald claimed that the Irish, like the Welsh, were habitually unfaithful: 'In addition, they always pursue treachery, more so than all other peoples; they never keep a pledge they have given'.[68] This propensity for treachery was particularly evident, according to Gerald, in the Irish custom of using an axe in place of a walking stick: 'So, when the Irishman sees the opportunity, and seizes the moment, no sword is drawn, no bow is bent, no lance is held out. Without any preparation, having raised that deadly instrument, he inflicts a wound'.[69] Once again, the treacherous character manifests itself in the breaking of oaths and unprovoked assaults, rather than employing stratagems. The use of false oaths, sworn on relics, to persuade the garrison of Wexford to surrender in 1171 is the most prominent example in the *Expugnatio* (see Chapter 7) but, beyond this, Gerald rarely credits the Irish with employing ruses in warfare. Considering his obvious interest in such stories, as demonstrated in his Welsh texts, we can reasonably conclude that this was a deliberate choice on Gerald's party, perhaps to emphasise the Cambro-Normans' superior intelligence and prowess.

Scots

Discussing English attitudes towards the Scots in the central Middle Ages is complicated by the fact that the very meaning of the term 'Scot' changed over this period. While the office 'king of Scots' was of considerable antiquity, up until the end of the thirteenth century 'Scotland' referred almost exclusively to the lands north of the Forth. Those who lived between Stirling and Berwick, although ruled by the king of Scots, identified variously as English, Cumbrian or Galwegian. Twelfth-century Scottish royal charters were addressed to 'French, English, Scots and Galwegians and very occasionally Welsh and Flemings'.[70] Over the course of the twelfth

---

[67] EH, pp. 245–53.
[68] EH, p. 165: 'Praeterea, prae omni alia gente proditionibus semper insistunt; fidem datam nemini servant'.
[69] EH, p. 165: 'Visa igitur opportunitate, et occasione captata, non haec ut gladius evaginatur, non ut arcus tenditur, non ut lancea protenditur. Citra omnem praeparatum parum elevata letale vulnus infligit'.
[70] Dauvit Broun, 'Becoming a Nation: Scotland in the Twelfth and Thirteenth Centuries', in Hirokazu Tsurushima (ed.), *Nations in Medieval Britain* (Donington, 2010), pp. 86–103, at p. 91.

and thirteenth centuries, as royal judicial power extended both north and south of the Forth, so the disparate *gens* of the kingdom all came to identify themselves as 'Scots', members of a single country and owing fealty to a single king. It is notable that it is precisely during this period, as the southerners began to self-identify as 'Scots', that we find the first recorded distinction between savage 'highlanders' and civilised 'lowlanders'.[71] With this in mind, it is necessary to treat attitudes towards the Scots during the two major Anglo-Scottish conflicts that fall within this period separately. When describing David I of Scotland's invasion of England in 1138, it was David's Galwegian troops who were specifically identified by the Anglo-Norman chroniclers as culturally 'other'. By the First War of Independence at the end of the thirteenth century, however, no distinction is drawn between the different regions: they are all 'Scots' and they are all 'other'.

According to the Anglo-Norman chroniclers, one of the ways Galwegians were distinguished from other *gentes* was their propensity for extreme violence and their primitive manner of fighting. Richard of Hexham's chronicle contains particularly lurid descriptions of the atrocities the Galwegians committed in northern England in 1138: sacking churches, ripping unborn babies from the womb, drinking children's blood and enslaving the surviving populace.[72] Whether any of these incidents actually occurred is debatable but they do conform to a general Anglo-Norman stereotype that the 'Celts' were excessively brutal: similar accusations were made against the Welsh and Irish. This brutality was manifested in their indiscriminate slaughter of prisoners, whether commoner or nobleman, and the taking of slaves. While there appear to have been both cultural (the Galwegians measured martial prowess in the number of heads taken in battle) and practical reasons for this (lacking strong fortifications to dominate territory, the only effective way of resolving military conflict was to kill one's opponents outright) the Anglo-Norman nobility, who expected to be captured for ransom if defeated, considered them illicit and a further demonstration that the 'Celts' were uncivilised barbarians.[73]

---

[71] Broun, 'Becoming a Nation', p. 101. See also David Ditchburn and Alastair MacDonald, 'Medieval Scotland, 1100–1560', in R. A. Houston and W. W. J. Knox (eds.), *The New Penguin History of Scotland: From the Earliest Times to the Present Day* (London, 2001), pp. 96–181, at pp. 150–4; Alexander Grant, 'Aspects of National Consciousness in Medieval Scotland', in Claus Bjørn, Alexander Grant, and Keith J. Stringer (eds.), *Nations, Nationalism and Patriotism in the European Past* (Copenhagen, 1994), pp. 68–95; Murray G. H. Pittock, *Scottish Nationality* (Basingstoke, 2001), pp. 29–34.

[72] RH, pp. 151–3.

[73] Gillingham, 'Conquering the Barbarians', p. 79; Matthew Strickland, *War and Chivalry: The Conduct and Perception of War in England and Normandy 1066–1217* (Cambridge, 1996), pp. 304–19.

Connected to this idea of Galwegian barbarity was their use of primitive equipment and tactics. Anglo-Norman accounts of the Battle of the Standard (22 August 1138) depict the Galwegians charging into battle naked, to be slaughtered by archers and mail-clad knights: 'The archers, who were intermingled with the knights, darkening the sky with arrows, pierced them, for they were evidently unarmed'.[74] Ailred of Rievaulx depicted Walter Espec, one of the Anglo-Norman commanders, declaring to his troops:

> So who would not laugh, rather than fear, that such a worthless Scot comes to fight us with half-naked buttocks? [...] They oppose our lances, swords and darts with naked skin; they are using calf's hide for a shield; they are inspired by an irrational contempt for death more than strength.[75]

Ronan Toolis has presented a compelling argument that such descriptions misrepresent the actual role played by the Galwegians, who were employed as skirmishers to disrupt the Anglo-Norman formation, and that it was the failure of David I's knights to break said formation, rather than Galwegian ineptitude, that was the decisive factor in the battle.[76] Nevertheless, it is significant that Ailred of Rievaulx credited Henry, son of David I, who commanded the Scottish cavalry, with employing a ruse to escape when his troop found itself cut off behind enemy lines (see Chapter 2): 'Now wisdom is needed, no less than strength [...] when you cannot overcome an enemy with force you must do so with wisdom'.[77] Henry, who was raised at the English royal court and who fought at the Standard in the manner of an Anglo-Norman knight, is the one credited with the *consilium* to devise a stratagem, rather than the primitive and irrational Galwegians. As with Gerald of Wales and the Irish, the ability to employ ruses is regarded as a mark of civilisation rather than barbarism.

Accounts of the First War of Independence offer more scope for analysing English attitudes towards Scottish trickery, as the Scots employed guerrilla-style tactics, retreating into the mountains and woods and rarely confronting the English in pitched battle. It is easy, however, to overstate the differences between the English and Scottish strategies. As previously

---

[74] HH, p. 716: 'Viri uero sagittarii equitibus inmixti obnubilantes eos nimirum inermes penetrabant'.

[75] BoS, p. 186: 'Quis igitur non rideat, potius quam timeat, quod adversus tales vilis Scottus seminudis natibus pugnaturus occurit? [...] lanceis nostris, gladiis et telis nostris nudum obiciunt corium; pelle vitulina pro scuto utentes; irrationabili mortis contemptu, magis quam viribus animati'.

[76] Ronan Toolis, '"Naked and unarmoured": A Reassessment of the Role of the Galwegians at the Battle of the Standard', *Transactions of the Dumfriesshire and Galloway Natural History and Antiquarian Society*, 78 (2004), 79–92.

[77] BoS, pp. 197–8: 'Nunc consilio non minus opus est quam virtute [...] quando non potes viribus, consilio superes inimicum'.

established, pitched battles were rare during the Middle Ages and most warfare consisted of raiding and swift manoeuvres. Although Alastair Macdonald has claimed that 'trickery was an unusually pronounced characteristic of the Scottish method of waging war', the evidence he cites for English condemnation of the Scots is very slight: a single fourteenth-century poem, a parliamentary record and Shakespeare's *Henry V*.[78] Contemporary histories generally do not remark on the Scottish use of trickery, either positively or negatively. When they do condemn the Scots for treachery, it appears to be connected to the act of rebellion itself rather than their method of fighting. The anonymous author of the *Vita Edwardi Secundi* even expressed admiration for the Robert Bruce's tactics. Describing how the Scots killed English foragers in an ambush in September 1310, they wrote:

> With such ambushes they frequently managed to do much harm to our men. For Robert Bruce, knowing that he was unequal to the king of England in strength as much as fortune, declared to his men that it would be better to move in arms against our king secretly than to contend for his right in open battle. In fact, I desired to extol the lord Robert Bruce with praises, except that the accusation of murder and the mark of treason compelled me to keep silent; however the accusation removes all honour.[79]

It was not the use of ambushes or the decision to fight 'secretly' that prevented the chronicler praising Bruce: it was the murder of John Comyn, his rival for the throne, before the high altar in Greyfriars Church, Dumfries. This was the most frequent charge laid against Bruce. By contrast, his period in the wilderness, or his supporters' preference for attacking strongholds under cover of darkness, attracted little ridicule or condemnation.

English historians were more willing to criticise William Wallace. The Lanercost chronicler introduced him as 'a bloody man [...] who had been a chief of robbers in Scotland'.[80] Later, following his account of the English victory at Falkirk, the chronicler composed a verse in which he accused

---

[78] Alastair Macdonald, 'Trickery, Mockery and the Scottish Way of War', *Proceedings of the Society of Antiquaries of Scotland*, 143 (2014), 319–38, at p. 325.
[79] VES, p. 24: 'Ex talibus insidiis frequenter inuenerunt homines nostri multa mala. Robertus enim de Brutz, sciens se tam ex uiribus quam ex fortuna sua regis Anglie imparem, decreuit sibi magis expedire contra regem nostrum arma latenter mouere quam in bello campestri de iure suo contendere. Reuera dominum Robertum de Brutz affectarem laudibus extollere nisi reatus homicidii et nota prodicionis cogerent me tacere; reatus autem excludit omnem honorem'.
[80] The Latin is ambiguous here: it is unclear whether the chronicler wished to say that Wallace was the chief of *all* the robbers or simply one chief among many. Lanercost, p. 190: 'virum sanguineum, Willelmum Waleis, qui prius fuerat in Soctia princeps latronum'.

Wallace of 'treason, slaughters, burnings, deceits and robberies'.[81] This is accompanied by another verse under the heading: 'On the impiety of the Scots'.[82] Peter Langtoft, one of the most virulently anti-Scottish chroniclers of the period, wrote: 'May Scotland be cursed by the mother of God and Wales sunk deep to the Devil! In neither one was there any truth'.[83] Wallace is called a *feloun* and a 'master of thieves' ('mestre de larouns').[84] Langtoft accuses the Scots of attempting to unexpectedly attack the English army besieging Dunbar during a period of truce (27 April 1296), which he describes as a *descait* ('deceit').[85] Similarly, Marmeduke Thweng, the English commander of Stirling castle, was persuaded to come out and treat with the Scots in 1297 under safe conduct, only for the Scots to break the agreement and capture him.[86] Even Robert Bruce does not escape censure. The continuator of Langtoft's chronicle described his retreat to the wilderness following the battle of Methven not as a daring exploit but as a fit of madness, similar to the Biblical king Nebuchadnezzar: 'Their king Robert, who lost cities and towns by his shield, has drunk of the drink of Sir [Fulk fitz] Warren. Afterwards he grazes on raw grass in the forest with the beasts, mad and naked'.[87]

Wallace may have attracted more censure than Bruce because he was relatively low-born and could be dismissed as a bandit, whereas Bruce was a nobleman of established lineage. Additionally, as with other conflicts discussed above, there is the problem of perception. To the English, the kings of England were the rightful rulers of Scotland. Wallace and Bruce's campaigns constituted treason. For the Scots, however, it was a war of independence against a foreign invader and, later, a war to establish Bruce's claim to the throne. When Wallace was put on trial, he strongly rejected the charge that he had committed treason, saying that he had never done homage nor sworn fealty to Edward I.[88] This also explains the English policy of executing noble Scots, such as Herbert de Morham, Simon, earl of Atholl and Nigel Bruce: they were not chivalrous opponents in a licit

---

[81] Lanercost, p. 193: 'proditio, caedes, incendia, frasque rapniae'.

[82] Lanercost, p. 192: 'De impietate Scottorum'.

[83] PL, p. 220: 'Escoce sait maudite de la mere Dé, / Et paround ad deable Gales efoundré! / En l'un ne l'autre fu unkes verité'.

[84] PL, p. 350 and p. 362.

[85] PL, pp. 240–2.

[86] PL, p. 304.

[87] 'Sir Warren' is a reference to Fulk Fitzwarren, whose legend is discussed in Chapter 1. PL, p. 372: 'Du boyvere dam Waryn luy rey Robyn ad bu, / Ke citez et viles perdist par l'escu, / Après en la forest, forsenez et nu, / Se pesceit ove la beste de cel herbe cru'.

[88] Michael Prestwich, 'England and Scotland during the Wars of Independence', in Michael Jones and Malcolm Vale (eds.), *England and Her Neighbours, 1066–1453: Essays in Honour of Pierre Chaplais* (London, 1989), pp. 181–98, at pp. 192–3.

war but forsworn traitors.[89] If the Scots were condemned during the Wars of Independence for treachery, it was because they were perceived to be rebels fighting an illicit war, not because they employed stratagems more frequently than the English.

Greeks

In contrast to the stereotypically bellicose Celts, Western chroniclers portrayed the subjects of the Byzantine empire (usually referred to by the catch-all term 'Greeks' or the pejorative 'Grifons') as unmanly and cowardly in warfare. This was already an established prejudice at the turn of the millennium. Liudprand, bishop of Cremona (c. 920–72), described the courtiers whom he encountered on an embassy to Constantinople on behalf of Otto I of Germany as 'soft, effeminate, long-sleeved, tiara-wearing, hooded, lying, unsexed, idle people'.[90] The twelfth-century Anglo-Norman courtier Walter Map described Greeks as 'soft and feminine, talkative and deceitful, neither faithful nor strong against enemies'.[91] This prejudice appears to have its roots in the profound cultural difference between the Latin and Byzantine nobility. While Latin noble culture prized martial ability and linked masculine honour to physical violence, the Byzantine nobility measured worth according to a man's place in the imperial bureaucracy. Advancement was more likely to be achieved through political manoeuvring than military service.[92]

One aspect of this 'unmanliness' was their fickle, unreliable character and propensity for treachery.[93] There was some truth to this, as the Byzantine courtiers did not consider it immoral to lie to 'barbarians', just as

---

[89] Prestwich, 'England and Scotland', pp. 193–4.
[90] Liudprand of Cremona, *The Complete Works*, ed. and trans. Paolo Squatriti (Washington, DC, 2000), p. 272.
[91] Walter Map, *De nugis curialium*, ed. and trans. M. R. James, rev. C. N. L. Brooke and R. A. B. Mynors (Oxford, 1983), p. 174: 'molles et femineos, loquaces et dolosos, nulliusque contra hostes fidei uel virtutis'.
[92] Marc Carrier, 'Perfidious and Effeminate Greeks: The Representation of Byzantine Ceremonial in the Western Chronicles of the Crusades, 1096–1204', *Annuario*, 4 (2002), 47–68, at pp. 48–50.
[93] Matthew Bennett, 'Virile Latins, Effeminate Greeks and Strong Women: Gender Definitions on Crusade?', in Susan B. Edgington and Sarah Lambert (eds.), *Gendering the Crusades* (Cardiff, 2001), pp. 16–30, p. 18; Leán Ní Chléirigh, 'The Impact of the First Crusade on Western Opinion towards the Byzantine Empire: The *Dei gesta per Francos* of Guibert of Nogent and the *Historia Hierosolymitana* of Fulcher of Chartres', in Conor Kostick (ed.), *The Crusades and the Near East* (London, 2011), pp. 161–88; Lindsay Diggelmann, 'Of Grifons and Tyrants: Anglo-Norman Views of the Mediterranean World during the Third Crusade', in Lisa Bailey, Lindsay Diggelmann and Kim M. Philips (eds.), *Old Worlds, New Worlds: European Cultural Encounters, c. 1000 – c. 1750* (Turnhout, 2009), pp. 11–30, at p. 21.

a parent might lie to a child for their own good.[94] The Greek reputation for treachery was further strengthened in Western minds following the First Crusade, aided in particular by Bohemond's campaign to recruit men for an expedition against Alexios Komnenos and the propaganda that accompanied it.[95] Many of the chronicles of the First Crusade claim that Alexios attempted to sabotage the crusade, blaming him for attacks on the crusaders' camps before Constantinople in 1097 and accusing him of passing information about the crusaders to the Turks.[96] By the time Orderic Vitalis wrote his narrative of the crusade (based substantially on the account of Baldric of Bourgueil), Alexios is portrayed as a Byzantine Bond villain, distributing coins among the crusaders simply to learn their numbers and unleashing tame leopards on the innocent Franks.[97]

While the Greeks are frequently portrayed as treacherous, chroniclers rarely criticise them for employing stratagems. Their treachery does not appear to have been understood in terms of cunning in battle but in a willingness to betray allies and break sworn promises. For example, Amatus of Montecassino described them as follows: 'And since the Greeks often defeated their enemies through malicious arguments and subtle treachery [...] the Greeks more often conquered through malice and treason than valour'.[98] Odo of Deuil, describing the difficulties Louis VII of France faced negotiating with Emperor Manuel I Komnenos for support for his crusading army in 1147, wrote: 'And then the Greeks were thoroughly degenerated into women; casting off all manly vigour of words and mind, they swore lightly to whatever they thought we wanted but neither kept their pledge to us nor respect for themselves'.[99] Robert of Clari, writing a generation later, repeated an apocryphal story that Manuel Komnenos had been urged by his Greek courtiers to expel the Frankish knights in his service. Manuel pretended to do so, then arranged for the supposedly banished Franks to return and stage an attack on him. The Greeks in his entourage promptly fled, exposing their cowardice and proving the Franks' superiority.[100]

When discussing specific stratagems, Western chroniclers did not commonly use negative vocabulary to describe the Greeks who carried

---

[94] Carrier, 'Perfidious and Effeminate Greeks', pp. 55–6.
[95] Jonathan Harris, *Byzantium and the Crusades*, 2nd edn (London, 2014), pp. 94–7.
[96] See BB, p. 17; FC, p. 519; GF, pp. 6, 11; GN, p. 130; GT, pp. 8–9, 15; RA, p. 236.
[97] OV, vol. 5, pp. 332, 336.
[98] AM, p. 248: 'Et que li Grex molt de foiz maliciouz argument et o subtil tradement [...] li Grex ont plus sovent vainchut per malice et par traïson que par vaillantize'.
[99] OD, p. 56: 'et tunc Graeci penitus frangebantur in feminas; omne virile robur et verborum et animi deponentes, leviter iurabant quicquid nos velle putabant, sed nec nobis fidem nec sibi verecundiam conservabant'.
[100] RC, pp. 16–18.

them out. Returning to Orderic Vitalis's account of a night attack supposedly carried out by Raymond of Poitiers on John II Komnenos outside Antioch in 1137 (see Chapter 3), Raymond is characterised as acting 'manfully' (*viriliter*) and 'boldly' (*audacter*) against the Greeks who 'lack boldness and fortitude in difficult things'.[101] Orderic's implication is that it takes courage to attempt a bold and risky stratagem, such as a night attack on an enemy camp, something that the effeminate Greeks would never be able to accomplish.

An unusual example of a Western chronicler criticising the Greek use of stratagems can be found in the first book of the *Itinerarium Peregrinorum*. Discussing the Greeks' alleged attempts to sabotage Frederick Barbarossa's crusade in 1189, the anonymous chronicler lamented that the once-valiant Greeks no longer possessed their ancestors' prowess:

> There is no successor to their ancestors' *virtus*, yet all hold fast to their ancestors' crimes: the lies of Sinon, the deceits of Ulysses, the cruelty of Atreus. But if the Greek's warlike spirit is sought, he fights by craft, not arms: if his faith is sought, he injures as a friend the one whom he cannot injure as a foe.[102]

The three 'criminals' named here are all exemplars of deceit and treachery. Sinon is the Greek who, in the *Aeneid*, pretends to desert the besiegers and convinces the Trojans to bring the wooden horse into the city. Ulysses, who devised the said horse, is a famous trickster (see p. 160). Atreus murdered his nephews, then tricked his brother, Thysetes, into eating their flesh.

It is noteworthy that, while the author of Book 1 of the *Itinerarium* used Ulysses as an example of illicit deception, the author of Book 2 used him as an example of the virtue of prudence: 'and, remarkable in such a famous knight, [Richard I of England possessed] the speech of Nestor [and] the prudence of Ulysses, which deservedly rendered him more distinguished than others in all activities, whether making speeches or deeds'.[103] Once again we find an ambiguity surrounding deceitful behaviour. When an author wished to criticise deceit Ulysses could be employed as an example of a famous liar but when they wished to praise it, he became an example of cleverness and skill.

---

[101] OV, vol. 6, p. 504: 'in arduis rebus audacia et fortitudine carent'.
[102] *Virtus* may mean courage, power, virtue, manliness or any combination of these qualities, so I have left it untranslated here. IP, p. 46: 'Virtutum siquidem nullus successor, scelerum omnes; nam Sinonis figmenta, Ulixis fallaciam. Atrei atrocitatem retinent. Quod si Graeci militia quaeritur; arte, non armis dimicat: si fides; amicus obest, inimicus obesse non potest'.
[103] Nestor was the wise old king of Pylos, famous for giving good advice. IP, p. 143: 'et quod in tam famoso milite perrarum esse solet, lingua Nestoris, prudentia Ulixis, in omnibus negotiis vel perorandis, vel gerendis, aliis merito reddebant excellentiorem'.

Muslims

Western attitudes to the Muslims they encountered in Sicily and Outremer were complex. Not only were they clearly racially and culturally distinct from Europeans, they were not Christian. The literature of the crusades regularly portrayed them as monstrous enemies of Christ, who must be destroyed in order to reclaim his patrimony in the Holy Land. At the same time, however, encounters with Muslims generated a more nuanced understanding of Islam and the diversity of its adherents.

The confused attitude towards Muslims in the chronicles is reflected in the variety of words used to describe them. In the *chansons de geste*, and in a number of crusader chronicles, they are pagans (*pagani*), polytheists who worship idols. John V. Tolan interpreted this depiction, which appears to have originated in the twelfth century, not as mere ignorance of Islam but a conscious effort to situate the crusades within a tradition of defending Christendom against pagans, such as the Vikings or Magyars.[104] The term 'gentile' was also employed for Muslims, linking the crusades to the Israelite conquest of Canaan.[105] Another common catch-all for Muslims was 'Saracen'. Initially a Roman term for inhabitants of the eastern part of the Arabian peninsula, during the Middle Ages it grew to encompass all Arabs, then all Muslims and finally non-Christians in general.[106] Nicholas Morton has demonstrated that, prior to the First Crusade, the crusaders had little knowledge of the peoples of the Near East, as evidenced by the very general references to 'barbarians', 'pagans' and 'Saracens' in crusader letters and charters.[107] This appears to have changed radically by the time that the first crusader chronicles came to be written. These chroniclers were aware that their foremost enemies were Turks, a *gens* distinct from both the native Christian *gentes* and other Muslims. Chroniclers continued to use 'Saracen' for Arabs and Egyptians but (usually) described the Turks as a distinct *gens*.[108]

---

[104] John V. Tolan, *Saracens: Islam in the Medieval European Imagination* (New York, 2002), pp. 106–11.

[105] Matthew Bennett, 'First Crusaders' Images of Muslims: The Influence of Vernacular Poetry?', *Forum for Modern Language Studies*, 22 (1986), 101–22.

[106] Sini Kangas, '*Inimicus Dei et sanctae Christianitatis*? Saracens and their Prophet in Twelfth-Century Crusade Propaganda and Western Travesties of Muhammad's Life', in Conor Kostick (ed.), *The Crusades and the Near East* (London, 2011), pp. 131–60, at pp. 138–9.

[107] Nicholas Morton, 'Encountering the Turks: The First Crusaders' Foreknowledge of their Enemy, Some Preliminary Findings', in Simon John and Nicholas Morton (eds.), *Crusading and Warfare in the Middle Ages: Realities and Representations, Essays in Honour of John France* (Farnham, 2014), pp. 47–68, at pp. 49–52.

[108] Thomas S. Asbridge, 'Knowing the Enemy: Latin Relations with Islam at the Time of the First Crusade', in Norman Housley (ed.), *Knighthoods of Christ: Essays on the History of the Crusades and the Knights Templar, Presented to Malcolm Barber* (Farnham,

From the very earliest accounts, chroniclers characterised the Turks as skilled in war. This is understandable as Turkish horsemen, whether tribal mercenaries or *mamlūk* slave-soldiers, made up the core of Muslim armies throughout the crusading period. The anonymous author of the *Gesta Francorum* praised the Turks' valour and skill:

> Who is so wise or learned to ever venture to describe the prudence, courage in battle and strength of the Turks? They thought to terrify the *gens* of the Franks with the threat of their arrows, as they terrified the Arabs, Saracens and Armenians, the Syrians and the Greeks. But, if it pleases God, they will never be as strong as our men. Nevertheless, they say that they are of the same lineage as the Franks and, because of this, no man is born to be a knight except the Franks and themselves.[109]

This passage occurs just after the crusaders' victory at Dorylaeum and serves to make the Franks look even stronger for having defeated this mighty *gens*. It is also noteworthy that prudence is listed as one of the Turks' virtues. Guibert of Nogent, adapting the *Gesta* for his own chronicle, described the Turks as 'acute in mind and active in arms'.[110]

While Turkish rulers such as Karbogha and Īlghāzī were typically portrayed as wicked and monstrously cruel, some of the later chroniclers expressed admiration for individual Muslim rulers. In visual art, Muslim rulers were set apart from the rest of their *gens*. In her study of illustrations of William of Tyre's chronicle, Svetlana Luchitskaya identified that Muslim rulers were usually presented as fair skinned and dressed in the style of Western kings, distinguishing them from the stereotypical depiction of dark skinned, turban-wearing 'Saracens'.[111] William of Tyre, who was born in Outremer and intimately involved in the kingdom of Jerusalem's diplomatic relations with neighbouring Muslim powers, described Nūr al-Dīn in 1174 as a 'just prince, crafty and provident and religious according to the

---

2007), pp. 17–26, at p. 19; Rosalind Hill, 'The Christian View of the Muslims at the Time of the First Crusade', in P. M. Holt (ed.), *The Eastern Mediterranean Lands in the Period of the Crusades* (Warminster, 1977), pp. 1–8, at p. 2; Alan V. Murray, 'From the Bosphorus to Kurasan: The Turkish Domination of Asia in the Perception of the Chroniclers of the First Crusade', *Elçuk University Journal of Seljuk Studies*, 8 (2018), 82–98.

[109] GF, p. 21: 'Quis unquam tam sapiens aut doctus audebit descrbiere prudentiam militiamque et fortitudinem Turcorum? Qui putabant terrere gentem Francorum minis suarum sagittarum, sicut terruerunt Arabes, Saracenos, et Hermenios, Suranios et Grecos. Sed, si Deo placet, nunquam tantum valebunt quantum nostri. Verumtamen dicunt se esse de Francorum generatione, et quia nullus homo naturaliter debet esse miles nisi Franci et illi'.

[110] GN, p. 158: 'adeo argutos animis ac strenuos armis'.

[111] Svetlana Luchitskaya, 'Muslims in Christian Imagery of the Thirteenth Century: The Visual Code of Otherness', *Al-Masāq: Islam and the Medieval Mediterranean*, 12 (2000), 37–67, at p. 54.

traditions of his *gens*'.¹¹² Towards the end of the *Itinerarium Peregrinorum*, the compiler imagined an interview between Saladin and Hubert Walter, bishop of Salisbury. When Saladin asked Hubert to described the character of Richard I of England, he replied: 'I judge that if anybody could join the well-ordered virtues with which you are endowed (your sins excepted) with those of king Richard, that each might be provided with the gifts of the other, two such princes would not be found in the whole world'.¹¹³ Saladin agreed with the assessment, stating that Richard, although courageous, was too reckless in battle. The chronicler appears to be suggesting here that Saladin possessed the virtues of moderation and prudence that Richard would have done well to emulate.

This admiration for Turkish prowess and the virtues of certain rulers sat side-by-side with the most extreme vilification. Robert the Monk depicted the Turks as bestial, gnashing their teeth and howling like dogs.¹¹⁴ Albert of Aachen called them 'wicked and impious men'.¹¹⁵ According to Geoffrey Malaterra, when the Muslim Benthumen agreed to betray the city of Catania to the emir of Syracuse in 1081 in return for money, he was acting according to his 'pagan name'.¹¹⁶ To Ambroise, Turks were *la gente haïe* (the hateful men) or *li poeples al diable* (the devil's people).¹¹⁷ They were depicted as lustful, greedy and treacherous, in implicit contrast to the ideal virtuous crusader.¹¹⁸ We have already examined how the Turks garrisoning Tarsos were alleged to have negotiated with Tancred in bad faith in September 1097 (see Chapter 7) and how Qilij Arslān, following his defeat at Dorylaeum, lied to the Christian towns he came to as he retreated through Cilicia in order to gain entry and plunder them (see Chapter 2). According to Walter the Chancellor, in August 1113 Īlghāzī swore an oath to spare the Christian citizens of Zardana if he was admitted,

---

¹¹² WT, p. 956: 'princeps tamen iustus, vafer et providus et secundum gentis sue traditiones religiosus'.

¹¹³ IP, pp. 437–8: 'Si quis, me judice, exceptis peccatis tuis, tuarum dotes virtutum simul cum regis Ricardi communicaret compositas, ut uterque vestrum utriusque dotaretur praeditus potentiis tales in orbe terrarum duo principes non invenirentur'.

¹¹⁴ Carol Sweetenham, 'Crusaders in a Hall of Mirrors: The Portrayal of Saracens in Robert the Monk's *Historia Iherosolimitana*', in Sarah Lambert and Helen Nicholson (eds.), *Languages of Love and Hate: Conflict, Communication, and Identity in the Medieval Mediterranean* (Turnhout, 2012), pp. 49–64, at p. 55.

¹¹⁵ AA, p. 37: 'impiis et sceleratis hominibus'.

¹¹⁶ GM, p 75: 'Paganus vero nominis sui competens imitator'.

¹¹⁷ Amb, lines 3490, 6354.

¹¹⁸ Marianne J. Ailes, 'The Admirable Enemy? Saladin and Saphadin in Ambroise's *Estoire de la guerre sainte*', in Norman Housley (ed.), *Knighthoods of Christ: Essays on the History of the Crusades and the Knights Templar Presented to Malcolm Barber* (Farnham, 2007), pp. 51–64, at p. 53; Sweetenham, 'Crusaders in a Hall of Mirrors', p. 55.

only to massacre them all once they had surrendered.[119] The Old French continuation of William of Tyre's chronicle, know to scholars as the *Estoire d'Eracles*, contains a fanciful variation on the story of Saphadin, Saladin's brother, sending a horse to Richard I of England so that he would not be dishonoured by fighting on foot.[120] The author of the *Eracles* claimed that the horse was mad and was given to Richard in the hope that it would throw him if he tried to mount it.[121]

With regard to military stratagems, the Turks appear to have frequently employed ambushes, if the chronicle evidence is to be relied upon: of the 132 ambushes recorded in the Appendix to this volume, 32 (24.2%) were set by Turkish or Muslim troops. This might be explained by the fact that they were operating in familiar terrain, whereas the Franks initially had very little knowledge of the region, making them easy to ambush. The other key ruse attributed to the Turks was the feigned flight. Although Morillo has claimed that this manoeuvre ran contrary to Western military norms and was regarded as cowardly, the truth seems to be more complex. Some chroniclers did express disdain for this habit of fighting on the run. In his account of Urban II's sermon to the Council of Clermont in 1095, William of Malmesbury drew on ancient theories of climate and its impact on physiology, preserved in Vegetius's *De rei militari*, to claim that the Turks were physically incapable of fighting any other way:

> It is a well known fact that every nation born in an Eastern clime is dried up by the great heat of the sun; they may have more good sense, but they have less blood in their veins, and that is why they flee from battle at close quarters: they know that they have no blood to spare.[122]

Other chroniclers, however, were more equivocal about this ruse. The compiler of the *Itinerarium Peregrinorum* described the experience of fighting Turkish horse archers as follows: 'when they are fleeing and they see that those pursuing them have stopped, then they themselves stop fleeing, like a wearisome fly which will fly away when you drive it off but which returns when you stop'.[123] While it is not precisely flattering to

---

[119] WC, p. 101.

[120] For a more plausible variation of the story, in which the horse is simply a gift, see Amb, lines 11512–33; IP, p. 419.

[121] Margaret Ruth Morgan (ed.), *La Continuation de Guillaume de Tyr, 1184–1197* (Paris, 1982), p. 147.

[122] GRA, vol. 1, p. 602: 'Constat profecto quod omnis natio quae in Eoa plaga nascitur, nimio solis ardore siccata, amplius quidem sapit, sed minus habet sanguinis; ideoque uicinam pugnam fugiunt, quia parum sanguinis se habere norunt'.

[123] IP, p. 247: 'Turcorum etiam moris est, ut quando persenserint se fugantes a persequendo cessare, tunc et ipsi fugere cessabunt, more muscae fastidiosae, quam si abegeris avolabit, cum cessaveris redibit, quamdiu fugaveris fugiet, cum desieries praesto est'. See also Amb, line 5629–66.

describe the Turks as an 'infuriating fly', the chronicler does not call the tactic dishonourable or cowardly. Rather, he criticised the crusaders who pursued them recklessly and were captured: 'And what ought by rights to have been reckoned glorious is adjudged to be foolishness'.[124] The chronicle of Fulcher of Chartres preserves a letter, written by the leaders of the First Crusade to Pope Urban II in September 1098, that describes the capture of Antioch and subsequent battle before the city on 28 June. In the letter, the crusaders describe how they had learned to anticipate the Turks' tactics:

> But they began to scatter in every direction, as is their custom. Occupying the hills and paths, they wanted to go around us wherever they could, for they thought to kill all of us this way. But since our men had been educated in many battles against their cunning tricks and devices, God's grace and mercy rescued us so that we, who were very few in comparison to them, forced them all into one place.[125]

This passage is another important reminder that medieval interpretations of a battle could be entirely different to those of twenty-first-century scholars. The second sentence is constructed so that victory is ascribed to the *gratia Dei et misericordia*. The crusaders' 'education' through repeated encounters with the Turks and their new strategy that prevented the Turks dispersing and surrounding them are first and foremost divine gifts, not the result of human skill or endeavour.

As discussed in Chapter 4, Western Europeans were unused to these kinds of hit-and-run tactics and presumed that the Turks were fleeing, prompting them to break formation and give chase. Experience taught them the importance of holding formation until they could launch a single, devastating charge. We can see the value of this experience in Odo of Deuil's account of Louis VII's crusade. Having suffered repeated losses from Turkish attacks on the march through Anatolia, Louis took the remarkable step of placing the entire army under the authority of Gerald, master of the Knights Templar:

> Those who had vexed us because they had readily fled from our enemies were ordered to be patient until they received an order and that they should have returned when commanded. They were warned to return immediately when recalled. When this law had been learned, they were also taught an order of march, that those at the front should not go to the rear, nor should those guarding the flanks disorder themselves.[126]

---

[124] IP, p. 246: 'et quod jure debuerat ascribi gloriae, addictum est insipientiae'.

[125] FC, p. 263: 'Ipsi autem, ut mos eorum est, undique se dispergere coeperunt, occupando colles et vias ubicumque poterant nos girare voluerunt. Sic enim nos omnes interficere putaverunt. Sed nobis multis bellis contra eorum calliditates et ingenia edoctis, gratia Dei et misericordia ita subvenit, ut qui paucissimi ad eorum comparationem eramus, omnes illos in unum coegimus'.

[126] OD, p. 124: 'Iubentur pati usque ad praeceptum (eos) qui nos vexant, quia cito

Louis's force appears to have faced problems similar to those encountered by Richard I of England at the battle of Arsuf (7 September 1191), when he struggled to prevent the Hospitallers, who were acting as the rearguard, from charging Saladin's horsemen before they were given an order.[127]

To conclude, Western attitudes towards Muslim stratagems were influenced by a variety of factors. Racially, culturally and, above all, religiously, they were perceived as 'other' and their actions were interpreted through the twin lenses of prejudice and religious ideology. While some chroniclers were willing to acknowledge that Turks were effective soldiers or generals, the need to portray them as the wicked opponents of a holy cause inevitably coloured their depiction in the narratives. The 'wickedness' of their tactics did not necessarily stem from the tactics themselves (after all, crusaders and other Westerners were willing to employ similar tactics) but the purpose for which they were employed: to frustrate God's purpose and prevent the recovery of Christ's patrimony.

Conclusion

It was common for Western literature to stereotype the 'other' as treacherous and deceitful. This seems to have had little relation to whether the treacherous *gentes* were thought to be dangerously warlike, such as the Irish and Scots, or inherently cowardly, such as the Greeks. This treachery does not appear to have been understood as a preference for employing military ruses. Rather, it was a general untrustworthiness and willingness to betray one's given word: a trait almost universally condemned in Western sources. Employing stratagems was often portrayed as a sign of courage and prudence, qualities that did not necessarily match the stereotype of an ignorant or cowardly *gens*. Western chroniclers could and did express admiration when the 'other' employed trickery in warfare, if only to make the Westerners appear more valiant by overcoming such a dangerous enemy.

---

refugiunt inimicos, et, cum iussi restituerint, ilico regredi praemonent revocatos. Cognita lege docentur et gradum, ne qui de primo est vadat ad ultimum vel ne se confundant custodes laterum'.

[127] IP, pp. 267–8.

Conclusion

'Stratagem slipped into disuse in Europe during the Middle Ages [...] As late as the Battle of Ravenna (1512) adversaries were accustomed to open battle, with chivalrous challenges and to conduct war, at least in theory, in accord with agreed rules and fixed means'.[1] At least, this was the view of the twentieth-century military theorist Barton Whaley. The medieval chroniclers studied in this volume would have been astonished. They clearly thought that stratagems were an integral part of warfare: they depicted kings and emperors, crusaders and Muslims, nobles and commoners employing deception to achieve their goals.

Did all these incidents take place exactly as described? Almost certainly not. Many of them are probably fiction, fabricated by boastful warriors or by writers seeking to embellish their narratives. Their true value lies in what they tell us about medieval culture. The chroniclers evidently thought these stories were worth recording and that their readers would be interested in reading them. They are colourful, dramatic, often comical, contradicting any ideas about chronicles being 'dry and dusty'. These incidents also tell us what qualities contemporaries admired in their fighting men, what kind of behaviour they thought was worthy of praise or censure. This is surely more useful to scholarship than whether Robert Guiscard *really did* have a 'fake corpse' carried into Montecassino or whether Louis the Fat *actually* infiltrated Gasny dressed in a monk's habit.

This study of the language and presentation of military deception has revealed a profound ambiguity towards the subject of trickery, not dissimilar to that found in our own culture. Different chroniclers could describe the same essential act as a nefarious fraud or a sound tactical decision. Deceitful behaviour could be ascribed to either treachery or prudence. The quality of 'cunning' could be attributed to both heroes and villains. Even the language used inhabited a grey zone of moral meaning, as the same phrases were also used for works of skill, engineering and rhetoric. Consider the subtle difference between 'craft', 'craftsman' and 'crafty' in modern English, or the range of meaning that be attached to words such as 'artifice' or 'subtle'.

When we do find medieval chroniclers making moral judgements about an act of military deception, they appear to have judged the ends rather

---

[1] Barton Whaley, *Stratagem: Deception and Surprise in War* (Norwood, MA, 2007), p. 47.

than the means. If deception was employed in a 'good' cause, the chroniclers tended to approve of the deception, or at least attempt to excuse it. If the deception was employed in a 'bad' cause, such as an unwarranted rebellion or in opposition to a holy crusade, then chroniclers would disapprove. The only form of deceit that was universally condemned was breaking a sacred oath. This was the charge most frequently laid against the 'other', the Celt, the Greek and the Muslim, who were often stereotyped as inherently untrustworthy. There are even exceptions to this, however, and we can find examples of chroniclers excusing the violation of this major cultural taboo.

For all the ambiguity surrounding the subject, it is clear that the medieval authors were able to admire cunning on the battlefield, even in an enemy. Biographers of notable individuals not only included incidents of trickery in their narratives, they actively celebrated them as displays of good sense and martial skill. When we consider how carefully chroniclers chose their material in order to bend events to suit their narrative, the fact that they chose to include these stories of guile tells us that they would be appreciated by their intended audience. There must have been considerable variation in individual opinion, of course, but the frequent appearance of such stories tells us that deception was a recognised aspect of warfare and one that people wanted to hear about.

We must be cautious about pushing this line of reasoning too far, however. To recognise that there is a strong element of fiction in medieval chronicles does not mean we must adopt a wholly relativist mindset and abandon any hope of learning anything meaningful about historical reality. The sheer number of incidents of military deception, reported in such a broad range of chronicles, at the very least demonstrates that contemporaries *expected* combatants to use guile and trickery in addition to brute force. Moreover, many of these incidents are no more implausible than the extraordinary stratagems recorded in the twentieth and twenty-first centuries. Hopefully this study is another nail in the coffin for the 'chivalric maniac' stereotype of medieval combatants: the mail-clad simpleton charging blindly at the foe without a thought for strategy or tactics. Although they lacked the benefits of a modern military education, medieval commanders were capable of displaying innovation and intelligence to rival generals from any other time and place. Similarly, the knighthood of medieval Europe could fight with great shrewdness and subtlety. They did not always do so, being guided as much by circumstance, social expectations or individual temperament as reason and exigency, but the same could be said of any soldier. This study demonstrates that medieval combatants could and did use cunning to achieve their goals.

What then does this mean for our understanding of 'chivalry'? The majority of sources studied above are Latin chronicles, written by churchmen for a predominantly clerical audience. There are sufficient parallels between the Latin and the vernacular chronicles of this period to demonstrate that admiration of *engin* or *slycht* was not confined to Latinate churchmen but the portrayal of deception in overtly 'literary' sources remains understudied. There is a wealth of material that might fruitfully be analysed in the romances and the *chansons de geste*: the anonymous red or black knight, the secret love affair and the various wiles of Tristan all indicate that deceit was a well-known topos in chivalric tales. A study of the 'trickster' hero in romance or the value of cunning in the *chansons* would complement this volume by delving further into vernacular culture and perhaps bring us closer to the mindset of the Francophone knights who listened to these tales.

There is also much scope to expand this field beyond the borders of Francophone Europe, to find parallels and variations in German, Italian or Spanish sources. A more ambitious undertaking would be to focus on the transcultural nature of deception. In Chapter 9, we considered Western perceptions of trickery when practiced by the culturally 'other' but a genuinely comparative study could be undertaken to study how one or more of these cultures perceived military deception and how they in turn perceived Western Europeans.[2] Another possible avenue for further research would involve shifting the focus forward in time and analysing the depiction of military stratagems in fourteenth- and fifteenth-century sources. Not only is this period rich in narrative histories and accounts of war, it would be instructive to note if there were any significant changes in the use or perception of trickery that coincided with the changes in European warfare, such as the dominance of waged soldiers or the growing tactical importance of foot soldiers.

The topic of deception touches closely on the difficult subjects of honour and shame. As noted above, the desire to avoid public shame and to defend one's good name had a powerful, if frequently indefinable, influence on combatants' behaviour. Yet the subject of knightly honour has, like stratagems, been overlooked by many scholars, who seem to assume that the term has universal meaning when, in fact, each society has a highly specific understanding of 'honour'. Contemporaries did not consider cunning to be an inherently shameful quality in a fighting man and it was possible for contemporaries to respect or praise a man who deceived his enemy. There is need for a study of exactly how honour was understood within medieval martial culture, what was considered honourable or dishonourable on the battlefield and how people sought to justify potentially shameful behaviour. There is an enduring fascination in a culture that prized a man for his courteous speech as much as for his

---

[2] Theotokis has already performed a study of this nature on the perception of trickery in both Byzantine and Latin sources. Georgios Theotokis, *Byzantine Military Tactics in Syria and Mesopotamia: A Comparative Study* (Edinburgh, 2018), pp. 29–41.

ability to batter another man's brains out with a sword, that taught people to preserve their good name above all else but could praise deception as an act of prudence and foresight. We may be shocked by the hypocrisy but we also see the paradoxes and contradictions of our own society reflected back at us and find a little empathy for these long-dead warriors.

Appendix

Taxonomy of Military Deceptions in Medieval Chronicles
c. 1000–1320

Summary

Category	Number of Incidents (Percentage of total)
Ambushes	135 (31.61%)
Bribery and Inducement	20 (4.68%)
Distraction	5 (1.17%)
Disguise	57 (13.34%)
Feigned Flight	39 (9.13%)
Hidden Traps	10 (2.34%)
Misinformation	46 (10.53%)
Night/Dawn Attacks	79 (18.50%)
Oaths and Truces	25 (5.85%)
Spies and Spying	12 (2.81%)
Total	427

Ambushes

Ambushes – Forest/Undergrowth

Date	Place	Description	Source(s)
c. 1070s	England, Northamptonshire	Hereward the Wake rescued in forest	GH, 402–3
1079	Sicily, Taormina	Roger I of Sicily ambushed by Slavs in myrtle thicket	GM, 146
c. 1085	Maine, Saint Suzanne	Richer, son of Engenulf of Langle, shot in ambush	OV, vol. 4, 49–51
1095	England, Northumberland	Plan to ambush William II of England in forest	OV, vol. 4, 281
1098	Maine, near Dangeul	Helias, count of Maine, ambushed in forest	OV, vol. 5, 239
1098, April	Syria, Antioch	Adelbero, archdeacon of Metz, and a knight are ambushed in a pleasure garden	AA, 208–12
1123 April 18	Cilicia, Samosata	Baldwin II of Jerusalem ambushed and captured in a wood	OV, vol. 6, 111; WT, 566–8
1130	Picardy, Coucy	Rebel garrison lay ambush for Louis VI of France	SSD, 143
1136 April 15	Wales, near Abergavenny	Iorweth of Caerleon kills Richard fitz Gilbert in an ambush	GS, 17; IK, 47–8; JW, 221
1148	Syria, Damascus	Citizens ambush crusaders in orchards	WT, 764–5
1157	Wales, near Hawarden	Henry II of England ambushed in wooded and marshy terrain	WN, vol. 2, 23–5
1169	Ireland, Leinster	MacDonnchadh of Ossory ambushed in a thicket by Maurice de Prendergast	Dermot, 49–53
1174 August	Normandy, Rouen	Henry II of England employs Welsh troops to ambush French supplies in forest	GRH, vol. 1, 74–5; RT, 265; WN, vol. 2, 153

Ambushes – Forest/Undergrowth (*concluded*)

Date	Place	Description	Source(s)
1190 May	Cyprus, near Nicosia	Isaac Komnenos ambushes Richard I of England in forest	IP, 192–4
1192 Jan 3	Palestine, near Casal of the Plains	Richard I of England attacks a Turkish force lying in ambush	IP, 303–4
1194 July 4	Loire Valley, Fréteval Forest	Richard I of England ambushes Philip II of France	GPA, 197; HPA, 330
1195 Nov	Normandy, near Dieppe	Richard I of England ambushes Philip II of France	GPA, 198; HPA, 334
1203	Thrace, near Philia	Mourtzouphlus ambushes Henry of Flanders	Clari, 65–8; GV, vol. 2, 26
1225	Gascony, near La Réole	Richard, earl of Cornwall, ambushes the count of Marche	RW, vol. 2, 457–8
1233, Dec 26	Wales, possibly Monmouthshire	John of Monmouth ambushed by Richard Marshal	RW, vol. 2, 580
1303 April	Flanders, near Bruges	William of Jülich ambushed by French troops	AG, 40
1314 June 24	Scotland, Bannockburn	Henry de Bohun ambushed by Robert Bruce from woodland	VES, 88

Ambushes – Swamp/Fenland

Date	Place	Description	Source(s)
1070–1	England, Ely	Hereward the Wake ambushes William, earl of Warenne in the fens	GH, 374–7
1099	Syria, near Antioch	Godfrey of Bouillon ambushes Turkish force in a 'marshy place'	AA, 370–2
1138 Feb 2	Scotland, Roxburgh	David I of Scotland attempts to ambush Stephen of England in a marsh	JH, 8; RH, 44
c. 1307	Scotland, Edirford	James Douglas ambushes Philip Mowbray in a marsh	Bruce, bk 8, lines 25–73

Ambushes – Mountains/Hills

Date	Place	Description	Source(s)
1077	Sicily, Trapani	Jordan of Sicily ambushes citizens from a 'hollow' outside the town	GM, 142
1096	Bucinat, Pelagonia	Raymond of Saint-Gilles ambushes a force of Pechenegs in the mountains	RA, 237
1098 Feb 9	Syria, near Antioch	Armenians and Syrians ambush Turks fleeing from the battle of the Lake	GF, 37; OV, vol. 5, 81
1113	Palestine, near Tyre	Baldwin I of Jerusalem ambushes garrison of Tyre in mountains	AA, 838
1115 Sept 4	Syria, near Sarmin	Bursuq of Hamadān deploys force behind a hill to attack Roger of Salerno	WC, 101–2
c. 1141	England, Wiltshire, Ludgershall	John Marshal ambushes Patrick, earl of Salisbury, in a valley	HWM, lines 302–6
1172	Ireland, Kildare	O'Dempsey, lord of Offaly, ambushes Richard Fitzgilbert in a pass	Dermot, 179–81
1179 Mar 21	Palestine, Zebulon Valley	Baldwin IV of Jerusalem lays ambushes for bandits	WT, 996–8
1190 May 3	Phrygia, near Iconium	Frederick Barbarossa ambushed by Turks while ascending 'steep cliffs'	IP, 50–1
1192 June 12	Palestine, near Jerusalem	Richard I surprises a Muslim ambush party in the mountains	IP, 369
1295	Aquitaine, near Belgarde	John of St. John is led into a French ambush by a treacherous spy	PL, vol. 2, 280–2

Ambushes – Urban/Siege

Date	Place	Description	Source(s)
946	Normandy, Rouen	Norman garrison ambushes Otto I of Germany	GND, vol. 1, 119
987–92	Anjou, Angers	Fulk Nerra ambushes the sons of Conan of Brittany	GCA, vol. 1, 92
1062 May	Campania, Capua	Richard of Aversa ambushes boats bringing supplies to the city	AM, 121
1071	Sicily, Palermo	Normans lure the besiegers into an ambush with loaves of bread	AM, 157
1096 Sept	Bithynia, Xerigordon	Participants in the Peoples' Crusade unsuccessfully lay ambush for Turks	BB, 14; GF, 3; GN, 124; RM, 85
1097 Oct 29	Syria, Antioch	Bohemond ambushes the garrison	BB, 39
1098	Syria, Antioch	Turks lay ambushes for crusaders	OV, vol. 5, 81
1098 March	Syria, Antioch	Garrison ambushes workmen constructing a siege castle	RM, 131
1098 April	Syria, Antioch	Tancred ambushes a Turkish supply train	RM, 139
1098	Syria, Talamania	Syrian Christians are ambushed by Turks	RM, 177
1099	Syria, Tripoli	Garrison lays an ambush for the crusaders	BB, 98–9
1099 June	Palestine, Jerusalem	Garrison lays ambushes for crusaders around water sources	AA, 410; BB, 105–6; GF, 89; GN, 128; OV, vol. 5, 163
1099 June	Palestine, Jerusalem	Crusaders set ambushes for messengers travelling between Egypt and Jerusalem	AA, 420
1099 June	Palestine, Ramla	Citizens of Ascalon ambush foragers from crusading army	AA, 408
1099 June	Palestine, Jerusalem	Garrisons attacks crusaders from 'hidden caves'	GT, 109
1099	Palestine, Arsuf	Godfrey of Bouillon ambushes garrison	AA, 494–502

—*(continued)*

Ambushes – Urban/Siege (*continued*)

Date	Place	Description	Source(s)
1103	Syria, Laodicea	Tancred lures garrison into an ambush with a giant tent	GT, 122–3
1107	Île-de-France, Goumay	Garrison attempt to ambush Louis VI of France from 'holes in the ground'	SSD, 57
1108 June	Syria, Tripoli	Egyptian soldiers placed in a cave to ambush Franks	AA, 784–6
1109	Palestine, Ascalon	William Jordan is killed in a night-time ambush while besieging the city	FC, 531–2
1110	Syria, Tyre	Baldwin I of Jerusalem ambushes treasure bound for the city	AA, 826–8
1112	Chartres, Toury	Ralph of Beaugency ambushes Louis VI of France's assault force	SSD, 99
1123	Normandy, Gisors	Baudry of Bray attempts to ambush Robert of Candos inside the town during market day	OV, vol. 6, 343–5
1127 Nov 11	Campania, Benevento	Rao of Fragento ambushes the garrison when they sally out to attack Roger II of Sicily	FB, 176
1136	England, Oxfordshire, Bampton	Stephen captures a member of the garrison in an ambush	GS, 29–30
1127 March	Flanders, Bruges	Both sides of siege lay ambushes for one another	GB, 57
1128 April	Flanders, Oostburg	Lambert of Aardenburg's besieging force is ambushed	GB, 165
1130	Anjou, l'Île-Bouchard	Geoffrey V of Anjou ambushes garrison as they sally out	HG, 267–8
1137	Campania, Benevento	Henry of Bavaria ambushes garrison as they sally out	FB, 218
1140	England, Bath	Stephen of England lays ambushes for garrison	JW, 291
1146–7	England, Coventry	Ranulf, earl of Chester, lays ambushes for Stephen of England on his approach to castle	GS, 199–201
1187	Palestine, Tyre	Conrad de Montferrat ambushes Muslim army from caves and houses	GRH, vol. 2, 25–6

Ambushes – Urban/Siege (*concluded*)

Date	Place	Description	Source(s)
1189	Maine, Le Mans	Geoffrey, count of Vendôme, ambushed by the viscount of Mont Double	GRH, vol. 2, 68; HowChr, vol. 2, 108
1211	Languedoc, Montgey	Raymond-Roger, count of Foix, ambushes a force of crusaders travelling to Lavaur	HA, vol. 1, 217–18
1216 Aug 15	Languedoc, Beaucaire	Crusaders attempt to ambush garrison by attacking during a diversionary assault	CCA, vol. 2, 178–92
1217	England, Lincoln	John Marshal ambushed by French while scouting the town	HWM, lines 16437–43
1233 Nov	Welsh Marches	Richard Marshal ambushes garrisons of the royal castles	RW, vol. 2, 576
c. 1306	Scotland, Cupar	Alexander Fraser ambushes Thomas Gray	TG, 68

Ambushes – Location Unspecified

Date	Place	Description	Source(s)
1035	England, Southampton	Edward the Confessor ambushed by followers of Harold Harefoot	GG, 3
1053	Normandy, Arques	Garrison ambushes Henry I of France	GG, 39–41; GRA, 433
c. 1060s	Flanders, Saint-Omer	Hereward the Wake ambushed by a knight of St. Valery	GH, 357
1063	Sicily, Agrigento	Roger I of Sicily's men ambushed by Muslims	GM, 113
1067 March	England, Northumbria	Copsi, earl of Northumberland, ambushed by 'men of his district'	OV, vol. 2, 209
c. 1070s	Wales, near Rhuddlan	Robert of Rhuddlan ambushes Bleddyn, king of Gwynedd and Powys	OV, vol. 4, 145
1071	Flanders, Cassel	Robert the Frisian ambushes William fitz Osbern and Arnulf III of Flanders	GRA, 475

—(*continued*)

Ambushes – Location Unspecified (*continued*)

Date	Place	Description	Source(s)
1071	Sicily, Castrogiovanni	Serlo, nephew of Roger I of Sicily, ambushed by his brother Brachiem	GM, 12627
c. 1073	Calabria, Santa Severina	Gerard of Buonalbergo ambushes Richard of Capua	AM, 176
1096	Scalvonia	Raymond of Saint-Gilles ambushed by locals	RA, 235–6; WT, 182–4
c. 1097	Syria, Antioch	Pakrad, an Armenian warlord, ambushes Nicusus of Turbessel's men	AA, 262
1097 Feb 18	Macedonia, River Vardar	Byzantine Turcopoles ambush Norman crusaders	GT, 8–9
1097	Constantinople	Baldwin of Bouillon ambushes Byzantine troops attacking crusader foraging parties	GF, 6; BB, 17; GN, 130; RM, 94
1097	Cappadocia, Heraclea Cybistra	Turks lay an ambush for crusaders	GF, 23–4
1097 Feb	Cilicia, Samosata	Garrison ambush Baldwin of Bouillon's cattle	FC, 51; WT, 234–6
1098	Syria, Antioch	Crusaders bringing supplies from St. Symeon ambushed by Turks	AA, 238–43; BB, 49–50; WT, 309–11
1098 Feb 8	Syria, Antioch	Crusaders ambush an army of Damascene Muslims	RM, 129; WT, 306–7
1098 June	Syria, Antioch	Turks ambush Roger of Barneville	RM, 151
1098 July	Bithynia, near Nicaea	Turcopoles ambush Baldwin, count of Hainault	AA, 340–2
1098 c. July	Syria, Azaz	Crusaders are ambushed by Turks while travelling from Antioch to Azaz	WT, 349–50
1099	Syria, near Damascus	Raymond of Saint-Gilles ambushes Damascene Turks	RA, 273; WT, 359–60
1100 Aug 15	Cappadocia, Melitene	Danishmend of Sivas ambushes and captures Bohemond	FC, 346–7

Ambushes – Location Unspecified (*continued*)

Date	Place	Description	Source(s)
1101	Paphlagonia, near Merzifon	Stragglers from Raymond of Saint-Gilles's army are ambushed by Turks	AA, 598
1101	Lycaonia, near Iconium	William, count of Nevers, ambushed by Turks	AA, 620
1103 July	Palestine, near Caesarea	Baldwin I of Jerusalem wounded in an ambush	AA, 662–4; FC, 460–1; WT, 484–5
1103 Aug	Ireland	Magnus of Norway is ambushed by the local Irish	OV, vol. 6, 49
1106	Palestine, near Ascalon	Arnold II of Oudenaarde is ambushed by Turks	AA, 712–16
1107 Nov	Palestine, near Jerusalem	Men of Ascalon ambush Franks travelling from Jaffa to Jerusalem	FC, 515–18; WT, 501
c. 1111	Wales, Pembrokeshire	Henry I of England shot by a 'stealthy arrow'	GRA, 727–9
1113 June 28	Palestine, Lake Tiberias	Baldwin I of Jerusalem ambushed by Muslims	FC, 567–70
1119	Normandy, Tillières	William of Chaumont ambushed by garrison	OV, vol. 6, 249
1128 June 12	Flanders, Bruges	William Clito lures citizens into ambush by burning a house	GB, 171–2
1128 June 21	Flanders, near Bruges	William Clito ambushes Thierry of Alsace at the battle of Akspoele	GB, 175
1137	Normandy, Cotentin	Reginald of Dunstanville ambushes Roger II, viscount of the Cotentin	OV, vol. 6, 513
1138	England, Bristol	Garrison lays ambushes for the citizens of Bristol	GS, 47
1139	Lazia, Gaullucio	Roger, duke of Apulia, lays ambush for Pope Innocent II	FB, 238
1144	England, Wiltshire, Crickdale	William de Dover sets ambushes for King Stephen's supporters	GS, 171
1146	England, Gloucestershire, Miserden	Philip, earl of Gloucester, captures Robert Musard and Reginald, earl of Cornwall in an ambush	GS, 186

—(*continued*)

Ambushes – Location Unspecified (*continued*)

Date	Place	Description	Source(s)
1147 Dec	Lydia, Laodicea ad Lycum	Bernard of Carinthia is led by the town governor into a Turkish ambush	OD, 113
1149	England, between York and Bristol	King Stephen lays ambushes for Henry Curtmantle but he avoids them	GS, 215–17
1150 May 5	Syria, near Aleppo	Joscelin II of Courtenay is captured in an ambush	WT, 774–5
1154 June 7	Between Egypt and Palestine	Abbas, former vizier of Egypt, is killed in an ambush	WT, 822–3
1157	Palestine, Jacob's Ford	Baldwin III of Jerusalem is ambushed by Nūr al-Dīn	RT, 194; WT, 828–30
1168 April	Poitou	Patrick, earl of Salisbury, is killed by Poitevin rebels in an ambush	HWM, lines 1645–51
1173	Normandy, Gournay	Hugh de Gournay is captured by Henry the Young King in ambush	RD, vol. 1, 369
1179 May	Syria, Banyas	Turks ambush Baldwin IV of Jerusalem	WT, 998–1000
1192 April	Palestine, near Acre	Christian foragers ambushed by Turks	IP, 344
1192 June 16	Palestine, near Jerusalem	Supply caravan from Jaffa ambushed by Turks	IP, 373–6
1194	Normandy, Fonatines	Robert, earl of Leicester, ambushed and captured by Philip II of France	HowChr, vol. 2, 326
1198	Île-de-France, Beauvais	The bishop of Beauvais and William de Mello are captured in an ambush by Angevin troops	HPA, 354
1204	Anatolia	Latin crusaders are captured en route to Antioch by Turks	GV, vol. 2, 30
1207	Bithynia, Nicodemia	Theodore of Lascaris, emperor of Nicaea, ambushes crusaders	GV, vol. 2, 298
1209	Languedoc, near Cabaret	Garrison captures a crusader, Bouchard de Marly, in an ambush	HA, vol. 1, 127–8
1211	Languedoc, near Fanjeaux	Simon and Geoffrey of Neauphle are ambushed by the men of Foix	HA, vol. 1, 279–80

Ambushes – Location Unspecified (*concluded*)

Date	Place	Description	Source(s)
1217	England, near Lincoln	French troops are ambushed as they flee to London after the battle of Lincoln	MFW, vol. 2, 238
1231 June	Brittany	Henry, count of Brittany, and Ralph, earl of Chester, ambushed Louis IX of France	RW, vol. 2, 541
1282	Wales, Snowdonia	Llewelyn ab Gruffudd ambushes Edward I of England's men as they cross a bridge	PL, vol. 2, 179; TG, 10
c. 1306	Scotland, Brodick	James Douglas ambushes provisions destined for the castle	Bruce, bk 4, lines 384–453
1308	Scotland, near Cupar	Walter Bickerton ambushes Thomas Gray	TG, 68
1310	Scotland	English foragers are ambushed by Scots	VES, 22

Bribery and Inducements

Date	Place	Description	Source(s)
991	Île-de-France, Melun	Odo of Chartres bribes a knight named Walter to betray the town for 'gifts'	GN, vol. 2, 33–5
c. 1053	Normandy, Arques	William, count of Arques, uses 'lavish gifts' to persuade the garrison to surrender	GRA, 433
c. 1064	Basilicata, Montepeloso	Robert Guiscard bribes Godfrey, keeper of the *castrum*, with promises of a larger castle	WA, 26
1081	Sicily, Catania	Benarvet of Syracuse bribes one Bethumen to admit his army to the town by night	GM, 160–1
1082 Feb	Nova Epirus, Dyrrachion	Robert Guiscard bribes Dominic, a Venetian, to betray the city	GM, 158–9; WA, 54–5
c. 1087	Calabria, Cosenza	Bohemond persuades the citizens to shift their allegiance with promises to demolish the Norman fortress there	GM, 185–6
1090	Normandy, Saint-Valéry and Aumale	William Rufus gains the castles by bribing the garrisons	GRA, 549; HH, 415

—(*continued*)

218

APPENDIX

Bribery and Inducements (*concluded*)

Date	Place	Description	Source(s)
1094	Calabria, Rossano	Roger Borsa bribes the townsfolk with promises to allow them to elect a Greek archbishop	GM, 201
1099 June	Syria, Antioch	Bohemond bribes a member of the garrison to help the crusaders scale the wall by night	AA, 270–8; BB, 53–9; FC, 57–9; GF, 46–7; GN, 90–2; GRA, 635–7; HH, 435; OV, vol. 5, 87–9; RA, 251; RM, 141–6; WT, 285–9
1105	Normandy, Caen	Henry I of England bribes the garrison	HH, 453
1137	Flanders, County of Guînes	Arnold of Ghent seizes the county's fortresses through 'pleas, money and promises'	LA, 94
1167	Syria, Banyas	Nūr al-Dīn bribes the commander, Walter de Quesnoy, to surrender the city	WN, vol. 2. 95; WT, 877
c. 1173	Ireland, Wicklow	Muircheratch, prince of Uí Chennselaig bribes Walter the German to surrender the castle	EH, 172
1173	Brittany, Combourg and Dol	Ralph of Fougères bribes the garrisons to surrender	RT, 259
1182 July	Palestine, Cave de Suète	Chronicler suggests fortress may have been surrendered due to bribery	WT, 1028–30
1196	Normandy, Nonancourt	Richard I of England bribes garrisons to surrender	GPA, 200; HPA, 340–2
1211	Lanuedoc, Puylaurens	Garrison allegedly bribed by Sicard de Puylaurens	HA, vol. 1, 251
1224	Aquitaine, La Rochelle	Louis VIII of France bribes the citizens to surrender	RW, vol. 2, 240
c. 1315	England, Norham	One of the garrison is bribed to kill the porter and open the gate to the Scots	TG, 84
1317 April 2	England, Berwick	One Peter Spalding betrays the town to the Scots for 'promises of riches and land'	Bruce, bk 17, lines 1–38; Lanercost, 234–5; TG, 78

Distraction

Date	Place	Description	Source(s)
1071 Aug 26	Upper Mesopotamia, Manzikert	Romanos Diogenes scatters gold and silver around his camp to distract the Turks from pursuing	WA, 29
1099 Jan–Feb	Syria, Hisn al-Akrad	Turkish garrison drive out herds of animals to distract crusaders while they escape	BB, 96–7; GF, 82; OV, vol. 5, 145; RM, 188
1099 Aug 12	Palestine, Ascalon	Egyptians drive herds of animals ahead of them to distract crusader army	AA, 458
1147 July 1	Portugal, Lisbon	Moors throw away their gear to distract crusaders as they retreat	DEL, 128
1154	Between Egypt and Palestine	Household of Abbas, vizier of Egypt, drops treasure to distract pursuers	WT, 822–3

Disguises

Disguises – Changing Appearance

Date	Place	Description	Source(s)
11th century	Southern Italy	Robert Guiscard pretends that one of his men has died and asks for permission to bury him in a monastery	WA, 23–4
c. 1013	Normandy, Tillières	Hugh, count of Maine, buries his hauberk and flees to Le Man disguised as a shepherd	GND, vol. 2, 25
1038 28 Jan	Berry, banks of the River Cher	Army of Aimon, archbishop of Bourges, mounts foot soldiers on asses to resemble cavalry	MSB, 196–7
1051	Calabria, Belvedre	Peasant smuggles himself into the castle inside a pile of logs then sets fire to the building	AM, 82
c. 1070	England, Ely	Wulfric the Black infiltrates a Norman garrison with his face daubed with charcoal	GH, 372

—(continued)

Disguises – Changing Appearance (*continued*)

Date	Place	Description	Source(s)
1070–1	England, Cottenham	Hereward the Wake disguises himself as a fisherman to enter a Norman camp	GH, 388–9
1070–1	England, Ely	Two of Hereward's men tonsure themselves to appear as priests	GH, 392
1070–1	England, Northamptonshire	Hereward the Wake's men put their horses' shoes on backwards	GH, 393
1097 April	Constantinople	Tancred crosses the Bosporus dressed as a foot soldier	GT, 15
c. 1097	Cilicia, Adana	Armenian Christians capture the city by hiding troops in hay wagons	GT, 39–41
1098 Feb	Syria, Antioch	Crusaders position troops behind a hill and raise extra banners to appear more numerous	GT, 55
1098 June	Syria, Antioch	Kemal ad-Din, ruler of Antioch, flees disguised as a beggar	RM, 148
1098 Nov-Dec	Syria, Antioch	Tancred moves troops into the citadel disguised under cloaks	GT, 84
1099 Feb 16–17	Syria, Tortosa	Raymond Pilet and Raymond of Turenne light fires by night to make their force appear more numerous	GF, 83–4; RM, 190
1099 June	Palestine, Jaffa	Crusaders raise a great cloud of dust which makes their force appear more numerous	RA, 294–5
1099 Aug 12	Palestine, Ascalon	Egyptians mistake animals marching with the crusaders for extra troops	AA, 462; FC, 81; WT, 434–5
1106–8	Palestine	Gervais de Bazoches has his troops fasten shirts to their lances to resemble banners	GN, 347–8
1109	Île-de-France, Ferté-Baudouin	Castle besieged by Louis VI of France. Hugh of Crécy attempts to pass through the siege lines in various disguises.	SSD, 67

Disguises – Changing Appearance (*continued*)

Date	Place	Description	Source(s)
1116	Normandy, Gasny	Louis VI of France disguises his men to attack the town	SSD, 112; OV, vol. 6, 185
1118 March	Sinai, al-Arīsh	Baldwin I of Jerusalem's body is embalmed and mounted on his horse to hide the fact of his death	AA, 869–71
1119	Normandy, Breteuil	Ralph of Gael, frequently changes his 'arms' to avoid being recognised	OV, vol. 6, 247
1119 Aug 20	Île-de-France, Noyon	Peter of Maule and other French knights escape by discarding their 'cognizances'	OV, vol. 6, 243
1123	Cappadocia, Kharput	A group of Armenians go in disguise to rescue Baldwin II of Jerusalem	FC, 678–9; GRA, 691; OV, vol. 6, 115
1123	Cappadocia, Kharput	Geoffrey le Grêle and Joscelin I, count of Edessa disguise themselves as Turkish peasants to reach Antioch unnoticed	OV, vol. 6, 115
1124 March	Normandy, near Rouen	William Lovel cuts his hair to look like a squire and flees, carrying a staff	OV, vol. 6, 353
1136	England, Exeter	Alured, son of Joel, and his men intermingle with Stephen of England's forces, as they were all dressed alike	GS, 34–5
1141	England, Winchester	Empress Matilda's forces discard their 'emblems of knighthood' to escape	GS, 88
1147	England, Kent	Gilbert de Clare escapes Stephen of England by 'hiding his face'	GS, 203
1147	Syria, Bostrum	Baldwin III of Jerusalem orders all the dead and wounded to be carried to hide the Franks' losses	WT, 730
1182 July	Palestine, Forbelet	Saladin orders all the dead and wounded to be carried to hide the Muslims' losses	WT, 1032

—(*continued*)

Disguises – Changing Appearance (*continued*)

Date	Place	Description	Source(s)
1189 Oct 4	Palestine, Acre	A crusader named Ferrand pretends to be dead and allows himself to be despoiled to escape Saracens	IP, 72
1190 Aug–Sept	Palestine, Acre	Saracen ships enter Acre disguised with Christian symbols and 'imitating Christian speech'	IP, 92
1191 June	Cyprus	Richard I of England encounters a Saracen ship flying French banners	GRH, vol. 2, 168; HowChr, vol. 2, 206; IP, 204–9
1192	Palestine, Galatia	Richard I of England sends out spies disguised as Bedouin	IP, 385–6
1213 Sept 12	Languedoc, Muret	Peter II of Aragon is killed in battle while wearing another knight's arms	HA, vol. 2, 153–4
1216 Dec 6	England, Hertfordshire, Berkhamsted	Garrison sallies out under a captured banner	RW, vol. 2, 382
1217 May	England, Lincoln	French overestimate size of royalist army due to number of banners	RW, vol. 2, 394
1234 Apr 1	Ireland, Kildare, Curragh Plain	Anglo-Irish nobles give their arms to others when planning to murder Richard Marshal at a parley	RW, vol. 2, 589
1263	England, Gloucester	John Giffard and John Balun enter the town disguised as wool merchants	RG, vol. 2, 740–1
1264	England, Gloucester	Edward, prince of Wales, enters town hidden aboard a ship captured from the abbot of Tewkesbury	RG, vol. 2, 744
1264 May 14	England, Lewes	Three citizens of London are placed inside a cart, decorated with Simon de Montfort's arms. Interpreted as a ruse	CM, 193–4; FH, vol. 2, 495; TW, 150–1; WG, 195; WR, 25–6

Disguises – Changing Appearance (*concluded*)

Date	Place	Description	Source(s)
1265 Aug 4	England, Evesham	Edward, prince of Wales, approaches under banners captured at Kenilworth	WG, 200
1265 Aug 4	England, Evesham	Henry III of England is forced to enter battle in another's arms	CM, 200–1; WG, 201
1304 Aug 18	Flanders, Mons-en-Pévèle	Philip IV of France's bodyguards strip off his coat armour to disguise him from the Flemings	AG, 71
1306 Apr 7	Scotland, Douglas	James Douglas enters the village church, his arms hidden under a mantle, to attack the English garrison	Bruce, bk 5, lines 335–428
1306 Jun 19	Scotland, Methven	Robert Bruce orders his men to wear white shirts over their coat armour	NT, 409–10; TG, 52; WR, 230
c. 1308	Scotland, Linlithgow	Scots take a peel by hiding soldiers in a hay wagon	Bruce, bk 10, lines 187–252
1308	Scotland, Cupar	Thomas Gray gives a banner to his grooms to make his force appear more numerous	TG, 68
1314 Jun 24	Scotland, Bannockburn	The Scottish commoners dismay the English by assembling into a company, using sheets as banners	Bruce, bk 13, lines 225–64
1317 Nov 11	England, Northallerton	Joseclin Deyville and his men invade a manor disguised as Cistercian lay brothers	JT, 208
1322 Mar 16–17	England, Boroughbridge	Thomas, earl of Lancaster, and his men attempt to flee disguised as beggars	VES, 212

Disguises – Other

Date	Place	Description	Source(s)
1112	Île-de-France, Toury	Monks of St. Denis pass through enemy siege force by 'pretending to be part of their company'	SSD, 87
1119	Normandy, Andely	French troops enter the citadel by crying the English royal battle cry	OV, vol. 6, 217
1187 July	Palestine, Acre	Conrad de Montferrat speaks Arabic to bypass Muslim blockade of port	IP, 18–19
1191 Sept 29	Palestine, near Jaffa	William de Préaux shouts the Arabic for 'king' to deceive Muslims into thinking he is Richard I of England	IP, 287
1210	Languedoc, Carcassonne	Peter-Roger escapes by shouting the crusaders' battle cry	HA, vol. 1, 171–2
1211	Languedoc, Castelnaudary	'Heretics' attempt to escape crusaders by copying their battle cry	HA, vol. 1, 270–1

Feigned Flight

Feigned Flight – Luring an Enemy into an Ambush

Date	Place	Description	Source(s)
946	Normandy, Rouen	Normans feign flight into city to lure Germans into range of an unexpected sally	Dudo, 27; GND, vol. 1, 39
1052	Normandy, Arques	Normans lure French troops into ambush	GND, vol. 2, 105
c. 1057	Calabria, Salerno	Richard I of Aversa lures Guaimar IV of Salerno into ambush by feigning flight	AM, 102–3
c. 1066–77	Apulia, Ortona	Robert of Lortello burns his siege castle and retreats through a pass to lure a relief force into an ambush	AM, 181–2

APPENDIX

Feigned Flight – Luring an Enemy into an Ambush (*continued*)

Date	Place	Description	Source(s)
c. 1097	Cilicia, Adana	Armenian Christians lure Turkish garrison away to allow troops to infiltrate city	GT, 39–41
1097	Cilicia, Tarsus	Tancred lures garrison into an ambush with a force of Turcopoles	GT, 35–6
1097	Syria, Artah	Garrison lures crusaders into an ambush	AA, 184; WT, 240–1
1097 Dec	Syria, Artah	Bohemond and Robert of Flanders lure garrison of Harim into an ambush	GN, 76; OV, vol. 5, 73; RM, 122–3
1098 June	Syria, Antioch	Roger of Barneville is killed after being lured into an ambush by Turks	AA, 286–90; WT, 307–8
1098 summer	Cilicia, Sorogia	Folbert of Chartres lures Turks into an ambush	AA, 364; WT, 350–2
1106 Oct	Palestine, Jaffa	Citizens of Ascalon lure garrison into an ambush in the mountains	AA, 728–30
1108 May	Palestine, Tiberias	Damascene Turks lure a knight named Gervase into an ambush	AA, 768
1113 June 28	Palestine, Lake Tiberias	Baldwin I of Jerusalem is lured into an ambush by Turks	WT, 523–4
1123	Palestine, Ascalon	Baldwin II of Jerusalem lures an Egyptian army into an ambush	WT, 607
1129	Anjou, Thouars	Geoffrey V of Anjou lures rebel garrison into an ambush	HG, 262–4
1134 July 17	Aragon, Fraga	Moors lure Christians into an ambush by having their baggage feign flight	OV, vol. 5, 415
1137 Aug	Palestine, near Ascalon	Renaud, head of the Order of St. George, is lured into an ambush by Saracens	WT, 666
1191 Sept 29	Palestine, near Jaffa	Richard I of England is lured into an ambush by Saracens	IP, 287

—(*continued*)

Feigned Flight – Luring an Enemy into an Ambush (*concluded*)

Date	Place	Description	Source(s)
1198	Normandy, Pacy-sur-Eure	Robert, earl of Leicester, lures the garrison into an ambush	HowChr, vol. 2, 431–2
1230 July	Ireland, Connaught, near Lough Key	Aedh, son of Rory of Connaught, is lured into an ambush by Geoffrey de Marisco	RW, vol. 2, 536
1307 May	Scotland, Douglas	James Douglas uses troops disguised as merchants to lure the castle garrison into an ambush	Bruce, bk 8, lines 416–87
c. 1308	Scotland, Douglas	James Douglas uses a herd of cattle to lure the castle garrison into an ambush	Bruce, bk 6, lines 375–452

Feigned Flight – To Lure an Enemy onto Unfavourable Ground and then Attack

Date	Place	Description	Source(s)
1060	Sicily, Messina	Roger I of Sicily lures the garrison out then turns to attack	GM, 30
1066 Oct 14	England, Battle	Norman army feigns flight to draw English off Senlac Hill	CDH, 26; GG, 133; GRA, 453; HH, 393; OV, vol. 2, 175
c. 1067	Zeeland	Flemings feign flight to draw Zeelanders away from their camp	GH, 362
1098	Syria, Antioch	Turks withdraw to the mountains, hoping to break up crusaders' formation	OV, vol. 5, 113
1098	Syria, Antioch	Robert Curthose feigns flight to lure Turks into unfavourable position	GRA, 703
1100 Oct 24–26	Syria, near Beirut	Baldwin I of Jerusalem feigns flight to draw Turks into a narrow place	AA, 536; GRA, 669; WT, 458–60
1104 May 7	Syria, Raqqa	Turks flee from before Edessa, drawing Bohemond onto unfavourable ground	GT, 124

Feigned Flight – To Lure an Enemy onto Unfavourable Ground and then Attack (*concluded*)

Date	Place	Description	Source(s)
1111	Syria, Baalbek	Bohemond lures garrison through a narrow pass	GRA, 665
1119 June	Syria, al-Athrab	Turks feign flight to draw Christian army away from their camp	WC, 116–18
1169	Ireland, Osraige	Diarmait Mac Murchada lures the men of Osraige out into the open	EH, 37
1205 April	Thrace, Adrianople	Cumans lure crusaders out of their camp by feigning flight	GV, vol. 2, 166
1219 Aug 29	Egypt, near Damietta	Egyptian relief force feigns flight, causing dispute among crusaders about whether to pursue	RW, vol. 2, 419
1231 July	Wales, Montgomery	Llewellyn ap Iorwerth feigns flight into a wood, causing the English garrison to become stranded in a marsh	RW, vol. 2, 540–1
1304 Aug 18	Flanders, Mons-en-Pévèle	French horsemen feign flight to break up Flemish formations	AG, 66

Feigned Flight – To Confuse/Terrify One's Allies

Date	Place	Description	Source(s)
1101–2	Île-de-France, Montmorency and Chambly	The two sieges are broken up when traitors in Louis VI of France's army pretend to panic and flee	SSD, 33; OV, vol. 6, 159
1102	Normandy, Vignants	Robert of Montfort and others set fire to their own tents and pretend to flee Robert Curthose's army	OV, vol. 6, 25
1187 July 4	Palestine, Meskenah	Allegation that Raymond III of Tripoli pretended to flee the battle of Hattin to break the Franks' formation	IP, 14–16

Hidden Traps

Date	Place	Description	Source(s)
992 July 27	Brittany, Conquereuil	Conan I of Brittany digs hidden pits on the battlefield then feigns flight, luring the Angevins into them	GCA, vol. 1, 94–5
c. 1013	Brittany, near Dol	Scandinavian raiders stop a Breton cavalry charge with hidden trenches	GND, vol. 2, 25–7
1099 July	Palestine, Jerusalem	Garrison digs hidden trenches before the gates	GN, 279
1107	Île-de-France, Gournay	Garrison places sharpened-stakes, hidden beneath straw, in the castle ditch	SSD, 57
c. 1144	England, Coventry	Robert of Marmion is killed when he falls into a hidden ditch he dug to trap Ranulf, earl of Chester	WN, vol. 1, 71–3
1147 Oct	Portugal, Lisbon	Flemings catch three Moors in nets, bated with figs	DEL, 145
1169	Ireland, Ferns	Diarmait Mac Murchada digs pits and creates hidden exits to defend his territory	EH, 40
1189	Normandy, near Le Mans	Henry II of England places stakes in the fords on the Huisne and digs trenches to defend the town	HWM, lines 8485–6
1189–90	Palestine, Acre	Crusaders construct 'secret traps' around their camp for the Saracens	IP, 102–3
1219	Egypt, Damietta	Saracens sink ships and drive stakes into the river bed to prevent the crusaders sailing up the Nile	OP, 196; RW, vol. 2, 415

Misinformation

Misinformation – Misleading an Enemy Regarding One's Intentions

Date	Place	Description	Source(s)
1070	England, Teesdale	Malcolm III of Scotland sends part of his army home with booty to convince the English that he has departed, then attacks with a concealed force when they return from hiding	HowChr, vol. 1, 145
c. 1071	Calabria, Sujo	Jordan, son of Richard I of Aversa, leaves the siege as if going to Capua but instead goes raiding in Aquino	AM, 162
1098 Feb	Syria, Antioch	Crusaders secretly leave their camp and hide in mountains to surprise Turks	RA, 246
1098	Syria, Orontes Valley	Raymond of Saint-Gilles launches a feigned attack to save his foot soldiers from an unexpected sally by a Turkish garrison	RA, 274
1105 Aug	Palestine, Jaffa	Saracens used a diversionary attack on Ramla while their main force attacks Jaffa	FC, 497; WT, 548–50
1112	Île-de-France, Toury	Hugh of Le Puiset convinces monks of St. Denis to go and petition the king on his behalf. While they are away, he takes their fortress	SSD, 96
1115 Aug–Sept	Syria, near Antioch	Bursuq of Hamadām pretends to retreat, waits for the Franks to disband their army, then returns	WC, 93–4; WT, 532
1119 June	Syria, Ruz Valley	Īlghāzī sends a force as if to besiege al-Atharib while they actually performing reconnaissance on Roger of Salerno's camp	WC, 115

—(continued)

Misinformation – Misleading an Enemy Regarding One's Intentions (*continued*)

Date	Place	Description	Source(s)
1138	England, Somerset, Harptree	Stephen of England pretends to march on Bristol to lure the garrison out	GS, 45–6
1138	England, Northumbria	David I of Scotland leaves town unburned to take the English army by surprise	JW, 253
1141	England, Lincoln	Robert, earl of Gloucester, does not tell his troops their destination on his march to Lincoln to 'conceal his purpose'	HN, 85
1169	Languedoc, Béziers	William of Trencavel pretends to bring Aragonese troops into the city of make war on the count of Saint-Gilles but instead uses them to attack the citizens who murdered his father	RT, 243; WN, vol. 2, 53–5
1183	Limousin, Limoges	Geoffrey of Brittany promises to go to the town to negotiate with his brother, Henry, only to loot the shrine of St. Martial instead	HowChr, vol. 2, 25
1188 Aug	Normandy, Gisors	William Marshal advices Henry II of England to disband his army to deceive Philip II of France	HWM, lines 7787–801
1189	Maine, Le Mans	Philip II of France pretends to travel to Tours but suddenly attack Le Mans	HowChr, vol. 2, 107
1189 Oct 4	Palestine, Acre	Garrison attacks the crusaders by advancing 'with twists and turns' to conceal their intended target	IP, 67–71
1197	Palestine, Acre	Henry of Brunswick and Hugh of Tiberias launch a feigned charge to intimidate a Saracen force	LE, 189–91

Misinformation – Misleading an Enemy Regarding One's Intentions (*concluded*)

Date	Place	Description	Source(s)
1197 May	Normandy, Gerberoy	Richard I of England secretly assembles an army to attack Milly	HWM, lines 11107–11
1210	Languedoc, Termes	Crusaders feign an attack on the town walls to save William of Ecureuil, who had become isolated	HA, vol. 1, 183
1221	England, Northamptonshire, Fotheringay	William de Foret pretends to travel to Westminster to answer a summons only to take Fotheringay castle by surprise	RW, vol. 2, 429
1265 Aug	England, Winchester	Edward, prince of Wales, marches north to deceive rebels then turns south for Evesham by night	TW, 171–2

Misinformation – Deceiving One's Allies

Date	Place	Description	Source(s)
1138 Aug 22	England, Thirsk	The English commoners rally when somebody holds up a severed head, claiming to have killed David I of Scotland	BoS, 196–7
1189	Palestine, Acre	Saladin tells his troops that the crusaders are not receiving many supply ships but are sailing the same ships back and forth across the horizon	IP, 67
1250 Feb 9	Egypt, Mansurah	Baybars displays Robert of Artois's coat to his troops, claiming that Louis IX of France is dead	VSL, 128–30
1314 Jun 24	Scotland, Bannockburn	Robert Bruce spreads false news that the English are approaching in poor order	Bruce, bk 11, lines 461–504

Appendix

Misinformation – Providing the Enemy with False Information

Date	Place	Description	Source(s)
1009	England, near Sandwich	Eadric, earl of Mercia, uses false reports to persuade Aethelred of England not to give battle with the Danes	HH, 347
1016 Oct 18	England, Ashingdon	Eadric, earl of Mercia, causes a rout by falsely announcing that Edmund Ironside has been killed	HH, 359
1079	Apulia, Giovinazzo	William fitz Ivo sends false warning that Roger Borsa is approaching, causing the besiegers to retreat	WA, 41
1092	Wales, Pembroke	The castellan, Gerald of Windsor, persuades besiegers he is very well-supplied, causing them to break the siege	IK, 89–90
1097 July	Syria	Following his defeat at Dorylaeum, Kilij Arslan tells Christian towns that the crusaders were defeated in order to gain access	BB, 34–5; GN, 69; GF, 23; OV, vol. 5, 65; RM, 114–15
1099 March	Syria, Jabala	Raymond of Saint-Gilles is bribed to send a false report about an approaching army to lure the crusader away	AA, 380–2; WT, 364–5
1099 May	Syria, 'Arqah	Muslim garrison spreads false rumours that the 'pope of the Turks' is approaching with a relief force, causing the crusaders to retreat	RA, 277–8
1102	Palestine, Jaffa	Besiegers dismember a captive and display the body to the garrison, claiming to have killed Baldwin I of Jerusalem	AA, 646
1106	Normandy, Dive	Robert Curthose sends false report to Henry I of England that the garrison wishes to surrender in order to trap him	OV, vol. 6, 81–3
1106	Palestine, Tiberias	A group of Turks give false reports to the atabeg of Damascus that Baldwin I of Jerusalem was on hand with a very large army	AA, 742
1106	Palestine, Valley of Moses	A Syrian priest gives an army of Damascene Turks false reports about Baldwin I of Jerusalem's strength, prompting them to flee	AA, 747

Misinformation – Providing the Enemy with False Information (*concluded*)

Date	Place	Description	Source(s)
1118	Normandy, Livet	William of Tancarville persuades Henry I of England to withdraw from siege of Laigle by false reports of William Clito's movements	OV, vol. 6, 198–201
1127 Apr 13	Flanders, Bruges	Garrison spreads a rumour that one of their commanders, Borsiard, has been killed in the hope of placating the besiegers	GB, 106
1128 Aug	Flanders, Aalst	Godfrey, duke of Louvain, conceals from the garrison that William Clito has died in order to safely withdraw under cover of negotiations	HT, 289
1147 Oct–Nov	Cappadocia	Conrad III of Germany's army is deliberately misled by Greek guides	WT, 744–5
1148 Jan	Pamphylia, Adalia	Louis VII of France hides his army's remaining warhorses and uses them to launch a surprise attack on the Turks, to make them think he is well-supplied	OD, 135
1163	Wales, Pencader	A deacon from Cantref Mawr deceives Henry II of England into thinking the approach to Dinevor is very difficult	IK, 81–2
1187	Palestine, Tyre	Conrad of Montferrat traps five Saracens ships in the harbour by sending false letters to Saladin	LE, 76–8
1194	England, Nottingham	The garrison believe the trumpets announcing Richard I of England's presence to be a deception	HowChr, 314
1211	Languedoc	Raymond-Roger, count of Foix, convinces many strongholds to surrender by spreading the rumour that Simon de Montfort had been killed	HA, vol. 1, 274
1231 July	Wales, Montgomery	Llewellyn ap Iorweth sends a Cistercian monk to convince the garrison to sally out and fight by giving them false information	RW, vol. 2, 540–1

Night and/or Dawn Attacks

Date	Place	Description	Source(s)
c. 962	Normandy, Ermentrudeville	Richard I of Normandy crosses the Seine by night to attack Theobald of Chartres	GND, vol. 1, 125
c. 1013	Normandy, Tillières	Odo of Chartres attacks the castle by night	GND, vol. 2, 23
1019	Denmark	Earl Godwine leads a contingent of Englishmen from King Cnut's army to attack the Wends by night	HH, 363–5
1041 March	Apulia, Melfi	Rainulf I of Aversa enters Melfi by night	AM, 70
c. 1061	Normandy, Échauffour	Arnold of Échauffour drives the ducal garrison out by night with only four knights	OV, vol. 2, 92
1061 March	Sicily, Messina	Garrison sallies out against Robert Guiscard by night	AM, 137
1061 May	Sicily, Tremestieri	Roger I of Sicily leads an advanced party to Sicily by night ahead of an invasion	AM, 138
1066 Oct 14	England, Battle	Harold Godwinson attempts to attack William II of Normandy by night	CDH, 18; GND, vol. 2, 169; OV, vol. 2, 173
1067	England, Dover	Eustace of Boulogne attempts to capture the castle by night	GG, 185; OV, vol. 2, 205
1069	England, Durham	Robert of Commine and five hundred of his men are killed in their sleep by citizens	OV, vol. 2, 223
c. 1087	Normandy, Évreux	High Estevel and Ralph Mauvoisin cross the Eure by night to go raiding	OV, vol. 4, 75
1097 April	Constantinople	Raymond of Saint-Gilles's camp is attacked at night by Greeks	WT, 187–8

Night and/or Dawn Attacks (*continued*)

Date	Place	Description	Source(s)
1097 June	Bithynia, Nicaea	A group of Byzantine Turcoples draw boats overland and launch them onto the lake by night	AA, 117; GF, 16; BB, 27; GN, 64; WT, 204–5
1097 Sept	Cilicia, Tarsus	Members of the garrison flee by night, killing some of the crusaders on their way	AA, 157
1097 Dec	Syria, Antioch	Bohemond and Robert Curthose are attacked by night while out foraging	AA, 218
1098 Feb	Phrygia, near Philomelium	Sweyn, son of Sweyn II of Denmark, is killed in a night attack by Turks	WT, 261–2
1098 June	Syria, Antioch	Turks attack the crusaders by scaling the city walls by night	AA, 300; GT, 69; WT, 316–17
1098 Dec 12	Syria, Ma'arrat-an-Nu'mān	The poorer members of the crusaders' army attack the city by night	RA, 269–70
1101	Palestine, east of the Jordan	Baldwin I of Jerusalem lead a night raid across the Jordan	WT, 464–5
1105	Upper Mesopotamia, Edessa	Tancred leads a sally against the Turkish besiegers by night	AA, 698
1107 Apr	Palestine, St. Abraham's Castle	Baldwin I of Jerusalem leads a night attack on the Saracens besieging the castle	AA, 749–50
1119	Syria, Hab	Īlghāzī attempts a dawn attack on Baldwin II of Jerusalem	WT, 560–2
1122	Auvergne, Monterraud	William VI of Auvergne attempts a night attack on Louis VI of France	SSD, 136
1127 Mar 19	Flanders, Bruges	Citizens scale the castle walls at dawn and seize the outer defences	GB, 72
c. 1128	Flanders, Ypres	William Clito escapes a night attack by Flemish enemies	OV, vol. 6, 375

—(*continued*)

Night and/or Dawn Attacks (*continued*)

Date	Place	Description	Source(s)
c. 1137–41	Flanders, Guînes, Amaurvial	Henry of Bourbourg has a wooden tower constructed and erected by night outside the town	LA, 98
1137	Syria, Antioch	Raymond of Antioch attacks John II Komnenos's siege force by night	OV, vol. 6, 505
1138	England, Northumberland, Carham	Walter, son of Duncan, attempts a night attack on the town	RH, 42
1139	England, Devon	Henry de Tracy captures William fitz Odo in a night attack	GS, 83
1139	England, Berkshire, Wallingford	Miles of Gloucester captures the town by night	GS, 93–5
1139	England, Malmesbury	Robert fitz Hubert enters the castle by night then burns the town	HN, 63
1140 Mar 26	England, Devizes	Robert fitz Hubert scales the walls by night and seizes the castle	HN, 77; GS, 105; JW, 287
1141	England, Belvoir	Alan, earl of Richmond, takes the castle by night	JH, 16
1143	England, Nottingham	William Peverel's troops scale the castle rock by night and expel the garrison	JH, 20
1158	Wales, Cardiff	Ivor Bach enters the castle and abducts William, earl of Gloucester, and his family by night	IK, 63–4
1167	Egypt, near Cairo	Amalric of Jerusalem and his Egyptian allies attempt a night attack on the forces of Shīrkūh, encamped on an island in the Nile	WT, 892–4

Night and/or Dawn Attacks (*continued*)

Date	Place	Description	Source(s)
1173	Ireland, Cashel	Domnall, prince of Limerick, attacks the men of Dublin in a dawn raid	EH, 139
1174	England, Belford	William I of Scotland sends troops to raid Belford by night	JF, 87
1182	Wales, Abergavenny	Welsh take the castle by hiding in the ditch then scaling the walls at night	IK, 49–51
1182	Wales, Llaningad	Men of Gwent killed Ralph Poer in a night raid	IK, 51–2
1184	Portugal, Santarem	Archbishop of Saint James leads night attack on Saracens besieging the town	RD, vol. 2, 29
1189 Sept 14	Palestine, Acre	Garrison launches night attack on Christian camp to allow one of Saladin's sons to escape	IP, 65–7
1191	Cyprus	Richard I of England attacks Isaac Komnenos's camp by night	GRH, vol. 2, 164; HowChr, vol. 2, 202
1191 July 5	Palestine, Acre	Saladin launches night attack on crusaders' camp in hope that it will allow garrison to escape	GRH, vol. 2, 174; HowChr, vol. 2, 212
1192	Palestine, Jaffa	Saladin's army attacks the crusaders by night	RC, 44–5
1192 Aug 5	Palestine, Jaffa	A force of Mamlūks and Kurds attempt to kidnap Richard I of England in his sleep	IP, 412–24
1194 July	Normandy, Vaudreuil	Philip II of France attacks John Lackland's camp by night	HPA, 330
1203	Normandy, Château-Gaillard	John of England attempts to attack French camp by night in conjunction with an attack on the river	GPA, 213–14

—(*continued*)

Night and/or Dawn Attacks (*continued*)

Date	Place	Description	Source(s)
1205 March	Peloponnesos, Corinth	Garrison launches a dawn assault on the Latins' camp	GV, vol. 2, 142
1209	Languedoc, Fanjeaux	Raymond-Roger, count of Foix, attempts to take the town by night	HA, vol. 1, 138
1210	Languedoc, Carcassonne	Garrison sallies out to burn crusaders' siege engines	CCA, vol. 1, 126–8; HA, vol. 1, 171–2
1210 June	Languedoc, Minerve	Garrison sallies out to burn crusaders' siege engines	HA, vol. 1, 156–7
1211	Languedoc, Lavaur	Garrison sallies out to burn the crusaders' siege engines	HA, vol. 1, 223–4
1211	Languedoc, Moissac	Garrison sallies out to burn the crusaders' siege engine	HA, vol. 2, 45–6
1213 June	Languedoc, Puycelsi	Garrison sallies out to burn the crusaders' siege engine	HA, vol. 2, 121–2
1214 June	Languedoc, Casseneuil	Garrison sallies out to attack the crusaders' camp	HA, vol. 2, 215
1214 June	Languedoc, Casseneuil	Garrison tries to burn the crusaders' siege tower with a 'fire boat' by night	HA, vol. 2, 220
1214 Nov	Languedoc, Séverac-le-Château, near Rodez	Guy de Montfort seizes the town by night	HA, vol. 2, 233
1218	Languedoc, Toulouse	Crusaders attack the city at dawn	CCA, vol. 3, 72–8
1218 Jun 25	Languedoc, Toulouse	Garrison launches a two-pronged assault on the crusaders' camp	HA, vol. 2, 310–12

Night and/or Dawn Attacks (*continued*)

Date	Place	Description	Source(s)
1218 Oct 26	Egypt, Damietta	Garrison attacks the Templars' camp before dawn	OP, 190–1
1219	Egypt, Damietta	Saracen relief force attacks crusaders' siege camp at dawn	RW, vol. 2, 416
1219 Nov 2	Egypt, Damietta	Al-Kāmil, sultan of Egypt, sends a force through a marsh to attack crusaders' camp	OP 224; RW, vol. 2, 423
1220 Aug	Egypt, near Mahalech	Crusaders are attack at night by Ethiopian troops	OP, 273
1233 Nov 11	Wales, Grosmont	Welsh attack Henry III of England's army by night and steal its baggage	RW, vol. 2, 573
1250 Feb 9	Egypt, Mansurah	Egyptians attack crusaders' camp by night	VSL, 126–8
1264	England, Berkshire, Wallingford	A royalist relief army attempts to storm the castle at dawn	RG, vol. 2, 751–2
1265 Aug 2	England, Warwickshire, Kenilworth	Edward, prince of Wales, surprises Simon de Montfort the Younger by night	CM, 198; FH, vol. 3, 4; RG, vol. 2, 761; TW, 170; WG, 199
1295	Wales	William de Beauchamp, earl of Warwick makes a night attack on Welsh camp	NT, 335–6; WR, 148
1298 Feb	Scotland, Roxburgh	Roger fitz Roger attacks Scottish siege camp at dawn	TG, 40–2
1302 May 18	Flanders, Bruges	Flemings attack French troops in the city at dawn	AG, 24
1303 Feb 24	Scotland, Roslin	John of Seagrave is captured in a Scottish night attack	NT, 400; TG, 44; WR, 214
1306	Scotland, Turnberry	Robert Bruce attacks Henry Percy's men while they are asleep in a nearby village	Bruce, bk 5, lines 61–122

—(*continued*)

Night and/or Dawn Attacks (concluded)

Date	Place	Description	Source(s)
1307 June	Scotland, Glen Trool	Aymer de Valence attempts to attack Robert Bruce by night	Bruce, bk 7, lines 495–642
1312 Dec 6	England, Berwick	Robert Bruce scales the walls and captures the town by night	Lanercost, 220
1313 Jan 10	Scotland, Perth	Robert Bruce scales the walls and captures the town by night	Bruce, bk 9, lines 371–419; Lanercost, 221
1314	Scotland, Edinburgh	Thomas Randolph takes the castle by climbing the rock by night	Bruce, bk 10, lines 511–642
1314 Feb 28	Scotland, Roxburgh	James Douglas scales the walls and captures the castle by night	Bruce, bk 10, lines 357–472; Lanercost, 223; VES, 84
1316 Jan 15	England, Berwick	Robert Bruce attempts to take the town by night	Lanercost, 232

Oaths and Truces

Date	Place	Description	Source(s)
c. 1096	Hungary, Pannonhalma	Hungarians trick German crusaders into surrendering their arms and money, then massacre them	AA, 45–6; WT, 154–5
1097 Sept	Cilicia, Tarsus	Turkish garrison claim to have entered into negotiations with Tancred in bad faith, hoping for a relief force to attack him	AA, 149
1101	Palestine, near Ascalon	Baldwin I of Jerusalem lures bandits out of their caves by offering bribes, then having them persuade their fellows to come out and be killed	AA, 544–6
1106 Sept 14	Syria, Apamea	Tancred agrees to let the traitor Botherus live. His allies protest but Tancred refuses to break his word.	AA, 740

Oaths and Truces (*continued*)

Date	Place	Description	Source(s)
1127 March	Flanders, Bruges	Besiegers make false promises of clemency to the garrison in return for treasure	GB, 57
1138	England, Bath	Gilbert de Lacy breaks an oath of safe conduct to the bishop of Bath	GS, 39–41
1152	England, Newbury	John Marshal uses a truce with Stephen of England to refortify and supply his castle	HWM, lines 493–508
1155	Syria, Banyas	Baldwin III of Jerusalem breaks a treaty to raid Turkoman herds	WT, 825
1171	Ireland, Wexford	Irish swear false oaths to garrison to persuade them to surrender	EH, 84–5
1173	England, Northumbria	Richard de Lacy conceals news of Robert of Leicester's invasion in order to persuade William I of Scotland to agree to a truce	JF, 63
1173 Aug	Normandy, Verneuil	Louis VII of France breaks an agreement with the townsfolk when he sacks it	GRH, vol. 1, 53; HowChr, vol. 1, 371
1174 Aug 10	Normandy, Rouen	Louis VII of France breaks a truce with the garrison and attack the town	WN, vol. 2, 147–51
1195 July	Normandy, Vaudreuil	Philip II of France continues to demolish the castle during negotiations with Richard I of England	HWM, lines 10537–48
1205	Macedonia, Serres	Johanitsa of Vlachia breaks agreement with the garrison, whom he attacks and imprisons	GV, vol. 2, 202–4
1209	Languedoc, Pamiers	Raymond-Roger, count of Foix, ambushes crusaders during a parley	HA, vol. 1, 206–7

—(*continued*)

Oaths and Truces (*concluded*)

Date	Place	Description	Source(s)
1213	Languedoc	Raymond VI of Toulouse raids the crusaders' lands during a truce	HA, vol. 2, 67–8
1226	Toulouse, Avignon	Louis VIII of France falsely claims he only wishes to pass through the city	RW, vol. 2, 478
1226 Oct	Toulouse, Avignon	Cardinal Romain, papal legate, arranges to enter the city to parley only for the French to storm inside	RW, vol. 2, 482
1233	Wales, Pembrokeshire	Henry III of England persuades Richard Marshal to surrender a castle to him on the false promise that he will return it	RW, vol. 2, 570–2
1264 Apr 5	England, Northampton	Philip Basset breaks into the city while the garrison are negotiating with Henry III of England	WG, 189–90
1296	Scotland, Stirling	Scots capture the English commander of the castle by breaking their promise of safe conduct	PL, vol. 2, 304
1296 Apr 27	Scotland, Dunbar	Garrison secure a three-day truce, then encourage their relief force to attack the besiegers unexpectedly	PL, vol. 2, 240–2
1304 Aug 13	Flanders, Mons-en-Pévèle	French request a truce in order to wear down the Flemish army	AG, 64–5
1306 June 19	Scotland, Methven	Aymer of Valence requests to postpone a battle with Robert Bruce only to sally out and attack	NT, 409–10
1318 Jan	England, Pontefract	Edward II orders his troops to take up arms near the castle, believing that Thomas of Lancaster intended to break his truce	VES, 140–2

Spies and Spying

Date	Place	Description	Source(s)
c. 1068	Sicily, Palermo	Robert Guiscard sends 'Peter the Deacon', who spoke Arabic, as an emissary to spy on Palermo	AM, 142
1070–1	England, Ely	Hereward the Wake disguises himself as a potter to infiltrate William I of England's court	GH, 384–8
c. 1070s	England, Northamptonshire	Leofric the Deacon pretends to be stupid in order to spy on Robert de Horepol	GH, 402
1097 May	Bithynia, Nicaea	Qilij Arslān sends two spies, posing as Christians, to spy on the crusaders	AA, 104
1097 Oct – 1098 June	Syria, Antioch	Turkish garrison use Armenian and Syrian Christians, posing as refugees, to spy on crusaders	AA, 220; BB, 39; GF, 29; GN, 75–6; OV, vol. 5, 71; RM, 121; WT, 265–6
1099 autumn	Palestine, Arsuf	Local chieftains send gifts of food to the crusaders to learn their numbers	WT, 446–7
1101	Constantinople	Alexios Komnenos distributes coins in order to learn crusaders' numbers	OV, vol. 5, 335

—(*continued*)

Spies and Spying (*concluded*)

Date	Place	Description	Source(s)
1119 June	Syria, Ruz Valley	Īlghāzī sends spies disguised as bird-sellers to Roger of Salerno's camp	WC, 115
1138	England, Bath	Geoffrey Talbot reconnoitres Bath by pretending to assist a 'straggler'	JW, 249
1152	England, Newbury	William Marshal accidentally betrays a spy sent into the royal siege camp	HWM, lines 623–34
1192	Palestine, Betenoble	Richard I of England sends spies into Egypt	IP, 384
1319	England, York	A Scottish spy betrays James Douglas's plan to kidnap Isabella, queen of England	VES, 162–6

Bibliography

Primary Sources

Aachen, Albert of, *Historia Ierosolimitana: History of the Journey to Jerusalem*, ed. and trans. Susan B. Edgington (Oxford, 2007)

Aguilers, Raymond of, 'Historia Francorum qui ceperunt Iheruslaem', in *Recueil des historiens des croisades: Historiens occidentaux tome troisième* (Paris, 1866), pp. 231–310

Ambrose, *De officiis*, ed. and trans. Ivor J. Davidson (2 vols, Oxford, 2001)

Andersson, Theodore M., and Kari Ellen Gade (eds.), *Morkinskinna: The Earliest Icelandic Chronicle of the Norwegian Kings, 1030–1157* (London, 2000)

'Annales de Dunstaplia,' in *Annales monastici*, ed. Henry Richard Luard, RS, 36 (5 vols, London, 1869), vol. 3, pp. 3–408

Apulia, William of, *La Geste de Robert Guiscard*, ed. and trans. Marguerite Mathieu (Palermo, 1961)

Aquinas, Thomas, *Summa theologiae*, ed. and trans. Thomas Gilby and others (61 vols, London, 1964–81)

Ardres, Lambert of, *Historia comitum Ghisensium*, MGH, Scriptores, 24 (Hanover, 1879), pp. 550–642

Augustine, *Quaestionum in Heptateuchum libri vii*, ed. Joseph Zycha (Vienna, 1895)

Bahā al-Dīn Ibn Shaddād, *The Rare and Excellent History of Saladin or al-Nawadir al-Sultaniyya wa'l-Mahasin al-Yusufiyya*, trans. D. S. Richards (Aldershot, 2002)

Barbour, John, *The Bruce*, ed. and trans. A. A. M. Duncan (Edinburgh, 1997)

Benevento, Falco of, 'Chronicle', in G. A. Loud (ed.), *Roger II and the Creation of the Kingdom of Sicily: Selected Sources* (Manchester, 2012), pp. 130–249

Berard, John, *Liber instrumentorum seu chronicorum monasterii Casauriensis seu chronicon Casauriense*, eds. Alessandro Pratesi and Paolo Cherubini (3 vols, Rome, 2017–18)

Bourgueil, Baldric of, *Historia Ierosolimitana*, ed. Steven Biddlecombe (Woodbridge, 2014)

Brault, Gerald J. (ed.), *The Song of Roland: An Analytical Edition* (2 vols, University Park, PA, 1978)

Breton, William the, 'Gesta Philippi Augusti', in François Delaborde (ed.), *Ouevres de Rigord et de Guillaume le Breton: Historiens de Philippe-Auguste* (2 vols, Paris, 1882), vol. 1, pp. 168–320

Bruges, Galbert of, *De multro, traditione, et occisione gloriosi Karoli comitis Flandriarum*, ed. Jeff Rider (Turnholt, 1994)

Burgess, Glyn S., *Two Medieval Outlaws: Eustace the Monk and Fouke Fitz Waryn* (Cambridge, 1997)

Caen, Ralph of, *Tancredus*, ed. Edoardo D'Angelo (Turnhout, 2011)
Certain, E. de (ed.), *Les Miracles de Saint Benoit* (Paris, 1858)
Chancellor, Walter the, *Bella antiochena*, ed. Heinrich Hagenmeyer (Innsbruck, 1896)
Chartres, Fulcher of, *Historia Hierosolymitana, 1095–1127*, ed. Heinrich Hagenmeyer (Heidelberg, 1913)
'Chronique française des rois de France par un anonyme de Béthune', in Léopold Delisle (ed.), *Recueil des historiens des Gaules et de la France* (24 vol, Paris, 1840–1904), vol. 24, pp. 750–76
Cicero, Marcus Tullius, *De officiis*, ed. C. Atzert (Leipzig, 1932)
Clari, Robert de, *La Conquête de Constantinople*, ed. Philippe Lauer (Paris, 1974)
Clausewitz, Carl von, *On War*, trans. Michael Howard and Peter Paret (Princeton, NJ, 1976)
Conlon, Denis Joseph (ed.), *Li Romans di Witasse le moine* (Chapel Hill, NC, 1972)
———, *The Song of Dermot and Earl Richard Fitzgilbert* (Frankfurt, 1992)
Coggeshall, Ralph of, *Chronicon Anglicanum*, ed. Joseph Stevenson (London, 1875)
Cremona, Liudprand of, *The Complete Works*, ed. and trans. Paolo Squatriti (Washington, DC, 2000)
David, Charles Wendell (ed. and trans.), *De expugnatione Lyxbonensi* (New York, 2001)
Denholm-Young, N., and Wendy R. Childs (eds.), *Vita Edwardi secundi* (Oxford, 2005)
Deuil, Odo of, *De profectione Ludovici VII in orientem*, ed. and trans. Virginia Gingerick Berry (New York, 1948)
Devizes, Richard of, 'De rebus gestis Ricardi primi', in Richard Howlett (ed.), *Chronicles of the Reigns of Stephen, Henry II and Richard I*, RS, 82 (4 vols, London, 1884–9), vol 3, pp. 381–454
Diceto, Ralph of, *Historical Works*, ed. William Stubbs, RS, 68 (2 vols, London, 1876)
Dostourian, Ara Edmond (trans.), *Armenia and the Crusades, Tenth to Twelfth Centuries: The Chronicle of Matthew of Edessa* (Lanham, MD, 1993)
Eadmer, *Historia in novorum in Anglia*, ed. Martin Rule, RS, 81 (London, 1884)
Edbury, Peter W., *The Conquest of Jerusalem and the Third Crusade: Sources in Translation* (Farnham, 1996)
Fantosme, Jordan, *Chronicle*, ed. and trans. R. C. Johnston (Oxford, 1981)
Freising, Otto von and Rahewin, *Die Taten Friedrichs oder richtiger Cronica*, ed. Franz-Josef Schmale, trans. Adolf Schmidt (Darmstadt, 1965)
Frontinus, Julius, *Strategems. Aqueducts of Rome*, ed. Mary B. McElwain, trans. Charles E. Bennett (Cambridge, MA, 1925)
———, *Strategemata*, ed. Robert I. Ireland (Leipzig, 1990)
'Gesta consulum Andegavorum et dominorum Ambaziensium', in Paul Marchegay and Andre Salmon (eds.), *Chroniques d'Anjou* (2 vols, Paris, 1856), vol. 1, pp. 1–226
'Gesta Herwardi incliti exulis et militis', in Thomas Duffy Hardy and Charles Trice Martin (eds.), *Lestorie des engles solum la translacion Maistre Geffrei Gaimar* (2 vols, London,1888), vol. 1, pp. 339–404

Gibb, H. A. R., *The Damascus Chronicle of the Crusades: Extracted and Translated from the Chronicle of Ibn Al-Qalānisī* (London, 1932)
Gloucester, Robert of, *Metrical Chronicle*, ed. William Aldis Wright, RS, 86 (2 vols, London, 1887)
Gratian, 'Decretum', in Emil Ludwig Richter (ed.), *Corpus iuris canonici*, rev. Emil Friedberg, rev edn (2 vols, Graz, 1955), vol. 1, pp. 1–1467
Gray, Thomas, *Scalacronica, 1272–1363*, ed. and trans. Andy King (Woodbridge, 2005)
Guisborough, Walter of, *Chronicle*, ed. Harry Rothwell (London, 1957)
Guy (bishop of Amiens), *Carmen de Hastingae proelio*, ed. and trans. Frank Barlow, 2nd edn (Oxford, 1999)
Hathaway, E. J., P. T. Ricketts, C. A. Robson, and A. D. Wilshere (eds.), *Fouke le fitz Waryn* (Oxford, 1975)
Hexham, John of, 'Historia', in *Historiae Anglicanae scriptores x*, ed. Roger Twysden (London, 1652), pp. 257–84
Hexham, Richard of, 'De gestis regis Stephani et de bello standardii', in Richard Howlett (ed.), *Chronicles of the Reigns of Stephen, Henry II and Richard I*, RS, 82 (4 vols, London, 1884–9), vol. 3, pp. 139–80
Hill, Rosalind (ed.), *Gesta Francorum et aliorum Hierosolimitanorum* (London, 1962)
'Historia Gaufredi ducis Noramnnorum et comitis Andegavorum', in Paul Marchegay and Andre Salmon (eds.), *Chroniques d'Anjou* (2 vols, Paris, 1856), vol. 1, pp. 227–310
Holden, A. J. (ed.), *History of William Marshal*, trans. S. Gregory (3 vols, London, 2002–6)
Howden, Roger of, *Chronica*, ed. William Stubbs, RS, 51 (4 vols, London, 1868–71)
Huntingdon, Henry of, *Historia Anglorum*, ed. and trans. Diana Greenway (Oxford, 1996)
Ibn al-Athīr, *Chronicle for the Crusading Period from al-Kamil fi'l-ta'rikh*, trans. D. S. Richards (3 vols, Aldershot, 2006–8)
Imād ad-Dīn al-Ifahānī, *Conquête de la Syrie et de la Palestine par Saladin (al-Fatḥ al-qussî fi l-fatḥ al-qudsî)*, trans. Henri Massé (Paris, 1972)
'Itinerarium peregrinoum et gesta regis Ricardi', in William Stubbs (ed.), *Chronicles and Memorials of the Reign of Richard I*, RS, 38 (2 vols, London, 1864–5), vol. 1, pp. 3–450
Johnstone, Hilda (ed.) *Annals of Ghent* (London, 1951)
Joinville, Jean de, *Vie de Saint Louis*, ed. and trans. Jacques Monfrin (Paris, 1995)
Knight, Stephen and Thomas Ohlgren (eds.), *Robin Hood and Other Outlaw Tales*, 2nd edn (Kalamazoo, MI, 2000)
Komnene, Anna, *The Alexiad*, trans. E. R. A. Sewter (London, 1969)
Langtoft, Peter of, *Chronicle*, ed. Thomas Wright, RS, 47 (2 vols, London, 1866–8)
Livy, Titus, *Ab urbe condita: Tomus i, libri i–v*, ed. Robert Maxwell Ogilvie (Oxford, 1974)
Loud, G. A., *The Crusade of Frederick Barbarossa: The History of the Expedition of the Emperor Frederick and Related Texts* (Farnham, 2010)
Luard, Henry Richards (ed.), *Flores historiarum*, RS, 95 (3 vols, London, 1890)
MacLean, Simon (ed. and trans.), *History and Politics in Late Carolingian and*

Ottonian Europe: The Chronicle of Regino of Prüm and Adalbert of Magdeburg (Manchester, 2009)

Malaterra, Geoffrey, *De rebus gestis Rogerii Calabriae et Siciliae comitis et Roberti Guiscardi ducis fratris eius*, ed. Ernesto Pontieri (Bologna, 1927)

Malmesbury, William of, *Gesta regum Anglorum*, ed. and trans. R. A. B. Mynors, R. M. Thomson and M. Winterbottom (2 vols, Oxford, 1998)

——, *Historia novella*, ed. Edmund King, trans. K. R. Potter (Oxford, 1998)

Map, Walter, *De nugis curialium: Courtiers trifles*, ed. and trans. M. R. James, rev. C. N. L. Brooke and R. A. B. Mynors, rev edn (Oxford, 1983)

Martin-Chabot, Eugéne (ed. and trans.), *La Chanson de la croisade albigeoise* (3 vols, Paris, 1931–61)

Maximus, Valerius, *Facta et dicta memorabilia*, ed. John Briscoe (Leipzig, 1998)

Michel, Francisque (ed.), *Histoire des ducs de Normandie et des rois d'Angleterre* (Paris, 1840)

Monk, Robert the, 'Historia Iherosolimitana', in *Recueil des historiens des croisades: Historiens occidentaux tome troisième* (Paris, 1866), pp. 717–882

Montecassino, Amatus of, *History of the Normans*, trans. Prescott N. Dunbar (Woodbridge, 2004)

——, *Ystoire de li Normant*, ed. Michèle Guéret-Laferté (Paris, 2011)

Morgan, Margaret Ruth (ed.), *La Continuation de Guillaume de Tyr* (Paris, 1982)

Myers, John Vernon (ed.), *Jehan de Lanson: Chanson de geste of the Thirteenth Century* (Chapel Hill, NC, 1965)

Newburgh, William of, *The History of English Affairs*, ed. and trans. P. G. Walsh and M. J. Kennedy (2 vols, Warminster, 1988–2007)

Nicolas, Nicholas Harris, *The Controversy between Sir Richard Scrope and Sir Robert Grosvenor in the Court of Chivalry A.D. MCCCLXXXV – MCCCXC* (2 vols, London, 1832)

Nogent, Guibert of, *Dei gesta per Francos et cinq autre textes*, ed. R. B. C. Huygens (Turnhout, 1996)

Ohlgren, Thomas H. (ed.), *Medieval Outalws: Ten Tales in Modern English* (Stroud, 1998)

Ovid Naso, Publius, *Fastorum libri sex*, ed. E. H. Alton, D. E. W. Wormell and E. Courtney (Leipzig, 1978)

Paderborn, Oliver of, 'Historia Damiatina', in H. Hoogeweg (ed.), *Die Schriften des Kölner Domscholasters, späteren Bischofs von Paderborn und Kardinal-Bischofs von S. Sabina, Oliverus* (Tübingen, 1894), pp. 159–282

Paris, Matthew, *Chronica majora*, ed. Henry Richards Luard, RS, 57 (7 vols, London, 1872–83)

Poitiers, William of, *Gesta Guillelmi*, ed. and trans. R. H. C. Davis and Marjorie Chibnall (Oxford, 1998)

Potter, K. R. (ed. and trans), *Gesta Stephani*, rev. R. H. C. Davis, rev edn (Oxford, 1976)

Prudentius Clemens, Aurelius, *Carmina*, ed. Maurice P. Cunningham (Turnhout, 1966)

Puylaurens, William of, *Chronique*, ed. and trans. Jean Duvernoy (Paris, 1976)

Regino of Prüm, *Chronicon cum continuatione Treverensi*, ed. Friedrich Kurze, MGH, Scriptores rerum Germanicarum, 50 (Hannover, 1890)

'Relatio Marchianensis', MGH, Scriptores, 26 (Hanover, 1882), pp. 390–1

Rievaulx, Aelred of, 'Relatio de standardo', in Richard Howlett (ed.), *Chronicles of the Reigns of Stehphen, Henry II and Richard I*, RS, 82 (4 vols, London, 1884–9), vol. 3, pp. 181–201

Rigord, *Histoire de Philippe Auguste*, ed. and trans. Élisabeth Carpentier, Georges Pon and Yves Chauvin (Paris, 2006)

Rishanger, William, *Chronica et annales*, ed. Henry Thomas Riley, RS, 28 (London, 1865)

Salisbury, John of, *Policraticus*, ed. Clemens C. I. Webb (2 vols, New York, 1979)

Searle, Eleanor (ed. and trans.), *Chronicle of Battle Abbey* (Oxford, 1980)

St Denis, Suger of, *Vie de Louis VI le Gros*, ed. and trans. Henri Waquet, 2nd edn (Paris, 1964)

St Quentin, Dudo of, *De moribus et actis primorum Normanniae ducum*, ed. Jules Lair (Caen, 1865)

Stevenson, J. (ed.), *Chronica de Mailros* (Edinburgh, 1835)

———, *Chronicon de Lanercost* (Edinburgh, 1839)

Stubbs, William (ed.), *Gesta regis Henrici secundi Benedicti abbatis*, RS, 49 (2 vols, London, 1867)

———, *Memoriale fratris Walteri de Coventria*, RS, 58 (2 vols, London, 1872–3)

Sturlson, Snorri, *Heimskringla: History of the Kings of Norway*, trans. Lee M. Hollander (Austin, TX, 1964)

Swanton, Michael, 'The Deeds of Hereward', in Thomas H. Ohlgren (trans.), *Medieval Outlaws: Ten Tales in Modern English* (Stroud, 1998), pp. 12–60

Thérouanne, Walter of, *Vita Karoli comitis Flandrie et Vita domi Ioannis Morinensis episcopi*, ed. Jeff Rider (Turnhout, 2006)

Trivet, Nicholas, *Annales sex regum Angliae, qui a comitibus Andegavensibus originem taxerunt*, ed. Thomas Hog (London, 1845)

Torigni, Robert of, 'Chronicle', in Richard Howlett (ed.), *Chronicles of the Reigns of Stephen, Henry II and Richard I*, RS, 82 (4 vols, London, 1884–9), vol. 4

Tournai, Herman of, *Liber de restauratione monasterii S. Martini Tornacensis*, MGH, Scriptores, 14 (Hanover, 1883) pp. 274–317

Troyes, Chrétien de, *Cligés*, ed. Stewart Gregory and Claude Luttrell (Cambridge, 1993)

Tynemouth, John of, 'Extracts from the *Historia aurea*', in V. H. Galbraith, 'Extracts from the *Historia aurea* and a French "Brut" (1317–47), *The English Historical Review* (1928), 203–17

Tyre, William of, *Chronique*, ed. R. B. C. Huygens (Turnholt, 1986)

Van Houts, Elisabeth M. C. (ed. and trans.), *The Gesta Normannorum of William of Jumièges, Orderic Vitalis, and Robert of Torigni* (2 vols, Oxford, 1992–5)

les Vaux-de-Cernay, Peter of, *Hystoria albigensis*, ed. Pascal Guébin and Ernest Lyon (2 vols, Paris, 1926–30)

Vegetius Renatus, Publius Flavius, *Epitome of Military Science*, trans. N. P. Milnes, 2nd edn (Liverpool, 1996)

———, *Epitoma rei militaris*, ed. M. D. Reeve (Oxford, 2004)

Vergil Maro, P. *Aeneid*, ed. Gian Biagio Conte (Berlin, 2009)

Villehardouin, Geoffrey de, *La Conquête de Constantinople*, ed. and trans. Edmond Faral, 2nd edn (2 vols, Paris, 1961)

Vitalis, Orderic, *Ecclesiastical History*, ed. and trans. Marjorie Chibnall (6 vols, Oxford, 1969–80)
Wace, *Roman de Brut: A History of the British*, ed. and trans. Judith Weiss, rev edn (Exeter, 2002)
———, *Le Roman de Rou*, ed. A. J. Holden (3 vols, Paris, 1970–3)
Wales, Gerald of, *Expugnatio Hibernica*, ed. and trans. A. B. Scott and F. X. Martin (Dublin, 1978)
———, 'Itinerarium Kambriae', in *Opera*, ed. J. S. Brewer, RS, 21 (8 vols, London, 1861–91), vol. 6, pp. 3–154
———, 'Descriptio Kambriae', in *Opera*, ed. J. S. Brewer, RS, 21 (8 vols, London, 1861–91), vol. 6, pp. 155–227
———, 'Topographia Hibernica', in *Opera*, ed. J. S. Brewer, RS, 21 (8 vols, London, 1861–91), vol. 5, pp. 3–206
Weber, Robert, Roger Gryson and Bonifatius Fischer (eds.), *Biblia sacra iuxta vulgatam versionem*, 5th edn (Stuttgart, 2007)
Wendover, Roger of, *Chronica*, ed. Henry O. Coxe (5 vols, London, 1841–4)
Worcester, John of, *Chronicle*, ed. and trans. P. McGurk (3 vols, Oxford, 1998)
Wykes, Thomas, 'Chronicon', in Henry Richards Luard (ed.), *Annales monastici*, RS, 36 (5 vols, London, 1864–9), vol. 4, pp. 6–354

Secondary Sources

Abels, Richard, and Stephen Morillo, 'A Lying Legacy? A Preliminary Discussion of Images of Antiquity and Altered Reality in Medieval Military History', *Journal of Medieval Military History*, 3 (2005), 1–13
Adams, Tracy, 'The Cunningly Intelligent Characters of BnF, fr 19152', *Modern Language Notes*, 120 (2005), 896–924
Ailes, Adrian, 'The Knight, Heraldry and Armour: The Role of Recognition and the Origins of Heraldry', in Christopher Harper-Bill and Ruth Harvey (eds.), *Medieval Knighthood IV: Papers from the Fifth Strawberry Hill Conference, 1990* (Woodbridge, 1992), pp. 1–21
Ailes, Marianne J., 'The Admirable Enemy? Saladin and Saphadin in Ambroise's *Estoire de la guerre sainte*', in Norman Housley (ed.), *Knighthoods of Christ: Essays on the History of the Crusades and the Knights Templar Presented to Malcolm Barber* (Farnham, 2007), pp. 51–64
Alban, J. R., and Christopher Allmand, 'Spies and Spying in the Fourteenth Century', in Christopher Allmand (ed.), *War, Literature and Politics in the Late Middle Ages* (Liverpool, 1976), pp. 73–101
Albu, Emily, 'Bohemond and the Rooster: Byzantines, Normans, and the Artful Ruse', in Thalia Gouma-Peterson (ed.), *Anna Komnene and her Times* (London, 2000), pp. 157–68
———, *The Normans in their Histories: Propaganda, Myth, and Subversion* (Woodbridge, 2001)
Allmand, Christopher, 'A Roman Text on War: The *Strategemata* of Frontinus in the Middle Ages', in Peter Coss and Christopher Tyerman (eds.), *Soldiers,*

Nobles and Gentlemen: Essays in Honour of Maurice Keen (Woodbridge, 2009), pp. 153–68

———, *The 'De re militari' of Vegetius: The Reception, Transmission and Legacy of a Roman Text in the Middle Ages* (Cambridge, 2011)

———, 'Vegetius' *De re militari*: Military Theory in Medieval and Modern Conception', *History Compass*, 9 (2011), 397–409

Amory, Frederick, 'The Viking Hasting in Franco-Scandinavian Legend', in Margot H. King and Wesley M. Stevens (eds.), *Saints, Scholars and Heroes: Studies in Medieval Culture in Honour of Charles W. Jones* (2 vols, Collegeville, MN, 1979), vol. 2, pp. 265–86

Anglo, Sydney, 'Vegetius's *De re militari*: The Triumph of Mediocrity', *Antiquaries Journal*, 82 (2002), 247–67

Archer, Christon I., John R. Ferris, Holger H. Herwig, and Timothy H. E. Travers, *World History of Warfare* (Lincoln, NE, 2002)

Asbridge, Thomas S., 'Knowing the Enemy: Latin Relations with Islam at the Time of the First Crusade', in Norman Housley (ed.), *Knighthoods of Christ: Essays on the History of the Crusades and the Knights Templar, Presented to Malcolm Barber* (Farnham, 2007), pp. 17–26

Ayalon, David, 'From Ayyūbids to Mamlūks', *Revue des etudes islamiques*, 49 (1981), 43–57

Ayton, Andrew, and J. L. Price, 'Introduction: The Military Revolution from a Medieval Perspective', in Andrew Ayton and J. L. Price (eds.), *The Medieval Military Revolution: State, Society and Military Change in Medieval and Early Modern Europe* (London, 1995), pp. 1–22

Bachrach, Bernard S., 'The Alans in Gaul', *Traditio*, 23 (1967), 476–89

———, 'The Feigned Retreat at Hastings', *Mediaeval Studies*, 33 (1971), 344–7

———, 'The Origins of Armorican Chivalry', *Technology and Culture*, 10 (1969), 166–71

———, 'The Practical Use of Vegetius' *De re militari* during the Early Middle Ages', *Historian*, 47 (1985), 239–55

Bachrach, David S., *Religion and the Conduct of War, c. 300–1215* (Woodbridge, 2003)

Baldwin, John W., *The Government of Philip Augustus: Foundations of French Royal Power in the Middle Ages* (Berkeley, CA, 1986)

Ballon, Roger, 'Trickery as an Element of the Character of Renart', *Forum for Modern Language Studies*, 22 (1986), 34–52

Barber, Malcolm, *The Two Cities: Medieval Europe, 1050–1320* (London, 1992)

Barber, Richard, 'Heralds and the Court of Chivalry: From Collective Memory to Formal Institutions', in Anthony Musson and Nigel Ramsay (eds.), *Courts of Chivalry and Admiralty in Late Medieval Europe* (Woodbridge, 2018), pp. 15–28

———, *The Knight and Chivalry*, rev edn (Woodbridge, 1995)

Barrow, G. W. S., *Robert Bruce and the Community of the Realm of Scotland*, 4th edn (London, 2005)

Bartlett, Robert, *Gerald of Wales: A Voice of the Middle Ages* (Stroud, 2006)

———, 'Medieval and Modern Concepts of Race and Ethnicity', *Journal of Medieval and Early Modern Studies*, 3 (2001), 39–56

Bates, David, *William the Conqueror* (New Haven, CT, 2016)

Beecham, K. J., *The History of Cirencester and the Roman City of Corinium* (Dursley, 1887)

Beeler, John, *Warfare in England 1066–1189* (Ithaca, NY, 1966)

Benham, Jenny, *Peacemaking in the Middle Ages: Principles and Practice* (Manchester, 2011)

Bennett, Charles E., 'The Life and Works of Sextus Julius Frontinus', in Mary B. McElwain (ed.), *The Stratagems and the Aqueducts of Rome* (London, 1925), pp. xiii–xxvii

Bennett, Matthew, 'First Crusaders' Images of Muslims: The Influence of Vernacular Poetry?', *Forum for Modern Language Studies*, 22 (1986), 101–22

———, 'The Myth of the Military Supremacy of the Knightly Cavalry', in Matthew Strickland (ed.), *Armies, Chivalry and Warfare in Medieval Britain: Proceedings of the 1995 Harlaxton Symposium* (Stamford, 1998), pp. 304–16

———, 'The Status of the Squire: The Northern Evidence', in Christopher Harper-Bill and Ruth Harvey (eds.), *The Ideals and Practices of Medieval Knighthood: Papers from the First and Second Strawberry Hill Conferences* (Woodbridge, 1986), pp. 1–11

———, 'Virile Latins, Effeminate Greeks and Strong Women: Gender Definitions on Crusade?', in Susan B. Edgington and Sarah Lambert (eds.), *Gendering the Crusades* (Cardiff, 2001), pp. 16–30

———, 'Wace and Warfare', in R. Allen Brown (ed.), *Anglo-Norman Studies XI: Proceedings of the Battle Conference 1988* (Woodbridge, 1989), pp. 37–57

Birk, Joshua C., 'The Betrayal of Antioch: Narratives of Conversion and Conquest during the First Crusade', *Journal of Medieval and Early Modern Studies*, 41 (2011), 463–86

Bjork, Robert E. (ed.), *Oxford Dictionary of the Middle Ages* (4 vols, Oxford, 2010)

Blakeslee, Merrit R., 'Tristan the Trickster in the Old French Tristan Poems', *Cultura Neolatina*, 44 (1984), 167–90

Bliese, John R. E., 'Rhetoric and Morale: A Study of Battle Orations from the Central Middle Ages', *Journal of Medieval History*, 15 (1989), 201–26

———, 'The Courage of the Normans: A Comparative Study of Battle Rhetoric', *Nottingham Medieval Studies*, 35 (1991), 1–26

———, 'When Knightly Courage May Fail: Battle Orations in Medieval Europe', *The Historian*, 53 (1991), 489–504

Blöndal, Sigfus, *The Varangians of Byzantium: An Aspect of Byzantine Military History*, trans. Benedikt S. Benedikz (Cambridge, 1978)

Bloomer, W. Martin, *Valerius Maximus and the Rhetoric of the New Nobility* (London, 1992)

Bolton, Timothy, *Cnut the Great* (New Haven, CT, 2017)

Bouchard, Constance Brittain, *Spirituality and Administration: The Role of the Bishop in Twelfth-Century Auxerre* (Cambridge, MA, 1979)

Bouet, Pierre, 'Hasting, le Viking pervers selon Dudon de Saint-Quentin', *Annales de Normandie*, 62 (2012), 215–34

Bradbury, Jim, 'Geoffrey V of Anjou, Count and Knight', in Christopher Harper-Bill and Ruth Harvey (eds.), *The Ideals and Practice of Medieval Knighthood III: Papers from the Fourth Strawberry Hill Conference, 1988* (Woodbridge, 1990), pp. 21–38

Brault, Gerard J., *Early Blazon: Heraldic Terminology in the Twelfth and Thirteenth Centuries with Special Reference to Arthurian Literature* (Oxford, 1972)

Broun, Dauvit, 'Becoming a Nation: Scotland in the Twelfth and Thirteenth Centuries', in Hirokazu Tsurushima (ed.), *Nations in Medieval Britain* (Donington, 2010), pp. 86–103

Brown, Paul, 'The *Gesta Roberti Wiscardi*: A Byzantine History?', *Journal of Medieval History*, 37 (2011), 162–79

Brown, R. Allen, 'The Battle of Hastings', in R. Allen Brown (ed.), *Anglo-Norman Studies III: Proceedings of the Battle Conference on Anglo-Norman Studies 1980* (Woodbridge, 1981), pp. 1–21

Buck, Andrew D., *The Principality of Antioch and its Frontiers in the Twelfth Century* (Woodbridge, 2017)

Canick, Hubert, and Helmuth Schneider (eds.), *Brill's New Pauly: Encyclopaedia of the Ancient World* (15 vols, Leiden, 2002)

Cannan, Fergus, 'The Myths of Medieval Heraldry', *Nottingham Medieval Studies*, 47 (2003), 198–216

Carey, Stephen Mark, 'Fictionality', in Albrecht Classen (ed.), *Handbook of Medieval Studies: Terms, Methods, Trends* (3 vols, Berlin, 2010), 1500–4

Carrier, Marc, 'Perfidious and Effeminate Greeks: The Representation of Byzantine Ceremonial in the Western Chronicles of the Crusades, 1096–1204', *Annuario*, 4 (2002), 47–68

Carter, C. J., 'Valerius Maximus', in T. A. Dorey (ed.), *Empire and Aftermath: Silver Latin II*, (London, 1975), pp. 26–56

Carter, John Marshall, 'Une réévaluation des interprétations de la fuite simulée d'Hastings', *Annales de Normandie*, 45 (1995), 27–34

Cheyette, Fredric L., 'Giving Each his Due', in Lester K. Little and Barbara H. Rosenwein (eds.), *Debating the Middle Ages: Issues and Readings* (Oxford, 1998), pp. 170–9

Chibnall, Marjorie, 'Orderic Vitalis on Castles', in C. Harper-Bill, C. J. Holdsworth, and J. L. Nelson (eds.), *Studies in Medieval History Presented to R. Allen Brown* (Woodbridge, 1989), pp. 43–56

———, *The World of Orderic Vitalis* (Oxford, 1984)

Chléirigh, Léan Ní, 'The Impact of the First Crusade on Western Opinion towards the Byzantine Empire: The *Dei gesta per Francos* of Guibert of Nogent and the *Historia Hierosolymitana* of Fulcher of Chartres', in Conor Kostick (ed.), *The Crusades and the Near East* (London, 2011), pp. 161–88

Church, S. D., *The Household Knights of King John* (Cambridge, 1999)

———, 'The Rewards of Royal Service in the Household of King John: A Dissenting Opinion', *English Historical Review*, 110 (1995), 277–302

Contamine, Philippe, *War in the Middle Ages*, trans. Michael Jones (Oxford, 1984)

Cook, David R., 'The Norman Military Revolution in England', in R. Allen Brown (ed.), *Anglo-Norman Studies I: Proceedings of the Battle Conference on Anglo-Norman Studies 1978* (Woodbridge, 1979), pp. 94–102

Cook, Robert, 'Russian History, Icelandic Story, and Byzantine Strategy in *Eymundar Þáttr Hringssonar*', *Viator*, 17 (1986), 65–90

Coulson, Charles L. H., *Castles in Medieval Society: Fortresses in England, France, and Ireland in the Central Middle Ages* (Oxford, 2003)

Coupland, Simon, 'The Vikings on the Continent in Myth and History', *History*, 88 (2003), 187–203

Crook, David, *Robin Hood: Legend and Reality* (Woodbridge, 2020)

Crouch, David, *The Birth of Nobility: Constructing Aristocracy in England and France 900–1300* (Harlow, 2005)

———, *William Marshal: Court, Career and Chivalry in the Angevin Empire 1147–1219* (London, 1990)

Cruickshank, Charles, *Deception in World War II* (Oxford, 1981)

Curry, Anne (ed.), *The Battle of Agincourt: Sources and Interpretations* (Woodbridge, 2000)

———, 'Disciplinary Ordinances for English and Franco-Scottish Armies in 1385: An International Code?', *Journal of Medieval History*, 37 (2011), 269–94

D'Arcq, Douët, *Collection de sceaux* (3 vols, Paris, 1863)

Davies, Sean, *War and Society in Medieval Wales 633–1283: Welsh Military Institutions* (Cardiff, 2004)

Davis, R. H. C., *The Medieval Warhorse: Origin, Development and Redevelopment* (London, 1989)

DeVries, Kelly, *A Cumulative Bibliography of Medieval Military History and Technology* (Leiden, 2002)

———, *Infantry Warfare in the Early Fourteenth Century: Discipline, Tactics and Technology* (Woodbridge, 1996)

DeVries, Kelly, and Robert Douglas Smith, *Medieval Military Technology*, 2nd edn (Toronto, 2012)

Diggelmann, Lindsay, 'Hewing the Ancient Elm: Anger, Arboricide, and Medieval Kingship', *Journal of Medieval and Early Modern Studies*, 40 (2010), 249–72

———, 'Of Grifons and Tyrants: Anglo-Norman Views of the Mediterranean World during the Third Crusade', in Lisa Bailey, Lindsay Diggelmann, and Kim M. Phillips (eds.), *Old Worlds, New Worlds: European Cultural Encounters, c. 1000 – c. 1750* (Turnhout, 2009), pp. 11–30

Ditchburn, David, and Alastair Macdonald, 'Medieval Scotland, 1100–1560', in R. A. Houston and W. W. J. Knox (eds.), *The New Penguin History of Scotland from the Earliest Times to the Present Day* (London, 2001), pp. 96–181

Du Cange and others, *Glossarium mediae et infimae latinitatis*, ed. Leopold Favre (Niort, 1883–7)

Duby, Georges, *The Legend of Bouvines: War, Religion and Culture in the Middle Ages*, trans. Catherine Tihanyi (Berkeley, CA, 1990)

Dunphy, Graeme, 'Chronicles', in Albrecht Classen (ed.) *Handbook of Medieval Studies: Terms, Methods, Trends* (3 vols, Berlin, 2010), 1714–21

Edgington, Susan B., 'Espionage and Military Intelligence during the First Crusade, 1095–99', in Simon John and Nicholas Morton (eds.), *Crusading and Warfare in the Middle Ages: Realities and Representations. Essays in Honour of John France* (Farnham, 2014), pp. 75–86

Flanagan, Marie Therese, 'Irish and Anglo-Norman Warfare in Twelfth-Century Ireland', in Thomas Bartlett and Keith Jeffery (eds.), *A Military History of Ireland* (Cambridge, 1996), pp. 52–75

Forey, A. J., 'The Failure of the Siege of Damascus in 1148', *Journal of Medieval History*, 10 (1984), 13–23

France, John, 'Crusading Warfare and its Adaptation to Eastern Conditions in the Twelfth Century', *Mediterranean Historical Review*, 15 (2000), 49–66

———, 'The Fall of Antioch during the First Crusade', in *Dei gesta per Francos: Etudes sur les croisades dédiées à Jean Richard*, ed. by Michel Balard, Benjamin Z. Kedar, and Jonathan Riley-Smith (Ashgate, 2001), pp. 13–20

———, *Victory in the East: A Military History of the First Crusade* (Cambridge, 1994)

———, *Western Warfare in the Age of the Crusades, 1000–1300* (London, 1999)

Friedman, Yvonne, 'Did Laws of War Exist in the Crusader Kingdom of Jerusalem?', in Yitzhak Hen (ed.), *De Sion exibit lex et verbum domini de Hierusalem: Essays on Medieval Law, Liturgy, and Literature in Honour of Amnon Linder* (Turnhout, 2001), pp. 81–103

Gaunt, Simon, *Gender and Genre in Medieval French Literature* (Cambridge, 1995)

Gay, Victor, *Glossaire archéologique du Moyen Âge et de la Renaissance*, ed. Henri Stein (2 vols, Paris, 1928)

Geary, Patrick J., *The Myth of Nations: The Medieval Origins of Europe* (Princeton, NJ, 2002)

Gerrard, Daniel M. G., *The Church at War: The Military Activities of Bishops, Abbots and Other Clergy in England, c. 900–1200* (London, 2017)

Gibb, Hamilton A. R., 'The Armies of Saladin', in S. J. Shaw and W. R. Polk (eds), *Studies on the Civilization of Islam* (Boston, 1962), pp. 74–90

Gilbert, Jane, 'The *Chanson de Roland*', in Simon Gaunt and Sarah Kay (eds.), *The Cambridge Companion to Medieval French Literature* (Cambridge, 2008), pp. 21–34

Gillingham, John, 'An Age of Expansion, *c.* 1020–1204', in Maurice Keen (ed.), *Medieval Warfare: A History* (Oxford, 1999), pp. 59–88

———, 'Conquering the Barbarians: War and Chivalry in Twelfth-Century Britain', *Haskins Society Journal*, 4 (1992), 67–84

———, *Richard the Lionheart*, 2nd edn (London, 1989)

———, 'William the Bastard at War', in Christopher Harper-Bill, Christopher J. Holdsworth, and Janet L. Nelson (eds.), *Studies in Medieval History Presented to R. Allen Brown* (Woodbridge, 1989), pp. 141–158

Given-Wilson, Chris, *Chronicles: The Writing of History in Medieval England* (London, 2004)

Gransden, Antonia, *Historical Writing in England* (2 vols, London, 1974–82)

Grant, Alexander, 'Aspects of National Consciousness in Medieval Scotland', in Claus Bjørn, Alexander Grant, and Keith J. Stringer (eds.), *Nations, Nationalism and Patriotism in the European Past* (Copenhagen, 1994), pp. 68–95

Guyot-Bachy, Isabelle, 'Cris et trompettes: Les Échos de la guerre chez les historiens et les chroniqueurs', in Didier Lett and Nicolas Offenstadt (eds.), *Haro! Noël! Oyé! Pratiques du cri au Moyen Âge* (Paris, 2003), pp. 103–16

Hanawalt, Emily A., 'Norman Views of Eastern Christendom, from the First Crusade to the Principality of Antioch', in Vladimir P. Goss (ed.), *The Meeting of Two Worlds: Cultural Exchange between East and West during the Period of the Crusades* (Kalamazoo, MI, 1986), pp. 115–21

Hanley, Catherine, *War and Combat 1150–1270: The Evidence from Old French Literature* (Cambridge, 2003)

Hanning, Robert W., *The Individual in Twelfth-Century Romance* (New Haven, CT, 1977)

Harari, Yitzak, 'The Military Role of the Frankish Turcopoles', *Mediterranean Historical Review*, 12 (1997), 75–116

Harari, Yuval Noah, 'Knowledge, Power and the Medieval Soldier', in Iris Shagrir, Ronnie Ellenblum, and Jonathan Riley-Smith (eds.), *'In laudem Hierosolymitani': Studies in Crusades and Medieval Culture in Honour of Benjamin Z. Kedar* (Aldershot, 2007), pp. 345–56

———, *Special Operations in the Age of Chivalry 1100–1550* (Woodbridge, 2007)

Harris, Jonathan, *Byzantium and the Crusades*, 2nd edn (London, 2014)

Harris, Julian, '*Munjoie* and *Reconuisance* in *Chanson de Roland*, l. 3620', *Romance Philology*, 10 (1956), 168–73

Hill, Rosalind, 'The Christian View of the Muslims at the Time of the First Crusade', in P. M. Holt (ed.), *The Eastern Mediterranean Lands in the Period of the Crusades* (Warminster, 1977), pp. 1–8

Hillenbrand, Carole, *The Crusades: Islamic Perspectives* (Edinburgh, 1999)

Hodgson, Natasha, 'Reinventing Normans as Crusaders? Ralph of Caen's *Gesta Tancredi*', in C. P. Lewis (ed.), *Anglo-Norman Studies XXX: Proceedings of the Battle Conference 2007* (Woodbridge, 2008), pp. 117–32

Hollander, L. M., 'The Battle of the Vin-Heath and the Battle of the Huns', *Journal of English and Germanic Philology*, 32 (1933), 33–43

Holt, J. C., *Robin Hood*, rev edn (London, 2011)

Hoppenbrouwers, Peter, 'Such Stuff as Peoples Are Made On: Ethnogenesis and the Construction of Nationhood in Medieval Europe', *Medieval History Journal*, 9 (2006), 195–242

Hosler, John D., *Henry II: A Medieval Soldier at War, 1147–1189* (Leiden, 2007)

———, *John of Salisbury: Military Authority of the Twelfth-Century Renaissance* (Leiden, 2013)

Isaac, Steven, 'Galbert of Bruges and the Urban Experience of Siege', in Jeff Rider and Alan V. Murray (eds.), *Galbert of Bruges and the Historiography of Medieval Flanders* (Washington, DC, 2009), pp. 89–106

Jefferson, Lisa, *Oaths, Vows and Promises in the First Part of the French Prose Lancelot Romance* (Bern, 1993)

Jenéy, Cynthia, 'Horses and Equitation', in Albrecht Classen (ed.), *Handbook of Medieval Culture: Fundamental Aspects and Conditions of the European Middle Ages* (2 vols, Berlin, 2015), vol. 1, pp. 674–96

John, Simon, 'Historical Truth and the Miraculous Past: The Use of Oral Evidence in Twelfth-Century Latin Historical Writing on the First Crusade', *English Historical Review*, 130 (2015), 263–301

Johnson, James Turner, *Ideology, Reason, and the Limitation of War: Religious and Secular Concepts 1200–1740* (Princeton, NJ, 1975)

———, *Just War Tradition and the Restraint of War: A Moral and Historical Inquiry* (Princeton, NJ, 1981)

Johnson, Lesley, 'Imagining Communities: Medieval and Modern', in Simon Forde, Lesley Johnson, and Alan V. Murray (eds.), *Concepts of National Identity in the Middle Ages* (Leeds, 1995), pp. 1–20

Jones, R. L. C., 'Fortifications and Sieges in Western Europe *c.* 800–1450', in Maurice Keen *Medieval Warfare: A History* (Oxford, 1999), pp. 163–85

Jones, Robert W., *Bloodied Banners: Martial Display on the Medieval Battlefield* (Woodbridge, 2010)

———, 'Heraldry and Heralds', in Robert W. Jones and Peter Coss (eds.), *A Companion to Chivalry* (Woodbridge, 2019), pp. 139–59

———, 'Identifying the Warrior on the Pre-Heraldic Battlefield', in C. P. Lewis (ed.), *Anglo-Norman Studies XXX: Proceedings of the Battle Conference, 2007* (Woodbridge, 2008), pp. 154–67

———, '"What banner thine?" The Banner as a Symbol of Identification, Status and Authority on the Battlefield', *Haskins Society Journal*, 15 (2004), 101–9

Jones, Robert W. and Peter Coss (eds.), *A Companion to Chivalry* (Woodbridge, 2019)

Jones, William Randolph, 'England against the Celtic Fringe: A Study in Cultural Stereotypes', *Journal of World History*, 13 (1971), 155–71

———, 'The Image of the Barbarian in Medieval Europe', *Comparative Studies in Society and History*, 13 (1971), 376–407

Jucker, Michael, 'Le Butin de guerre au Moyen Âge: Aspects symboliques et économiques', *Francia*, 36 (2009), 113–33

Kaeuper, Richard, *Medieval Chivalry* (Cambridge, 2016)

Kangas, Sini, '*Inimicus Dei et sanctae Christianitatis*? Saracens and their Prophet in Twelfth-Century Crusade Propaganda and Western Travesties of Muhammad's Life', in Conor Kostick (ed.), *The Crusades and the Near East* (London, 2011), pp. 131–60

Keegan, John, *The Face of Battle* (London, 1976)

Keen, Maurice, *Chivalry* (New Haven, CT, 1984)

———, *The Laws of War in the Late Middle Ages* (London, 1965)

——— (ed.), *Medieval Warfare: A History* (Oxford, 1999)

———, *The Outlaws of Medieval Legend*, rev edn (London, 1977)

Kennedy, Hugh, *Crusader Castles* (Cambridge, 1994)

———, *The Armies of the Caliphs: Military and Society in the Early Islamic State* (London, 2001)

Knight, Stephen, *Robin Hood: A Complete Study of the English Outlaw* (Oxford, 1994)

Kostick, Conor, 'The Terms *milites*, *equites* and *equestres* in the Early Crusading Histories', *Nottingham Medieval Studies*, 50 (2006), 1–21

Lacy, Norris J., 'Trickery, Trubertage, and the Limits of Laughter', in Kristin Burr, John F. Moran, and Norris J. Lacy (eds.), *The Old French Fabliaux: Essays on Comedy and Context* (Jefferson, NC, 2007), pp. 82–92

Lake, Justin, 'Authorial Intention in Medieval Historiography', *History Compass*, 12 (2014), 344–60

Lambert, Sarah, 'Translation, Citation, and Ridicule: Renart the Fox and Crusading in the Vernacular', in Sarah Lambert and Helen Nicholson (eds.), *Languages of Love and Hate: Conflict, Communication, and Identity in the Medieval Mediterranean* (Turnhout, 2012), pp. 65–86

Landon, Lionel, *The Itinerary of King Richard I* (London, 1935)

Latham, R. E. and D. R. Howlett, 'arma', *Dictionary of Medieval Latin from British Sources* (3 vols, Oxford, 1975–2013), vol. 1, p. 216

Lawson, M. K., *Cnut: England's Viking King 1016–35*, 2nd edn (Stroud, 2011)

Lemmon, Charles H., *The Field of Hastings*, 3rd edn (St. Leonards-On-Sea, 1964)

Lesdain, L. Bouly de, 'Etudes historiques sur le xiie siècle', *Annuaire du conseil heraldique de France*, 20 (1907), 185–244

Levine, Robert, 'The Pious Traitor: Rhetorical Reinventions of the Fall of Antioch', *Mittellateinisches Jahrbuch*, 33 (1998), 59–80

Lewis, Charlton T., and Charles Short, *A Latin Dictionary* (Oxford: Clarendon Press, 1879)

Lodge, R. Anthony, and Kenneth Varty (eds.), *The Earliest Branches of the Roman de Renart* (Leuven, 2001)

Loud, Graham, *The Age of Robert Guiscard: Southern Italy and the Norman Conquest* (London, 2000)

——, 'Some Reflections on the Failure of the Second Crusade', *Crusades*, 4 (2005), 1–14

Luchitskaya, Svetlana, 'Muslims in Christian Imagery of the Thirteenth Century: The Visual Code of Otherness', *Al-Masāq: Islam and the Medieval Mediterranean*, 12 (2000), 37–67

Macdonald, Alastair, 'Trickery, Mockery and the Scottish Way of War', *Proceedings of the Society of Antiquaries of Scotland*, 143 (2014), 319–38

MacEvitt, Christopher, *The Crusades and the Christian World of the East: Rough Tolerance* (Philadelphia, 2008)

MacLean, Simon, 'Introduction', in Simon MacLean (ed. and trans.), *History and Politics in Late Carolingian and Ottonian Europe: The Chronicle of Regino of Prüm and Adalbert of Magdeburg* (Manchester, 2009), pp. 1–60

Makarius, Laura, 'Le Mythe du "trickster"', *Revue de l'histoire Des Religions*, 75 (1969), 17–46

Martin, F. X., 'Diarmait Mac Murchada and the Coming of the Anglo-Normans', in Art Cosgrove (ed.), *A New History of Ireland II: Medieval Ireland, 1169–1534* (Oxford, 1987), pp. 43–66

Marvin, Laurence W., '"…Men Famous in Combat and Battle…": Common Soldiers and the Siege of Bruges, 1127', *Journal of Medieval History*, 24 (1998), 243–58

Mittman, Asa Simon, 'The Other Close at Hand: Gerald of Wales and the "Marvels of the West"', in Bettina Bildhauer and Robert Mills (eds.), *The Monstrous Middle Ages* (Cardiff, 2003), pp. 97–112

Moffat, Ralph, 'The Importance of Being Harnest: Armour, Heraldry and Recognition in the Melee', in Lorna Bleach and Keira Borrill (eds.), *Battle and Bloodshed: The Medieval World at War* (Newcastle upon Tyne, 2013), pp. 5–24

Morillo, Stephen, 'A General Typology of Transcultural Wars - The Early Middle Ages and Beyond', in Hans-Henning Kortüm (ed.), *Transcultural Wars from the Middle Ages to the 21st Century* (Berlin: Akademie Verlag, 2006), pp. 29–42

——, 'Expecting Cowardice: Medieval Battle Tactics Reconsidered', *Journal of Medieval Military History*, 4 (2006), 65–73

——, 'Hastings: An Unusual Battle', in Stephen Morillo (ed.), *The Battle of Hastings: Sources and Interpretations* (Woodbridge, 1996), pp. 219–28

———, 'The "Age of Cavalry" Revisited', in Donald J. Kagay and L. J. Andrew Villalon (eds.), *The Circle of War in the Middle Ages: Essays on Medieval Military and Naval History* (Woodbridge, 1999), pp. 45–58

Morse, Ruth, *Truth and Convention in the Middle Ages: Rhetoric, Representation and Reality* (Cambridge, 1991)

Morton, Nicholas, 'Encountering the Turks: The First Crusaders' Foreknowledge of Their Enemy, Some Preliminary Findings', in Simon John and Nicholas Morton (eds.), *Crusading and Warfare in the Middle Ages: Realities and Representations, Essays in Honour of John France* (Farnham, 2014), pp. 47–68

———, *The Field of Blood: The Battle for Aleppo and the Remaking of the Medieval Middle East* (New York, 2018)

Murray, Alan V., 'Biblical Quotations and Formulaic Language in the Chronicle of William of Tyre', in Susan B. Edgington and Helen Nicholson (eds.), *Deeds Done Beyond the Sea: Essays on William of Tyre, Cyprus and the Military Orders Presented to Peter Edbury* (Farnham, 2014), pp. 25–34

——— (ed.), *The Crusades: An Encyclopaedia* (2 vols, Oxford, 2006)

———, 'Ethnic Identity in the Crusader States: The Frankish Race and the Settlement of Outremer', in Simon Forde, Lesley Johnson, and Alan V. Murray (eds.), *Concepts of National Identity in the Middle Ages* (Leeds, 1995), pp. 59–74

———, 'From the Bosphorus to Kurasan: The Turkish Domination of Asia in the Perception of the Chroniclers of the First Crusade', *Elçuk University Journal of Seljuk Studies*, 8 (2018), 82–98

———, 'The Origin of Money-Fiefs in the Latin Kingdom of Jerusalem', in John France (ed.), *Mercenaries and Paid Men: The Mercenary Identity in the Middle Ages. Proceedings of a Conference Held at the University of Wales, Swansea, 7–9th July 2005* (Leiden, 2008), pp. 275–86

Nakashian, Craig M., *Warrior Churchmen of Medieval England, 1000–1250: Theory and Reality* (Woodbridge, 2016)

Nash, Owain, 'Elements of Identity: Gerald, the Humours and National Characteristics', in Georgia Henley and A. Joseph McMullen (eds.), *Gerald of Wales: New Perspectives on a Medieval Writer* (Cardiff, 2018), pp. 203–20

Nicholson, Helen, *Medieval Warfare: Theory and Practice of War in Europe 300–1500* (Basingstoke, 2004)

Oram, Richard, *Domination and Lordship: Scotland 1070–1230* (Edinburgh, 2011)

Otter, Monika, 'Functions of Fiction in Historical Writing', in Nancy F. Partner (ed.), *Writing Medieval History* (London, 2005), pp. 109–30

———, *Inventiones: Fiction and Referentiality in Twelfth-Century English Historical Writing* (Chapel Hill, NC, 1996)

Partner, Nancy F., 'Making Up Lost Time: Writing on the Writing of History', *Speculum*, 61 (1986), 90–117

———, *Serious Entertainments: The Writing of History in Twelfth-Century England* (Chicago, 1977)

Pastoureau, Michel, 'La Diffusion de armoiries et les débuts de l'héraldique', in Robert-Henri Bautier (ed.), *La France de Philippe Auguste: Le Temps des mutations* (Paris, 1982), pp. 737–60

———, 'L'Apparition des armoiries en Occident: État du problème', *Bibliothèque de l'école des chartes*, 134 (1976), 281–300

Pennington, Kenneth, 'Feudal Oath of Fidelity and Homage', in Kenneth Pennington and Melodie Harris Eichbauer (eds.), *Law as Profession and Practice in Medieval Europe* (Farnham, 2011), pp. 93–116

Perron, Anthony, 'The Face of the "Pagan": Portraits of Religious Deviance on the Medieval Periphery', *Journal of the Historical Society*, 9 (2009), 467–92

Phillips, Jonathan, *The Second Crusade: Extending the Frontiers of Christendom* (New Haven, CT, 2007)

Pittock, Murray G. H., *Scottish Nationality* (Basingstoke, 2001)

Pohl, Benjamin, *Dudo of Saint-Quentin's Historia Normannorum: Tradition, Innovation and Memory* (York, 2015)

Prestwich, J. O., 'Military Intelligence under the Norman and Angevin Kings', in George Garnett and John Hudson (eds.), *Law and Government in Medieval England and Normandy: Essays in Honour of Sir James Holt* (Cambridge, 1994), pp. 1–30

Prestwich, Michael, 'England and Scotland during the Wars of Independence', in Michael Jones and Malcolm Vale (eds.), *England and her Neighbours, 1066–1453: Essays in Honour of Pierre Chaplais* (London, 1989), pp. 181–98

———, '*Miles in armis strenuus*: The Knight at War', *Transactions of the Royal Historical Society*, 6 (1995), 201–10

Prinet, M., 'Séance du 15 décembre. Présidence de M. M. Prou, président', *Bulletin de la société nationale des antiquaires de France* (1909) 363–9

Purton, Peter, *The Medieval Military Engineer, from the Roman Empire to the Sixteenth Century* (Woodbridge, 2018)

Ramseyer, Valerie, 'Pastoral Care as Military Action: The Ecclesiology of Archbishop Alfanus I of Salerno, 1058–1085', in John S. Ott and Anna Trumbore Jones (eds.), *The Bishop Reformed: Studies in Episcopal Power and Culture in the Central Middle Ages* (Aldershot, 2007), pp. 189–208

Regalado, Nancy Freeman, 'Tristan and Renart: Two Tricksters', *L'Espirit créateur*, 16 (1976), 30–8

Reichberg, Gregory M., *Thomas Aquinas on War and Peace* (Cambridge, 2017)

Reynolds, Susan, *Kingdoms and Communities in Western Europe, 900–1300*, 2nd edn (Oxford, 1997)

Robinson, F. C. R., and P. C. Hughes, 'Lampron: Castle of Armenian Cilicia', *Anatolian Studies*, 19 (1969), 183–207

Rogers, Clifford J., 'Tactics and the Face of Battle', in Frank Tallett and D. J. B. Trim (eds.), *European Warfare, 1350–1750* (Cambridge, 2010), pp. 203–35

———, 'The Age of the Hundred Years War', in Maurice Keen (ed.), *Medieval Warfare: A History* (Oxford, 1999), pp. 136–62

———, 'The Military Revolutions of the Hundred Years' War', *Journal of Military History*, 57 (1993), 241–78

Rogers, R., *Latin Siege Warfare in the Twelfth Century* (Oxford, 1992)

Rossenbeck, Klaus, *Die Stellung Der Riddarassogur in Der Altnordischen Prosaliteratur : Eine Untersuchung an Hand Des Erzählstils* (Bamberg, 1970)

Rothwell, William and others (eds.), *Anglo-Norman Dictionary: Online Edition* (London, 1977–92)

Rozier, Charles C., Daniel Roach, Giles E. M. Gasper, and Elisabeth van Houts (eds.), *Orderic Vitalis: Life, Works and Interpretations* (Woodbridge, 2016)

Runciman, Steven, *A History of the Crusades* (3 vols, Cambridge, 1951)
Russell, Frederick H., *The Just War in the Middle Ages* (Cambridge, 1975)
Russell, P. E., 'San Pedro de Cardeña and the Heroic History of the Cid', *Medium Aevum*, 27 (1958), 57–79
Schullian, Dorothy, 'Valerius Maximus', in *Catalogus translationum et commentariorum: Mediaeval and Renaissance Latin Translations and Commentaries* (11 vols, Washington, DC, 1960), vol. 5, 287–404
Schwinges, Rainer Christoph, 'William of Tyre, the Muslim Enemy, and the Problem of Tolerance', in Michael Gervers and James M. Powell (eds.), *Tolerance and Intolerance: Social Conflict in the Age of the Crusades* (Syracuse, NY, 2001), pp. 124–34
Shirling, Victor, *Die Verteidigungswaffen im altfranzösischen Epos* (Marburg, 1887)
Slitt, Rebecca L., 'Justifying Cross-Cultural Friendship: Bohemond, Firuz, and the Fall of Antioch', *Viator*, 38 (2007), 339–49
Smail, R. C., *Crusading Warfare, 1097–1193* (Cambridge, 1956)
Sommerstein, A. H., 'What Is an Oath?', in A. H. Sommerstein and Isabelle C. Torrance (eds.), *Oaths and Swearing in Ancient Greece* (Berlin, 2014), pp. 1–5
Spiegel, Gabrielle M., 'History, Historicism, and the Social Logic of the Text in the Middle Ages', *Speculum*, 65 (1990), 59–86
———, 'Theory into Practice: Reading Medieval Chronicles', in Erik Kooper (ed.), *The Medieval Chronicle: Proceedings of the First International Conference of the Medieval Chronicle* (Amsterdam, 1999), pp. 1–12
Stafford, Pauline, 'The Meanings of Hair in the Anglo-Norman World: Masculinity, Reform, and National Identity', in Mathilde van Dijk and Renée Nip (eds.), *Saints, Scholars, and Politicians: Gender as a Tool in Medieval Studies* (Turnhout, 2005), pp. 153–72
Stein, Robert M., 'Literary Criticism and the Evidence for History', in Nancy F. Partner (ed.), *Writing Medieval History* (London, 2005), pp. 67–87
Stone, John, 'Technology, Society, and the Infantry Revolution of the Fourteenth Century', *Journal of Military History*, 68 (2004), 361–80
Strayer, Joseph R. (ed.), *Dictionary of the Middle Ages* (13 vols, New York, 1982–9)
Strickland, Matthew, *War and Chivalry: The Conduct and Perception of War in England and Normandy 1066–1217* (Cambridge, 1996)
Suppe, Frederick C., *Military Institutions on the Welsh Marches: Shropshire, A.D. 1066–1300* (Woodbridge, 1994)
Sweetenham, Carol, 'Crusaders in a Hall of Mirrors: The Portrayal of Saracens in Robert the Monk's *Historia Iherosolimitana*', in Sarah Lambert and Helen Nicholson (eds.), *Languages of Love and Hate: Conflict, Communication, and Identity in the Medieval Mediterranean* (Turnhout, 2012), pp. 49–64
———, 'What Really Happened to Eurvin de Créel's Donkey? Anecdotes in Sources for the First Crusade', in Marcus Bull and Damien Kempf (eds.), *Writing the Early Crusades: Text, Transmission and Memory* (Woodbridge, 2014), pp. 75–88
Taylor, Craig, *Chivalry and the Ideals of Knighthood in France during the Hundred Years War* (Cambridge, 2013)
Theotokis, Georgios, *Byzantine Military Tactics in Syria and Mesopotamia: A Comparative Study* (Edinburgh, 2018), pp. 29–41

———, *The Norman Campaigns in the Balkans 1081–1108* (Woodbridge, 2014)

Thomas, Hugh M., 'The *Gesta Herwardi*, the English and their Conquerors', in Christopher Harper-Bill (ed.), *Anglo-Norman Studies xxi: Proceedings of the Battle Conference 1998* (Woodbridge, 1999), pp. 213–32

Thompson, Kathleen, 'Orderic Vitalis and Robert of Bellême', *Journal of Medieval History*, 20 (1994), 133–41

———, 'Robert of Bellême Reconsidered', in Marjorie Chibnall (ed.), *Anglo-Norman Studies XIII: Proceedings of the Battle Conference, 1990* (Woodbridge, 1991), pp. 263–86

Thompson, Stith, *Motif-Index of Folk Literature: A Classification of Narrative Elements in Folktales, Ballads, Myths, Fables, Mediaeval Romances, Exempla, Fabliaux, Jest-Books and Local Legends*, rev edn (6 vols, Copenhagen, 1955)

Tolan, John V., *Saracens: Islam in the Medieval European Imagination* (New York, 2002)

Toolis, Ronan, '"Naked and unarmoured": A Reassessment of the Role of the Galwegians at the Battle of the Standard', *Transactions of the Dumfriesshire and Galloway Natural History and Antiquarian Society*, 78 (2004), 79–92

Tsurushima, Hirokazu, 'What Do We Mean by "Nations" in Early Medieval Britain?', in Hirokazu Tsurushima (ed.), *Nations in Medieval Britain* (Donington, 2010), pp. 1–18

Tuley, K. A., 'A Century of Communication and Acclimatization: Interpreters and Intermediaries in the Kingdom of Jerusalem', in Albrecht Classen (ed.), *East Meets West in the Middle Ages and Early Modern Times: Transcultural Experiences in the Premodern World* (Berlin, 2013), pp. 311–40

Van Houts, Elisabeth, 'Hereward and Flanders', *Anglo-Saxon England*, 28 (1999), 201–23

Varty, Kenneth, *Reynard the Fox: A Study of the Fox in Medieval English Art* (Leicester, 1967)

Verbruggen, J. F., *The Art of Warfare in Western Europe during the Middle Ages from the Eighth Century to 1340*, trans. Summer Willard and Sheila C. M. Southern, 2nd edn (Woodbridge, 1998)

———, *The Battle of the Golden Spurs: Courtrai, 11 July 1302*, ed. Kelly DeVries, trans. David Richard Ferguson, rev edn (Woodbridge, 2002)

———, 'La Tactique militaire des armées de chevaliers', *Revue du Nord*, 29 (1947), 161–80

Walter, Bastian, 'Urban Espionage and Counterespionage during the Burgundian Wars (1468–1477)', *Journal of Medieval Military History*, 9 (2011), 132–45

Ward, James P., 'Security and Insecurity, Spies and Informers in Holland during the Guelders War, 1506–1515', *Journal of Medieval Military History*, 10 (2012), 173–96

Warlop, E., *The Flemish Nobility before 1300* (2 vols, Kortrijk, 1975)

Weiler, Björn, 'Knighting, Homage and the Meaning of Ritual', *Viator*, 37 (2006), 275–300

Whaley, Barton, *Stratagem: Deception and Surprise in War* (Norwood, MA, 2007)

Wheeler, Everett L., *Stratagem and the Vocabulary of Military Trickery* (Leiden, 1988)

Whetham, David, *Just Wars and Moral Victories: Surprise, Deception and the Normative Framework of European War in the Later Middle Ages* (Leiden, 2009)

Web-based Sources

Rasmussen, Sune Engel, 'Afghan defence officials quit over Taliban attack as Pentagon chief flies in', *The Guardian*, 24 Apr. 2017 <https://www.theguardian.com/world/2017/apr/24/afghan-defence-officials-resign-deadly-taliban-attack> [accessed 24 Oct. 2020].

Index

Aachen, Albert of 34, 36, 40, 95, 105, 128, 138, 198
Acre, siege of 32, 70, 112–13, 136–7, 164
Adana (Cilicia) 95
Aimon, archbishop of Bourges 101
Andely (Normandy) 107
Antalya (Turkey) 32
Aeneid, The 145, 166
Aguilers, Raymond of 33, 55, 105
Akspoele, battle of 81
Alasce, Thierry of 34, 81
Ambroise, French poet 32
Annales Gandenses 177–8
Antioch 43–4, 66, 86, 88, 103, 130–3, 163
Apamea (Syria) 138
Apulia, William of 98, 124–5, 128, 159–62
Aquinas, Thomas 173–4
Ardres, Lambert of 68
Arthurian literature 6, 11, 24, 119
Arqah (Syria) 33
Arslān, Qilij, sultan of Rūm 35
Ascalon, battle of 104–5
Augustine 54, 172–3

Badges 120–1
Bahā al-Dīn 109, 113
Baldwin I, king of Jerusalem 33, 35–6, 79, 103, 140, 168
Baldwin II, king of Jerusalem 62, 93
Baldwin III, king of Jerusalem 38, 129
Banners
  as a sign of readiness for combat 62
  as an instrument of deception 102–4, 110–13
Bannockburn, battle of 5, 103
Banyas (Syria) 127
Barbour, John, author of *The Bruce* 95, 103, 144, 165, 169, 178–9
Bath, English town 146–7
Battle Abbey, Chronicle of 76
Battle-cries 106–10
Bellême, Robert of 152–4
Belvedre (Italy) 94
Berkhamsted (Hertfordshire) 110
Bible
  Genesis 54
  Joshua 39, 75, 174
  Judges 64
Blood, Field of 44, 86, 156–8

Bohemond of Taranto, Norman crusader 78, 130, 166
  advocates bribery 124
  persuades Pirrus to betray Antioch 131–2
  use a dead rooster to fake his death 3, 99
  use of 'professional' spies 40–1
Borsa, Roger 34, 130
Bouillon, Godfrey of 68, 128
Boulogne, Eustace, count of 69
Bourgueil, Baldric of 43, 124
Bouvines, battle of 48, 117–18, 121
Bovet, Honoré 3
Brémule, battle of 29, 120
Breteuil, Robert of 83
Breton, William the 48, 69, 176
Bruce, The, poem *see* Barbour, John
Bruce, Robert, king of Scotland 144, 169, 178–9, 191
Bruges 66–7, 82, 148–49, 177–8
Bruges, Galbert of 37, 60, 66, 81–2, 148–9
Busquet, Eustace 10

Caen, Ralph of 90, 95, 97, 103, 132, 166
Canon law 171–5
Castrogiovanni (Sicily) 130
Cavalry, *see* Knights
Chancellor, Walter the 44, 86, 156–8, 168, 179–80, 198
Chanson de la croisade albigoise 63
Chanson de Roland 62, 107
Chartres, Fulcher of 36, 80, 93, 104, 132, 168, 200
Chester, Ranulf of, 2
Chivalry 1–2, 13, 135
Chronicles
  problems of interpretation 5, 20–6
  use of classical material 17, 23
Cid, El 36
Clari, Robert of 56
Clausewtiz, Carl von 27
Clerics, used as spies 46–51
Clito, William 34, 81
  death of 37
Cnut, king of Denmark and England 64–5
Cornwall, Richard, earl of 60

Courtrai, battle of, 5, 117
Crécy, Hugh de 93
Crusade
    First 33, 34, 35, 43, 55, 68, 86, 88, 97–8, 103–5, 128, 130–3, 163, 168, 194, 200
    Second 32, 129–30, 140, 200
    Third 58, 108, 201
    Fourth 56, 165
    Albigensian 108, 118
Curthose, Robert 153, 163

Damascus 34, 55, 62, 79, 127, 129
David I, king of Scotland 29, 36, 57
De re militari, see Vegetius
Devizes, Richard of 136
Dinevor (Carmarthenshire) 50
Disjunction, rhetorical device 166–70
Dorylaion, battle of 35
Dudo of St Quentin, see St Quentin, Dudo of
Duqāq, ruler of Damascus 79
Dyrrachion 124, 127, 161

Edinburgh 137, 165, 179
Edward I, king of England 110, 137
Engineering 163–6
Evesham, battle of 110–11, 121
Exeter 40, 48, 106, 164

Facta et dicta memorabilia, see Maximus, Valerius
Fantosme, Jordan 141
Fleury, Andrew of 101
Foot Soldiers 4–5, 76–7, 86, 90, 101, 116, 136, 204
Fox, Renart the see Renart
Freising, Otto of 99
Frontinus, Julius 18–20, 31, 75, 101, 123, 175

Galwegians 189–90
Geoffrey V, count of Anjou 82
Gesta Francorum 40, 104, 131, 197
Gesta Normannorum Ducum 89, 155 n. 15
Gesta Stephani 28, 48, 54, 116, 125, 146–7, 164
Gingers see Red hair
Giovinazzo (Apulia) 34
Gloucester, Miles of 54
Greeks
    and warfare 56, 66, 98–9, 127–8, 194–5
    Western prejudice against 66, 193–5
Guisborough, Walter of 139, 144
Guiscard, Robert
    1079 rebellion against 34
    advises his men not to use trickery 162
    character of, according to William of Apulia 159
    sends a bilingual spy to Palermo 49
    use of bribery 124–5, 127–8
    use of the 'fake corpse' trick 97–9
Guy, bishop of Amiens, author of the *Carmen de Hastingae* 70, 75, 168

Hardrada, Harald see Sigurðarson, Haraldr
Harptree (Somerset) 28
Hasting, semi-legendary Viking warlord 96–7, 100–1
Hastings, battle of 72–8, 119, 136
Henry I, king of England 29, 34
Henry I, king of France 82
Henry II, king of England 16, 30, 50, 55
Henry III, king of England 65, 139, 143
Heraldry 113–21
Herbert, count of Maine 155
Hereward, English rebel 10–11, 57
Hexham, John of 57
Hood, Robin 9–10
Horses
    concealed to deceive an enemy 32
    mad horse sent to Richard I of England as a trick 199
    shoes put on backwards as a ruse 11
    simulated using baggage animals 101
    suitable/unsuitable for combat 61
Howden, Roger of 29, 55, 70, 83, 113, 141, 146
Hugh III, count of Maine 89
Huntingdon, Henry of 64, 77, 126

Ibn al-Athīr 44, 109, 129
Ibn al-Qalānisī 129, 132, 139
Īlghāzī 44, 156, 158, 168, 179, 198
Infantry, see Foot Soldiers
Iorwerth, Llewelyn ap, king of Gwynedd 50
Ireland
    character of the Irish 167, 186–8
    warfare in 79, 187
Itinerarium Peregrinorum 32, 44, 58, 63, 85, 113, 150, 195, 198–9

Jabala (Syria) 34
Jaffa (Palestine) 35
Jerusalem, siege of (1099) 59, 68, 105
John, king of England 13, 33, 69, 176
Joinville, Jean de 63
Just War Theory 171–2

INDEX

Kharput, fortress in northern Mesopotamia 93
Knights 1, 5, 11, 13, 37, 41, 48, 50–1, 55, 58, 62, 65–6, 76–7, 80, 83, 86, 92, 101, 103, 105, 106, 109, 114–18, 120–1, 127, 136, 145, 168, 173, 183–4, 190, 194, 197
   ability to perform feigned flight 74–5
   distinctive appearance of 89–91
Komnene, Anna 3, 99, 161 n. 37
Komnenos, Alexios 68, 90, 161, 194

Lanercost chronicler 137, 191
Les Vaux-de-Cernay, Peter of 108, 118
Lewes, battle of 111–12
Linguistic turn 21
Linlithgow (Scotland) 94
Lionheart, Richard the, *see* Richard I, king of England
Louis VI, king of France 29, 58, 91–3, 107, 115
Louis VII, king of France 32, 55, 141–2, 144–6, 200
Louis VIII, king of France 124
Louis IX, king of France 63
Lovel, William 89

Malaterra, Geoffrey 128, 130, 160, 167
Malcolm III, king of Scotland 29
Malmesbury, William, of 77, 79, 127, 136, 169, 199
Mansurah, battle of 63
Map, Walter 168, 193
Marshal, Richard 65, 116
Marshal, William, earl of Pembroke
   advocates a ruse against Philip II of France 30
   returns to Ireland 13
   unintentionally betrays his father's spy 43
Maximus, Valerius 17–18, 20, 31
Monmouth, Geoffrey of, 24
Mons-en-Pévèle, battle of 118
Montecassino (Italy) 97
Montecassino, Amatus of 49, 59, 94
Montfort, Simon de, the elder 110–12
Montfort, Simon de, the younger 139
Muret, battle of 118

Nerra, Fulk, count of Anjou 16
Newburgh, William of 144
Nogent, Guibert de 103, 132
Normans
   propensity for deception 78, 160–1, 169
   uses of stratagems 3, 34, 49, 56, 57, 59, 65, 72–9, 83, 89, 98–9, 108–9, 115, 124, 126–7, 130, 152–6, 159–62

Northallerton 29
Northampton 139
Nottingham 9, 33

Oaths, in medieval society 134–6
Odysseus *see* Ulysses

Palermo (Sicily) 49, 59
Paris, Matthew 97
Pembroke 31
Peter-Roger, lord of Cabaret 108
Philip II, king of France 30, 48, 136, 139
Philip IV, king of France 118
Poitiers, William of 76, 168

Racial theory, medieval 180–3
Red hair, as mark of treachery 132
Regio, abbot of Prüm 73–4
Renart the Fox 12–13, 14
Richard, count of Aversa 83
Richard I, king of England 33, 41, 108, 113, 126, 139, 164, 201
   use of local spies on crusade 44–5
Rievaulx, Aelred of 36, 108, 120, 190
Robert the Monk 88, 132, 163, 198
Roger I, Norman ruler of Sicily 78, 99, 130, 167
Roman de Brut 59, 119, 165, 169
Roman de Rou 77, 89, 106, 119
Rossano (Italy) 130
Rouen (Normandy) 34, 55, 144–6

Saint-Denis, Suger of 58, 91–3, 96–7, 123
Saint-Gilles, Raymond of, crusade leader 104, 166
   potential treachery at Arqah 33–4
   use of scouts 41
Saint Quentin, Dudo of 64
Saladin 38, 70, 112–13, 150, 198
Salisbury, John of 20
Salisbury, Patrick, earl of 60
Scots 188–93
Seville, Isidore of 22
Siege warfare 4, 7, 19, 28, 31–4, 37, 41, 43–4, 48–9, 55, 59–60, 66–70, 93–4, 103, 105–6, 108, 110, 112–13, 115, 124–33, 136–50, 153, 163–6, 169, 176, 187
Sigurðarson, Haraldr 100–1
Song of Dermot and Earl Richard fitz Gilbert 57, 63, 143
Spies, difficulty identifying in texts 39–42
Standard, battle of the 35, 47, 108, 120, 190
Stephen, king of England 28, 43, 57, 106, 125
   captures Harptree 28
   siege of Newbury 43, 140

Stratagemata, *see* Frontinus
Swabia, Frederick, duke of 58, 63

Tancarville, William 34
Tancred, prince of Galilee 90, 95, 97, 138, 140
Tartūs (Syria) 104
Templar, Order of the Knights 129, 200
Trans-cultural war 182–3
Turks 32
  admired as warriors 197
  demonised in Christian chronicles 196–8
  distinctive tactics of 84–7, 199–201
Tyre, William of 37–8, 66, 94, 126–7, 197–8

Ulysses 160, 195
Ursinus, possibly historical Cilician ruler 95

Vales-ès-Dunes, battle of 106, 120
Vegetius, Publius 15–17, 19, 23, 27
Verneuil (Normandy) 141
Villehardouin, Geoffrey de 137, 142, 165
Vita Edwardi Secundi 191
Vitalis, Orderic 29, 34, 65, 89, 92, 107, 115, 120, 151–6, 163, 195

Wake, Hereward the *see* Hereward
Wales
  warfare in 31–2, 49–51, 183–6
  Welsh character 183–6
  Welsh troops as specialists in rough terrain 55, 183–4
Wales, Gerald of 31, 50, 78, 143, 167, 183–8
Wallace, William 191–3
War-cry *see* Battle-cry
Waryn, Fulk fitz 10, 192
Wendover, Roger of 50, 60, 65, 102, 116, 124, 142
Wexford 13, 143, 167
William I, king of England 40, 70, 82, 136
William II, king of England 126
William of Préaux 108–10, 109 n. 87
Winchester 116, 164

Warfare in History

The Battle of Hastings: Sources and Interpretations, *edited and introduced by Stephen Morillo*

Infantry Warfare in the Early Fourteenth Century: Discipline, Tactics, and Technology, *Kelly DeVries*

The Art of Warfare in Western Europe during the Middle Ages, from the Eighth Century to 1340 (second edition), *J.F. Verbruggen*

Knights and Peasants: The Hundred Years War in the French Countryside, *Nicholas Wright*

Society at War: The Experience of England and France during the Hundred Years War, *edited by Christopher Allmand*

The Circle of War in the Middle Ages: Essays on Medieval Military and Naval History, *edited by Donald J. Kagay and L.J. Andrew Villalon*

The Anglo-Scots Wars, 1513–1550: A Military History, *Gervase Phillips*

The Norwegian Invasion of England in 1066, *Kelly DeVries*

The Wars of Edward III: Sources and Interpretations, *edited by Clifford J. Rogers*

The Battle of Agincourt: Sources and Interpretations, *Anne Curry*

War Cruel and Sharp: English Strategy under Edward III, 1327–1360, *Clifford J. Rogers*

The Normans and their Adversaries at War: Essays in Memory of C. Warren Hollister, *edited by Richard P. Abels and Bernard S. Bachrach*

The Battle of the Golden Spurs (Courtrai, 11 July 1302): A Contribution to the History of Flanders' War of Liberation, 1297–1305, *J.F. Verbruggen*

War at Sea in the Middle Ages and the Renaissance, *edited by John B. Hattendorf and Richard W. Unger*

Swein Forkbeard's Invasions and the Danish Conquest of England, 991–1017, *Ian Howard*

Religion and the Conduct of War, c.300–1215, *David S. Bachrach*

Warfare in Medieval Brabant, 1356–1406, *Sergio Boffa*

Renaissance Military Memoirs: War, History and Identity, 1450–1600, *Yuval Harari*

The Place of War in English History, 1066–1214, *J.O. Prestwich, edited by Michael Prestwich*

War and the Soldier in the Fourteenth Century, *Adrian R. Bell*

German War Planning, 1891–1914: Sources and Interpretations, *Terence Zuber*

The Battle of Crécy, 1346, *Andrew Ayton and Sir Philip Preston*

The Battle of Yorktown, 1781: A Reassessment, *John D. Grainger*

Special Operations in the Age of Chivalry, 1100–1550, *Yuval Noah Harari*

Women, Crusading and the Holy Land in Historical Narrative, *Natasha R. Hodgson*

The English Aristocracy at War: From the Welsh Wars of Edward I to the Battle of Bannockburn, *David Simpkin*

The Calais Garrison: War and Military Service in England, 1436–1558, *David Grummitt*

Renaissance France at War: Armies, Culture and Society, c.1480–1560, *David Potter*

Bloodied Banners: Martial Display on the Medieval Battlefield, *Robert W. Jones*

Alfred's Wars: Sources and Interpretations of Anglo-Saxon Warfare in the Viking Age, *Ryan Lavelle*

The Dutch Army and the Military Revolutions, 1588–1688, *Olaf van Nimwegen*

In the Steps of the Black Prince: The Road to Poitiers, 1355–1356, *Peter Hoskins*

Norman Naval Operations in the Mediterranean, *Charles D. Stanton*

Shipping the Medieval Military: English Maritime Logistics in the Fourteenth Century, *Craig L. Lambert*

Edward III and the War at Sea: The English Navy, 1327–1377, *Graham Cushway*

The Soldier Experience in the Fourteenth Century, *edited by Adrian R. Bell and Anne Curry*

Warfare in Tenth-Century Germany, *David S. Bachrach*

Chivalry, Kingship and Crusade: The English Experience in the Fourteenth Century, *Timothy Guard*

The Norman Campaigns in the Balkans, 1081–1108, *Georgios Theotokis*

Welsh Soldiers in the Later Middle Ages, 1282–1422, *Adam Chapman*

Merchant Crusaders in the Aegean, 1291–1352, *Mike Carr*

Henry of Lancaster's Expedition to Aquitaine, 1345–1346: Military Service and Professionalism in the Hundred Years War, *Nicholas A. Gribit*

Scotland's Second War of Independence, 1332–1357, *Iain A. MacInnes*

Military Communities in Late Medieval England: Essays in Honour of Andrew Ayton, *edited by Gary P. Baker, Craig L. Lambert and David Simpkin*

The Black Prince and the Grande Chevauchée of 1355, *Mollie M. Madden*

Military Society and the Court of Chivalry in the Age of the Hundred Years War, *Philip J. Caudrey*

Warfare in the Norman Mediterranean, *edited by Georgios Theotokis*

Chivalry and Violence in Late Medieval Castile, *Samuel A. Claussen*

The Household Knights of Edward III: Warfare, Politics and Kingship in Fourteenth-Century England, *Matthew Hefferan*

Elite Participation in the Third Crusade, *Stephen Bennett*

Printed in the United States
by Baker & Taylor Publisher Services